Revolutionary World

CW01083137

Throughout the modern age, revolutions have spread across state borders, engulfing entire regions, continents, and, at times, the globe. *Revolutionary World* examines the spread of upheavals during the major revolutionary moments in modern history: the Atlantic Revolutions, Europe's 1848 revolts, the commune movement of the 1870s, the 1905–15 upheavals in Asia, the communist revolutions around 1917, the "Wilsonian" uprisings of 1919, the "Third World" revolutions, the global Islamic revolt of 1978–79, the events of 1989, and the rise and fall of the "Arab Spring." The chapters explore the nature of these revolutionary waves, tracing the exchange of radical ideas and the movements of revolutionaries around the world. Bringing together a group of distinguished historians, *Revolutionary World* shows that the major revolutions of the modern age, which have so often been studied as isolated national or imperial events, were almost never contained within state borders and were usually part of broader revolutionary moments.

David Motadel is Associate Professor of International History at the London School of Economics and Political Science (LSE). He is the author of *Islam and Nazi Germany's War* (Harvard University Press, 2014), which was awarded the Fraenkel Prize, and the editor of *Islam and the European Empires* (Oxford University Press, 2014). In 2018, he received the Philip Leverhulme Prize for History.

Revolutionary World

Global Upheaval in the Modern Age

Edited by

David Motadel

London School of Economics and Political Science

CAMBRIDGE
UNIVERSITY PRESS

CAMBRIDGE
UNIVERSITY PRESS

University Printing House, Cambridge CB2 8BS, United Kingdom

One Liberty Plaza, 20th Floor, New York, NY 10006, USA

477 Williamstown Road, Port Melbourne, VIC 3207, Australia

314–321, 3rd Floor, Plot 3, Splendor Forum, Jasola District Centre, New Delhi – 110025, India

79 Anson Road, #06–04/06, Singapore 079906

Cambridge University Press is part of the University of Cambridge.

It furthers the University's mission by disseminating knowledge in the pursuit of education, learning, and research at the highest international levels of excellence.

www.cambridge.org
Information on this title: www.cambridge.org/9781107198401
DOI: 10.1017/9781108182409

First published 2021

A catalogue record for this publication is available from the British Library.

Library of Congress Cataloging-in-Publication Data
Names: Motadel, David, editor.
Title: Revolutionary world : global upheaval in the modern age / edited by David Motadel, London School of Economics and Political Science.
Description: 1 Edition. | New York : Cambridge University Press, 2021. | Includes bibliographical references and index.
Identifiers: LCCN 2020046980 (print) | LCCN 2020046981 (ebook) | ISBN 9781107198401 (hardback) | ISBN 9781108182409 (ebook)
Subjects: LCSH: Revolutions–History. | World politics. | History, Modern.
Classification: LCC HM876 .R448 2021 (print) | LCC HM876 (ebook) | DDC 303.6/409–dc23
LC record available at https://lccn.loc.gov/2020046980
LC ebook record available at https://lccn.loc.gov/2020046981

ISBN 978-1-107-19840-1 Hardback
ISBN 978-1-316-64817-9 Paperback

Contents

Figures and Tables

Figures

Tables

Contributors

ABBAS AMANAT is William Graham Sumner Professor of History at Yale University and Director of the Yale Program in Iranian Studies. He is the author of numerous books on modern Middle Eastern history, including *Iran: A Modern History* (Yale University Press, 2017), *Pivot of the Universe: Nasir al-Din Shah Qajar and the Iranian Monarchy, 1831–1896* (University of California Press, 1997), and *Resurrection and Renewal: The Making of the Babi Movement in Iran, 1844–1850* (Cornell University Press, 1989).

DAVID A. BELL is Sidney and Ruth Lapidus Professor at Princeton University. His publications include *Lawyers and Citizens* (Oxford University Press, 1994), *The Cult of the Nation in France* (Harvard University Press, 2001), and *The First Total War* (Houghton Mifflin, 2007). He is currently working on a book on the Atlantic Revolutions.

CHRISTOPHER CLARK is Regius Professor of History at the University of Cambridge. He is the author of *The Politics of Conversion: Missionary Protestantism and the Jews in Prussia, 1728–1941* (Oxford, 1995), *Iron Kingdom: The Rise and Downfall of Prussia, 1600–1947* (Penguin, 2006), *The Sleepwalkers: How Europe Went to War in 1914* (Penguin, 2012), and *Time and Power: Visions of History in German Politics, from the Thirty Years' War to the Third Reich* (Princeton University Press, 2019). He is currently working on a book on the revolutions of 1848.

JOHN CONNELLY is Professor of History at the University of California, Berkeley. His publications include *Captive University: The Sovietization of East German, Czech, and Polish Higher Education, 1945–1956* (University of North Carolina Press, 2000) and *From Enemy to Brother: The Revolution in Catholic Teaching on the Jews* (Harvard University Press, 2012). He is currently working on a book on the end of the Cold War.

QUENTIN DELUERMOZ is Professor of Modern History at the University of Paris. He is the author of *Policiers dans la ville: La construction d'un ordre public à Paris (1854–1914)* (Publications de la Sorbonne, 2012), *Le Crépuscule des Révolutions, 1848–1871* (Seuil, 2012), and *Commune(s), 1870–1871: Une traversée des mondes au XIXe siècle* (Seuil, 2020).

ANNE ELLER is Associate Professor of Latin American and Caribbean History at Yale University. She is the author of *We Dream Together: Dominican Independence, Haiti, and the Fight for Caribbean Freedom* (Duke University Press, 2016).

JAMES L. GELVIN is Professor of History at the University of California, Los Angeles. He is the author of *Divided Loyalties: Nationalism and Mass Politics in Syria at the Close of Empire* (University of California Press, 1998), *The Modern Middle East* (Oxford University Press, 2004), *Israel–Palestine Conflict: One Hundred Years of War* (Cambridge University Press, 2005), and *The Arab Uprisings* (Oxford University Press, 2012).

RACHEL G. HOFFMAN is a historian in Cambridge, working on modern Europe. She is currently preparing a book manuscript entitled *Germany's Age of Assassins.*

CHARLES KURZMAN is Professor of Sociology at the University of North Carolina at Chapel Hill. He is the author of *The Unthinkable Revolution in Iran* (Harvard University Press, 2004) and *Democracy Denied, 1905–1915: Intellectuals and the Fate of Democracy* (Harvard University Press, 2008).

EREZ MANELA is Professor of History at Harvard University. He is the author of *The Wilsonian Moment: Self-Determination and the International Origins of Anticolonial Nationalism* (Oxford University Press, 2007) and the coeditor of *The Shock of the Global: The 1970s in Perspective* (Harvard University Press, 2010), *Empires at War, 1911–1923* (Oxford University Press, 2014), and *The Development Century: A Global History* (Cambridge University Press, 2018).

DAVID MOTADEL is Associate Professor of International History at the London School of Economics and Political Science (LSE). He is the author of *Islam and Nazi Germany's War* (Harvard University Press, 2014), which was awarded the Fraenkel Prize, and the editor of *Islam and the European Empires* (Oxford University Press, 2014). In 2018, he received the Philip Leverhulme Prize for History.

ODD ARNE WESTAD is Elihu Professor of History and Global Affairs at Yale University. His publications include *The Global Cold War: Third World Interventions and the Making of Our Times* (Cambridge University Press, 2005) and *Restless Empire: China and the World since 1750* (Bodley Head, 2012). He is the coauthor of *Penguin History of the World* (Penguin, 2013) and *The Cold War: A World History* (Penguin, 2017). He is also the coeditor of *The Cambridge History of the Cold War* (Cambridge University Press, 2010).

Acknowledgments

Revolutions have captured the attention of historians for generations. This book has greatly benefitted from the wealth of their scholarship. It is the result of several years of work, and, along the way, I was fortunate to discuss it with many extraordinary scholars. I am particularly grateful to David Armitage, Houchang E. Chehabi, Sir Richard J. Evans, Tim Hochstrasser, Mark Jones, Jeppe Mulich, Nikos Papadogiannis, Jonathan Singerton, and John Slight for their invaluable feedback and advice. I would also like to thank James Swarbrick, Iona Tait, Jeremy Lowe, and Marie Deer for their assistance during the final phase of the editorial process. James Swarbrick, with a great eye for detail, also prepared the index. Moreover, I would like to express my gratitude to the anonymous readers, whose insightful reports helped to improve the book. Finally, I owe a great debt of thanks to our editor at Cambridge University Press, Michael Watson, who took an early interest in the project, for his unwavering support, guidance, and patience. It was a pleasure to work with Cambridge University Press's Emily Sharp, Becca Grainger, Lisa Carter, and Lauren Simpson, as well as with our copy-editor, Akash Udayakumar, and our production manager, Jayavel Radhakrishnan. I am also indebted to the team of the Wylie Agency, particularly James Pullen, who oversaw the process. A book like this could not have been produced by a single author, and it was a real privilege to work with the remarkable group of distinguished historians who provided the essays that brought it to life.

Global Revolution

David Motadel

In his lectures on the philosophy of history, given at the University of Berlin between 1822 and 1831, only a few decades after the storming of the Bastille, G. W. F. Hegel noted that the significance of the French Revolution, with its "external expansion," had been "world historical," changing the history of not only one country, but the globe.[1] His view reflected the vision many French and other revolutionaries of the time had had themselves. Some years later, in 1848, as revolutions spread across Europe and beyond, Marx and Engels considered the prospect of world revolution, calling for the "workers of the world" to "unite."[2] Similarly, after the Russian Revolution of 1917, Lenin claimed that the time had come for the revolutionaries across "all countries and nations throughout the world" to rise in "alliance and unity."[3] And amidst the global upheaval of 1989, Francis Fukuyama pondered whether the fundamental transformations that engulfed "many regions in the world" would affect "world history."[4]

Strikingly, contemporaries of all major revolutions of the modern age considered them to be of global significance – the beginning of a new era for humanity. This was the result of the universalist ideas these revolts represented, fought in the name of all humankind. Yet it also reflected

---

[1] Georg Wilhelm Friedrich Hegel, *Vorlesungen über die Philosophie der Geschichte*, ed. by D. Eduard Gans (Berlin, 1837), 444, originally given between 1822 and 1831; for the English translation, Georg W. F. Hegel, *The Philosophy of History* (New York, 1956), 285. Joachim Ritter, *Hegel und die Französische Revolution* (Cologne, 1957), provides the context.

[2] Karl Marx and Frederick Engels, "The Manifesto of the Communist Party," in *Karl Marx and Frederick Engels: Collected Works*, 50 vols. (London, 1975–2004), vol. 6 (*Marx and Engels: 1845–48*) (London, 1976), 477–519, 519, which was first published as Karl Marx and Friedrich Engels, *Manifest der Kommunistischen Partei* (London, 1848), 23. The sentence of the manifesto ("Proletarier aller Länder, vereinigt euch!") was translated as "Working Men of All Countries, Unite!"

[3] V. I. Lenin, "Preliminary Draft Theses on the National and the Colonial Questions," in *V. I. Lenin: Collected Works*, 45 vols. (London, 1960–1980), vol. 31 (*April-December 1920*) (London, 1966), 144–51, 151, originally published on June 5, 1920.

[4] Francis Fukuyama, "The End of History?," *The National Interest* 16 (1989), 3–18, 3, and, more detailed, Idem, *The End of History and the Last Man* (New York, 1992).

their actual geographical reach. Contemporary observers witnessed that revolutions were rarely confined within one country. Most revolutions of the modern era spread across state borders, engulfing entire regions, continents, and, at times, the globe.

The earliest revolutionary wave in modern history was that of the Atlantic Revolutions, which began with the American Revolution of 1776 and, in 1789, swept over to France. Inspired by the idea of liberty, revolutionaries fought against the old aristocratic elites and colonial rulers. They sparked the Haitian Revolution of 1791, the Irish Rebellion of 1798, and the revolutionary wars in Latin America. Around the same time, similar revolutions broke out in the Netherlands, Belgium, Poland, and the Ottoman Empire. Even more closely linked were the upheavals of 1848. Across Europe, revolutionaries radicalized by ideas of liberalism and nationalism went to the barricades to confront absolutist regimes. Revolts began in January in the streets of Palermo, soon sparking unrest on the Italian peninsula. The February Revolution in France toppled King Louis Philippe and led to an escalation of events. Civil war spread across the German states, the Habsburg Empire, the Netherlands, Denmark, and Ireland. In many places, martial law was declared and most of the protests were put down, with thousands killed. In the end, revolutionary turmoil even reached Europe's overseas empires. In Asia, the events of 1848 were echoed in the constitutional revolutions of the early twentieth century. Japan's defeat of Russia and the ensuing Russian Revolution of 1905 sparked the Persian Constitutional Revolution in the same year, the Young Turk Revolution of 1908 in the Ottoman Empire, and, finally, the Chinese Revolution of 1911. In the Russo-Japanese War, a non-European country with a constitution had prevailed over a European country without one. Meiji Japan thus became a shining model of modernization in the eyes of many activists and reformers in Asia, eager to confront traditional society and the autocratic political order. Soon, the constitutional revolutionary wave spread beyond the Middle East and East Asia, reaching Europe – with the Greek Revolution of 1909, the Portuguese Revolution of 1910, and the 1910 Constitutional Revolution of Monaco – and even America.

The Russian Revolution of 1917 had similarly profound global repercussions. Inspired by the events in St. Petersburg, revolutionaries across the world rose to overthrow the existing order, leading to the proclamation of the Munich Soviet Republic, the Hungarian Revolution and the foundation of the Hungarian Soviet Republic, the Limerick Soviet, and the Galician Soviet Socialist Republic. The Bolsheviks also inspired countless movements beyond Europe, perhaps most notably the Iranian insurgents under the charismatic guerrilla leader Mirza Kuchik Khan, who, in 1920, declared the short-lived Persian Socialist Soviet Republic in Gilan. Almost equally intense was the wave of anticolonial upheavals after the First World War. Fuelled by President Wilson's (and European statesmen's) promises of national self-determination, in 1919 anti-colonial demonstrations broke out in Egypt, Tunisia, India, Korea, China, French Indochina, and beyond. In Cairo, Egyptian women, for the first time in history, took to the streets to join in public protest. In the end, this wave of upheaval receded. Hopes for independence remained unfulfilled. Yet, soon however, anticolonial revolutionaries would rise again. During the Cold War, several chains of "Third World" revolutions shook Africa, Southeast Asia, the Middle East, and Latin America. Marxist slogans of world revolution fired American paranoia about the spread of communism through a domino effect. Ironically, the Cold War ended in a wave of demonstrations that overthrew most of the world's communist regimes. In Europe, protests began in Poland, spread to Hungary, East Germany, Bulgaria, and Czechoslovakia, and finally, in late 1989, reached Ceaușescu's Romania. Earlier that year, in China, the Tiananmen Square protests were crushed in a bloodbath, while communist rule was abandoned across most of Asia and Africa. Since then, new waves of revolution, most importantly the Color Revolutions in Georgia, Ukraine, and Kyrgyzstan, and the upheavals of the "Arab Spring," have followed. This book traces and examines the nature of these revolutionary waves. It shows that the major nineteenth- and twentieth-century revolutions and revolutionary movements, which have mainly been studied as isolated national or imperial events, were in fact all remarkably international.

The following chapters examine similarities and differences, through comparison, between revolutions that broke out at around the same time in different countries (and the volume as a whole compares the revolutionary waves to each other).[5] They show that these revolutions were often defined as much by their differences as they were by their similarities. Comparison is of course not without epistemological problems: We

---

[5] Patrick O'Brien, "Historiographical Traditions and Modern Imperatives for the Restoration of Global History," *Journal of Global History* 1, 1 (2006), 3–39; and the contributions to Heinz-Gerhard Haupt and Jürgen Kocka (eds.), *Geschichte und Vergleich: Ansätze und Ergebnisse international vergleichender Geschichtsschreibung* (Frankfurt, 1996); Heinz-Gerhard Haupt and Jürgen Kocka (eds.), *Comparative and Transnational History: Central European Approaches and New Perspectives* (New York, 2009); and, more generally, the contributions to Anil Bhatti and Dorothee Kimmich (eds.), *Ähnlichkeit: Ein kulturtheoretisches Paradigma* (Konstanz, 2015), on comparative history. Michel Espagne, "Sur les limites du comparatisme en histoire culturelle," *Genèses: Sciences Sociales et Histoire* 17 (1994), 112–21; and, more generally, R. Radhakrishnan, "Why Compare?," *New Literary History* 40, 3 (2009), 453–71, provide critical reflections.

always need to keep in mind that in any comparison, the cases being compared and the criteria used to compare them have been consciously chosen. Also, our units of comparison are not necessarily independent from one another – in some cases they are connected and in other cases not.

The book also, and perhaps more importantly, traces the links, both indirect and direct, between simultaneous revolutions.[6] Some of these connections were seen by contemporaries. Others can be reconstructed by historians, but were not visible to those living through the events at the time. First, there could be indirect connections between simultaneous revolutions through similar external (structural) transformations – such as major wars, global economic crises, or the collapse of empires – that led to conjunctural revolutionary power struggles in different countries. A prominent example is the First World War, causing political instability across continents, which led to the global revolutionary moments of 1917 and 1919.

Second, there could be direct links between revolutionary movements across state borders. After all, modern revolutions took place in a world of thickening global connections that resulted from imperialism, trade and commerce, and modern means of communication and transport. As the world became more integrated, the spread of revolutions across towns and provinces, nations and empires, regions and continents, and indeed the globe, accelerated.

Important hereby was often the movement of rebels. Major revolutionary figures, from Thomas Paine to M. N. Roy, as well as lesser-known itinerant rebels, roamed the globe. They often created new transimperial and transnational spaces of cooperation and global revolutionary sociability. At times, they were connected to revolutionary regimes attempting to export their revolutions to other countries. Throughout the modern era, such states provided military and non-military assistance to revolutionary movements abroad; examples range from the aid the Bolsheviks

---

[6] Sanjay Subrahmanyam, "Connected Histories: Notes towards a Reconfiguration of Early Modern Eurasia," *Modern Asian Studies* 31, 3 (1997), 735–62; and, identically, Idem, "Connected Histories: Toward a Reconfiguration of Early Modern Eurasia," in Victor B. Lieberman (ed.), *Beyond Binary Histories: Reimagining Eurasia to c. 1830* (Ann Arbor, MI, 1997), 289–316; Michael Werner and Bénédicte Zimmermann, "Vergleich, Transfer, Verflechtung: der Ansatz der Histoire croisée und die Herausforderung des Transnationalen," *Geschichte und Gesellschaft* 28, 4 (2002), 607–36; Idem, "Beyond Comparison: Histoire Croisée and the Challenge of Reflexivity," *History and Theory* 45, 1 (2006), 30–50; and Caroline Douki and Philippe Minard, "Histoire globale, histoires connectées: un changement d'échelle historiographique?," *Revue d'histoire moderne et contemporaine* 54-4bis, 5 (2007), 7–21, on connective history.

sent across the Caspian Sea to northern Persia in 1920–21 to the Cuban mission to Congo in 1965.

More importantly, revolutionary ideas (and the language in which they were conveyed) frequently resonated beyond state borders. Most of the revolutionaries of the modern age made universal claims, promoting ideas such as republicanism, constitutionalism, communism, or liberalism, and sought to replace the old rulers with popular forms of government, which all had a genuine attraction to revolutionary movements across the world. Also, the adoption of revolutionary ideas from abroad had a pragmatic appeal, since they had proven to be successful elsewhere and since they could help a revolutionary group appear to be part of a powerful global movement. The following chapters examine the ways in which revolutionary ideas and slogans spread and changed their meanings in different local contexts, taking into account differences in political and social conditions. The media used to circulate revolutionary messages were diverse, ranging from letters, pamphlets, newspapers, and books to radio, television, computers, and mobile phones. Ideas could be conveyed in scholarly texts, photographs, songs, poems, artworks, and many other forms. The transmission of ideas changed dramatically over the centuries. In the Atlantic Revolutions, which stretched over nearly five decades, revolutionary thoughts could only cross the oceans on sailing vessels. As modern communication became more advanced, the pace of revolutionary waves increased. In 1905, when the Constitutional Revolutions shook Asia, revolutionary slogans were circulated by telegraph and modern means of transport – railways and steamers – within hours. Over the course of the twentieth century, technological innovations became ever more important for the global expansion of political mass mobilization.

To be sure, when examining the spread of revolts we need to avoid the assumption of a simple diffusion from center to periphery.[7] This also means that in various cases, Europe was not the epicenter of global revolutionary moments. Although several of the global revolutionary waves of the modern age originated in Europe, most European revolutions were themselves influenced by global transformations. Movements in the colonial world, such as the American Revolution, could have a remarkable impact on the imperial centers of Europe and on Europe's global imperial webs. In fact, as this volume shows, there was often more than one center, and that transfers could go in more than one direction, as

---

[7] James M. Blaut, *The Colonizer's Model of the World: Geographical Diffusionism and Eurocentric History* (New York, 1993), 1–49, offers a more general critique of Eurocentric diffusionism.

revolutionary movements influenced each other. Moreover, the authors point to the limits of the spread of revolutions, examining the peaking, breaking, and ebbing of revolutionary waves.

Finally, there could be another form of direct connection between simultaneous revolutions, which did not necessarily involve the movement of revolutionaries or the transfer of ideas. A revolution in one state could cause major political, economic, and social instability in another, leading to a revolutionary situation there. The most prominent example of such a shock is the Atlantic upheaval, when the American Revolution, which was supported by substantial French funds, led to the French economic crisis, one of the causes of the French Revolution.[8]

The concept of "revolution," although central to our political vocabulary, lacks semantic clarity. Its definition has differed dramatically across time and space. "Revolution," as a historical concept, could mean very different things in different settings, from the *thawra* of the Arab world to China's *gemin*.[9] Using the Western (European and American) concept of "revolution" to study upheavals across the world may obscure as much as it allows us to see.[10] Also, its use may implicitly impose standards that make non-Western upheavals look deficient. And yet, compared to most other political concepts, the meaning of "revolution" has often been surprisingly similar in different parts of the world.

Moreover, the idea of "revolution" has evolved over time. The English word "revolution," for example – a term used with only

---

[8] Lynn Hunt, "The Global Financial Origins of 1789," in Suzanne Desan, Lynn Hunt, and William Max Nelson (eds.), *The French Revolution in Global Perspective* (Ithaca, NY, 2013), 32–43, provides an excellent discussion of these connections.

[9] Reinhard Koselleck, "Der neuzeitliche Revolutionsbegriff als geschichtliche Kategorie," *Studium Generale* 22 (1969), 825–38, reprinted as "Historische Kriterien des neuzeitlichen Revolutionsbegriff," in Idem, *Vergangene Zukunft: Zur Semantik geschichtlicher Zeitung* (Frankfurt, 1979), 68–9, translated as "Historical Criteria of the Modern Concept of Revolution," in Idem, *Futures Past: On the Semantics of Historical Time* (New York, 2004), 43–57, as well as Reinhard Koselleck, Neithard Bulst, Jörg Fisch, and Christian Meier, "Revolution, Rebellion, Aufruhr, Bürgerkrieg" in Otto Brunner, Werner Conze, and Reinhart Koselleck (eds.), *Geschichtliche Grundbegriffe: Historisches Lexikon zur politisch-sozialen Sprache in Deutschland*, 8 vols. (Stuttgart, 1972–1997), vol. 5 (Stuttgart, 1984), 653–788, provide good overviews of the history of the concept of "revolution." A classic is Eugen Rosenstock, "Revolution als politischer Begriff," in *Festgabe der rechts- und staatswissenschaftlichen Fakultät in Breslau für Paul Heiborn zum 70. Geburtstag, 6. Februar 1931* (Breslau, 1931), 83–124. More detailed discussions provide Karl Griewank, *Der neuzeitliche Revolutionsbegriff: Entstehung und Entwicklung* (Weimar, 1955); and Karl-Heinz Bender, *Revolutionen: Die Entstehung des politischen Revolutionsbegriffes in Frankreich zwischen Mittelalter und Aufklärung* (Munich, 1977).

[10] Dipesh Chakrabarty, *Provincializing Europe: Postcolonial Thought and Historical Difference* (Princeton, NY, 2000), problematizes the universal use of European concepts to study societies around the world. Hajimr Nakamura, *Parallel Developments: A Comparative History of Ideas* (New York, 1975), argues that some concepts are (and become) similar across the globe.

small spelling variations ("révolution," "revolución," "revolyutsiya," and so on) from Eastern Europe to Latin America – has significantly changed its meaning over the centuries. Indeed, it is worth reminding ourselves that its pre-modern and modern meanings were quite different. Prior to the French Revolution, the term signified the cyclical return to a previous political order in the course of history, a natural rotation back to a starting point. Originally an astronomical concept, popularized through Copernicus's *De revolutionibus orbium coelestium* (1543), describing the revolving motion of the planets, it entered political language in the seventeenth century. This pre-modern political conception of "revolution" was in fact similar to the classical political theories of Plato's change of states, *metavoli politeion*, or Polybius's cycle of states, *politeion anakyklosis*, the natural motion of different forms of political order returning to a point of departure – for example, monarchy, to aristocracy, to oligarchy, to democracy, to ochlocracy, to monarchy.[11] It was based on the assumption that the creation of an entirely new political and social order was impossible, and that every major political change was a preordained stage in the cycle of political orders. Moreover, it assumed that the entire historical process was beyond human control, a natural event leaving no agency to mortals. It was a "metahistorical" or "transhistorical concept of revolution," as Reinhardt Koselleck once put it.[12] Thus, Hobbes, for example, used the word "revolution" to characterize the upheavals in England from the 1640s to the 1660s, which may be seen as a full cycle of political orders (monarchy, parliaments, Cromwell's dictatorship, oligarchies, monarchy): "I have seen in this revolution a circular motion of the sovereign power."[13] Similarly, the "Glorious Revolution" of 1688 was termed a "revolution" by contemporaries in the sense that it constituted a cycle that started with the overthrow of the monarchy of James II and ended with the establishment of the monarchy of William and Mary. To be sure, the meaning of the early modern concept of revolution, as Keith Baker pointed out, could have nuances, at times simply implying sudden change, rupture, and

---

[11] Peter Derow, "Historical Explanation: Polybius and his Predecessors," in Simon Hornblower (ed.) *Greek Historiography* (Oxford, 1994), 73–90, provides a good overview. On *politeion anakyklosis*, see *Polybius: The Histories*, ed. by W. R. Paton, 6 vols. (London 1922–1927), vol. 6 (London, 1927); and on *metavoli politeion*, see book 8 of *Plato: The Republic*, ed. by Paul Shorey, 2 vols. (London, 1930–1935), vol. 2 (London, 1935).

[12] Koselleck, *Futures Past*, 46, 47, and 48, for "transhistorical"; and 50, for "metahistorical."

[13] Thomas Hobbes, *Behemoth or the Long Parliament* (London, 1889), 204, which was first published in 1679. Mark Hartman, "Hobbes's Concept of Political Revolution," *Journal of the History of Ideas* 47, 3 (1986), 487–95, provides the context.

disorder.[14] In any case, before 1789, the sort of violent political and social upheaval that we would call "revolution" today was commonly termed "rebellion", "revolt", "uprising", "riot", or "insurrection". Hannah Arendt once observed that "revolutions, properly speaking, did not exist prior to the modern age," which is hard to dispute if we compare her modern notion of "revolution" with that of pre-modern thinkers.[15]

Over the course of the eighteenth century, particularly during the Enlightenment, as the term became more widespread, its meaning began to change. A revolution was seen less and less as a natural, irresistible phenomenon and more as an act rooted in human agency. At the same time, the idea of the "people" became important, as revolutions came to be seen as a collective act. Moreover, it was increasingly thought to result in an entirely new political and social order; this was to some extent the result of a new understanding of time, in which older cyclical notions of human history were replaced by new linear conceptions. And finally, the new understanding of revolution had increasingly optimistic connotations of emancipation, liberation, and progress. When Marx, in the mid-nineteenth century, identified revolutions as the "locomotives of history," it was exactly this idea of progress that he was emphasizing.[16] It is also worth noting that this modern transformation of the meaning of the word "revolution" can also be observed in some other linguistic universes, most notably perhaps in the case of the Arabic word *inqilab*, which is used in Persian (more than in Arabic).

After the Atlantic Revolutions, this new notion of "revolution" became the norm, even globally. Still, as a historical concept it has always had different meanings in different places and at different times; those uprisings termed "revolution" by contemporaries could differ significantly in character. This book will take into account the historical concept of "revolution" as it was used by contemporaries, yet it will employ the term first and foremost as an analytic, not historical, concept.

Scholars have proposed a wide range of definitions of "revolution" as an analytic concept to study past and present societies. Some of them are rather broad, such as Crane Brinton's (classic) definition of revolution as a violent and successful upheaval that leads to the "drastic, sudden substitution of one group in charge of the running of a territorial political

---

[14] Keith Michael Baker, "Revolutionizing Revolution," in Keith Michael Baker and Dan Edelstein (eds.), *Scripting Revolution: A Historical Approach to the Comparative Study of Revolutions* (Stanford, CA, 2015), 71–102.

[15] Hannah Arendt, *On Revolution* (New York, 1963), 2.

[16] Karl Marx, "The Class Struggles in France, 1848 to 1850," in *Karl Marx and Frederick Engels: Collected Works*, vol. 10 (*Marx and Engels: 1849–51*) (London, 1978), 45–145, 122, which was first published as Karl Marx, "Die Klassenkämpfe in Frankreich, 1840-1850," *Neue Rheinische Zeitung* 1, 2, 3, 5, 6 (1850).

entity by another group hitherto not running that government."[17] Others are narrower, like Theda Skocpol's (now equally classic) definition of revolutions – "social revolutions," as she termed them – as successful (though not necessarily violent) upheavals that lead to a "rapid" and "basic" transformation of not only the political order but also society and class structure.[18] Some scholars have put forward more complex definitions. Charles Tilly conceptualized revolutions as a successful "forcible transfer of power over a state in the course of which at least two distinct blocs of contenders make incompatible claims to control the state, and some significant portion of the population subject to the state's jurisdiction acquiesces in the claims of each bloc."[19] He understood a revolution as a combination of a "revolutionary situation," which is a situation in which two incompatible blocs claim control over a polity, and a "revolutionary outcome," which is the actual transfer of state power.

The chapters in this book follow a basic definition of revolution as a condition in which a substantial part of the population challenges its rulers' claim to power over the state – leading to a split in the polity – and which results in abrupt (and often violent) political change. Yet it should be mentioned that major attempted revolutions, which only fulfill parts of this definition, will also be considered. After all, even unsuccessful revolts could have a profound impact on individuals, changing their lives forever, and, in any case, the results of revolutions have not always been unambiguous. Still, there are of course various forms of inner-state conflict that lead to abrupt political change which do not constitute revolutions, such as coup d'états, succession struggles, and civil wars (although they can overlap).[20] Although our definition is strictly political, it should be noted that revolutions have always had a significant cultural dimension, shaping political cultures and social milieus, transforming

---

[17] Crane Brinton, *The Anatomy of Revolution* (New York, 1965), 4; a first version of the text was published in 1938.

[18] Theda Skocpol, *States and Social Revolutions: A Comparative Analysis of France, Russia, and China* (Cambridge, 1979), 4–5. Karl Marx had already written: "Every revolution dissolves the *old society* and to that extent it is *social*. Every revolution overthrows the *old power* and to that extent it is *political*", see Karl Marx, "Critical Marginal Notes on the Article 'The King of Prussia and Social Reform. By a Prussian'," in *Karl Marx and Frederick Engels: Collected Works*, vol. 3 (*Marx and Engels: 1843–44*) (London, 1975), 189–206, 205, which was first published as Karl Marx, "Kritische Randglossen zu dem Artikel 'Der König von Preußen und die Sozialreform: Von einem Preußen'," *Vorwärts!* 63 (August 7, 1844) and 64 (August 10, 1844).

[19] Charles Tilly, *European Revolutions, 1492–1992* (Oxford, 1993), 1–20.

[20] Koselleck, Bulst, Fisch, and Meier, "Revolution, Rebellion, Aufruhr, Bürgerkrieg," on the concepts of "revolution" and "civil war." David Armitage, *Civil Wars: A History in Ideas* (New Haven, CT, 2017), provides an excellent discussion of ideas of "civil war."

political languages and worldviews, evoking hopes and fears. Considering revolutions to be neither progressive nor regressive per se, the following chapters will, as far as possible, avoid value judgments. Revolutions could be as emancipatory as they could be authoritarian. Finally, the concept of a revolutionary wave will be defined as a series of revolutions with similar aims which break out in different states around the same time and which are connected by common external causes or (and) because they directly impact each other.

Scholars have studied the mechanics of revolutions for decades, examining their reasons (both deeper long-term causes – material and ideological – and short-term triggers), actors, objectives, means, and courses, starting from individual acts of civil disobedience, developing into collective acts of civil disobedience, pivoting with the emergence of a movement with its own internal dynamics, and possibly ending with transfers of control of the state apparatus and the breakdown of the hegemony of the old rulers' world views. Ultimately, however, every revolution is unique, shaped by its specific contexts and contingencies, and any attempt to establish some sort of general theory of revolution is bound to suffer from the reductionism. The diversity in the character of revolutions also makes writing their global history a complicated matter. And yet, a global history may provide general insights into the nature of revolutions while avoiding the temptation to make wild theoretical generalizations.

The major revolutions of the modern age are often considered to have been distinct, isolated national events: The French Revolution is and remains "French" in French popular memory, just like the Egyptian Revolution of 1919 is remembered as an "Egyptian" revolt by Egyptians, and the Iranian Revolution of 1978–79 as "Iranian" in Iran. In Germany, the image prevails that it was the protesters on the streets of Leipzig, Dresden, and Berlin, chanting the nationalist slogan "We are the people" ("Wir sind das Volk"), who brought down the Berlin wall, not events beyond German borders. National exceptionalism remains at the heart of the popular narratives of modern revolutions. In the age of the nation-state, we have come to see (and glorify) revolutions as *national* events. Most of the time, however, they have in fact been strikingly international and part of broader revolutionary waves. No scholar studying revolutions can afford not to take into account their transnational and transimperial environments.

Over the years, social and political scientists have produced a vast body of works on revolutions. It includes more theoretical works, such as the classics of Lyford Edwards, George Pattee, Crane Brinton, Chalmers Johnson, and Jean Baechler, which use historical examples (often selectively) to build (or simply illustrate) general theories of revolutions.[21] It also includes studies of comparative historical sociology, such as the works of Eric Wolf, Theda Skocpol, and Charles Tilly, which examine a number of historical case studies in more depth to find recurrent mechanisms.[22] This research has often been connected to research on collective action more generally.[23] Strikingly, most of these theoretical studies compare revolutions only vertically and rarely examine the nature of revolutionary waves.[24]

Historians have naturally shown an equally profound interest in the subject. Yet they, too, have studied revolutions and revolutionary movements predominantly within national or imperial frameworks, as separate events; to be sure, their research has resulted in some of the finest works of historical scholarship, among them the writings of François Furet on the

---

[21] Lyford Edwards, *The Natural History of Revolution* (Chicago, 1927); George Sawyer Pattee, *The Process of Revolution* (New York, 1938); Crane Brinton, *The Anatomy of Revolution* (New York, 1938); Chalmers Johnson, *Revolutionary Change* (Boston, MA, 1966); and Jean Baechler, *Les phénomènes révolutionnaires* (Paris, 1970), are the classics. Moreover, important insights are also offered by the essays in Carl J. Friedrich (ed.), *Revolution* (New York, 1966); and Jack A. Goldstone (ed.), *Revolutions: Theoretical, Comparative, and Historical Studies* (San Diego, CA, 1986). Michael S. Kimmel, *Revolution: A Sociological Interpretation* (Philadelphia, 1990), provides an excellent survey of the most important theories of revolution.

[22] Eric R. Wolf, *Peasant Wars of the Twentieth Century* (New York, 1969); Skocpol, *States and Social Revolutions*; and Charles Tilly, *European Revolutions*; and also, though less substantial, John Dunn, *Modern Revolutions: An Introduction to the Analysis of a Political Phenomenon* (Cambridge, 1972). A more recent work of comparative historical sociology is George Lawson, *Anatomies of Revolution* (Cambridge, 2019). A fascinating study of comparative historical sociology of counterrevolutions is offered by Amir A. Farman-Farma, "A Comparative Study of Counter-Revolutionary Mass Movements during the French, Mexican and Russian Revolutions with Contemporary Application" (DPhil dissertation, University of Oxford, 1990).

[23] Ted Gurr, *Why Men Rebel* (Princeton, NJ, 1970); Mancur Olson, *The Logic of Collective Action: Public Goods and the Theory of Groups* (Cambridge, MA, 1971); Charles Tilly, *From Mobilization to Revolution* (Reading, MA, 1978); and Idem, *Social Movements 1768–2004* (London 2004) are classics. The chapters in Timothy Garton Ash and Adam Roberts (eds.), *Civil Resistance and Power Politics: The Experience of Non-Violent Action from Gandhi to the Present* (Oxford, 2009) offer important insights into the nature of non-violent collective action.

[24] Mark. N. Katz, *Revolutions and Revolutionary Waves* (New York, 1997) is, despite of its title, a study of the great power politics of revolutionary regimes and their support for client regimes, focusing on the Cold War. Colin J. Beck, *Ideological Roots of Waves of Revolution* (Ph.D., Stanford, 2009); and Kurt Weyland, *Making Waves: Democratic Contention in Europe and Latin America since the Revolutions of 1848* (Cambridge, 2014), provide important theoretical insights into revolutionary waves. Moreover, major communist writers have naturally written theoretical reflections on revolutionary waves, which forms the basis of the concept of world revolution, including Karl Marx and Friedrich Engels, Rosa Luxemburg, V. I. Lenin, and Leon Trotsky. George Lawson, "Revolutions and the International," *Theory and Society* 44, 4 (2015), 299–319, offers some general thoughts on the international dimension in theories of revolution.

French Revolution, Orlando Figes on the Russian Revolution, and Said Amir Arjomand on the Iranian Revolution.[25] Moreover, there are also general (vertically) comparative historical (not historical-sociological) studies of individual revolutions, including the classic surveys of revolutions in Europe, from A. J. P. Taylor to Charles Tilly.[26] And finally, and this brings us to the subject of this volume, historians have shown a growing interest in the impact of revolutions beyond state borders.

So far, there are only scattered historical studies that look at individual cases of transnational and transimperial revolutionary waves. The best-researched by far are the Atlantic Revolutions, which have been studied in a wide range of works, from the traditional histories by R. R. Palmer, Jacques Godechot, and Eric Hobsbawm to the global histories by Joseph Klaits and Michael Haltzel, by David Armitage and Sanjay Subrahmanyam, and by Suzanne Desan, Lynn Hunt, and William Max Nelson.[27] It is worth noting

---

[25] François Furet, *La Révolution*, 2 vols. (Paris, 1988), translated into English as François Furet, *The French Revolution, 1770–1814* and *Revolutionary France, 1770–1880* (Oxford, 1992); as well as the classic François Furet and Denis Richet, *La Révolution*, 2 vols. (Paris, 1965), translated, abbreviated, as *The French Revolution* (London, 1970); Orlando Figes, *A People's Tragedy: The Russian Revolution: 1891–1924* (London, 1996); and Said Amir Arjomand, *The Turban for the Crown: The Islamic Revolution in Iran* (Oxford, 1988).

[26] Eric Hosbawm, *Primitive Rebels: Studies in Archaic Forms of Social Movement in the 19th and 20th Centuries* (London, 1959); and Idem, *Revolutionaries* (London, 1973); A. J. P. Taylor, *Revolutions and Revolutionaries* (London, 1980); Yves-Marie Bercé, *Révoltes et Révolutions dans l'Europe moderne* (Paris, 1980); Jack A. Goldstone, *Revolution and Rebellion in the Early Modern World* (Berkeley, CA, 1991); Charles Tilly, *European Revolutions, 1492–1992* (Oxford, 1993), are major (vertically) comparative histories of revolution. Notable more specific (vertically) comparative studies are as Arno J. Mayer, *The Furies: Violence and Terror in the French and Russian Revolutions* (Princeton, NJ, 2000); and S. A. Smith, *Revolution and the People in Russia and China: A Comparative History* (Cambridge, 2008). A broader global (vertically) comparative history of revolutions in the modern age provide the contributions to Baker and Edelstein (eds.), *Scripting Revolutions*.

[27] R. R. Palmer, *The Age of Democratic Revolution: A Political History of Europe and America, 1760–1800*, 2 vols. (Princeton, NJ, 1959 and 1964); Jacques Godechot, *Les institutions de la France sous la Révolution et l'émpire* (Paris, 1951); Idem, *La Grande Nation: L'expansion révolutionnaire de la France dans le monde de 1789 à 1799* (Paris, 1956); Idem, *Les Révolutions, 1770–1799* (Paris, 1963), translated as *France and the Atlantic Revolution of the Eighteenth Century, 1770–1799* (New York, 1965); Eric Hobsbawm, *The Age of Revolution: Europe, 1789–1948* (New York, 1962); Wim Klooster, *Revolutions in the Atlantic World: A Comparative History* (New York, 2009); Janet Polasky, *Revolutions without Borders: The Call to Liberty in the Atlantic World* (New Haven, CT, 2015); and the contributions to Pierre Serna (ed.), *Républiques soeurs: La Directoire et la Révolution atlantique* (Rennes, 2009), are the classics on the Atlantic Revolutions. A pioneering study remains Alphonse Aulard, *Études et leçons sur la révolution française*, 9 vols. (Paris, 1908–1924), vol. 8 (Paris, 1921). Groundbreaking works on the global history of the Atlantic Revolutions are C. A. Bayly, *The Birth of the Modern World 1780–1914: Global Connections and Comparisons* (London, 2004); Idem, "The 'Revolutionary Age' in the Wider World, c. 1790-1830," in Richard Bessel, Nicholas Guyatt, and Jane Rendall (eds.), *War, Empire and Slavery, 1770–1830* (New York, 2010), 21–43; and the chapters in Joseph Klaits and Michael H. Haltzel (eds.), *The Global Ramifications*

that early research on the Atlantic revolutionary wave took shape not only in the western hemisphere, in the work of Godechot, Palmer, and Hobsbawm, but also in the Soviet world, in the work of the Leipzig scholars Walter Markov and, more importantly, Manfred Kossok.[28] Hannah Arendt's *On Revolution* was another early text that sought to look at the American and French Revolutions together, an important study despite its factual inaccuracies, which were rather mercilessly pointed out by Eric Hobsbawm.[29] Other revolutionary moments have been examined to different degrees and at different levels of sophistication. William Langer, Jonathan Sperber, and Mike Rapport have studied the spread of the 1848 revolts in Europe, while Édouard de Lépine, Miles Taylor, Kurt Weyland, and others have explored their influences in the wider world.[30] Charles Kurzman, Nader Sohrabi, and Pankaj Mishra

of the French Revolution (Cambridge, 1994); David Armitage and Sanjay Subrahmanyam (eds.), *The Age of Revolutions in Global Context, c. 1760–1840* (New York, 2010); Desan, Hunt, and Nelson (eds.), *The French Revolution in Global Perspective*; and Maria O'Malley, Denys van Renen, and Edward N. Simon (eds.), *Beyond 1776: Globalizing the Cultures of the American Revolution* (Charlottesville, VA, 2018). It is also worth mentioning that already nineteenth-century scholars like Heinrich von Sybel, *Geschichte der Revolutionszeit von 1789 bis 1795 (1800)*, 5 vols. (Düsseldorf, 1853–1879) and Albert Sorel, *L'Europe et la Révolution française*, 8 vols. (Paris, 1885–1904), wrote histories of the French Revolution which transcended French borders.

[28] Walter Markov, *Weltgeschichte im Revolutionsquadrat* (East Berlin, 1979); as well as Manfred Kossok, *Ausgewählte Schriften*, 3 vols. (Leipzig, 2000), especially the articles in vol. 2 (*Vergleichende Revolutionsgeschichte der Neuzeit*), but also those in vol. 1 (*Kolonialgeschichte und Unabhängigkeitsbewegung in Lateinamerika*), and, to a lesser extent, in vol. 3 (*Zwischen Reform und Revolution: Übergänge von der Universal- zur Globalgeschichte*). Manfred Kossok, *In tyrannos: Revolutionen der Weltgeschichte* (Leipzig, 1989), provides a broader overview.

[29] Hannah Arendt, *On Revolution* (New York, 1963); and, for the review, Eric Hobsbawm, Review of On Revolution by Hannah Arendt, *History and Theory* 4, 2 (1965), 252–58, reprinted in Eric Hobsbawm, *Revolutionaries* (London, 2007), 267–75, which was first published in 1973, noted critically: "The historian or sociologist, for instance, will be irritated, as the author plainly is not, by a certain lack of interest in mere fact. This cannot be described as inaccuracy or ignorance, for Miss Arendt is learned and scholarly enough to be aware of such inadequacies if she chooses, but rather as a preference for metaphysical construct or poetic feeling over reality."

[30] William Langer, *The Revolutions of 1848* (New York, 1971); Jonathan Sperber, *The European Revolutions, 1848–1851* (Cambridge, 1994); Mike Rapport, *1848: Year of Revolution* (New York, 2010); and the essays in R. J. W. Evans and Hartmut Pogge von Strandmann (eds.), *The Revolutions in Europe, 1848–1849: From Reform to Reaction* (Oxford, 2000); Dieter Dowe, Heinz-Gerhard Haupt, Dieter Langewiesche, and Jonathan Sperber (eds.), *Europe in 1848: Revolution and Reform* (New York, 2001), which was first published as Dieter Dowe, Heinz-Gerhard Haupt, and Dieter Langewiesche (eds.), *Europa 1848: Revolution und Reform* (Bonn, 1998); Axel Körner (ed.), *1848: A European Revolution? International Ideas and National Memories of 1848* (New York, 2000); and, with a focus on intellectual history, Douglas Moggach and Gareth Stedman Jones (eds.), *The 1848 Revolutions and European Political Thought* (Cambridge, 2018), examine the waves of revolution in Europe. Édouard de Lépine, *Dix semaines qui ébranlèrent la Martinique, 25 mars – 4 Juin 1848* (Paris, 1999); Miles Taylor, "The 1848 Revolutions and the British Empire," *Past*

have traced the Asian revolutions of 1905.[31] Silvio Pons and others have explored the Russian Revolution's impact on the world.[32] Erez Manela has studied the "Wilsonian" upheavals.[33] John Foran has examined the "Third World" Revolutions.[34] Victor Sebestyen, Pierre Grosser, and others have chronicled the world's 1989.[35] James L. Gelvin and many

and Present 166 (2000), 146–80; Timothy M. Roberts and Daniel W. Howe, "The United States and the Revolutions of 1848," in Evans and Strandmann (eds.), *The Revolutions in Europe*, 157–79; Kurt Weyland, "The Diffusion of Revolution: '1848' in Europe and Latin America," *International Organization* 63, 3 (2009), 391–423, and the contributions to Guy Thomson (ed.), *The European Revolutions of '1848' and the Americas* (London, 2002), look at the impact of 1848 beyond Europe.

[31] Charles Kurzman, *Democracy Denied, 1905–1915: Intellectuals and the Fate of Democracy* (Cambridge, MA, 2008); Nader Sohrabi, *Revolution and Constitutionalism in the Ottoman Empire and Iran* (Cambridge, 2011); and, more concisely, Idem, "Historicizing Revolutions: Constitutional Revolutions in the Ottoman Empire, Iran, and Russia, 1905-1908," *American Journal of Sociology* 100, 6 (1995), 1383–1447; and Idem, "Global Waves, Local Actors: What the Young Turks Knew about Other Revolutions and Why It Mattered," *Comparative Studies in Society and History* 44, 1 (2002), 45–79. Houri Berberian, *Roving Revolutionaries: Armenians and the Connected Revolutions in the Russian, Iranian, and Ottoman Worlds* (Berkeley, CA, 2019), traces a group of itinerant revolutionaries. Klaus Kreiser, "Der japanische Sieg über Russland (1905) und sein Echo unter den Muslimen," *Die Welt des Islams* 21, 1 (1981), focuses on the impact of Japan's victory over Russia and constitutionalism in Muslim lands. Pankaj Mishra, *From the Ruins of Empire: The Revolt against the West and the Remaking of Asia* (London, 2012), provides an excellent picture of the broader context.

[32] Silvio Pons, *The Global Revolution: A History of International Communism 1917–1991* (Oxford, 2014), 7–42; Robert Service, *Comrades: Communism: A World History* (London, 2007), 83–163; Peter Hopkirk, *Setting the East Ablaze: Lenin's Dream of an Empire in Asia* (London, 1984); and the chapters in Stefan Rinke and Michael Wildt (eds.), *Revolutions and Counter-Revolutions: 1917 and its Aftermath from a Global Perspective* (Frankfurt, 2017). On the immediate impact of the Russian Revolution in Europe, see also Robert Gerwarth, *The Vanquished: Why the First World War Failed to End, 1917–1923* (London, 2016), and, more generally, the chapters in Idem and John Horne (eds.), *War in Peace: Paramilitary Violence in Europe after the Great War* (Oxford, 2012). A good overview of the European revolutionary wave is provided by John Paul Newman, "Revolution and Counterrevolution in Europe 1917-1923," in Silvio Pons and Stephen A. Smith (eds.), *The Cambridge History of Communism*, 3 vols. (Cambridge, 2017), vol. 1 (*World Revolution and Socialism in One Country, 1917–1941*), 96–120. A fascinating contemporary text is C. L. R. James, *World Revolution 1917–1936: The Rise and Fall of the Communist International* (London, 1937).

[33] Erez Manela, *The Wilsonian Moment: Self-Determination and the International Origins of Anticolonial Nationalism* (Oxford, 2007); and, for an excellent summary, Idem, "Dawn of a New Era: The "Wilsonian Moment" in Colonial Contexts and the Transformation of World Order, 1917–1920," in Sebastian Conrad and Dominic Sachsenmaier (eds.), *Competing Visions of World Order: Global Moments and Movements, 1880s–1930s* (New York, 2007), 121–49; and, on the broader context, Arno J. Mayer, *Wilson vs. Lenin: Political Origins of the New Diplomacy, 1917–1918* (New York, 1967).

[34] John Foran, *Taking Power: On the Origins of the Third World Revolutions* (Cambridge, 2005).

[35] Victor Sebestyen, *Revolution 1989: The Fall of the Soviet Empire* (London, 2009); and Pierre Grosser, *1989: L'année où le monde a basculé* (Paris, 2009). Patrick Kenney, *A Carnival of Revolution: Central Europe 1989* (Princeton, NJ, 2002) offers a history from below. Robert Service, *The End of the Cold War, 1985–1991* (London, 2015); and

others have looked at the spread of revolts during the "Arab Spring."[36] All of these historians have examined various kinds of connections, including the spread of ideas and the movement of revolutionaries.[37] They have contributed significantly to our knowledge of the revolutionary waves. And yet, despite looking at similar questions and problems, most scholars studying simultaneous revolts and the impact of revolutions beyond state borders have taken little notice of each other's work. Bringing together the research of leading historians who work on revolutionary moments in history, this volume provides the first general account of the global history of revolutionary waves in the modern age.

It begins with the best-known revolutionary wave, the Atlantic Revolutions, which started with the American Revolution of 1776 and, in 1789, swept over to France.[38] Soon, revolutionaries challenged aristocratic and colonial rule in places as diverse as Warsaw, Geneva, Granville Town, and Dublin. They sparked the slave revolution in the French colony of Saint-Domingue (Haiti) of 1791, led by the liberated slave

---

the essays in George Lawson, Chris Armbruster, and Michael Cox (eds.), *The Global 1989: Continuity and Change in World Politics* (Cambridge, 2010), provide the more general context. Paul Betts, "1989 at Thirty: A Recast Legacy," *Past and Present* 244, 1 (2019), 271–305, discusses the complex political nature (and legacy) of the revolutionary wave. Timothy Garton Ash, *The Magic Lantern: The Revolution of '89 Witnessed in Warsaw, Budapest, Berlin, and Prague* (London, 1990), offers a fascinating eyewitness account.

[36] James L. Gelvin, *The Arab Uprisings* (Oxford, 2012); as well as Jean-Pierre Filiu, *The Arab Revolution* (London, 2011); Asef Bayat, *Revolution without Revolutionaries: Making Sense of the Arab Spring* (Stanford, CA, 2017); and the contributions to Adam Roberts, Michael J. Willis, Rory McCarthy, and Timothy Garton Ash (eds.), *Civil Resistance in the Arab Spring: Triumphs and Disasters* (Oxford, 2016).

[37] David Malet, *Foreign Fighters: Transnational Identity in Civic Conflicts* (Oxford, 2013); Nir Arielli, *From Byron to bin Laden: A History of Foreign War Volunteers* (Cambridge, MA, 2018); and the contributions to Idem and Bruce Collins (eds.), *Transnational Soldiers: Foreign Military Enlistment in the Modern Era* (New York, 2012), examine the history of foreign fighters in civil wars and revolutionary conflicts.

[38] Gordon S. Wood, *The American Revolution: A History* (New York, 1982); and Alan Taylor, *American Revolutions: A Continental History, 1750–1804* (New York, 2016), are classics on the American Revolution; an excellent overview offer the contributions to Edward G. Gray and Jane Kamensky (eds.), *The Oxford Handbook of the American Revolution* (Oxford, 2013). Georges Lefebvre, *The French Revolution: From its Origins to 1793* (London, 1962), which was first published as Georges Lefebvre, *La Révolution française* (Paris, 1951); Furet and Richet, *La Révolution*; François Furet, *Penser la Révolution française* (Paris, 1978), translated as François Furet, *Interpreting the French Revolution* (Cambridge, 1981); Furet, *La Révolution*; Lynn Hunt, *Politics, Culture, and Class in the French Revolution* (Berkeley, CA, 1984); and Ernst Schulin, *Die Französische Revolution* (Munich, 1988), are classics on the French Revolution; a good overview is provided by the chapters in David Andress (ed.), *The Oxford Handbook of the French Revolution* (Oxford, 2015); and an excellent overview of the historiography is offered by Erich Pelzer (ed.), *Revolution und Klio: Die Hauptwerke zur Französischen Revolution* (Göttingen, 2004).

Toussaint Bréda, soon to be Louverture (or L'Ouverture).[39] Addressing the insurgents of Saint-Domingue in spring 1797 Louverture, the "black Jacobin," made a powerful plea to overcome "the barriers that separate nations" to "unite the human species into a single brotherhood" and to bring "liberty" to all mankind.[40] Haiti, the richest of the Caribbean plantation colonies, became independent in 1804. "The transformation of slaves, trembling in hundreds before a single white man, into a people able to organize themselves and defeat the most powerful European nations of their day, is one of the great epics of revolutionary struggle and achievement," celebrated C. L. R. James in his 1938 classic *The Black Jacobins*.[41] Indeed, various slave rebellions of the following decades, from Demerara-Essequibo (Guyana) to Barbados, took inspiration from the Haitian Revolution. The wave also hit Latin America, where it led to the revolutionary wars.[42] On the other side of the Atlantic, on the

[39] Eugene Genovese, *From Rebellion to Revolution: Afro-American Slave Revolts in the Making of the Modern World* (Baton Rouge, LA, 1979); Laurent Dubois, *Avengers of the New World: The Story of the Haitian Revolution* (Cambridge, MA, 2004); Laurent Dubois, *A Colony of Citizens: Revolution and Slave Emancipation in the French Caribbean, 1787–1804* (Chapel Hill, NC, 2004); Ada Ferrer, *Freedom's Mirror: Cuba and Haiti in the Age of Revolution* (Cambridge, 2014); Anne Eller, *We Dream Together: Dominican Independence, Haiti, and the Fight for Caribbean Freedom* (Durham, NC, 2016); and the contributions to David P. Geggus (ed.), *The Impact of the Haitian Revolution in the Atlantic World* (Columbia, SC, 2001); and David Patrick Geggus and Norman Fiering (eds.), *The World of the Haitian Revolution* (Bloomington, IN, 2009).

[40] Toussaint L'Ouverture, "Address to the Soldiers for the Universal Destruction of Slavery," in *Toussaint L'Ouverture: The Haitian Revolution*, ed. by Jean-Bertrand Aristide (London), 28, which was first published in *Bulletin officiel de St-Domingue* (May 18, 1797).

[41] C.L.R. James, *The Black Jacobins* (London, 2001), first published in 1938, quote on xviii.

[42] Richard Graham, *Independence in Latin America: A Comparative Approach* (New York 1972); John Lynch, *The Spanish American Revolutions, 1808–1826* (New York, 1973); Michael P. Costeloe, *Response to Revolution: Imperial Spain and the Spanish American Revolutions, 1810–1840* (Cambridge, 1986); Maria T. Berruezo León, *La lucha de Hispano-America por su independencia en Inglaterra, 1800–1830* (Madrid, 1989); Ernesto de la Torre Villar, *La independencia de México* (Madrid, 1992); François-Xavier Guerra, *Modernidad e independencias: Ensayos sobre las revoluciones hispánicas* (Madrid, 1992); Jay Kinsbruner, *Independence in Spanish America: Civil Wars, Revolution, and Underdevelopment* (Albuquerque, NM, 1994); John Lynch, *Latin American Revolutions, 1808–1826: Old and New World Origins* (Norman, OK, 1994); Charler F. Walker, *Smoldering Ashes: Cuzco and the Creation of Republican Peru, 1780–1840* (Durham, NC, 1999); Robert Harvey, *Liberators: Latin America's Struggle for Independence* (New York, 2000); Jeremy Adelman, *Sovereignty and Revolution in the Iberian Atlantic* (Princeton, NJ, 2006); John Charles Chasteen, *Americanos: Latin America's Struggle for Independence* (Oxford, 2008); Gabriel Paquette, *Imperial Portugal in the Age of Atlantic Revolutions: The Luso-Brazilian World, c. 1770–1850* (Cambridge, 2013); and the contributions to Leslie Bethell (ed.), *The Independence of Latin America* (Cambridge, 1987); Alberto Flores Galindo (ed.), *Independencia y revolución, 1780–1840*, 2. vols. (Lima, 1987); and, for comparisons among the American revolutions more generally, "AHR Forum: Revolutions in the Americas," *American Historical Review* 105, 1 (2000), 92–152, are some of the most important studies on the subject. A good historiographical overview is

shores of Sierra Leone, "black" loyalists, called "Jacobins" by the British authorities, rose to demand freedom.[43] In Europe, revolutionary upheaval shook the Dutch Republic, with the Batavian Revolution, the Austrian Netherlands, with the Brabant Revolution, Poland, with the Kościuszko Uprising, and Ireland, with the Irish Rebellion.[44] Even England, often considered untouched by revolutionary troubles, was by no means a haven of peace. At the height of the Gordon Riots of 1780, as London was burning, the army was called in.[45] Similar conflicts also broke out in the Ottoman Empire, with the revolts of 1807 and 1808.[46] And around the same time, revolutionary independence movements shook the sultan's realm, most notably with the 1804 Serbian Revolution and the 1821 Greek Revolution. In the end, the revolutionary wave was felt as far away as in China and the Maghrib.[47] It is therefore hardly surprising that contemporaneous observers understood the uprisings to be universal. "Over half of the globe, all men utter but one cry, they

---

provided by Victor M. Uribe, "The Enigma of Latin American Independence: Analyses of the Last Ten Years," *Latin American Research Review* 32, 1 (1997), 236–55.

[43] Joseph Miller, "The Dynamics of History in Africa and the Atlantic 'Age of Revolutions'," in Subrahmanyam and Armitage (eds.), *The Age of Revolutions in Global Context, c. 1760–1840*, 101–24; and, on West Africa in the Age of Revolution, also Manuel Barcia, "An Atlantic Islamic Revolution: Dan Fodio's *Jihād* and Slave Rebellion in Bahia and Cuba, 1804-1844," *Journal of African Diaspora Archaeology and Heritage* 2, 1 (2013), 6–18; and Paul E. Lovejoy, *Jihad in West Africa during the Age of Revolutions* (Athens, OH, 2016).

[44] Simon Schama, *Patriots and Liberators: Revolution in the Netherlands 1780–1813* (New York, 1977); S. R. E. Klein, *Patriots Republikanisme: Politieke cultuur in Nederland (1766–1787)* (Amsterdam, 1995), as well as the classic R. R. Palmer, "Much in Little: The Dutch Revolution of 1795," *Journal of Modern History* 26, 1 (1954), 15–35, on Batavian Revolution. Janet L. Polasky, *Revolution in Brussels, 1787–1793* (Hanover, NH, 1987); and Henri Pirenne, *Les États Belgiques Unis: Histoire de la Révolution belge de 1789–1790* (Paris, 1992), on the Brabant Revolution. Alex Storozynski, *The Peasant Prince: Thaddeus Kosciuszko and the Age of Revolution* (New York, 2009), on the Kościuszko Uprising. Thomas Pakenham, *The Year of Liberty: The Great Irish Rebellion of 1798* (London, 1969); Eckhardt Rüdebusch, *Irland im Zeitalter der Revolution: Politik und Publizistik der United Irishmen 1791–98* (Frankfurt, 1989); and E. W. McFarland, *Ireland and Scotland in the Age of Revolution* (Edinburgh, 1994), on the Irish Rebellion.

[45] George F. E. Rudé, "The Gordon Riots: A Study of the Rioters and their Victims," *Transactions of the Royal Historical Society*, 5th ser., 6 (1956), 93–114; Nicholas Rogers, *Crowds, Culture and Politics in Georgian Britain* (Oxford, 1998), 152–75; Edward Royle, *Revolutionary Britannia? Reflections on the Threat of Revolution in Britain, 1789–1848* (Manchester, 2000), 13–66; and, for an excellent collection of primary sources, Iain Hampsher-Monk (ed.), *The Impact of the French Revolution: Texts from Britain in the 1790s* (Cambridge, 2005).

[46] Ali Yaycioglu, *Partners of the Empire: The Crisis of the Ottoman Order in the Age of Revolutions* (Stanford, CA, 2016).

[47] Jeng-Guo Chen, "The Tea Not Consumed: Cultural and Political Meanings of the American Revolution in China," in O'Malley, Renen, and Simon (eds.), *Beyond 1776*, 206–25; and Ian Coller, "Barbary and Revolution: France and North Africa, 1789–1798," in Patricia M. E. Lorcin and Todd Shepard (eds.), *French Mediterraneans: Transnational and Imperial Histories* (Lincoln, NE, 2016), 52–75.

share but one desire," proclaimed a pamphlet in Brussels: All "humanity, united in action" was "rising up to reclaim a majestic and powerful liberty."[48] "All circumstances taken together, the French revolution is the most astonishing that has hitherto happened in the world," Edmund Burke claimed in 1790, anxious about the global impact of the revolutionary fervor.[49] The revolutionary wave may even be seen as a global phenomenon; C. A. Bayly considered it part of a "world crisis" that engulfed the globe between the Atlantic and the Pacific in the late eighteenth and early nineteenth centuries, also involving the Wahhabi revolution on the Arabian Peninsula and the Sikh revolution in northern India.[50]

Focusing on the Atlantic world, David A. Bell's chapter "The Atlantic Revolutions" traces the diverse connections between the upheavals. It examines indirect structural changes – such as economic, social, and cultural-literary transformations, as well as increasing strains between imperial centers and peripheries – which destabilized the aristocratic Atlantic order, as well as direct connections. The latter could be forged by itinerant revolutionaries inspired by the idea of global liberation.[51] The list of examples is long. Having fought as a European volunteer in the American Revolution, the Marquis de Lafayette, for instance, later participated in revolutionary activities in France, Prussia, and Austria.[52] The most prominent of these figures was perhaps the English-born American revolutionary Thomas Paine, who was at the forefront of the French Revolution. "A Share (sic) in two revolutions is living to some purpose," he wrote to George Washington in autumn 1789 – "I am going over to France."[53] His comrade (and later cellmate), the Prussian revolutionary

[48] Ct. in Janet Polasky, *Revolutions without Borders*, 2.

[49] Edmund Burke, *Reflections on the Revolution in France: And the Proceedings in Certain Societies in London Relative to that Event* (Cambridge, 2013), 11, which was first published in 1790.

[50] Bayly, *The Birth of the Modern World 1780–1914*, 86–120; and Idem, "The 'Revolutionary Age' in the Wider World, c. 1790-1830."

[51] Alfred Hasbrouck, *Foreign Legionaries in the Liberation of Spanish South America* (New York, 1928); Matthew Brown, *Adventuring through Spanish Colonies: Simón Bolívar, Foreign Mercenaries and the Birth of New Nations* (Liverpool, 2006); Polasky, *Revolutions without Borders*; Nathan Perl-Rosenthal, *Citizen Sailors: Becoming American in the Age of Revolution* (Cambridge, MA, 2015); Maya Jasanoff, *Liberty's Exiles: American Loyalists in the Revolutionary World* (New York, 2011); Friedemann Pestel, *Kosmopoliten wider Willen: Die "monarchiens" als Revolutionsemigranten* (Berlin, 2015); and Pascal Firges, *French Revolutionaries in the Ottoman Empire: Diplomacy, Political Culture, and the Limiting of Universal Revolution, 1792–1798* (Oxford, 2016), are important works on the mobility of peoples during and after the Atlantic revolutions.

[52] Lloyd Kramer, *Lafayette in Two Worlds: Public Cultures and Personal Identities in an Age of Revolutions* (Chapel Hill, NC, 1996).

[53] Thomas Paine to George Washington, October 16, 1789, London, in *The Papers of George Washington: Presidential Series*, 20 vols. (Charlottesville, VA, 1988–2016), vol. 4

Johann Baptist Hermann Maria, Baron de Cloots, known as Anacharsis
Cloots, who was charged with treason by the Jacobins, proclaimed, as he
mounted the scaffold of the guillotine in 1794: "Hurrah for the fraternity
of nations! Long live the Republic of the world!"[54] Most of the itinerant
rebels saw their struggle as part of a global movement. "God grant that
not only the love of liberty, but a thorough knowledge of the rights of man,
may pervade all Nations of the Earth," wrote Benjamin Franklin, who had
spent a decade in Europe, to a British friend in late 1789, "so that
a Philosopher may set his Foot anywhere on its Surface, and say, 'This
is my Country'."[55] Nicolas de Condorcet celebrated this global intellectual fraternity similarly: "Men whom the reading of philosophic books
had secretly converted to the love of liberty became enthusiastic over the
liberty of a foreign people while they waited for the moment when they
could recover their own, and they seized with joy this opportunity to avow
publicly sentiments which prudence had prevented them from
expressing."[56] His *Influence de la Révolution d'Amérique sur l'Europe*, published three years before the storming of the Bastille, had discussed early
on the importance of intellectual exchange across continents. Indeed,
more important than the movement of revolutionaries was the circulation
of political ideas. In some cases, texts were literally transferred, for
example when French revolutionaries used Virginia's bill of rights as a
model for their *Déclaration des Droits de l'Homme*. Around the world,
authors of new constitutional texts influenced one another.[57] To simplify,
it was the ideas of the global enlightenment, Peter Gay's "party of
humanity," that influenced revolutionaries across borders, whether
Louverture, who was said to have read the Abbé Raynal, or Simón
Bolívar, who studied Adam Smith, Montesquieu, and Rousseau.[58] The

---

(September 1789-January 1790), ed. by Dorothy Twohig (Charlottesville, VA, 1993),
196–97, 197.

[54] Ct. in Michael Rapport, *Nationality and Citizenship in Revolutionary France: The
Treatment of Foreigners 1789–1799* (Oxford, 2000), 2.

[55] Benjamin Franklin to David Hartley, December 4, 1789, Philadelphia, published in
Richard N. Rosenfeld, *American Aurora: A Democratic-Republican Returns* (New York,
1997), 496.

[56] Nicolas de Condorcet, "Éloge de Franklin," in *Oeuvres de Condorcet*, ed. by A. Condorcet
O'Connor and M. F. Arago, 12 vols. (Paris, 1847–1849), vol. 3 (Paris, 1847), 372–423,
406–07.

[57] Linda Colley, "Empires of Writing: Britain, America and Constitutions, 1776–1848,"
Law and History Review 32, 2 (2014), 237–66, is an outstanding study of the phenom-
enon. David Armitage, *The Declaration of Independence: A Global History* (Cambridge,
MA, 2007), provides a pathbreaking case study.

[58] Peter Gay, *The Party of Humanity* (New York, 1964). On the Enlightenment, see the
overviews by Dorinda Outram, *The Enlightenment* (Cambridge, 1995); Anthony Pagden,
The Enlightenment (Oxford, 2013); and the opus of Jonathan Israel, including Idem,
Radical Enlightenment: Philosophy and the Making of Modernity, 1650–1750 (Oxford,

forbidden tracts that Robert Darnton has shown to have been so important in 1789 were not just read within the borders of one country.[59] And it was not only political texts but also other media, such as art and songs, that connected revolutionaries across borders. Often, they shared a common culture, from letter writing to forms of sociability. Bell also looks at external shocks – another form of direct connection – showing that revolutions in the Atlantic world often destabilized the social and political situation in other countries, leading to political unrest there. Yet, his chapter also makes clear that connections had limits and that local conditions and internal dynamics made each revolutionary upheaval unique. In the end, the Atlantic Revolutions provoked a wave of counter-revolutions by the old elite, determined to preserve its privileges and properties. The smaller post-Atlantic revolutionary wave of the 1920s, which swept across Spain, Naples, and Russia, and the 1830s uprisings, which shook France, Poland, Switzerland, the Italian peninsula, Portugal, Brazil, England and Wales, and the Netherlands were, with few exceptions, soon broken by the forces of restoration.[60]

The upheavals of 1848 engulfed greater parts of Europe than any other revolutionary wave in history. Revolutionaries, imbued with the ideas of liberalism and nationalism, rose in rapid sequence from Naples, Turin, Prague, Budapest, Amsterdam, and Jassy to Copenhagen, Berlin, Munich, Vienna, Venice, and Paris.[61] It was an amalgam of protests – rural and

---

2001); Idem, *Enlightenment Contested: Philosophy, Modernity, and the Emancipation of Man, 1670–1752* (Oxford, 2006); Idem, *Democratic Enlightenment: Philosophy, Revolution, and Human Rights 1750–1790* (Oxford, 2011), as well as Idem, *A Revolution of the Mind: Radical Enlightenment and the Intellectual Origins of Modern Democracy* (Princeton, NJ, 2009); Idem, *Revolutionary Ideas: An Intellectual History of the French Revolution from The Rights of Man to Robespierre* (Princeton, NJ, 2014); and Idem, *The Expanding Blaze: How the American Revolution Ignited the World, 1775–1848* (Princeton, NJ, 2017). Sebastian Conrad, "The Enlightenment in Global History: A Historiographical Critique," *American Historical Review* 117, 4 (2012), 999–1027, provides an excellent global perspective on the Enlightenment.

[59] Robert Darnton, *The Forbidden Best-Sellers of Pre-Revolutionary France* (London, 1995).

[60] Richard Stites, *The Four Horsemen: Riding to Liberty in Post-Napoleonic Europe* (Oxford, 2014), discusses the revolutionary wave of the 1820s. David H. Pinkney, *The French Revolution of 1830* (Princeton, NJ, 1973); Pamela M. Pilbeam, *The 1830 Revolution in France* (New York, 1991); J. S. Fishman, *Diplomacy and Revolution: The London Conference of 1830 and the Belgian Revolt* (Amsterdam, 1988); and Royle, *Revolutionary Britannia?*, 67–91, provide overviews of some of the 1830s revolutions.

[61] Wolfgang J. Mommsen, *1848: Die ungewollte Revolution* (Frankfurt, 1989); Justine Davis Randers-Pehrson, *Germans and the Revolution of 1848–1849* (New York, 1999); and Hans Joachim Hahn, *The 1848 Revolutions in German-Speaking Europe* (London, 2001), on Germany; Georges Duveau, *1848: The Making of a Revolution* (New York, 1967); and Arnaud Coutant, *1848, quand la République combattait la Démocratie* (Paris, 2009), on France; István Deák, *Lawful Revolution: Louis Kossuth and the Hungarians 1848–1849* (New York, 1979), on the Habsburg Empire; Paul Ginsborg, *Daniele Manin and the Venetian Revolution of 1848–49* (Cambridge, 1979), on Italy;

agrarian, urban and proletarian, bourgeois constitutional and national. State authorities put down most of these uprisings with an iron fist. The numbers of victims rose into the thousands. The revolt of 1848 also had a global impact. It shook the British imperial world, leading to tensions from Ceylon to the Cape Colony.[62] Its influence was also felt across South and North America.[63] In the French West Indies, it fueled the Martinican slave revolt of 1848, which soon spilled over to neighboring Caribbean colonies.[64] In most places the revolts failed. Comparing the Parisian coup d'état of 1851 with Napoleon's seizure of power in 1799, Marx famously bemoaned in *The Eighteenth Brumaire of Louis Bonaparte* that "the revolution of 1848 knew nothing better to do than to parody."[65]

In his chapter "The Revolutionary Waves of 1848," Christopher Clark traces the spread of unrest across the world, exploring various forms of connectivity that made the simultaneity of these tumults possible. Structural transformations – social and economic crises affecting several countries similarly – were crucial. Yet the revolts were also directly entangled. Ideas, carried by a growing number of newspapers, spread across borders, traveling for example by packet boat from Paris to Martinique, from London to New South Wales. Itinerant revolutionaries fought on barricades across Europe. Transnational exile networks which had emerged in the European radical milieu since the 1820s to some extent shaped these revolutions. Mikhail Bakunin famously marched alongside revolutionaries in places like Baden, Prague, and Dresden. "The world is split into two camps; on one side the revolution, on the other the counterrevolution," he wrote in autumn 1848: "It is a sacred duty for all of us, soldiers of the revolution, democrats of all countries, to unite our forces, to come to an understanding and to organize."[66] But lesser-known figures, like the Polish revolutionary Ludwig Mieroslawski, who between 1846 and 1850 participated in

Royle, *Revolutionary Britannia?*, 92–138, on Britain; and Selda Kilich-Cafer Güler and Hamiyet Sezer Feyzioğlu, "Revolutions of 1848 and the Ottoman Empire,"*Bulgarian Historical Review* 37, 3/4 (2009), 196–205, on influences on the Ottoman Empire.

[62] Taylor, "The 1848 Revolutions and the British Empire."

[63] Roberts and Howe, "The United States and the Revolutions of 1848"; Weyland, "The Diffusion of Revolution: '1848' in Europe and Latin America"; and the contributions to Thomson (ed.), *The European Revolutions of 1848 and the Americas*.

[64] Lépine, *Dix semaines qui ébranlèrent la Martinique, 25 mars – 4 Juin 1848.*

[65] Karl Marx, "The Eighteenth Brumaire of Louis Bonaparte," in *Karl Marx and Frederick Engels: Collected Works*, vol. 11 (*Marx and Engels: 1851–53*) (London 1979), 99–197, 104; which was first published as Karl Marx, "Der 18te Brumaire des Louis Napoleon," *Die Revolution* 1 (1852).

[66] Mikhail Bakunin, "Appeal to the Slavs," in *Bakunin on Anarchy: Selected Works by the Activist-Founder of World Anarchism*, ed. by Sam Dolgoff (London, 1973), 63–68, 63 and 65, which was first published as Michael Bakunin, *Aufruf an die Slaven: Von einem russischen Patrioten* (Koethen, 1848).

protests in places like Berlin, Paris, Posen, and Baden (and later supported the Paris Commune), were also part of this story.[67] The movement of rebels peaked in the aftermath of 1848, with thousands of forty-eighters going into exile, flocking to Great Britain, the United States, and Latin America, where many of them continued their political activities.[68] Overall, 1848 may well be seen as part of another global crisis; Jürgen Osterhammel has even raised the question as to whether it may be seen as part of a global though unconnected "revolutionary cluster," which also included the Taiping Revolution of 1850–64, the Indian Revolt of 1857–59, and the American Civil War of 1861–65.[69]

The Paris Commune of spring 1871, which ended in a bloodbath with thousands massacred, is often considered a local revolt.[70] And yet, as Quentin Deluermoz shows in his chapter "The World of the Paris Commune," it was far more than an isolated urban event.[71] Many of the revolutionaries were foreigners. The French Republican War of 1870 had brought thousands of international volunteers, organized in Giuseppe Garibaldi's Army of the Vosges, to France to fight to replace the oppressive monarchy with a universal republic. Among them were Italians, Poles, Spaniards, Belgians, Irishmen, Greeks, Uruguayans, and citizens of the United States.[72] Many of them had previously fought across

---

[67] Norman Davies, *God's Playground: A History of Poland*, 2 vols. (Oxford, 1981), vol. 2 (*1975 to the Present*), 35.

[68] Bruce Levine, *The Spirit of 1848: German Immigrants, Labor Conflict, and the Coming of the Civil War* (Urbana, IL, 1992); Wolfram Siemann, "Asyl, Exil und Emigration der 1848er," in Dieter Langewiesche (ed.), *Demokratiebewegung und Revolution 1847 bis 1849: Internationale Aspekte und europäische Verbdungen* (Karlsruhe, 1998), 70–91; and the contributions to Charlotte L. Brancaforte (eds.), *The German Forty-Eighters in the United States* (New York, 1989).

[69] Jürgen Osterhammel, *The Transformation of the World: A Global History of the Nineteenth Century* (Princeton, NJ, 2014), 543–57, which was first published as Jürgen Osterhammel, *Die Verwandlung der Welt: Eine Geschichte des 19. Jahrhunderts* (Munich, 2009), 777–98. Michael Geyer and Charles Bright, "Global Violence and Nationalizing Wars in Eurasia and America: The Geopolitics of War in the Mid-Nineteenth Century," *Comparative Studies in Society and History* 38, 4 (1996), 619–57, looks at the mid-century moment of violent conflict more generally. Rajmohan Gandhi, *A Tale of Two Revolts: India's Mutiny and the American Civil War* (London, 2011), provides a comparison between the upheavals in America and India.

[70] Jacques Rougerie, *La Commune de 1871* (Paris, 2009); Pierre Milza, *L'année terrible: La Commune (mars-juin 1871)* (Paris, 2009); and John Merriman, *Massacre: The Life and Death of the Paris Commune* (New York, 2014), provide good overviews. Robert Le Quillec, *Bibliographie critique de la Commune de Paris* (Paris, 2006), offers an excellent historiographical overview.

[71] Quentin Deluermoz, *Commune(s), 1870–1871: Une traversée des mondes au XIXe siècle* (Paris, 2020).

[72] Lucy Riall, *Garibaldi: Invention of a Hero* (New Haven, CT, 2007), 352–55; and, focusing on the international struggle of the revolutionaries, Gilles Pécout, "The International Armed Volunteers: Pilgrims of a Transnational Risorgimento," *Journal of Modern Italian Studies* 14 (2009), 413–26.

the continent, in the conflicts in Italy, Poland, Spain, Ireland, and some even in America. In March 1871, several joined the Paris Commune, and some soon served in its higher ranks. After the movement was crushed, thousands of revolutionaries were deported, particularly to New Caledonia in the South Pacific, or forced into exile, to places from Switzerland to America, where they continued to promote their revolutionary ideas.[73] Yet it was not just the Paris Commune itself that was international. Protest marches in its support, led by republicans, socialists, and other radicals, took place in metropolises like London, Geneva, Brussels, Hamburg, Florence, and New York.

At the same time, the events in Paris led to uprisings in towns as far apart as Marseille, Algiers, and Fort-de-France. In Martinique, news of the proclamation of the French republic in autumn 1870 triggered the Southern Insurrection, the biggest uprising there since 1848.[74] Even stronger was the impact in French North Africa, where the events in France led to the Kabyle Insurrection, which lasted from early to late 1871.[75] The Algerian insurrection was an Arab anticolonial movement as well as a republican movement, which took on the name "Commune of Algiers," led by deported European 1848 veterans who, in autumn 1870, took control of Algiers and other main cities and, in spring 1871, sided with the Paris communards. It was to some extent triggered by the Franco-Prussian war, which forced Paris to send "African" troops to France, thereby weakening its position in Algeria, and by the proclamation of the Third Republic and the Paris Commune. To be sure, the uprisings also had deeper, local causes, but connections to the events in France – the movement of ideas and revolutionaries, as well as the shock of the military events in Europe which led to a change in the military status quo in Algeria – were crucial. In the end, the revolts were swiftly crushed. Still, as Deluermoz's chapter demonstrates, the Commune was a global media event and inspired revolutionaries from Latin America to East Asia, although its interpretations around the world were diverse. In Mexico, the paper *La Comuna* (*The Commune*), founded in the early 1870s and later renamed *La Comuna Mexicana* (*The Mexican Commune*), stated that: "As long as there is a man or a woman alive, the Commune will continue to exist, because great principles are immortal" and that the

---

[73] Julia Nicholls, *Revolutionary Thought after the Paris Commune, 1871–1885* (Cambridge, 2019), 207–68.
[74] Gilbert Pago, *L'insurrection de Martinique, 1870–1871* (Paris, 2011).
[75] Idir Hachi, *Histoire sociale de l'insurrection de 1872 et du procès de ses chefs (Constantine, 1873)* (PhD dissertation, Aix-Marseille University, 2017); and, on the global context, Tony Ballantyne and Antoinette Burton, *Empires and the Reach of the Global, 1870–1945* (Cambridge, MA, 2014), 147.

"Commune is alive in France as in Mexico, in the United States as in Germany, in China as in Arabia."[76]

Of even wider global reach were the Constitutional Revolutions of the early twentieth century, which Charles Kurzman discusses in his chapter "The Global Wave of Constitutional Revolutions, 1905–1915." Imperial Japan's victory over the tsarist empire and the subsequent Russian Revolution of 1905 forced Tsar Nicholas II, on October 30, 1905, to sign a one-page document promising to respect civil rights, share power with a parliament, and hold free elections.[77] Within a week, newspapers across the world had published accounts of the events in Russia. They marked the beginning of a global wave of constitutional revolutions that would engulf more than a quarter of the world's population. The events in Russia were followed first by the Persian Constitutional Revolution of 1905–11, which compelled the shah to accept a constitution, a parliament, and elections, then by the Young Turk Revolution of 1908 in the Ottoman Empire, where radical officers forced Abdülhamid II to restore the long-suspended 1876 constitution, and finally by the Chinese Revolution of 1911–16, which led to the collapse of the Qing dynasty and the foundation of the Chinese Republic.[78] In the end, the constitutional revolutionary wave even swept across Europe, with the 1909 Greek Goudi revolt, Portugal's revolution of

---

[76] Bruno Bosteels, "The Mexican Commune," in Shannon Brincat (ed.), *Communism in the Twenty-First Century*, (Santa Barbara, CA, 2013), 161–89, quotation on 169.

[77] Abraham Ascher, *The Revolution of 1905*, 2 vols. (Stanford, CA, 1988–1994); and, more concisely, Abraham Ascher, *The Revolution of 1905: A Short History* (Stanford, CA, 2004).

[78] Ahmad Kasravi, *Tarikh-i Mashrutah-yi Iran* (*History of the Constitutional Revolution in Iran*) (Tehran, 1319 [1941]); Mangol Bayat, *Iran's First Revolution: Shi'ism and the Constitutional Revolution of 1905–1909* (Oxford, 1991); Janet Afary, *The Iranian Constitutional Revolution, 1906–1911: Grassroots Democracy, Social Democracy, and the Origins of Feminism* (New York, 1996); and the contributions to H. E. Chehabi and Vanessa Martin (eds.), *Iran's Constitutional Revolution: Popular Politics, Cultural Transformations and Transnational Connections* (London, 2010), on Qajar Iran, and, on its international connections, Abdul-Hadi Hairi, "European and Asian Influences on the Persian Revolution of 1906," *Asian Affairs* 62, 2 (1975), 155–64; and Mansour Bonakdarian, "Iranian Nationalism and Global Solidarity Networks, 1906–1918: Internationalism, Transnationalism, and Nationalist Cosmopolitanism," in Houchang Chehabi, Peyman Jafari, and Maral Jefroudi (eds.), *Iran in the Middle East: Transnational Encounters and Social History* (London, 2015), 77–119. Şerif Mardin, *Genesis of Young Ottoman Thought* (Princeton, NJ, 1962); M. Naim Turfan, *The Rise of the Young Turks: Politics, the Military and Ottoman Collapse* (London, 2000); and M. Şükrü Hanioğlu, *Preparation for a Revolution: The Young Turks, 1902–1908* (Oxford, 2001), on the Ottoman Empire. Michael Gasster, *Chinese Intellectuals and the Revolution of 1911* (Seattle, WA, 1969); Joseph W. Esherick, *Reform and Revolution in China: The 1911 Revolution in Hunan and Hubei* (Berkeley, CA, 1976); Xiaowei Zheng, *The Politics of Rights and the 1911 Revolution in China* (Stanford, CA, 2018); and, for a concise overview, Rana Mitter, "1911: The Unanchored Chinese Revolution," *The China Quarterly* 208 (2011), 1009–20, on Qing China; and on its international dimension, L. Eve Armentrout Ma, *Revolutionaries, Monarchists, and Chinatowns: Chinese Politics in the Americas and the 1911 Revolution* (Honolulu, HI, 1990).

1910, and the Monegasque constitutional revolution of 1910, as well as the Americas, with the Mexican Revolution of 1910–20, which was perhaps the most extreme of all of these uprisings, leading to the fall of the country's strongman, Porfirio Díaz.[79] All of these revolutions challenged autocratic states and sought to legally circumscribe the absolute authority of their rulers. Their most prominent proponents were intellectuals.

The movements were interconnected on multiple levels. First, there were indirect structural conditions which affected all of the countries simultaneously, most importantly an intellectual current, a zeitgeist, that was centered on ideals of constitutionalism, liberalism, and positivism, and, related to this, the emergence of a global class of modern intellectuals.[80] Second, the revolutions were directly entangled with each other. Ideas circulated among these different revolutionary societies, inspiring the revolutionary intellectuals at their core. It was the first revolutionary wave that was covered live by international telegraph services around the world. Itinerant revolutionaries, on the other side, were less important. In the end, most of these revolts were either smashed or quickly reversed. And yet many of the reforms they advocated – educational, judicial, and medical – endured. Looking back, there is no doubt that this wave of liberal constitutional revolutions shaped the world for years to come.[81]

More momentous even was the global impact of the Russian Revolution.[82] When red revolutionaries stormed the tsar's Winter Palace, the world was electrified. "The October Revolution laid the foundation of a new culture taking everybody into consideration, and for that very reason immediately acquiring international significance," Trotsky later wrote in

[79] Douglas L. Wheeler, "The Portuguese Revolution of 1910," *Journal of Modern History* 44, 2 (1972), 172–94, on Portugal. S. Victor Papacosma, *The Military in Greek Politics: The 1909 Coup D'état* (Kent, OH, 1977), on Greece. Jean-Baptiste Robert, *Histoire de Monaco* (Paris, 1973), 82–83, on Monaco. James D. Cockcroft, *Intellectual Precursors of the Mexican Revolution 1900–1913* (Austin, TX, 1968); Adolfo Gilly, *The Mexican Revolution* (London, 1983), which was first published as Adolfo Gilly, *La revolución interrumpida* (Mexico City, 1971); Alan Knight, *The Mexican Revolution*, 2 vols. (Cambridge, 1986); John Mason Hart, *Revolutionary Mexico: The Coming and Process of the Mexican Revolution* (Berkeley, CA, 1987); and Michael J. Gonzales, *The Mexican Revolution: 1910–1940* (Albuquerque, NM, 2002), on Mexico.

[80] Denis Sdvižkov, *Das Zeitalter der Intelligenz: Zur vergleichenden Geschichte der Gebildeten in Europa bis zum Ersten Weltkrieg* (Göttingen, 2006).

[81] Bruce Ackerman, *Revolutionary Constitutions: Charismatic Leadership and the Rule of Law* (Cambridge, MA, 2019), and, with a focus on the Middle East, Elizabeth F. Thompson, *Justice Interrupted: The Struggle for Constitutional Government in the Middle East* (Cambridge, MA, 2013), on the wider context of twentieth-century constitutionalism.

[82] William H. Chamberlin, *The Russian Revolution*, 2 vols. (London, 1935); Sheila Fitzpatrick, *The Russian Revolution* (Oxford, 1982); and Figes, *A People's Tragedy*, are the classics. The classic eyewitness account remains John Reed, *Ten Days That Shock the World* (New York, 1919).

his monumental *History of the Russian Revolution* (1932).[83] In her chapter "The Global Red Revolution," Rachel G. Hoffman assesses the shock waves that the events in St. Petersburg sent across the globe. Stirred by the social, political, and economic turmoil of the First World War, and inspired by the upheaval in Russia, revolutionaries across the world rose in an effort to overthrow the old order. The revolutionary wave included the November 1918 Revolution in Germany and the proclamation of the Munich Soviet Republic, the Hungarian Revolution of 1919 and the foundation of the Hungarian Soviet Republic, the Slovak Soviet Republic of 1919, the Limerick Soviet, proclaimed in western Ireland in spring 1919, and the Galician Soviet Socialist Republic, established in 1920.[84] At the same time, Iranian revolutionaries, led by guerrilla commander Mirza Kuchik Khan, proclaimed the Persian Socialist Soviet Republic in Gilan.[85] Socialist uprisings and general strikes erupted across the world, spanning Glasgow, Genoa, Le Havre, Seattle, and Los Angeles. In some countries, they led to longer periods of social unrest, from the Biennio Rosso in Italy to Spain's Trienio Bolchevique.[86] In Turin, Antonio Gramsci's revolutionary journal *L'Ordine Nuovo* called for "the systematic suppression of private property, and the bourgeois class in all its forms of

---

[83] Leon Trotsky, *History of the Russian Revolution* (London, 2017), xvi, which was first published in 1932.

[84] Rudolf Coper, *Failure of a Revolution Germany in 1918–1919* (Cambridge, 1955); Sebastian Haffner, *Failure of a Revolution: Germany, 1918–19* (New York, 1973), originally published as *Die verratene Revolution: Deutschland 1918/19* (Hamburg, 1969); Richard Grunberger, *Red Rising in Bavaria* (London, 1973); Ulrich Kluge, *Die deutsche Revolution 1918/1919* (Frankfurt, 1985); Mark Jones, *Founding Weimar: Violence and the German Revolution of 1918–19* (Cambridge, 2016); and Volker Ulrich, *Die Revolution von 1918/19* (Munich, 2018), on Germany. Rudolf L. Tokes, *Béla Kun and the Hungarian Soviet Republic: The Origins and Role of the Communist Party of Hungary in the Revolutions of 1918–1919* (New York, 1967); and Sándor Szilassy, *Revolutionary Hungary, 1918–1921* (Astor Park, FL, 1971), on Hungary. Peter A. Toma, "The Slovak Soviet Republic of 1919," *American Slavic and East European Review* 17, 2 (1958), 203–15, on Slovakia. Liam Cahill, *Forgotten Revolution: Limerick Soviet 1919* (Dublin, 1990), on Ireland. Norman Davies, *White Eagle, Red Star: The Polish-Soviet War, 1919–20* (New York, 1972), on Galicia.

[85] Schapour Ravasani, *Sowjetrepublik Gilan: Die sozialistische Bewegung im Iran seit Ende des 19. Jh. bis 1922* (Berlin, 1973); Ibrahim Fakhrayi, *Sardar-i Jangal (The Commander of the Jungle)* (Tehran, 1362 [1983]); and Cosroe Chaqueri, *The Soviet Socialist Republic of Iran, 1920–21* (Pittsburgh, PA, 1994). A very insightful eyewitness account is offered by Jan Kulaj, *Biganah'i dar Kanar-i Kuchak Khan (A Stranger with Kuchik Khan)* (Tehran, 1394 [2015]).

[86] Stefano Caretti, *La rivoluzione russa e il socialismo italiano (1917–1921)* (Pisa 1974); Giuseppe Maione, *Il biennio rosso: Autonomia e spontaneità operaia nel 1919–1920* (Bologna, 1975); Roberto Bianchi, *Pace, pane, terra: Il 1919 in Italia* (Rome, 2006); and Fabio Fabbri, *Le origini della guerra civile: L'Italia dalla Grande Guerra al Fascismo, 1918–1921* (Turin, 2009); and Nives Banin, *Il biennio rosso 1919–1920* (Arezzo, 2013), on Italy; and Ángeles Barrio Alonso, *La modernización de España (1917–1939): Política y sociedad* (Madrid, 2004), on Spain.

domination: parliaments, newspapers, political parties, banks, professional armies" to forge a Soviet society.[87] Fears of socialist unrest even spread to London. "Thrones are everywhere crashing and the men of property everywhere secretly trembling," Beatrice Webb, co-founder of the LSE, wrote in her diary on November 11, 1918, asking: "How soon will the tide of revolution catch up with the tide of victory? That is a question which is exercising Whitehall and Buckingham Palace and which is causing anxiety even among the more thoughtful democrats."[88] Ultimately, the events in Russia also resonated in the colonial world. Inspired by Lenin's vision of "self-determination" for the oppressed peoples, anticolonial revolutionaries were invigorated. There was a Leninist moment in the lands of Europe's empires, reaching from Southeast Asia to West Africa. Everywhere the specter of socialist unrest began to haunt colonial officials. And yet, in the end, most attempts to establish socialist states outside of the Soviet Union were shattered by anti-Bolshevik and right-wing counter-movements.

The trajectories of the upheavals inspired by the events in the tsarist empire had many similarities. In all cases, revolutionaries borrowed ideas from the Russian Revolution to justify and popularize their actions. All of the revolutions were connected through structural transformations that affected different countries simultaneously, most importantly the First World War and the collapse of Europe's continental empires. Yet they also inspired one another. Soviet ideology gained new traction across the world after the successful dethroning of the tsar. Revolutionaries moved between countries. The most remarkable of them was M. N. Roy, who roamed between India, the Dutch East Indies, Japan, Korea, China, the United States, Mexico, and the Soviet Union, becoming a founding member of the communist party not only in India but also in Mexico.[89]

As they consolidated their power in the lands of the former tsarist empire, the Bolsheviks began to support revolutionaries abroad, from Budapest to Rasht. Moscow sought to coordinate the wave of revolutions through the Soviet-led (Third) Communist International (Comintern).

---

[87] Antonio Gramsci (unsigned), "La tendenza centrista," *L'Ordine Nuovo* 1, 12 (August 2, 1919). Martin Clark, *Antonio Gramsci and the Revolution that Failed* (New Haven, CT, 1977), provides the context.

[88] *Beatrice Webb's Diaries 1912–1924*, ed. by Margaret I. Cole (London, 1952), 136 (Entry of November 11, 1918).

[89] John Patrick Haithcox, *Communism and Nationalism in India; M. N. Roy and Comintern Policy, 1920–1939* (Princeton, NJ, 1971); S. M. Ganguly, *Leftism in India: M. N. Roy and Indian Politics, 1920–1948* (Columbia, MO, 1984); Kris Manjapra, *M. N. Roy: Marxism and Colonial Cosmopolitanism* (Delhi, 2010); and, for a concise account, Michael Goebel, "Geopolitics, Transnational Solidarity or Diaspora Nationalism? The Global Career of M. N. Roy, 1915-1930," *European Review of History* 21, 4 (2014), 485–99.

Significant efforts were also made to incite anticolonial movements.[90] In classic Marxist ideology, the colonial world had been of only peripheral concern. Lenin, however, made anti-imperialism a tenet of communist ideology, extending the slogan of the Communist Manifesto to "Proletarians of all countries and oppressed peoples, unite!"[91] As early as March 1917, he declared that if the Bolsheviks' revolution was successful in Russia, their peace plan was to include the "liberation of *all* colonies" and of "*all* dependent, oppressed and unequal nations."[92] And after the Bolsheviks seized power, Trotsky, as newly appointed Commissar of Foreign Affairs, sharply denounced the Western wartime rhetoric of self-determination, asking whether they were "willing on their part to give the right of self-determination to the peoples of Ireland, Egypt, India, Madagascar, Indochina, et cetera," in order to proclaim: "For it is clear that to demand self determination for the peoples that are comprised within the borders of enemy states and to refuse self determination to the peoples of their own state or of their own colonies would mean the defense of the most naked, the most cynical imperialism."[93] Shortly

---

[90] Stephen White, "Communism and the East: The Baku Congress, 1920," *Slavic Review* 33, 3 (1974), 492–514; Idem, "Colonial Revolution and the Communist International, 1919–1924," *Science and Society* 40, 2 (1976), 173–93; Idem, "Soviet Russia and the Asian Revolution, 1917–1924," *Review of International Studies* 10, 3 (1984), 219–32; Ronald Grigor Suny, "'Don't Paint Nationalism Red': Nationalist Revolution and Socialist Anti-Imperialism," in Prasenjit Duara (ed.), *Decolonization: Perspectives from Now and Then* (New York, 2003), 176–98; Jean-François Fayet, "1919," in Stephen A. Smith (ed.), *The Oxford Handbook of the History of Communism* (Oxford, 2014), 109–24, especially 119–24; Frederik Petersson, "Imperialism and the Communist International," *Journal of Labor and Society* 20, 1 (2017), 23–42; Alp Yenen, "The Other Jihad: Enver Pasha, Bolsheviks, and Politics of Anticolonial Muslim Nationalism during the Baku Congress 1920," in T. G. Fraser (ed.), *The First World War and its Aftermath: The Shaping of the Middle East*, (London, 2015); and, more generally, Silvio Pons, *The Global Revolution*, 43–101. The major studies of the Baku congress are John Riddell, *To See the Dawn: Baku, 1920-First Congress of the Peoples of the East* (New York, 1993); and John Sexton, *Alliance of Adversaries: The Congress of the Toilers of the Far East* (Leiden, 2018). On the case of the British dominions, see Oleksa Drachewych, *The Communist International, Anti-Imperialism and Racial Equality in British Dominions* (London, 2018). On the case of British India, see Satyabrata Rai Chowdhuri, *Leftism in India, 1917–1947* (New York, 2007); Kama Maclean, *A Revolutionary History of Interwar India: Violence, Image, Voice and Text* (Oxford, 2015); and the chapters in Kama Maclean and J. Daniel Elam (eds.), *Revolutionary Lives in South Asia: Acts and Afterlives of Anticolonial Political Action* (London, 2015).

[91] Ct. in White, "Colonial Revolution and the Communist International, 1919–1924," 173.

[92] V. I. Lenin, "Letters from Afar: Fourth Letter: How to Achieve Peace," March 25, 1917, in *V. I. Lenin: Collected Works*, vol. 23 (*August 1916-March 1917*) (London, 1964), 333–39, 338.

[93] Leon Trotsky, "To the Peoples and Governments of Allied Countries," December 31, 1917, included in David Rowland Francis to Robert Lansing, December 31, 1917, Petrograd, published in Arthur S. Link (ed.), *The Papers of Woodrow Wilson*, 69 vols. (Princeton, NJ, 1966–1994), vol. 45 (*November 11, 1917 – January 15, 1918*) (Princeton, NJ, 1984), 411–14, 412–13.

afterward, the Bolsheviks issued appeals to Arabs, Indians, and "all the toiling Muslims of Russia and the East" to rise against imperialism.[94] The Comintern trained revolutionaries from China, India, the Dutch East Indies, Korea, the Arab world, and Africa at the newly established Communist University for the Toilers of the East, and published various anticolonial publications. Most importantly, the Kremlin organized a number of large anticolonial congresses in the interwar period. The first one, held in Baku in 1920, brought together almost 2,000 revolutionaries from around the world. "Many violent speeches were made," it was reported, "but the general effect was in many cases spoiled by large numbers of the Moslem representatives going outside to say their prayers."[95] And yet, despite Moscow's support of various communist anticolonial movements, it took some years until these movements grew.

More immediate was the impact of liberal nationalism on the colonial and semi-colonial world at the end of the First World War, which is discussed in Erez Manela's chapter "The Wilsonian Uprisings of 1919." Woodrow Wilson's (and European statesmen's) promises of national self-determination during the war and at the Paris Peace Conference had sparked hopes among anticolonial nationalists around the world.[96] But as it became clear that the old empires were not willing to relinquish their overseas possessions, a wave of anticolonial nationalist revolts erupted, the May Fourth Movement in China, the Indian nationalist protest that marked the beginning of Mahatma Gandhi's civil disobedience movement, the Egyptian Revolution of 1919, and the March First Movement in Korea. In the end, all of these revolts were brutally suppressed, with thousands killed. Even so, they irrevocably transformed the anticolonial struggle, strengthening the commitment to an uncompromising anticolonial nationalist agenda. In their aftermath, many anticolonial revolutionaries turned to communism or to anti-liberal right-wing nationalism.

---

[94] Ct. in Fayet, "1919," 119.

[95] Ct. in White, "Colonial Revolution and the Communist International, 1919–1924," 181.

[96] Tse-Tsung Chow, *The May Fourth Movement: Intellectual Revolution in Modern China* (Cambridge, MA, 1960); Vera Schwarcz, *The Chinese Enlightenment: Intellectuals and the Legacy of the May Fourth Movement of 1919* (Berkeley, CA, 1986); and, for a broader view, Rana Mitter, *A Bitter Revolution: China's Struggle with the Modern World* (Oxford, 2004), on China. Alfred Draper, *The Amritsar Massacre: Twilight of the Raj* (London, 1985); and Kim A. Wagner, *Amritsar 1919: An Empire of Fear and the Making of a Massacre* (New Haven, CT, 2019), on India. 'Abd al-Rahman al-Rafi'i, *Thawrat Sanat 1919*, 2 vols. (Cairo, 1946); and Reinhard Schulze, *Die Rebellion der ägyptischen Fallahin 1919* (Berlin, 1981), on Egpyt. Frank Prentiss Baldwin, *The March First Movement: Korean Challenge and Japanese Response* (PhD dissertation, Columbia University, 1969), on Korea.

Although the similarities between the revolts – most importantly the aim (and language) of "self-determination" – are striking, Manela cautions that we should not underestimate their local particularities. They were all connected by the same broader global tectonic shifts, most importantly the First World War and promises of self-determination. Direct linkages between them were rare, however. The revolutionaries between Cairo and Calcutta were certainly aware of events elsewhere, feeling part of a worldwide movement, but the impact of the global centers of power, most notably the events and promises made at the imperial centers of power, were far more important than the circulation of revolutionary ideas between the countries of the colonial and semi-colonial world.

The twentieth-century revolt against colonialism reached its most important phase after the Second World War. In his chapter "The Third World Revolutions," Odd Arne Westad discusses the waves of revolutions that engulfed Africa, Southeast Asia, the Middle East, and Latin America during the Cold War. Focusing on the decade between the Bandung Conference of 1955 and the aborted Algiers Conference of 1965, he examines the key revolutions – in Algeria, Vietnam, and Cuba, for instance – as well as the struggles among the elites of "Third World" states – in Indonesia, Ghana, Egypt, and so on – who considered the building of a new kind of state and society in which all forms of exploitation would be abolished as part of this global revolutionary, anti-imperial moment.[97] To be sure, the revolutions were diverse in nature, ranging from struggles against colonial regimes, to rebellions against domestic class oppression, to upheavals against foreign intervention. And yet, the movements all fought for a radical redistribution of political, social, and economic power both within their own countries and on a global scale. Westad demonstrates that "Third World" revolutionaries were all

---

[97] Alistair Horne, *A Savage War of Peace: Algeria 1954–1962* (London, 1978); Benjamin Stora, *Histoire de la guerre d'Algérie, 1954–1962* (Paris, 1993); Annie Rey-Goldzeiguer, *Aux origines de la guerre d'Algérie* (Paris, 2002); Matthew Connelly, *A Diplomatic Revolution: Algeria's Fight for Independence and the Origins of the Post-Cold War Era* (Oxford 2002); and Jeffrey James Byrne, *Mecca of Revolution: Algeria, Decolonization, and the Third World Order* (Oxford, 2016), on Algeria; Jonathan C. Brown, *Cuba's Revolutionary World* (Cambridge, MA, 2017); and Rachel A. May, Alejandro Schneider, and Roberto González Arana, *Caribbean Revolutions: Cold War Armed Movements* (Cambridge, 2018), on the Caribbean; Aldo Marchesi, *Latin America's Radical Left: Rebellion and Cold War in the Global 1960s* (Cambridge, 2017), on Latin America; James L. Gelvin, *The Israel-Palestine Conflict* (Cambridge, 2005); and Paul Thomas Chamberlin, *The Global Offensive: The United States, the Palestine Liberation Organization, and the Making of the Post-Cold War Order* (Oxford, 2012), on the Israel-Palestine conflict; and Abdel Razzaq Takriti, *Monsoon Revolution: Republicans, Sultans, and Empires in Oman, 1965–1976* (Oxford, 2013), on Oman, are important studies on these "Third World" upheavals, among many others.

inspired by earlier modern revolutions, most importantly the Atlantic Revolutions, 1848, and the Russian Revolution, drawing on ideas of sovereignty, justice, liberty, equality, fraternity, progress, and the nation. Most of these movements were moreover united through some form of "Third World" solidarity. Ideas developed in one revolutionary country could easily inspire political transformation in another. International revolutionaries like the Argentinian Ernesto "Che" Guevara, who fought guerrilla wars from Congo to Bolivia, tried to spread socialist revolt across Africa and Latin America, in 1967, in his last text, calling his followers to rise in global revolt: "We must bear in mind that imperialism is a world system, the last stage of capitalism – and it must be defeated in a world confrontation."[98] Some of these itinerant revolutionaries also targeted Europe, such as the Venezuelan jet-setting militant Ilich Ramírez Sánchez, "Carlos the Jackal," hero of the anti-imperialist terrorist international.[99]

A late variant of these "Third World" revolutions was the Islamic upheavals of the late 1970s, discussed in Abbas Amanat's chapter "The Global Islamic Revolution." The most important of them was the Iranian Revolution, which ousted the Pahlavi potentate Muhammad Riza Shah and ended with Khomeini's establishment of the Islamic Republic, the first theocracy in the country's history.[100] One of the most excited supporters of the Islamic Republic, Michel Foucault, who met Khomeini at his exile residence outside Paris and visited Iran during the revolutionary months, and who wrote as enthusiastically as he did uncritically about the events in the pages of various European papers, from *Corriere della*

---

[98] Ernesto Che Guevara, "Create Two, Three, Many Vietnams," *Tricontinental* (April 1967). Jon Lee Anderson, *Che Guevara: A Revolutionary Life* (New York, 1997); Jorge G. Castañeda, *Compañero: The Life and Death of Che Guevara* (New York, 1998); and Frank Niess, *Che Guevara* (London, 2007), are some among the many biographies. Ernesto Che Guevara, *Reminiscences of the Revolutionary War* (New York, 1968), which was first published as *Pasajes de la guerra revolucionaria* in 1963; Idem, *The African Dream: The Diaries of the Revolutionary War in the Congo* (London, 2000), which was first published as *Pasajes de la guerra revolucionaria: Congo* in 1999; and *The Complete Bolivian Diaries of Che Guevara and other Captured Documents* (New York, 1968), which was first published as *El diario del Che en Bolivia* in 1968, provide good insights into his global revolutionary life.

[99] Bernard Violet, *Carlos: Les réseaux secrets du terrorisme international* (Paris, 1996); John Follain, *Jackal* (New York, 1998); and Oliver Schröm, *Im Schatten des Schakals: Carlos und die Wegbereiter des internationalen Terrorismus* (Berlin, 2002).

[100] Arjomand, *The Turban for the Crown*; Mohsen M. Milani, *The Making of Iran's Islamic Revolution: From Monarchy to Islamic Republic* (Boulder, CO, 1988); and Charles Kurzman, *The Unthinkable Revolution in Iran* (Cambridge, MA, 2004). Iradj Motadel, *Von der Schah-Dynastie zum Islamischen Gottesstaat* (Pfaffenweiler, 1987) provides insights into the actual institutional changes. On the global influences of the Iranian revolution, see the contributions to John L. Esposito (ed.), *The Iranian Revolution: Its Global Impact* (Miami, FL, 1990). On the broader context of the long Islamic resurgence, see David Motadel, "Islamic Revolutionaries and the End of Empire," in Martin Thomas and Andrew S. Thompson (eds.), *The Oxford Handbook of the End of Empires* (Oxford, 2018), 555–79.

Sera to *Le Monde*, not only praised the revolution as a radically new moment of modernity, untied from Western liberalism or Soviet socialism, but also saw early its international impact. "Thus, it is true that, as an "Islamic" movement, it can set the entire region afire, overturn the most unstable regimes, and disturb the most solid ones," he wrote in early 1979.[101]

Indeed, the Iranian revolution mobilized Muslim activists across the world. In the months between autumn 1978 and spring 1979, Islamic movements – Shi'ite and Sunni – from West Africa to Southeast Asia, gained momentum. Abu al-A'la Mawdudi spoke for many when declaring that "all Muslims in general and the Islamic movements in particular should support this revolution totally and cooperate with it in all aspects."[102] In autumn 1979, Sunni militants seized the Great Mosque of Mecca, Islam's holiest site, calling for the overthrow of the Saudi dictatorship, which they saw as heretical and corrupted by the West.[103] The revolt was swiftly put down, with hundreds killed and wounded. As the news of the siege in Mecca spread around the world, rumors emerged alleging that Washington was behind the attack on the holy site. Khomeini supposedly claimed that "the United States and its corrupt colony, Israel" were responsible for the events, calling all "Moslems" to "rise up and defend Islam."[104] Anti-American protests quickly spread around the world, from Turkey to Bangladesh, from the Arab Emirates to the Philippines. In Pakistan, hundreds of infuriated protesters stormed the American embassy in Islamabad; some embassy staff, both American and Pakistani, were killed.[105] In Libya, Islamist protesters attacked and burned down the American embassy in Tripoli, shouting pro-Khomeini

---

[101] During the Iranian revolution, he filed several sympathetic reports for the Italian daily *Corierre della Sera*. The reports have been published in English translation in Janet Afary and Kevin B. Anderson, *Foucault and the Iranian Revolution: Gender and the Seductions of Islamism* (Chicago, 2005), 67–162; and Behrooz Ghamari-Tabrizi, *Foucault in Iran: Islamic Revolution After the Enlightenment.* The quote is from Michel Foucault, "A Powder Keg Called Islam," in Afary and Anderson, *Foucault and the Iranian Revolution*, 239–41, 241, which was first published as Michel Foucault, "Una polveriera chiamata Islam," *Corriere della Sera* (February 13, 1979).

[102] Ct. in Shireen T. Hunter, "Iran and the Spread of Revolutionary Islam," *Third World Quarterly* 10, 2 (1988), 730–49, 740–41, which refers to an interview in *Al-Da'wa* (August 1979).

[103] Yaroslav Trofimov, *The Siege of Mecca* (New York, 2007).

[104] John Kifner, "Khomeini Accuses U.S. and Israel of Attempt to Take Over Mosques," *New York Times* (November 25, 1979).

[105] Graham Hovey, "Troops Rescue 100 in Islamabad; U.S. Offices Are Burned in 2 Cities," *New York Times* (November 22, 1979). Steve Coll, *Ghost Wars: The Secret History of the CIA, Afghanistan and Bin Laden from the Soviet Invasion to September 10, 2001* (London, 2005), 21–37, provides an excellent account of the storming of the Pakistani embassy.

slogans.[106] To some extent, this upheaval may be seen as part of a wider global Islamist revolutionary wave that began with the Islamist uprising in Syria in 1976–1982, brutally crushed during the Hama massacre, and the revolt of the mujahidin against the communist government and its Soviet backers in Afghanistan in 1979–89.[107]

Although each of these Islamic upheavals was shaped by its local, national, and regional conditions, the similarities among them are remarkable, with revolutionaries advocating not only a complete transformation of their societies and states but also an alternative global order. And the events were closely connected, not so much by structural global transformations as by entanglements among these countries, particularly with ideas from places like Iran, Afghanistan, and Pakistan inspiring movements elsewhere.

The wave of upheavals that overthrew the communist regimes across the globe at the end of the Cold War is studied in John Connelly's chapter "The Anticommunist Revolts of 1989." Protests began in Poland, spread to Hungary, East Germany, Bulgaria, and Czechoslovakia, and finally reached Romania, where revolutionaries put neo-Stalinist dictator Nicolae Ceauşescu and his wife Elena before a military tribunal and had them executed by firing squad in front of television cameras on Christmas Eve.[108] Southeastern Europe's communist states, Yugoslavia and Albania, were next. "After many a winter, this was spring," wrote the

---

[106] Anonymous, "Embassy of the U.S. in Libya is Stormed by a Crowd of 2,000," *New York Times* (December 3, 1979).

[107] Raphaël Lefèvre, *Ashes of Hama: The Muslim Brotherhood in Syria* (Oxford, 2013), 81–136, on Syria; and Olivier Roy, *Islam and Resistance in Afghanistan* (Cambridge, 1986), on Afghanistan.

[108] Hans-Hermann Hertle, *Chronik des Mauerfalls: Die dramatischen Ereignisse um den 9. November 1989* (Berlin, 1996); Charles S. Maier, *Dissolution: The Crisis of Communism and the End of East Germany* (Princeton, NJ, 1997); Karsten Timmer, *Vom Aufbruch zum Umbruch: Die Bürgerbewegung in der DDR 1989* (Göttingen, 2000); Jens Schöne, *Die friedliche Revolution: Berlin 1989/90* (Berlin, 2008); Ilko-Sascha Kowalczuk, *Endspiel: Die Revolution von 1989 in der DDR* (Munich, 2009); and Wolfgang Schuller, *Die deutsche Revolution 1989* (Berlin, 2009), on Germany. Hartmut Kühn, *Das Jahrzehnt der Solidarność: Die politische Geschichte Polens 1980–1990* (Berlin, 1999); and Agnieszka Zaganczyk-Neufeld, *Die geglückte Revolution: Das Politische und der Umbruch in Polen, 1976–1997* (Paderborn, 2014), on Poland. George Galloway and Bob Wylie, *Downfall: The Ceauşescu and the Romanian Revolution* (London, 1991); and Peter Siani-Davies, *The Romanian Revolution of December 1989* (Ithaca, NY, 2005), on Romania. Michael Andrew Kukral, *Prague 1989: Theater of Revolution* (New York, 1997), on Czechoslovakia. Branka Magas, *The Destruction of Yugoslavia: Tracking the Break-Up 1980–1992* (London, 1993); Carole Rogel, *The Breakup of Yugoslavia and Its Aftermath* (Westport, CT, 2004); and Fred C. Abrahams, *Modern Albania: From Dictatorship to Democracy in Europe* (New York, 2015), on the Balkans. Philip J. Cunningham, *Tiananmen Moon: Inside the Chinese Student Uprising of 1989* (Lanham, MD, 2009); and the contributions to Peter Li, Steven Mark, and Marjorie H. Li (eds.), *Culture and Politics in China: An Anatomy of Tiananmen Square* (New Brunswick, NJ, 1991), on China.

most famous chronicler of the events, Timothy Garton Ash, in *The Magic Lantern*, who experienced "1989" as "a year of solidarity both within and between nations": "By a mixture of popular protest and élite negotiation, prisoners became prime ministers and prime ministers became prisoners."[109] Outside Europe, communist rule was abandoned from Mongolia to Somalia. In China, however, the demonstrations of Tiananmen Square were put down with brute force, leaving an unknown number of protesters dead.

Focusing on the upheavals in Eastern Europe, Connelly points to the striking variety of anti-communist protests in 1989. Whereas in countries like Poland and Hungary the transitions of power were negotiated between regime and opposition, without violence, in places like East Germany and Romania, people took to the streets; in Bucharest, hundreds were killed. In all cases, however, as state socialism had proven to be irreparably dysfunctional and the Soviet vision of modernity had lost its appeal, Soviet-style rule was abolished.

All of the anti-communist revolutions were the result of structural transformations that affected countries across Europe, Asia, and Africa. Crucial thereby were the rapid changes in the Soviet Union, where Mikhail Gorbachev, embarking on his path of restructuring (*perestroika*) and openness (*glasnost*), showed no real interest in maintaining Soviet control in the states of the Eastern Bloc. Yet the upheavals also influenced one another. Protesters were from the outset inspired by protests (and their successes) in neighboring countries. They were usually well informed, mainly through television, about what was happening elsewhere. Oppositional ideas – ideals of freedom, democracy, citizenship, and the nation – were crossing borders rapidly. The program of Poland's Solidarity movement in particular provoked massive interest across Eastern Europe and beyond. In Budapest, for example, the oppositional student leader Victor Orbán, a law student from provincial central Hungary, wrote his master's thesis on Solidarity. Less important was the movement of revolutionaries. Western diplomatic officials and non-governmental organizations, however, played an important role in supporting dissenters. Also, the revolutionary situation in one country frequently affected the political situation in another. The transformations in Hungary and Poland, for instance, had a profound impact on East Germany. When the Hungarians opened the border to Austria in spring 1989, East Germans flooded into the country to escape to the West, shaking the German Democratic Republic politically.

History did not end with the fall of the Wall. In the post-Cold War era, several new revolutionary waves have spread across regions and even

---

[109] Ash, *The Magic Lantern*, 13, 145, and 20.

continents. In the early 2000s, the Color Revolutions swept across Ukraine, Georgia, and Kyrgyzstan. The revolts of the "Arab Spring" in 2010–12 came in faster waves than any experienced in history. Beginning in Tunisia, unrest spread across Egypt, Libya, Algeria, Morocco, Syria, Jordan, Bahrain, Oman, and Yemen within weeks.[110] But although these revolts led to the fall of some dictators, such as bin 'Ali of Tunisia, Mubarak of Egypt, and Qadhdhafi of Libya, they most often ended with the restoration of the old regimes or in bloody civil wars.

In his chapter "The Arab Uprisings," James L. Gelvin demonstrates that the revolts arose at the conjuncture of long-term regional structural transformations, most importantly the global diffusion of a rights-based discourse that privileged individual human rights and neo-liberal economic policies, as well as an uneven population growth, a youth bulge, that affected all countries simultaneously. The rebellions were also connected with each other, with revolutionary news and slogans spreading via internet and satellite television within seconds, inspiring protesters across borders.

Revolutions and revolutionary waves have been an integral part of modern history. No doubt, the increasing strength of the modern state has made them more and more difficult to occur. More than half a century ago, in the aftermath of the Second World War, Albert Camus proclaimed that "the seizure of power by violent means" had become "a romantic idea consigned to fantasy by advances in the technology of weaponry" as the "repressive apparatus can avail itself of the force of tanks and planes."[111] "Hence it would take tanks and planes merely to equal its power. 1789 and 1917 remain dates, but they are no longer examples," he concluded. And yet, as history has shown since then, even the strongest state is not immune to revolutionary upheaval.

This book is not intended to provide either a comprehensive or a definitive account of the global history of revolution and revolutionary waves. It is, rather, an attempt to offer some first insights into the phenomenon and to draw a broad picture that can be taken further in the future. Among the various revolutions left out are the hundreds of smaller

---

[110] Pierre Puchot, *La Révolution confisquée: Enquête sur la transition démocratique en Tunisie* (Paris, 2012), on Tunisia; Lindsey Hilsum, *Sandstorm: Libya in the Time of Revolution* (London, 2012), on Libya; Neil Ketchley, *Egypt in a Time of Revolution: Contentious Politics and the Arab Spring* (Cambridge, 2017), on Egypt; and Nikolaos van Dam, *Destroying a Nation: The Civil War in Syria* (London, 2017), on Syria, provide important insights into these upheavals.

[111] Albert Camus, "Neither Victims nor Executioners: The Revolution Travestied," in *Camus at Combat: Writing 1944–1947*, ed. by Jacqueline Lévi-Valensi (Princeton, NJ, 2006), 264–66, 264–65, which was first published as Albert Camus, "Ni victimes ni bourreaux," *Combat* (November 23, 1946).

European nineteenth-century revolts, peasant uprisings, and worker strikes, the 1930s revolutions, and the 1968 protests, which were considered a revolution by some contemporaries, prompting Hannah Arendt to ask at the time whether "children in the next century will learn about the year 1968 the way we learned about the year 1848."[112]

More generally, this book may contribute to our understanding of territoriality in the history of revolutionary upheavals. Historians have in fact looked at a wide range of spaces when studying revolutions. No doubt, the nation-state still constitutes the most important one.[113] But over the last decades, a considerable number of local and urban histories of revolutions have appeared.[114] And some scholars have adopted larger regional, continental, and even global spatial lenses.

One issue addressed by all of these studies – local and urban, national and imperial, regional, continental, and global – concerns the ways in which revolutions spread. Urban historians may be particularly interested in the expansion of revolutionary activity across neighborhoods, national historians in their dissemination within one country, and so on. Adopting

---

[112] Hannah Arendt to Karl Jaspers and Gertrud Jaspers, June 26, 1968, in *Hannah Arendt and Karl Jaspers: Correspondence 1926–1969*, ed. by Lotte Kohler and Hans Saner (New York, 1992), 680–81, 681, which was first published as *Hannah Arendt und Karl Jaspers: Briefwechsel 1926–1969* (Munich, 1985), 715–16. On the context of Hannah Arendt's elaborations and on the global history of 1968, see Alex Lichtenstein (ed.), "AHR Reflections: 1968," *American Historical Review* 123, 3 (2018), 706–78. More specific studies are Martin Klimke, *The Other Alliance: Student Protest in West Germany and the United States in the Global Sixties* (Princeton, NJ, 2010); Quinn Slobodian, *Third World Politics in Sixties West Germany* (Durham, NC, 2012); Timothy Scott Brown, *West Germany and the Global Sixties* (Cambridge, 2013); Christoph Kalter, *The Discovery of the Third World: Decolonization and the Rise of the New Left in France, c. 1950–1976* (Cambridge, 2016), which was first published as Christoph Kalter, *Die Entdeckung der Dritten Welt: Dekolonisierung und neue radikale Linke in Frankreich* (Frankfurt, 2011); and Madigan Fichter, "Yugoslav Protest: Student Rebellion in Belgrade, Zagreb, and Sarajevo in 1968," *Slavic Review* 75, 1 (2016), 99–121; as well as the chapters in Samantha Christiansen and Zachary Scarlett (eds.), *The Third World in the Global 1960s* (New York, 2013); Robert Gildea, James Mark, and Anette Warring (eds.), *Europe's 1968: Voices of Revolt* (Oxford, 2013); and Philipp Gassert and Martin Klimke (eds.), *1968: On the Edge of World Revolution* (Chicago, 2018). Jeremi Suri, *Power and Protest: Global Revolution and the Rise of Détente* (Cambridge, MA, 2003) focuses on the power politics. Idem (ed.), *The Global Revolutions of 1968* (New York, 2007), offers a valuable collection of documents. Stefan Aust, *The Baader-Meinof Complex* (London, 2008); and Petra Terhoeven, *Deutscher Herbst in Europa: Der Linksterrorismus der Siebziger Jahre als transnationales Phänomen* (Munich, 2014), give insights into the radicalization of the revolutionary moment.

[113] Reference 23 lists some important works on national space and revolution.

[114] Paul Ginsborg, *Daniele Manin and the Venetian Revolution of 1848–49* (Cambridge, 1979); Jill Harsin, *The War of the Streets in Revolutionary Paris* (New York, 2002); and, for a combination of local and global (comparative) history, Mike Rapport, *Rebel Cities: Paris, London, and New York in the Age of Revolution* (London, 2017), are important studies on urban and spaces and revolution.

a macro-perspective, the chapters of this volume examine the spread of revolts across regions, continents, and the globe.

In the end, revolutionary moments evolved on various spatial scales, from the local to the global. Thus, even global waves of revolutions manifest themselves in specific regional, national, local, and urban spaces. Looking at the intersection of revolutionary spaces within one polity, Charles Maier has perceptively pointed out that even if "revolutions have usually involved the dramaturgy of the city square," this urban space has often been closely related to the national: "Territory is contested at the micro level in front of the television cameras such that a small bit of acreage becomes a synecdoche for national space. The public square – whether the Sorbonne in 1968, Tiananmen and Leipzig in 1989, or Tahrir 2013 and Kiev's Maidan shortly after – reveals the power or impotence of the national regime."[115] Overall, it seems indisputable that we will have to consider different scales if we want to fully understand the history of a phenomenon like revolution. The question of the spatiality of revolutions – the ways in which revolutions relate to one another in space (and time) – will no doubt require further study, but I hope that the following chapters will make a contribution to our understanding of this subject.

Ultimately, this volume shows that revolutions have seldom been constrained to one space alone. At times, they have even engulfed regions, continents, and the globe. Revolutions that have usually been studied within national frameworks were often significantly influenced by developments in the wider world and, in turn, had a profound impact across state borders. Perhaps "world revolution" has always been more than a utopian dream.

---

[115] Charles S. Maier, *Once within Borders: Territories of Power, Wealth, and Belonging since 1500* (Cambridge, MA, 2016), 292.

1   The Atlantic Revolutions

David A. Bell

In 1775, the Atlantic world was utterly dominated by four monarchies: those of Great Britain, France, Spain, and Portugal. Between them, they largely controlled the seaways. They laid claim to vast territories, including most of the two American continents. They mustered the region's strongest land armies. Their subjects carried out nearly all of its most dynamic economic activity, much of which was supported by slave labor. Only a tiny percentage of these subjects had a voice in how they were governed.

Fifty years later, this dominion was at an end. Each of the four monarchies had been shaken to the core by the wave of revolutions that began in Lexington, Massachusetts, on April 19, 1775. At a minimum, the Atlantic territories affected by revolution included the United States, France, present-day Belgium, the Netherlands, Ireland, Haiti, and the vast mainland American possessions of Spain and Portugal. As a result of the revolutions, all four of the monarchies lost large, wealthy imperial territories, and in three of the four cases (all but Great Britain) the monarchy itself was temporarily toppled. New, radical political principles were proclaimed that challenged the very foundations of the old political orders. The effects of these events spread well beyond the Atlantic, spurring reform and revolution in locations that included Eastern Europe and the Arab Middle East.[1] And in the western hemisphere, new states rose up that contested, to one degree or another, the older monarchies' naval, military, and economic powers. A powerful symbolic threshold was crossed on December 2, 1823, when the elected president of the American republic, James Monroe, wrote to Congress that the political systems of the United States and the European powers were "essentially

---

[1] C. A. Bayly, "The 'Revolutionary Age' in the Wider World, c. 1790–1830," in Richard Bessel, Nicholas Guyatt, and Jane Rendall (eds.), *War, Empire and Slavery, 1770–1830* (New York, 2010), 21–43; and the contributions in David Armitage and Sanjay Subrahmanyam (eds.), *The Age of Revolutions in Global Context, c. 1760–1840* (New York, 2010).

different."[2] As a result, he continued: "we should consider any attempt on their part to extend their system to any portion of this hemisphere as dangerous to our peace and safety." The Monroe Doctrine forcefully asserted that the Atlantic was no longer a European, monarchical domain.

The participants themselves recognized that deep connections existed between the different revolutions of the period. The French revolutionaries, for instance, frequently acknowledged their debt to their American predecessors. "A French patriot must be a universal patriot, and most of all an American one," wrote Jacques-Pierre Brissot in August of 1789.[3] Americans agreed. In 1790, the American poet Philip Freneau effused: "From that bright spark which first illumed these lands / See Europe kindling, as the blaze expands."[4] Thomas Jefferson, in his autobiographical writings, claimed that "The appeal to the rights of man, which had been made in the U.S., was taken up by France, first of the European nations." He continued that from there the cause was spreading throughout the old continent.[5] In 1821, the Ecuadorian leader Vicente Rocafuerte praised the American founding fathers for creating "sublime institutions" and called them "great men whose wisdom the world admires and always will admire."[6] All these observers also noted the extraordinary rapidity with which revolutionary change in one part of the Atlantic world could spur effects elsewhere. While the speed at which the ocean was crossed remained limited by the wind, it nonetheless seemed as if the region was experiencing an acceleration of historical time.[7]

Historians were somewhat slow to devote systematic attention to the "Atlantic Revolutions" as a distinct phenomenon. It was only in the 1950s, in the context of the Cold War and the foundation of the North Atlantic Treaty Organization, that the American historian R. R. Palmer and his French colleague Jacques Godechot convened an international panel to discuss what they termed "the problem of Atlantic history."

[2] Monroe to Congress, December 2, 1823, Washington, in Dennis Merrill and Thomas G. Paterson (eds.), *Major Problems in American Foreign Relations*, 2 vols. (Boston, MA, 2009), vol. I, 147, which was first published in 1978. The document cited was largely written by Secretary of State John Quincy Adams.

[3] Anonymous (Jacques-Pierre Brissot), *Le patriote françois* (August 1, 1789), 1.

[4] Ct. in Jonathan Israel, *The Expanding Blaze: How the American Revolution Ignited the World, 1775–1848* (Princeton, NJ, 2017), v. On the continuing American sense of the links between the Atlantic Revolutions, see also Caitlin Fitz, *Our Sister Republics: The United States in an Age of American Revolutions* (New York, 2016).

[5] Ct. in Israel, *The Expanding Blaze*, 271.

[6] Anonymous (Vicente Rocafuerte), *Ideas necesarrias à todo pueblo americano independiente que quiera ser libre* (Philadelphia, PA, 1821), 7–8; see also Israel, *The Expanding Blaze*, 449.

[7] Lynn Hunt, *Measuring Time, Making History* (Budapest, 2008), 41–92.

A number of important works followed, including especially Palmer's own *The Age of the Democratic Revolution: A Political History of Europe and America, 1760–1800*.[8] In this same period, several other leading scholars – notably Hannah Arendt – placed the American and French Revolutions into a single frame of analysis.[9] But this scholarly moment was brief. As the center of gravity in the historical discipline shifted from political and military history to social and then cultural history, sweeping political syntheses like Palmer's lost favor, while, seen "from below," the differences between the various Atlantic societies of the time looked more important than their similarities. Nor, by the late 1960s, did many historians have sympathy for projects like Palmer's that, in their eyes, seemed designed to provide a genealogy for the Western alliance.[10]

But since the 1990s, a new shift in the discipline's center of gravity – this time toward global and transnational history – has renewed the subject. A generation of historians keenly aware of globalization in the present has drawn powerful attention to Atlantic connections in the past. These historians have gone back to the work of Palmer and his colleagues, but they have also sharply criticized this earlier work for its concentration on Europe and North America to the exclusion of the Caribbean and Latin America.[11] The Haitian Revolution has particularly benefitted from a new surge of interest, with some scholars arguing that it was here, amid the greatest slave insurrection the world has ever seen, that the promise of universal democracy was first truly glimpsed.[12] A plethora of books and articles have appeared on the "Atlantic Revolutions," and teaching positions in the Atlantic history of the period have multiplied.[13]

Needless to say, the historical profession remains deeply divided on the chronological and geographical boundaries of the phenomenon, and

---

[8] R. R. Palmer, *The Age of the Democratic Revolution: A Political History of Europe and America, 1760–1800* (Princeton, NJ, 2014). The work was originally published in two volumes in 1959 and 1964. On Palmer, see *Robert Roswell Palmer: A Transatlantic Journey of American Liberalism*, a special issue of *Historical Reflections/Réflexions Historiques* 37, 3 (2011); see also Jacques Godechot, *La grande nation: l'expansion révolutionnaire de la France dans le monde de 1789 à 1799* (Paris, 1983), originally published in 1956.

[9] Hannah Arendt, *On Revolution* (New York, 1963); see also Louis Hartz, *The Liberal Tradition in America: An Interpretation of American Political Thought since the Revolution* (New York, 1955).

[10] David Armitage, "Foreword," to Palmer, *The Age of the Democratic Revolution*, xv–xxii.

[11] Robin Blackburn, "Haiti, Slavery, and the Age of the Democratic Revolution," *The William and Mary Quarterly* 63, 4 (2006), 643–74.

[12] Laurent Dubois, *Avengers of the New World: The Story of the Haitian Revolution* (Cambridge, MA, 2004); and Nick Nesbitt, *Universal Emancipation: The Haitian Revolution and the Radical Enlightenment* (Charlottesville, VA, 2008), provide good overviews.

[13] See the titles listed in Armitage, "Foreword," xxi–xxii, and particularly Wim Klooster, *Revolutions in the Atlantic World: A Comparative History* (New York, 2009).

indeed on the utility of "Atlantic Revolutions" as an overall interpretive framework. For the influential Italian historian Franco Venturi, the revolutions of the eighteenth century did not begin in America in 1775 but earlier, in the Mediterranean – notably in the Corsican struggle for independence against Genoa that raged throughout much of the mid-eighteenth century.[14] Jonathan Israel, more recently, has argued that there was indeed "a single Atlantic Revolution," but he casts it as the beginning of a larger Western revolutionary moment that continued through the European revolutions of 1848 (he thereby continues Palmer's attention to continental Europe).[15] Pierre Serna, in a different vein, considers the Atlantic Revolutions as part of an essentially early modern conflict, again beginning well before 1775, that pitted governing elites against subjugated masses within nearly all Western states and empires.[16] Roberto Breña protests that the Spanish-American independence movements owed more to what he calls the "liberal revolution" of 1808–14 in Spain than to other Atlantic Revolutions.[17] Some scholars like Christopher Bayly have tried to extend the concept of an "age of revolutions" to the entire globe.[18] Meanwhile, Keith Michael Baker and Dan Edelstein see most modern revolutions as following a revolutionary "script" first worked out, above all, in the French Revolution of 1789.[19] The place of the American Revolution elicits particular disagreement. For Alan Taylor, it was virtually inseparable from the period's multifaceted military conflicts between European empires, while for Justin du Rivage it should be seen arising out of a broad crisis of governance within the British Empire.[20]

---

[14] Franco Venturi, *The End of the Old Regime in Europe, 1768–1776: The First Crisis* (Princeton, NJ, 1979), ix and xiv.

[15] Israel, *The Expanding Blaze*, 4; see also Palmer, *The Age of the Democratic Revolution*, 280–325, 473–504, 568–662.

[16] Pierre Serna, "Toute révolution est guerre d'indépendance," in Jean-Luc Chappey, Bernard Gainot, Guillaume Mazeau, Frédéric Régent, and Pierre Serna, *Pour quoi faire la Révolution* (Marseille, 2012), 19–44.

[17] Roberto Breña, "The Cádiz Liberal Revolution and Spanish American Independence," in John Tutino (ed.), *New Countries: Capitalism, Revolutions and Nations in the Americas, 1750–1870* (Durham, NC, 2016), 71–104.

[18] Christopher. Bayly, *The Birth of the Modern World, 1780–1914* (Oxford, 2004), 86–120; and the contributions in Armitage and Subrahmanyam (eds.), *The Age of Revolutions in Global Context*.

[19] Keith Michael Baker and Dan Edelstein, "Introduction," in Keith Michael Baker and Dan Edelstein (eds.), *Scripting Revolution: A Historical Approach to the Comparative Study of Revolutions* (Stanford, CA, 2015), 1–24.

[20] Alan Taylor, *American Revolutions: A Continental History, 1750–1804* (New York, 2016); Justin du Rivage, *Revolution against Empire: Taxes, Politics, and the Origins of American Independence* (New Haven, CT, 2017); and, in a similar vein to du Rivage, Steve Pincus, *The Heart of the Declaration: The Founders' Case for an Activist Government* (New Haven, CT, 2016).

Yet regardless of these differences of interpretation, a strong case can be made that the Atlantic Revolutions did constitute a discrete phenomenon. They did so by virtue of the connections between them, their closeness in time, their proximity to a body of water crossed annually by at least 4,000 mercantile vessels alone, and important shared ideas, practices, and political structures.[21] I would in no sense deny that multiple affiliations exist backwards and forwards in time from the revolutions of 1775–1825, and to multiple areas of the globe beyond the Atlantic. But the purpose of this chapter is above all to explore how different revolutions connect to each other. The particularly close and intense relationship between the revolutionary states around the Atlantic makes it the most useful prism for observing and understanding the phenomenon in the period often called "the Age of Revolutions," as well as for understanding its significance.

For the purposes of this chapter, I will divide the ways that different revolutions can be connected to each other into three broad categories (and I will do so, let it be noted, in a slightly different way from the editor of this volume). First, there are what could be termed "structural connections." When similar structural conditions pertain in different locales, they can generate similar tensions and ultimately bring about similar revolutionary explosions. Marxist historiography has of course tended to emphasize this sort of connection, arguing that revolutions have taken place when changes in the mode of production created tension between social classes that could only be resolved by revolutionary action. If revolutions happened across several countries in the same period, it was above all because these countries had reached similar stages of social and economic development. It is worth noting that while R. R. Palmer was no Marxist, his own approach to the Atlantic Revolutions was a heavily structural one. He attributed these revolutions in large part to the fact that rising social formations across the Atlantic world attacked the power of aristocratic elites in the context of political struggles between monarchies and older "constituted bodies," such as the French *parlements*. The term "structures," I should note, can apply to elements of governance and culture as well as to economies and social hierarchies.

Second, there are connections that follow from *transmission*: of news and concepts and practices, and often of people as well. A revolution or radical movement in one locality can give people elsewhere ideas that they had not considered before, and might even inspire them to take similar

---

[21] Ruggiero Romano, "Per una valuazione della flotta mercantile europea alle fine del secolo xviii," in *Studi in onore di Amintore Fanfani* (Milan, 1962), 573–91. My thanks to Nathan Perl-Rosenthal for this reference, and the estimates based upon it.

action. Intellectual and cultural historians naturally put particular emphasis on these sorts of connections. Israel's *The Expanding Blaze* provides a particularly uncompromising example, attributing the Atlantic Revolutions almost entirely to the spread of Enlightenment democratic ideas from Europe to America, where they triggered a revolution that then spread these ideas further throughout the world. Janet Polasky's *Revolutions without Borders* approaches the topic in a more nuanced and complex way, focusing particularly on "itinerant revolutionaries" who played a role in more than one country.[22] Whether a common attachment to "democracy" binds the Atlantic Revolutions to each other remains very much an open question, given the survival of slavery in many of the countries in question, and also the fact that in very few of them did democratic systems initially survive for long.[23] But nearly all the regimes did at least temporarily embrace the principle of popular sovereignty and institute representative systems of government that guaranteed a wide range of human rights. Again, these ideas and practices were in no sense limited to the Atlantic world.

Finally, there are what might be called "connections by disruption." A revolution in one locality leads to severe disruptions in the politics, economy, and/or social structure of another, thereby triggering revolutionary activity there, even in the absence of shared structural conditions or direct transmission of ideas. Bayly's sweeping history of the modern world often emphasizes such connections – for instance, the way that the debt incurred by the French monarchy in order to help the American revolutionaries achieve independence helped lead to French national bankruptcy, and therefore to the origins of the French Revolution.[24]

In practice, of course, any good history of the Atlantic Revolutions must take all of these different sorts of connections into account. Indeed, arguably it was the presence of all three sorts of connections in such concentrated form that explained why so many significant revolutionary episodes took place in such a concentrated fashion in the Atlantic world over the half-century from 1775 to 1825. It is also crucial to keep in mind that revolutions do not just develop neatly along the fault lines of underlying structural conditions, and they do not simply put preexisting ideas into practice. They are enormously volatile, dynamic events – examples of what Emile Durkheim called "collective

---

[22] Janet Polasky, *Revolutions without Borders: The Call to Liberty in the Atlantic World* (New Haven, CT, 2016), quote from 9.

[23] Joanna Innes and Mark Philp (eds.), *Re-Imagining Democracy in the Age of Revolutions: America, France, Britain, Ireland, 1750–1850* (Oxford, 2013), offers contributions with stimulating reflections.

[24] Bayly, *The Birth of the Modern World*, 86–120.

effervescence."[25] They radicalize. They turn violent. They spin off in directions wholly unpredictable at their beginnings. They sometimes collapse before they gain momentum. And the connections between such events do not always run smooth.

Structural Preconditions for Revolution

The Atlantic states that would experience revolution between 1775 and 1825 all underwent significant transformations in their politics, economics, and cultural life in the decades before revolution broke out. These transformations, of course, varied considerably from place to place but still had important features in common, and created what can be seen as the common structural preconditions for revolution. That is to say, without making a revolution inevitable, they made it possible under certain circumstances.[26] The common features, moreover, were in large part related to changes in trade, communication, and imperial competition across the Atlantic Ocean.

The first transformation was simply the enormous increase in trade across the Atlantic. In the eighteenth century, it was Britain and France that drove this increase: in both cases, between 1670 and 1787 the annual tonnage shipped in their vessels across the Atlantic went up ninefold (Spanish, Portuguese, and Dutch shipping grew by much less).[27] The vessels brought colonial products – tobacco, furs, hides, woods, fish, dyes, cotton, cacao, coffee, and especially sugar – from the Americas to Europe, along with precious metals from American mines. They brought a variety of products, including an increasing share of manufactured products, from Europe to American markets. And of course they brought people: permanent migrants, temporary migrants, merchants, administrators, sailors, soldiers, and millions of African slaves. Between 1751 and 1775 alone, close to two million Africans were transported into slavery in the Americas.[28] The increase in trade was both driven by and drove in turn a rapid increase in American populations. The population of the British

[25] Émile Durkheim, *The Elementary Forms of the Religious Life*, trans. by Joseph Ward Swain (London, 1915), 210–12.

[26] Lawrence Stone, *The Causes of the English Revolution, 1529–1642* (London, 1972), for the still-useful model, which distinguishes between "preconditions," "precipitants," and "triggers" of revolution.

[27] David Hancock, "Atlantic Trade and Commodities, 1402–1815," in Nicholas Canny and Philip Morgan (eds.), *The Oxford Handbook of the Atlantic World: 1450–1850* (Oxford, 2011), 324–39, at 332.

[28] "Trans-Atlantic Slave Trade: Estimates," Slave Voyages, Online; see also David Eltis, "Africa, Slavery, and the Slave Trade, Mid-Seventeenth to Mid-Eighteenth Centuries," in Canny and Morgan (eds.), *The Oxford Handbook of the Atlantic World*, 271–85.

colonies more than doubled between 1750 and 1770; that of New Spain came close to doing so between 1760 and 1790.[29]

This increase in trade generated enormous wealth on both sides of the Atlantic. It was the largest single factor driving economic expansion in both the British and the French Empires. Port cities around the ocean's edge grew in size and wealth, from Cádiz to Bordeaux to Bristol, Buenos Aires to Le Cap François to Philadelphia and Boston. The trade also fueled the so-called consumer revolution of the eighteenth century, as city-dwellers in particular came to use a much larger range of consumer products in their daily lives, including household furnishings, clothes, food and drink, art objects, inexpensive books, and printed periodicals.[30] In the city of Paris, by 1789 nearly half of all households owned equipment for making coffee or tea.[31]

Cultural practices also shifted among these wealthier, more mobile, and increasingly consumer populations. Especially in cities, men and women on both sides of the Atlantic frequented theaters, coffeehouses, learned societies, and lending libraries. As goods, fashions, books, ideas, and people traveled around the region, populations generally became more cosmopolitan, and indeed more similar to each another. They used the same products, attended similar plays, read similar books and periodicals, and discussed similar ideas. Colonies like Massachusetts and South Carolina came to have more in common – and both came to resemble Great Britain more greatly – than in the early decades of the century.[32] Through the spread of wildly popular epistolary novels like Samuel Richardson's *Pamela* and Jean-Jacques Rousseau's *Julie*, reading publics around the Atlantic came to appreciate the quality of "sensibility" – a quivering sensitivity, in one's very nerve endings, to the world around one. They also received lessons in "sentimentalism," which meant, above all, the ability to feel and express sympathy and compassion for others.[33]

---

[29] Joyce Chaplin, "The British Atlantic," in ibid., 219–34, at 228; and Craig Muldrew, "Atlantic World 1760–1820: Economic Impact," in ibid., 618–32, at 623.

[30] Frank Trentmann, *Empire of Things: How We Became a World of Consumers, from the Fifteenth Century to the Twenty-First* (London, 2016), is the most significant recent addition to a burgeoning bibliography.

[31] Daniel Roche, *The People of Paris: An Essay in Popular Culture in the 18th Century*, trans. by Marie Evans and Gwynne Lewis (Berkeley, CA, 1987), 118–19.

[32] T. H. Breen, *The Marketplace of Revolution: How Consumer Politics Shaped American Independence* (New York, 2004).

[33] David Denby, *Sentimental Narrative and the Social Order in France, 1760–1820* (Cambridge, 1994); Jessica Riskin, *Science in the Age of Sensibility: The Sentimental Empiricists of the French Enlightenment* (Chicago, IL, 2002); Anne C. Vila, *Enlightenment and Pathology: Sensibility in the Literature and Medicine of Eighteenth-Century France* (Baltimore, MA, 1998); and Sarah Knott, *Sensibility and the American Revolution* (Williamsburg, VA, 2009).

It has been argued that these reading experiences helped beget a new "emotional regime" throughout the Atlantic world that allowed readers to acknowledge people of different social backgrounds – even different nationalities – as equally deserving of what were coming to be called the "rights of man."[34]

These economic and cultural transformations did not, by themselves, necessarily have revolutionary political consequences. Although the economic changes certainly contributed to the increased wealth and cosmopolitanism of the groups the British called the "middling sorts," these groups had no real consciousness of themselves as a class, and displayed little if any political unity, either before or during the Atlantic Revolutions.[35] On the other hand, by the late eighteenth century members of the middle and upper classes around the Atlantic knew far more about events elsewhere in the world, had a far better knowledge of political and social systems different from their own, were far more accustomed to encountering a range of political viewpoints in print, and were far more experienced in discussing and debating political issues themselves – and possibly taking a critical stance toward their own governments – than in previous decades. Although formal systems of censorship still prevailed in the French, Spanish, and Portuguese empires, by the late eighteenth century these systems still allowed for the expression of a much larger range of viewpoints than previously, and many more radical ones circulated illegally, "under the cloak."[36]

More specifically, by the 1760s these populations also had access through books and periodicals to the ideas of the European Enlightenment and to a long tradition of writing generally referred to as "classical republicanism."[37] These ideas did not have a single or even a dominant political valence. Despite the arguments of Jonathan Israel, they cannot be neatly grouped into coherent, competing strands of "radical" and "moderate" Enlightenment.[38] The

---

[34] Lynn Hunt, *Inventing Human Rights: A History* (New York, 2007).

[35] Sarah Maza, *The Myth of the French Bourgeoisie: An Essay on the Social Imaginary, 1750–1850* (Cambridge, MA, 2005), for a look at the once-archetypal French case.

[36] The fundamental work articulating the argument advanced here is Jürgen Habermas, *The Structural Transformation of the Public Sphere: An Inquiry into a Category of Bourgeois Society*, trans. by Thomas Burger and Frederick Lawrence (Cambridge, MA, 1989), originally published in German in 1962.

[37] The classic work on this subject remains J. G. A. Pocock, *The Machiavellian Moment: Florentine Political Thought and the Atlantic Republican Tradition* (Princeton, NJ, 1975).

[38] Israel, *The Expanding Blaze*, and previously, among other works, Jonathan Israel, *Democratic Enlightenment: Philosophy, Revolution and Human Rights* (Oxford, 2011). Among the many critiques of Israel's work, see Antoine Lilti, "Comment écrit-on l'histoire intellectuelle des Lumières? Spinozisme, radicalisme et philosophie," *Annales: Histoire, Sciences Sociales* 64, 1 (2009), 171–206; and David A. Bell, "Where Do We Come From? The Enlightenment and the Age of Revolutions," in David A. Bell (ed.), *Shadows of Revolution: Reflections on France, Past and Present* (New York, 2016), 122–138.

ideas of the French *philosophes* could be used to bolster the claims of despotism as well as the claims of democracy. But thanks to the century's intellectual and cultural ferment, including the cult of "sensibility," readers around the Atlantic world could now draw on a storehouse of ideas and arguments with which to construct radical critiques of nearly every aspect of the existing order, including existing political, religious, and social establishments and hierarchies. From this storehouse came ways of understanding corruption and abuses of power not as isolated problems but as symptoms of a deeper social and political rot that only radical political action could satisfactorily address. At the same time, the emergence of shared cultural practices and shared cultural references across the Atlantic world ensured that when revolution occurred in one locality, its aims and ideas would be easily understood and appreciated in others.[39]

These changing ideas and practices would ultimately have the most profound consequences in regard to an institution that lay at the heart of eighteenth-century economic expansion: human slavery. By the end of the slave trade in the early nineteenth century, some 12.5 million Africans had been transported across the Atlantic to slave colonies throughout the Americas.[40] Opposition to slavery had begun well before the Enlightenment, with Quakers playing a particularly important role in calling the institution immoral.[41] But in the late eighteenth century formal movements opposing the slave trade, and slavery itself, took shape and grew in strength, especially in the British and French Empires. At the time they attracted only limited support, but it is no coincidence that during the period's revolutions, the metaphor of choice for those presenting themselves as victims of tyranny and injustice was "slavery." The overt reference may have been mostly to ancient Greek and Roman slavery, but those casting themselves as wearers of chains knew perfectly well that their own countries had enslaved millions. Indeed, as Samuel Johnson's famous quip so painfully underlined ("How is it that we hear the loudest yelps for liberty among the drivers of Negroes?"), many of them owned slaves themselves.[42]

Newly informed and critical populations would have a chance to deploy radical ideas in a series of crises that erupted around the Atlantic world

---

[39] Nathan Perl-Rosenthal, "Atlantic Cultures and the Age of Revolution," *William and Mary Quarterly* 74, 5 (2017), 667–96.

[40] See https://slavevoyages.org/.

[41] See Marcus Rediker, *The Fearless Benjamin Lay: The Quaker Dwarf Who Became the First Revolutionary Abolitionist* (Boston, MA: Beacon Press, 2017); Christopher Leslie Brown, *Moral Capital: Foundations of British Abolitionism* (Chapel Hill, NC: University of North Carolina Press, 2006).

[42] Samuel Johnson, "Taxation No Tyranny," in *The Works of Samuel Johnson*, 16 vols. (Troy, NY: Pafraets Press, 1903), vol. 14, p. 144.

beginning in the 1760s, and that derived in large part from the strains placed upon states and empires by the pressure of imperial competition and war. These strains represent the other crucial structural precondition for revolution that was widely shared around the Atlantic world.[43] They derived in large part from the intensifying warfare between the European empires – especially the British and French – for territory, glory, and control of the burgeoning wealth generated by global commerce. The Seven Years' War of 1756–63, often referred to as the first global war, involved significant hostilities in North America, the Caribbean, the Indian subcontinent, and Europe, as well as throughout the world's oceans, especially the North Atlantic. Britain and France both transported regular land armies to North America. The expense involved put the finances of each of these powers under unprecedented pressure. In just the six years from 1757 to 1763, the British public debt rose 70 percent.[44] The Seven Years' War in fact marked a crucial inflection point, after which imperial competition became unsustainable for all the major powers.

These rapidly mounting pressures in turn contributed to an ongoing, comprehensive rethinking of the governance of the empires. Even before the Seven Years' War started in 1756, the British parliament increasingly saw the British Empire as a cohesive whole whose component parts each had particular purposes to serve within it.[45] After 1763, it not only imposed heavy new taxes on its American colonies but also placed severe restrictions on these colonies' westward expansion into the North American interior. During the same period, the Spanish monarchy as well imposed higher taxes on its American possessions and moved to increase the power and influence of Spanish-born colonial officials at the expense of American-born white (creole) elites. In Madrid, policymakers increasingly came to see the monarchy's far-flung possessions as a cohesive "commercial machine."[46] Portugal also engaged in far-reaching reform, much of it inspired by the British.[47] Far less rethinking

---

[43] Jeremy Adelman, "An Age of Imperial Revolutions," *American Historical Review* 113, 2 (2008), 319–40, for a general overview.

[44] Walter S. Dunn, Jr., *The New Imperial Economy: The British Army and the American Frontier, 1764–1768* (Westport, CT, 2001), 15; and, for a comparative account, David Stasavage, *Public Debt and the Birth of the Democratic State: France and Great Britain, 1688–1789* (Cambridge, 2003).

[45] David Armitage, *The Ideological Origins of the British Empire* (Cambridge, 2000).

[46] Klooster, *Revolutions in the Atlantic World*, 122–27; Gabriel Paquette, *Enlightenment, Governance and Reform in Spain and its Empire, 1759–1808* (New York, 2008); and Fidel José Tavárez, "The Commercial Machine: Reforming Imperial Commerce in the Spanish Atlantic, c. 1740–1808" (PhD dissertation, Princeton University, 2016).

[47] Gabriel Paquette, *Imperial Portugal in the Age of Atlantic Revolutions: The Luso-Brazilian World, c. 1770–1850* (Cambridge, 2013).

took place in France, whose defeat in the Seven Years' War left it with drastically reduced imperial possessions – principally, the Caribbean colonies of Saint-Domingue (modern Haiti), Martinique, and Guadeloupe.

The strains, and the policy changes they prompted, played out in different ways in the various parts of the different empires. In the thirteen British colonies of the eastern seaboard, they sparked the tensions that would eventually boil over in the American Revolution. In Spain's mainland colonies, they contributed to scores of fiscal revolts, and to the major Túpac Amaru rebellion of 1780–82 in Peru, but not at first to sustained independence movements. In Caribbean colonies where slaves vastly outnumbered whites, plantation owners saw imperial military force as a safeguard against slave uprisings, and imperial restructuring had less important effects. As to the imperial metropoles, Britain handled the strains with relatively little internal strife, thanks to its sophisticated fiscal system and national bank, and an efficient tax collection apparatus.[48] France was another case entirely, especially after its monarchy sent another major expedition across the Atlantic in 1780–81, this time to help the United States in its battle for independence against Great Britain. Not only did the French debt rise massively, France had to pay significantly higher interest rates than Britain, and the French crown attempted to remedy the situation through inviting risky speculation on its credit instruments. The result, in the end, was its national bankruptcy.[49]

America

In the 1770s, these structural preconditions, which prevailed to one degree or another across the Atlantic world, helped to make revolution possible in America. Historians of course continue to debate the relative significance of each factor, and the role of other causes, and this is not the place to resolve their quarrels. But it is undeniable that together the structural preconditions had a crucial effect.

From the preconditions alone, however, it would have been impossible to predict the course taken by the American Revolution after 1775. The ideas articulated by the revolutionaries, particularly in the Declaration of Independence, may have been drawn from the classical republican

---

[48] John Brewer, *The Sinews of Power: War, Money and the English State, 1688–1788* (London, 1989), remains the work of reference.

[49] Lynn Hunt, "The Global Financial Origins of 1789," in Suzanne Desan, Lynn Hunt and William Max Nelson (eds.), *The French Revolution in Global Perspective* (Ithaca, NY, 2013), 32–43.

tradition and the Enlightenment, but nothing in this intellectual background could have predicted the effect of using the ideas to justify the establishment of a new sovereign state in defiance of an old one. The Declaration not only became what Pauline Maier called "American scripture" but also transformed international relations and international law, setting a precedent that scores of other states would copy over the following decades.[50] Arguably, even the French Declaration of the Rights of Man and Citizen of 1789 can be seen as a declaration of the French nation's independence from its monarchy.[51] In nearly every case, the documents enshrined popular sovereignty and a guarantee of individual rights as the only legitimate basis on which to found a government. The American constitution, along with the individual state constitutions, had a similar international resonance, above all in the Atlantic world, spreading the principle that popular sovereignty and individual rights had to be guaranteed by positive, written law.[52]

The preconditions by themselves might have led to new standards and practices of civic equality, but what actually followed, as Gordon Wood has compellingly argued, was something more: "a radical alteration in the nature of American society."[53] The revolution dealt a grievous blow to the aristocratic, hierarchical social conventions that had largely prevailed in the thirteen colonies before 1775 and introduced a new ethos of social equality. It transformed politics from an (at least theoretically) high-minded elite exercise into raucous, free-wheeling contests between parties and interests. It gave new energy and scale to commerce and the pursuit of profit, and also to evangelical religion. And the revolution also took place amidst large-scale violence that drove a significant proportion of the white American population into exile.[54] This radicalism and violence contributed powerfully to French perceptions of the American Revolution as "not merely an overthrow of British political and economic control, but ... a mass assertion of the inalienable rights of man ... a social rather than a political revolution," to quote the historian Durand Echeverria.[55]

[50] Pauline Maier, *American Scripture: Making the Declaration of Independence* (New York, 1997); and David Armitage, *The Declaration of Independence: A Global History* (Cambridge, MA, 2007).
[51] Marcel Gauchet, *La revolution des droits de l'homme* (Paris, 1989).
[52] Linda Colley, "Empires of Writing: Britain, America and Constitutions, 1776-1848," *Law and History Review* 32, 2 (2014), 237–66.
[53] Gordon Wood, *The Radicalism of the American Revolution* (New York, 1993), 275.
[54] See for instance Holger Hoock, *Scars of Independence: America's Violent Birth* (New York, 2017); see also Maya Jasanoff, *Liberty's Exiles: American Loyalists in the Revolutionary World* (New York, 2011).
[55] Durand Echeverria, *Mirage in the West: A History of the French Image of American Society to 1815* (Princeton, NJ, 1957), 70.

It is in fact hard to overestimate the impact of the American Revolution on the new reading publics that had emerged in the Atlantic world over the course of the eighteenth century. Much of the European press covered the events obsessively (despite the months it took for news to reach Europe from the western hemisphere) and from a perspective largely favorable to the American cause, while books on the subject circulated widely.[56] Even the British press tended to interpret the Revolution as a civil war between brothers more than as a treasonous revolt against legitimate authority, while giving George Washington particularly positive treatment.[57] As R. R. Palmer noted in the 1950s, the Revolution impressed readers not simply because of its principles but because of its astonishing drama.[58] It seemed nearly impossible, especially to European readers, that colonists generally perceived as uncouth woodsmen, and even as degenerate humans by virtue of their birth in the western hemisphere, could defeat the regular forces of the most powerful empire in the world.[59] Over the course of the revolution these images faded, often giving way to images of Americans as heroes of classical antiquity reborn.[60]

France

The French Revolution of 1789 had multiple, thick connections to the drama that had begun in America fourteen years before. It was made possible in large part by the same structural preconditions that previously played a role across the Atlantic. The American Revolution also helped directly to trigger it because the resultant French national bankruptcy and the subsequent collapse of French monarchical authority forced King Louis XVI to convoke a representative body, the Estates General, that had not met since 1615. It was in this context that the French Revolution began. As already noted, this connection offers a classic example of the way that one revolution can help trigger another through its disruptive effects. King Louis XVI and his ministers had hardly imagined that

[56] Palmer, *The Age of the Democratic Revolution*, 177–213; and also Luis Ángel García Melero, *La independencia de los Estados Unidos a traves de la prensa española: los precedentes (1763–1776)* (Madrid, 1977).

[57] Troy O. Bickham, *Making Headlines: The American Revolution as Seen through the British Press* (DeKalb, IL, 2009), esp. 185–205, on Washington; and Dror Wahrman, *The Making of the Modern Self: Identity and Culture in Eighteenth-Century England* (New Haven, CT, 2004), 218–64.

[58] Palmer, *The Age of the Democratic Revolution*, 178.

[59] On views of Americans as degenerate, see Philippe Roger, *The American Enemy: The History of French Anti-Americanism* (Chicago, IL, 2005), 1–29.

[60] Julia Osman, "Ancient Warriors on Modern Soil: French Military Reform and American Military Images in 18th Century France," *French History* 22, 2 (2008), 175–96.

French intervention in the American Revolution would help weaken the French state to the point of collapse. To the contrary, they hoped that France would emerge from the war greatly strengthened, thanks to the prestige and trade benefits associated with victory. But here, as in most of the other contexts where they operated, disruptive connections between revolutions offer an object lesson in the historical importance of unforeseen consequences.

As for the transmission of revolutionary ideas, practices, and personnel, the channels of influence can be difficult to define precisely. Did the Declaration of the Rights of Man and Citizen owe more to Anglo-American precedents or to French Enlightenment thought? Lively scholarly debate on the subject has taken place since the late nineteenth century.[61] Did the French officers who served in America in 1780–81 return home as proto-revolutionaries? Probably not. The presence of some prominent American revolutionaries in France – Franklin, Jefferson, Paine – likely counted for more.[62] French Revolutionaries often insisted, in the words of Jean-Paul Rabaut Saint-Etienne, that their country "was made, not to follow examples, but to give them."[63] But the intense, and intensely favorable coverage of the American Revolution in the French press, the model of radical political action the Americans provided, the hope they seemed to offer that the virtues of the ancient republics might reawaken, and specific actions such as the issuing of the Declaration of Independence and the Constitution together had an unmistakable influence upon French events. Significantly, the American constitution and the individual state constitutions were quickly translated into French, and widely commented upon in 1788–89.[64] For many French observers, the connection between the two revolutions was entirely obvious. As the philosopher and radical revolutionary Condorcet wrote in his sweeping history of human progress, published posthumously in 1795: "The American Revolution would therefore soon spread to Europe."[65]

[61] Keith Michael Baker, "The Idea of a Declaration of Rights," in Dale van Kley (ed.), *The French Idea of Freedom: The Old Regime and the Declaration of Rights of 1789* (Stanford, CA, 1994), 154–98.

[62] Gilbert Bodinier, *Les officiers de l'armée royale combattants de la guerre des États-Unis, De Yorktown à l'an II* (Vincennes, 1983); and Polasky, *Revolutions without Borders*, esp. 48–74.

[63] Ct. in Mona Ozouf, "La Révolution française et la formation de l'homme nouveau," in Mona Ozouf, *L'homme régénéré: Essais sur la Révolution française* (Paris, 1989), 116–57, 125.

[64] Palmer, *The Age of the Democratic Revolution*, 200–201.

[65] Jean-Antoine-Nicolas de Caritat Condorcet, *Esquisse d'un tableau historique des progrès des l'esprit humain* (Paris, 1795), 274.

Like the American Revolution, the French Revolution quickly radicalized in ways that no one could have predicted at its start, and that had
massively disruptive effects on France itself, on Europe, and on much of
the rest of the world. It abolished the French monarchy and nobility, and
overthrew the Catholic Church in the country. It established a republic
grounded in universal manhood suffrage, developed ambitious plans for
social welfare and education, and presided over massive transfers of
property and wealth. It began a war that soon expanded to include most
major European powers as adversaries, while it also battled multiple
insurgencies at home. A reign of terror took place that claimed hundreds
of thousands of victims, including massacres in the wake of insurgencies.
All this happened within five years of 1789, but in many ways the
Revolution continued to play itself out for another two decades, as the
wars continued and Napoleon Bonaparte, an authoritarian leader forged
in the Revolution, took power.

Many books have traced the impact of the French Revolution throughout the world, and particularly in the Atlantic world. Its ideas and practices were widely transmitted, discussed, copied, appropriated, and
adapted, while the disruptions it caused played a major role in triggering
revolution elsewhere, especially in the Caribbean and Latin America.[66]
Hundreds of political clubs in the United States, Britain, Western
Europe, the Caribbean, and Latin America formally affiliated with the
radical Jacobin Club in France.[67] The revolution also prompted coordinated attempts by conservative European monarchies to resist its spread.[68]

The impact of the French Revolution also involved one particular form
of transmission that the American Revolution, with the exception of its
brief, failed invasion of Canada, did not employ: namely direct proselyt-
ization, often using military force.[69] As early as 1791, revolutionary

---

[66] Alan Forrest and Matthias Middell (eds.), *The Routledge Companion to the French
Revolution in World History* (London, 2016); and also the contributions in Desan,
Hunt, and Nelson (eds.), *The French Revolution in Global Perspective*; Baker and
Edelstein (eds.), *Scripting Revolution*; Joseph Klaits and Michael Haltzel (eds.), *Global
Ramifications of the French Revolution* (Cambridge, 2002); and Geoffrey Best (ed.), *The
Permanent Revolution: The French Revolution and its Legacy, 1789–1989* (London, 1988).

[67] Jean Boutier and Philippe Boutry, *Atlas de la Révolution française: Les sociétés politiques*
(Paris, 1992).

[68] Adam Zamoyski, *Phantom Terror: The Threat of Revolution and the Repression of Liberty
1789–1848* (London, 2014); see also Brian Vick, *The Congress of Vienna: Power and Politics
after Napoleon* (Cambridge, MA, 2014).

[69] On the expansion of revolutionary France, see Palmer, *The Age of the Democratic
Revolution*; David A. Bell, *The First Total War: Napoleon's Europe and the Birth of
Warfare As We Know It* (Boston, MA, 2007); Edward James Kolla, *Sovereignty,
International Law and the French Revolution* (Cambridge, 2017); and Marc Belissa,
Fraternité universelle et intérêt national (1713–1795): Les cosmopolitiques du droit des gens
(Paris, 1998).

Figure 1.1 Allegorical French engraving on the decree of May 15, 1791, giving rights to free people of color in the Caribbean colonies. (Bibliothèque nationale de France)

France annexed a foreign territory – the papal city of Avignon – after its inhabitants voted for the change. A year later, the revolutionary government promised it would "grant fraternity and aid to all peoples who wish to recover their liberty": a direct incitement to revolution elsewhere.[70] Many leading revolutionaries, particularly those associated with the so-called Girondins, called for their movement to spread across the entire world. Over the course of the revolutionary and Napoleonic wars, France either directly annexed or set up dependent regimes in the Low Countries, all of Italy, Spain, western Germany, central Poland, the Croatian coast of the Adriatic, the Ionian Islands, and Egypt. Although Maximilien Robespierre, early on an opponent of the wars, quipped that "no one likes armed missionaries," in many of these areas the French received considerable indigenous support (Figure 1.1).[71]

[70] Ct. in Belissa, *Fraternité universelle*, 322.
[71] Maximilien Robespierre, *Discours de Maximilien Robespierre sur la guerre: Prononcé à la Société des amis de la constitution, le 2 janvier 1792* (Paris, 1792), 18.

The French Revolution made yet another major contribution to the shape of future revolutions, in the Atlantic world and beyond: it gave birth to the modern conception of "revolution" itself.[72] Before 1789, in the Western world, the word generally connoted a sudden, unpredictable, uncontrollable upheaval in human affairs. Eighteenth-century historians spoke commonly of "the revolutions" of a country to refer to events such as changes of dynasty and civil wars. But in the extraordinary laboratory of political thinking that was Paris in 1789 and 1790, the word came to signify something new and original: an extended process driven by human will and aimed at a wholesale transformation of a country's politics and society. For the first time, it became possible to think of people as "revolutionaries," and also to use "revolutionary" as an adjective (these words did not exist before 1789). It became possible to speak "in the name of the revolution." In the words of Keith Michael Baker, revolutions were no longer facts, but acts.[73] This shift contributed the most important element to what Baker and Dan Edelstein call a "script" for revolutions and prompted subsequent revolutionary actors in the Atlantic world to think of themselves as cousins to the French revolutionaries and their actions as a counterpart to, or even a continuation of, what had begun in France.[74]

Western Europe

Even before 1789, significant agitation for democratic reform had taken place in many parts of Western Europe, most significantly in England, Ireland, the Dutch Republic, the Austrian Netherlands (present-day Belgium), and Switzerland. The same structural preconditions that helped bring about the American and French Revolutions contributed to these movements as well. The American Revolution itself played a role, providing general inspiration, an example to follow, and disrupting existing political arrangements. For instance, the Anglo-Dutch War of 1780–84, a by-product of the American Revolutionary War, badly damaged the Dutch economy and prompted newly intense attacks by reform-minded "patriots" against the ruling elites. But these early movements mostly foundered on the shoals of determined repression. In 1787,

---

[72] Keith Michael Baker and Dan Edelstein, "Introduction," and Keith Michael Baker, "Revolutionizing Revolution," in Baker and Edelstein (eds.), *Scripting Revolution*, 1–24 and 71–102.

[73] Baker, "Revolutionizing Revolution," 71; and also Dan Edelstein, "Do We Want a Revolution Without Revolution? Reflections on Political Authority," *French Historical Studies* 35, 2 (2012), 269–89.

[74] David A. Bell, "Afterword," in Baker and Edelstein (eds.), *Scripting Revolution*, 335–44.

Prussian forces crushed the Dutch patriots and came to the rescue of the ruling House of Orange.[75]

The French Revolution quickly and massively disrupted these earlier patterns. In August of 1789, scarcely a month after the fall of the Bastille in Paris, a revolutionary government inspired by the French seized power in the episcopal principality of Liège and quickly issued a declaration of rights modeled after the one recently voted in Versailles. Liège provided a base for reformers persecuted by the authorities in the neighboring Austrian Netherlands, contributing to the outbreak of a revolution in that larger territory. French revolutionaries hailed the spread of revolution to their northern neighbor. But divisions quickly hardened between conservatives focused on national independence for the southern Netherlands and democratic forces inspired by the earlier Atlantic struggles. The conservatives won the day, only to see their movement suppressed by Austria at the end of 1790.

The game changed decisively in the areas where France's "armed missionaries" arrived after 1792, but the conquering armies did not simply impose French ideas and practices upon captive populations. French policy itself vacillated. At some moments, the revolutionary state aimed at annexation and full integration of conquered territories into the French Republic. But what more generally prevailed in French ruling circles in the 1790s was the ideal of a federation of free states – admittedly, led by France and supportive of it, including through financial extractions – but with its members allowed significant latitude to choose their form of government.[76] The numerous "sister republics" established after 1795 (by which time the radical regime of the Terror had given way in France to a more limited democracy) amounted to more than just satellite states and often demonstrated what Pierre Serna has called "republican inventiveness."[77] The Batavian Republic established in the Netherlands, for instance, retained important federalist structures inherited from the old Dutch Republic, while democratic forces there successfully defied a French envoy who wished to limit the extent of popular political participation.[78] Even so,

---

[75] Palmer, *The Age of the Democratic Revolution*, 242–79, remains the best summary of these movements. On the Netherlands, see Simon Schama, *Patriots and Liberators: Revolution in the Netherlands, 1780–1813* (New York, 1992); and Annie Jourdan, *La Révolution batave entre la France et l'Amérique (1795–1806)* (Rennes, 2008).

[76] Belissa, *Fraternité universelle*; and Marc Belissa, *Repenser l'ordre européen (1795–1802): De la société des rois aux droits des nations* (Paris, 2006).

[77] Pierre Serna, "The Sister Republics, or the Ephemeral Invention of a French Republican Commonwealth," in Forrest and Middell (eds.), *The Routledge Companion to the French Revolution in World History*, 39–59; see also the contributions in Pierre Serna (ed.), *Les Républiques sœurs, le Directoire et la Révolution atlantique* (Rennes, 2009).

[78] Serna, "The Sister Republics," 48.

the political structures throughout Western Europe tended strongly to resemble those established by the French Constitution of 1795. The constitution of the short-lived Roman Republic was actually written by four French commissioners.[79]

And, in general, the federative experiment did not survive for long. The sister republics mostly crumbled when the Second Coalition drove back the French armies in 1798–99, and their existence finally proved incompatible with the need of Bonaparte's regime to extract as much revenue and manpower as possible from the territories under his control. Napoleon's First Empire and his Kingdom of Italy annexed most of the territories of the former sister republics and subjected them to the tender mercies of the soldiers and bureaucrats Stuart Woolf has called "professionals of annexation."[80] The parts annexed by France were divided into French-style *départements*, the Napoleonic Code became their law, and they experienced the same authoritarian version of French revolutionary reform that Napoleon was imposing on the rest of his empire.

Outside the zones of French influence and occupation, the French Revolution remained a potent spur to revolutionary action. For example, during the 1790s the revolutionary wars put such pressure on the British state that Irish revolutionaries hoped they might successfully throw off the yoke of their larger neighbor and took considerable inspiration from the French example. The inaugural resolution of the Society of United Irishmen spoke hopefully of "the present great era of reform, when unjust Governments are falling in every quarter of Europe."[81] But the inability of the French to land significant forces in Ireland doomed the nascent Irish Revolution, which would only bear fruit more than a century later. The French example also spurred revolutionary activity in Poland and helped to inspire reformist activity in the Muslim Middle East.[82]

Saint-Domingue (Haiti) and the Caribbean

In the slave societies of the Caribbean, the structural preconditions discussed earlier did not contribute to the outbreak of revolution, at least not in the same way they did in North America and Europe. These societies stood at the heart of the eighteenth century's new commercial

---

[79] Palmer, *The Age of the Democratic Revolution*, 630.
[80] Stuart Woolf, *Napoleon's Integration of Europe* (London, 1991), 69.
[81] Ct. in Ultán Gillen, "Irish Revolutionaries and the French Revolution," in Forrest and Middell (eds.), *The Routledge Companion to the French Revolution in World History*, 225–39, 233.
[82] See for instance Khaled Fahmy, *All the Pasha's Men: Mehmed Ali, His Army and the Making of Modern Egypt* (Cairo, 2003).

prosperity, and white plantation owners participated in its new cultural practices and institutions. In 1790 white colonists in Saint-Domingue, inspired in part by the American Revolution and reacting to the political turmoil in France, demanded a large measure of autonomy for themselves within the French empire.[83] But the most important revolutionary actors in the Caribbean were not educated white patrons of coffeehouses, lending libraries, and learned societies. They were black slaves, rising up against one of the most brutal systems of oppression ever seen on the planet, in which as much as 5 percent of the workforce was literally worked to death each year.[84]

But this oppression alone was not enough to trigger a revolution; similarly oppressive systems in British Jamaica and Spanish Cuba did not experience anything like the massive uprising of slaves in French Saint-Domingue in August 1791, which still stands as the largest and most successful such uprising in human history. It was the French Revolution that made the difference, through both the transmission of ideas and the enormous disruption that the colonies experienced as a result of the political crisis in the metropole.

The proclamation that "men are born and remain free and equal in rights," included in the Declaration of the Rights of Man and Citizen in August 1789, could hardly fail to strike people of color under French rule as a monstrous hypocrisy.[85] In the French Caribbean, the first of them to claim rights for themselves were not slaves, but free people of color – largely of mixed race – who had suffered from increased discrimination since the 1760s. Their agitation led to an unsuccessful revolt in 1790, and eventually, after considerable legislative vacillation in Paris, to their receiving full civil rights.[86] But there is little evidence from before 1791 as to the circulation of revolutionary ideas among the slaves who, in Saint-Domingue, represented nine-tenths of the population.

But the revolt of people of color, coming on top of violent dissension among white colonists that accompanied the creation of an autonomous colonial assembly, threw the colony into chaos and weakened white control. It was in this context that the slave uprising could begin.

---

[83] Laurent Dubois, *Avengers of the New World: The Story of the Haitian Revolution* (Cambridge, MA, 2004), 24.

[84] Trevor Burnard and John Garrigus, *The Plantation Machine: Atlantic Capitalism in French Saint-Domingue and British Jamaica* (Philadelphia, PA, 2016), esp. 43 and 250, on slavery in Saint-Domingue.

[85] National Constituent Assembly of France, "Declaration of the Rights of Man and Citizen," 26 August 1789, Paris, in Lynn Hunt (ed.), *The French Revolution and Human Rights: A Brief History with Documents* (Boston, MA, 2016), 74.

[86] Dubois, *Avengers of the New World*, 60–90; and John Garrigus, *Before Haiti: Race and Citizenship in French Saint-Domingue* (New York, 2006).

Initially, the rebels professed their loyalty to the King of France, and at one point several of their leaders even promised to lay down their arms in exchange for only their own freedom and that of their families.[87] A number of them, including the man who would eventually come to rule Saint-Domingue, Toussaint Louverture, briefly took their followers into the service of Spain, which ruled the other half of the island of Hispaniola. But as control of Saint-Domingue slipped away from the French government, and especially after the burning of the capital, Le Cap François, in June, 1793, French commissioners took the momentous step of abolishing slavery in the colony so as to secure the support of the black majority.[88] The next winter, the National Convention in Paris formally ended slavery throughout the French empire. Within a few months, Louverture accepted a generalship in the French army, and in his correspondence and public proclamations professed his loyalty to the Republic, and to the political principles of the French Revolution.[89]

Over the course of the 1790s, revolution spread through many Caribbean islands, including the French colonies of Guadeloupe and Martinique, and British colonies in the Windward Islands. As in Saint-Domingue, these were not simply revolts "from below" against slavery. In each case, the disruptive effects of the French Revolution and the revolutionary wars between France and Britain, and the promise of liberty associated with France, played a major role. Throughout these islands, as in Saint-Domingue, former slaves taking up arms professed their loyalty to the French Republic, and former slaves fought alongside white revolutionaries. There is little evidence, Paul Friedland has recently argued in the case of the British colonies, for seeing the conflicts as driven principally by race.[90]

But at the same time, as Laurent Dubois has powerfully argued, the Caribbean revolutionaries did not simply act as passive receptacles for ideas flowing outwards from Paris. While they quoted revolutionary documents and slogans, and spoke of rights in a manner reminiscent of the 1789 Declaration, they tended to do so strategically – for instance, adopting Jacobin language to tar wealthy white planters as dangerous

---

[87] Philippe Girard, *Toussaint Louverture: A Revolutionary Life* (New York, 2016), 118.

[88] Jeremy Popkin, *You Are All Free: The Haitian Revolution and the Abolition of Slavery* (Cambridge, 2010).

[89] Toussaint Louverture, *Lettres à la France, 1794–1798: Idées pour la libération du peuple noir d'Haïti*, ed. by Antonio Maria Baggio and Ricardo Augustin (Bruyères-le-Châtel, 2011).

[90] Paul Friedland, "Every Island is not Haiti: The French Revolution in the Windward Islands," in David A. Bell and Yair Mintzker (eds.), *Rethinking the French Revolution* (New York, 2018), 41–79. On Guadeloupe, see the seminal work by Laurent Dubois, *A Colony of Citizens: Revolution and Slave Emancipation in the French Caribbean, 1787–1804* (Chapel Hill, NC, 2004).

royalists.[91] They adapted the revolutionary principles to their own needs, and interpreted these principles within their own African-derived cultural contexts.[92] And by forever attaching these principles to the cause of slave emancipation and universal human rights, they transformed the meaning of the age of revolutions as a whole.[93]

In most of the Caribbean, the turmoil of the 1790s ended with the violent reaffirmation of colonial rule and slavery (which Napoleon formally reintroduced to Guadeloupe and Martinique in 1802). The Saint-Domingue revolution, on the other hand, like its American and French predecessors, underwent a process of profound and unpredictable radicalization. After Toussaint Louverture became the official French Governor General in the late 1790s, he attempted to introduce a new constitution for the island which would have given it autonomy from France, under his own virtually absolute rule (including a reduction of the former slave population to virtual serfdom in order to restart the ruined plantation economy).[94] Napoleon Bonaparte refused to tolerate this act of defiance from a man he called a "gilded negro," and sent a massive expedition, led by his own brother-in-law, to return Saint-Domingue to full French rule.[95] Although this expedition initially succeeded, and captured Louverture himself (who died in captivity in France), it was decimated by yellow fever, and the conflict with black forces on the island degenerated into an all-out race war. Finally, the French were driven out, and on the first day of 1804, the former slave Jean-Jacques Dessalines proclaimed the establishment of the independent state of Haiti (supposedly the original Carib Indian name for Saint-Domingue). During this last conflict, the revolution itself acquired an explicitly racial content. Dessalines's new constitution defined all Haitian citizens as black, and his forces carried out massacres of white colonists.[96] Haitian society itself was militarized, and for much of the next century power would rest with an army that struggled to defend the new nation, while ruling over exploited agricultural laborers.[97] While Haiti and its revolution became a symbol of black liberation and universal equality for many admirers throughout the Western world (especially African-Americans), they also became symbols of ferociously racialized fears about revolution in general, and black revolution in particular.[98]

[91] Ibid., 124–55.   [92] Ibid., 110–23.   [93] Dubois, *Avengers of the New World*, 7.

[94] Ibid., 251–79; Claude Moïse, *Le projet national de Toussaint Louverture et la Constitution de 1801* (Port-au-Prince, 2001); and Philippe Girard, *The Slaves Who Defeated Napoleon: Toussaint Louverture and the Haitian War of Independence, 1801–1804* (Tuscaloosa, AL, 2011).

[95] Ct. in Dubois, *Avengers of the New World*, 255.   [96] Ibid., 280–301.

[97] Laurent Dubois, *Haiti: The Aftershocks of History* (New York, 2012).

[98] David Patrick Geggus (ed.), *The Impact of the Haitian Revolution in the Atlantic World* (Columbia, SC, 2001); and Ashli White, *Encountering Revolution: Haiti and the Making of*

Latin America

The last acts of the Atlantic Revolutions played out largely in Latin America. Here, the skein of connections to the earlier revolutions was thick and unmistakable, and involved all three of the different sorts of connections discussed above: shared structural preconditions, direct transmission, and disruption. These revolutions also of course involved forces and developments unique to Latin America and to its different regions, but by this point in the history of the Atlantic, the shadow of revolution fell heavily on all the ocean's shores, except Africa's.

Among the structural preconditions, the most important for Latin America were the increasing strains placed on imperial structures of governance as a result of intensifying imperial warfare, and the resulting attempts to tighten imperial control. In Spanish America, as already noted, these attempts provoked considerable resentment and even revolt. In Brazil, they proved, on balance, less divisive.[99] In neither the Spanish nor the Portuguese Empire, however, were these structural preconditions sufficient by themselves to trigger events of the magnitude of the American, French, or Haitian Revolutions.

Although the future Latin American revolutionaries looked first and foremost to Great Britain for both political and military support, and as a cultural model, they also paid very close attention to the American and French Revolutions.[100] Some American texts – notably Thomas Paine's *Common Sense* and the Declaration of Independence – circulated widely in the Spanish colonies.[101] The French Revolution aroused similar interest. But after 1793, a year which brought the execution of King Louis XVI – cousin to the Spanish Bourbon monarchs – and the outbreak of war between France and Spain, the Spanish authorities attempted to close off the Empire from French influence.[102] Even so, the earliest violent uprisings in northern South America that aimed at independence from Spain had clear connections to France. The 1797 conspiracy of Manuel Gual and José Maria España, which sought to create a republic that would abolish slavery and institute racial equality, borrowed liberally from French revolutionary documents such as the Declaration of the Rights

---

the *Early Republic* (Baltimore, MD, 2012); and James Alexander Dun, *Dangerous Neighbors: Making the Haitian Revolution in Early America* (Philadelphia, PA, 2016).

[99] Paquette, *Imperial Portugal*, 17–83.

[100] On the British influence, see Karin Racine, "'This England and This Now': British Cultural and Intellectual Influence in the Spanish American Independence Era," *Hispanic American Historical Review* 90, 3 (2010), 423–54.

[101] Peggy H. Liss, *Atlantic Empires: The Network of Trade and Revolution* (Baltimore, MD, 1983), 210; and Armitage, *The Declaration of Independence*, 118–19.

[102] Michael Zeuske, "The French Revolution in Spanish America," in Forrest and Middell (eds.), *The Routledge Companion to the French Revolution in World History*, 77–96, 80–81.

of Man, which the Colombian Antonio Nariño had distributed in Spanish translation in 1794.[103]

An attempt to invade Venezuela in 1806 and establish its independence was led by Francisco Miranda, a former general in the French Revolutionary armies, who also received significant help from Americans and Haitians. Simón Bolívar, the single most important Latin American revolutionary leader, visited both France and the United States in the first decade of the nineteenth century, and saw the latter in particular as a model of liberty. Both these examples show how the mobility of persons, as well as of ideas, constituted an important vector of revolutionary "transmissions." Bolívar doubted, however, that the Anglo-American political system represented an appropriate model for Spanish America. "It would be better," he wrote, "for South America to adopt the Koran rather than the United States' form of government."[104]

But as Michael Zeuske has keenly observed, Europe in particular was a distant world for slave-owning Latin American elites: "For them, the real revolution was the Saint-Domingue Revolution of 1791–1803."[105] The slave uprising in the Caribbean terrified these elites, and the worry that a struggle for independence might trigger similar uprisings by their own slaves severely dampened their own revolutionary enthusiasms. Nonetheless, once a struggle for independence began in earnest in Venezuela, Haiti served as a base and refuge for Bolívar on more than one occasion.[106] Alexandre Pétion, president of the southern Haitian republic in this period, had close relations both with Bolívar, and with leaders of Venezuelan mixed-race (*pardo*) forces.[107]

The most important factor triggering the Latin American revolutions was a disruptive one. In 1807, the Napoleonic regime born out of the French Revolution invaded Portugal in an attempt to enforce Napoleon's closure of continental Europe to British trade, and the Portuguese royal family fled to Brazil. A year later, Napoleon overthrew the Bourbon dynasty in Spain, imprisoned the King and the King's son in France, and placed his own brother Joseph on the Spanish throne. The long, brutal Peninsular War began, with Britain sending expeditions to aid resistance to the French, while Spanish opponents of the Bonapartes set up their own government in the southern port city of Cádiz. There, in

---

[103] Ibid., 81–82; and also Carmen Michelena, *Luces revolucionarias: de la rebelión de Madrid (1795) a la rebelión de La Guaira (1797)* (Caracas, 2010).
[104] Ct. in John Lynch, *Simó n Bolívar: A Life* (New Haven, CT, 2006), 261.
[105] Zeuske, "The French Revolution in Spanish America," 78.
[106] Lynch, *Simón Bolívar*, 99–103. Bolívar sought the support reluctantly, because he would have preferred British backing.
[107] Ibid., 106.

1812, delegates from throughout the Spanish Empire approved a new, liberal constitution that defined the Spanish nation as "the union of the Spanish of both hemispheres," and gave citizenship to all whites of Spanish descent, and also to Native Americans.[108] This constitution would have lasting importance for Latin America, and to the extent that it took inspiration from the French Revolution (especially the moderate French constitution of 1791), it served as an important vector of transmission from that earlier revolution.[109] At the same time, however, the Cádiz junta insisted on preserving the metropole's commercial privileges vis-à-vis the American colonies, angering the American delegates.[110] And then, little more than a year afterwards, as the Napoleonic Empire collapsed, the Bourbon Fernando VII returned to rule Spain and soon renounced the Cádiz constitution.

As Jeremy Adelman has written, these events and forces "external" to Latin America combined to create "a power vacuum across the [Spanish] empire."[111] Contrary to what earlier generations of nationalist historians claimed, it was not an opportunity for fully formed American nations to break free of colonial rule. Rather, it gave the final blow to older, imperial forms of sovereignty and forced Spanish Americans – outraged by what they saw as multiple promises broken by the metropole – to seek new forms of sovereignty, often finding models in the earlier Atlantic Revolutions. It was in this context that there began the long, bloody series of independence struggles, from Mexico to Cape Horn, which ended with nearly all of the Americas (although not the Caribbean) largely consisting of independent states, with declarations of independence and constitutions that owed much to the American and French precedents.[112] Brazil followed a different, more peaceful (though by no means entirely amicable and non-violent) path, owing in part to the presence of the Portuguese royal family in Rio de Janeiro.[113]

Concluding Thoughts

If the Atlantic in 1825 was no longer a dominion of European empires, it had not become a dominion of democracy. Nearly all of the regimes born out of the Atlantic Revolutions quickly fell prey to political instability,

---

[108] "Constitución española de 1812" (March 19, 1812), Wikisource, Online.
[109] Breña, "The Cádiz Liberal Revolution," 79, 81.
[110] Jeremy Adelman, *Sovereignty and Revolution in the Iberian Atlantic* (Princeton, NJ, 2006), 175–219.
[111] Ibid., 177 and 180.
[112] In addition to Adelman, see here the classic work of Jaime E. Rodríguez O., *The Independence of Spanish America* (Cambridge, 1998).
[113] Ibid., 308–343; and Paquette, *Imperial Portugal*, 140–163.

violence, and the lure of authoritarianism. Few of them managed to last for long without a charismatic military figure assuming the political leadership – a Washington, a Louverture, a Bonaparte, a Bolívar. In most cases these figures ended up trampling constitutional restraints and assuming, at least in part, a dictatorial role. Even Washington could most likely have seized dictatorial power had he wished to.[114] But dictators had short political half-lives as well, and in France, Haiti, and much of Spanish America, the decades after the Atlantic Revolutions were marked by a merry-go-round of governments and constitutions. In France, it would take until 1895 for a post-revolutionary regime to survive to its twenty-fifth anniversary.

Yet if the Atlantic Revolutions did not give birth to "democracy," they most certainly gave birth to a radically new political universe. Throughout the Atlantic world, the idea of popular sovereignty became the unchallenged basis of political legitimacy. Throughout the Atlantic world, this sovereignty was now firmly associated with nation-states that proclaimed their rightful existence through declarations of independence and ordered themselves by means of constitutions that included guarantees of rights. Even authoritarian rulers still claimed, for the most part, to respect these principles, staging plebiscites and staging other shows of public support. Finally, throughout the Atlantic world, it was now recognized that fundamental political change could take place through revolution – that is, through an unsettlingly rapid, but controlled, sustained process of change carried out by self-consciously "revolutionary" forces. Nor were revolutions necessarily limited to a single place. They could spread from country to country, and even across the great ocean, with disconcerting speed and violence. And while the principle was not yet accepted in most of the Atlantic world, the Haitian revolutionaries in particular had asserted that this new political universe belonged to all, regardless of race, and that slavery should have no place in it.

As already noted, this new political universe was not limited to the Atlantic world. Its borders already extended over much of Europe beyond the Atlantic seaboard, and by the early twentieth century, they would extend to most of the world. But it was arguably the Atlantic Revolutions that, happening in such close temporal and geographical proximity to each other, bound by such a thick web of connections and thereby reinforcing each other, gave this political sea-change its force and permanence and contributed to the disconcerting sense that had the new political principles and practices been associated with a single place, they

---

[114] David A. Bell, *Men on Horseback: The Power of Charisma in the Age of Revolution* (New York, 2020), on charismatic leadership and dictatorship.

might easily have perished with that place's revolutionary regime or been damned by association with that place's revolutionary excesses. But when so many lands, separated by vast distances but attached to each other by the common space of this ever more frequently traversed ocean, participated in what seemed, even at the time, a common project, then the changes were far more likely to endure.

2   The Revolutionary Waves of 1848

Christopher Clark

In their combination of intensity and geographical extent, the 1848 revolutions were unique – at least in European history. Neither the great French Revolution of 1789, nor the July Revolution of 1830, nor the Paris Commune of 1870, nor the Russian revolutions of 1905 and 1917 sparked a comparable transcontinental cascade. The year 1989 looks like a better comparator, but there is still controversy as to whether these uprisings can be characterized as "revolutions," and, in any case, their direct impact was limited to the Warsaw Pact states. In 1848, by contrast, parallel political tumults broke out across the entire continent, from Spain and Portugal to Wallachia and Moldavia, from Norway, Denmark, and Sweden to Naples and Palermo. And across the continent, the movements challenging the old regime – radical, democratic, or liberal – developed strikingly similar repertories of claims and objectives. This was the only truly European revolution that there has ever been.

The revolutions exhibit a complex and highly compacted chronology. In February and March 1848, upheaval spread like a brush fire across the continent, leaping from city to city and starting numerous spot fires in towns and villages in between. Metternich fled from Vienna, the Prussian army was withdrawn from Berlin, and the Bourbon king of Naples issued a constitution. This was the 1848 moment: one could be forgiven for thinking that European societies were united against the old regime and that victory was certain. But the divisions within the upheaval soon become apparent: by May 1848, radical demonstrators were already attempting to storm and overthrow the National Assembly created by the February revolution in Paris, while in Vienna Austrian democrats protested against the slowness of liberal reforms and established a Committee of Public Safety. In June there were violent clashes between the liberal (or in France, republican) leaderships and radical crowds on the streets of the larger cities in Prussia and France.

In other words, the early history of the revolutions was marked – roughly speaking – by two phases: apparent unanimity and open conflict. The autumn of 1848 offered a more complex picture. The narrative divides into two parallel strands: on the one hand, counterrevolution unfolded in Berlin, Prague, and the Kingdom of Naples; on the other hand, a second-phase radical revolt dominated by democrats and socialists of various kinds broke out in southern Germany, Vienna, and Rome, where the radicals, after the flight of the pope, eventually declared a Roman Republic. In Vienna, both things happened in rapid succession: there was a second-phase radical revolution and then a counterrevolutionary repression. In the south of Germany, the radical challenge to the old order was extinguished only in the summer of 1849, when Prussian troops finally captured the fortress of Rastatt in Baden, the last stronghold of the radical insurgency, in July 1849. In the following month, the Roman Republic fell under the assault of a French army now fighting under conservative auspices, the papacy was restored, the Venetian Republic of San Marco was shut down, and the bitter war over the future of Hungary was brought to an end as Austrian and Russian troops occupied the country.

As even this bare outline suggests, the revolutions of 1848 were characterized by extreme temporal compression, as unexpected successes were followed by setbacks and drastic reversals over the space of seventeen months. And since the events began at different times and unfolded at different speeds, driven by very diverse local circumstances in a wide variety of dispersed settings, the asynchrony of the process of revolution and counterrevolution across dispersed theaters generated countercurrents that militated against a convergence of revolutionary impulses across the continent. When revolution broke out in Wallachia in June 1848, triggered in part by the arrival in Bucharest of some Romanian students who had been living in Paris, the new provisional government sent an envoy to France in the hope of securing money and weapons, only to find that Lamartine, the patron of the Parisian Romanians, had disappeared from public life and a new conservative administration had taken control in Paris that had no interest whatsoever in offering practical assistance. By the time the German national parliament at Frankfurt am Main finished the long work of drafting a German constitution, public sympathy for the revolution had ebbed and Prussia had seized de facto control of the German national question. In the summer of 1849, those Roman Republicans who had looked to Paris for support found instead that the France of Bonaparte's presidential republic preferred to crush the Roman Republic and restore the papacy. The dynamics of connection and disconnection could become paradoxically intertwined: when the cohort of Romanian radical students in Paris decided to leave the city in March in order to foment revolution at home in Bucharest, were they connecting or disconnecting the two theaters? Might it not, as one Romanian historian has suggested, have been better to leave someone in the city to manage relations with the new provisional government?[1]

This complex pattern of interactions greatly complicates the task of tracing the contours of 1848 as a "global revolution." Diasporal and religious networks, migration, and the movement of students and political exiles certainly facilitated the transoceanic passage of ideas. Empire was another powerful form of connectivity, as we shall see, but close cultural affinities persisted even in postcolonial settings, such as the independent republics of South America. In a few exceptional cases (the French, Dutch, and Danish Caribbean, for example) they even triggered insurrections. In most places, the response was ambivalent, filtered through processes of contestation already under way in each locality. But what, one might ask, was being diffused or received when the news of revolution crossed oceans? Even those upheavals whose development was relatively closely synchronized could evolve into an antipathetic relationship with each other. This problem was especially salient in Central Europe, where conflicting programs focused on national or ethnic empowerment sometimes pitted revolutionaries against each other, obscuring the common impulses that had once shaped their respective struggles. The politically conflicted character of the revolutions confronted responders in remote locations with choices. With which strand of the revolution should they engage? With the radical revolution of democrats and socialists, or the gradualist revolution of the liberals? The fast politics of streets, clubs, and rallies, or the slow politics of constitutionally elected chambers? It may be true, as one historian has claimed, that the 1848 revolutions, unlike the French Revolution, formulated no "new universal principles."[2] But they changed and recombined many established ideas and arguments. There was no single issue at the heart of the revolutions but rather a multitude of questions – about democracy, representation, social equality, the organization of labor, gender relations, religion, forms of state power, among many other things – and an even greater multitude of competing answers. This, too, complicates the task of tracing the revolutions' impact on the wider world.

The European Revolution

What made such rapid transcontinental proliferation possible? Until quite recently, the literature on the revolutions was only marginally

[1] Traian Ionescu, "Misiunea lui Al. Gh. Golescu la Paris în 1848," *Revista de Istorie* 27 (1974), 1727–46.

[2] Jürgen Osterhammel, *The Transformation of the World. A Global History of the Nineteenth Century* (Princeton, NJ, 2014), 546.

interested in this question. Relatively few works offered an overview of the revolutions as a transcontinental event; national, regional, and municipal accounts dominated.[3] There are good reasons for this. The revolution really was a highly dispersed event with a correspondingly fragmented source base. No single historian – even if he or she possessed all the requisite languages – could master all those archives. A deeper reason is simply the power of the nation-state as a way of framing historical thought and memory. As Axel Körner showed in a book subtitled *International Ideas and National Memories of 1848*, these revolutions were nationalized in retrospect, as the historians of the nations absorbed them into specific national teleologies and path dependencies.[4] The revolutions were disaggregated into a plurality of parallel, nation-state-focused narratives. Their transnational dimension was lost to view.

Yet the problem of simultaneity remained, even if the structure of the literature made it difficult to address. Were the revolutions of 1848 the cognate expressions of a single common cause, such as social and economic pressures that spanned the continent as a whole? Did revolutionary ideas that had germinated in one place diffuse across national boundaries as newspaper copy, like the wind-borne seeds dispersed by a certain species of tree? Or were they carried and promulgated by traveling revolutionaries and political exiles?

These are not mutually exclusive explanations, and all of them have merit. The 1848 revolutions were undeniably preceded by a social and economic crisis that transcended political boundaries. The combination of population

---

[3] Jonathan Sperber, *The European Revolutions, 1848–1851* (Cambridge, 1994); Mike Rapport, *1848: Year of Revolution* (London, 2008); there are also some outstanding compiled volumes, such as Dieter Langewiesche (ed.), *Die Revolutionen von 1848 in der europäischen Geschichte* (Munich, 2000); and Dieter Dowe, Heinz-Gerhard Haupt, and Dieter Langewiesche (eds.), *Europe in 1848: Revolution and Reform* (Bonn, 1998). Excellent national, regional, and urban studies include (small selection): Rüdiger Hachtmann, *Berlin 1848: Eine Politik- und Gesellschaftsgeschichte der Revolution* (Bonn, 1997); Paul Ginsborg, *Daniele Manin and the Venetian Revolution of 1848–49* (Cambridge, 1979); István Deák, *The Lawful Revolution: Louis Kossuth and the Hungarians 1848–1849* (London, 2001); Jill Harsin, *The War of the Streets in Revolutionary Paris* (New York, 2002); Mark Traugott, *Armies of the Poor: Determinants of Working-Class Participation in the Parisian Insurrection of June 1848* (Princeton, NJ, 1985); Mauric Agulhon, *The Republican Experiment*, translated by Janet Lloyd (Cambridge, 1983); Maria Manuela Tavares Ribeiro, *Portugal e a Revolução de 1848* (Coimbra, 1990); Giuseppe Monsagrati, *Roma senza il Papa: Le Repubblica romana del 1849* (Rome, 2014); Karl-Joseph Hummel, *München in der Revolution von 1848/49* (Göttingen, 1987); Brian E. Vick, *Defining Germany: The 1848 Frankfurt Parliamentarians and National Identity* (Cambridge, 2002); and Mary Lynn Stewart-McDougall, *The Artisan Republic: Revolution, Reaction, and Resistance in Lyon, 1848–1851* (Kingston Ont., 1984).

[4] Axel Körner (ed.), *1848: A European Revolution? International Ideas and National Memories of 1848* (New York, 2000).

growth, stagnant productivity, and a decline in the real value of wages heightened the precarity of entire social groups across Europe, exposing them to subsistence crisis when the food supply failed, as it did in 1846–47. And the downturns in the business cycle that followed such disruptions struck hard at the overcrowded artisan trades in the cities, endowing urban protest with a strikingly consistent social profile.[5] Newspapers and news play a prominent role in countless contemporary reports of the upheavals in the European cities.[6] "It is really and truly a newspaper revolution," the *New York Herald* observed from across the Atlantic on March 20, 1848.[7] Transnational networks of exiles – Polish, Spanish, Russian, Italian, and German – had been a feature of the European radical milieu since the 1820s, and the return of Romanian students from Paris helped to escalate the unrest in Bucharest and Iasi in the summer of 1848.[8]

Yet these arguments all fall short, at least individually, of explaining what happened in 1848. Subsistence riots reached a peak in 1847, but they tended to embody a retrograde moral economy rather than revolutionary aspirations, and the areas most afflicted by socioeconomic distress were not usually the most politically active.[9] The upheavals cascaded across the continent faster than print was capable of broadcasting information about them, and, in any case, newspaper readers and barricade fighters were not necessarily the same people.[10] Once the revolutions

---

[5] Sperber, *The European Revolutions*, 5–55; Helge Berger and Mark Spoerer, "Economic Crises and the European Revolutions of 1848," *The Journal of Economic History* 61, 2 (2001), 293–326; Hans-Werner Hahn, "Die sozioökonomische Ordnung der Nation," in Christof Dipper and Ulrich Speck (eds.), *1848: Revolution in Deutschland* (Frankfurt, 1998), 366–80; Peter N. Stearns, *The Revolutions of 1848* (London, 1974), esp. 11–35; Charles, Louise, and Richard Tilly, *The Rebellious Century, 1830–1930* (London, 1975); for a Marxist account of economic origins, see Jürgen Kuczynski, "Wirtschaftliche und soziale Voraussetzungen der Revolution von 1848/49," in Elisabeth Todt and Hans Radandt (eds.), *Zur Frühgeschichte der deutschen Gewerkschaftsbewegung* (East Berlin, 1950), 7–32.

[6] Domokos G. Kosáry, *The Press during the Hungarian Revolutions of 1848–1849* (Boulder, CO, 1986); and Hanno Tauschwitz, *Presse und Revolution 1848/49 in Baden: Ein Beitrag zur Sozialgeschichte der periodischen Literatur und zu ihrem Einfluss auf die Geschichte der badischen Revolution* (Heidelberg, 1981), are notable studies on the subject.

[7] Anonymous, "The New Revolution in France – the Position of the United States" (Editorial), *New York Herald* (March 20, 1848).

[8] Angela Jianu, *A Circle of Friends: Romanian Revolutionaries and Political Exile, 1840–1859* (Leiden, 2011); for exiles elsewhere, see also Leopold G. Glueckert, *Between Two Amnesties: Former Political Prisoners and Exiles in the Roman Revolution of 1848* (New York, 1991); and the contributions in Sabine Freitag (ed.), *Exiles from European Revolutions: Refugees in Mid-Victorian England* (New York, 2003).

[9] Manfred Gailus, *Strasse und Brot: Sozialer Protest in den deutschen Staaten unter besonderer Berücksichtigung Preussens, 1847–1849* (Göttingen, 1990).

[10] Mark Traugott, *The Insurgent Barricade* (Berkeley, CA, 2010); and Mark Traugott, *Armies of the Poor: Determinants of Working-Class Participation in the Parisian Insurrection of June 1848* (Princeton, NJ, 1985).

were underway, it was difficult for revolutionaries to travel without for-
feiting their ability to shape events. The best and most thorough analysis
to date of the revolution in Berlin, Rüdiger Hachtmann's *Berlin 1848*,
found no evidence whatsoever for the claim – often advanced by the
authorities and the police – that foreign exiles or members of international
conspiratorial "clubs" were behind the outbreak of violence during the
"March days" of 1848.[11] Many contemporary accounts of the outbreak of
violence convey a sense of spontaneous combustion that defies historical
assumptions about causation. In his *History of the 1848 Revolution*, published in Brussels in 1849, Alphonse de Lamartine described the expect-
ant crowds in Paris on February 22, the first day of the revolution:
"Curious and inoffensive crowds continually moved along the boule-
vards, gathering numbers as they went; other crowds streamed from the
suburbs of Paris; they appeared, however, rather to observe what was
passing than to meditate any act. The event seems to have been engendered by the curiosity that attended it."[12]

The wavelike, sequential structure of the upheavals suggests an outward proliferation from a point of common origin. The older literature
tended to presume a diffusion of revolutionary contagion from Paris
across the continent, and this view certainly captures the extraordinary
impact of the news of the February revolution in many European cities.
On the other hand, a Paris-centered narrative conceals from view those
upheavals in Switzerland and the Kingdom of Naples (which included
Sicily) that occurred before the signal from Paris and also exhibited –
albeit in a more modest register – diffusion effects. It also misses the
importance of other centers, such as Vienna and Rome, which became
centers of revolutionary diffusion in their own right – Rome because of its
importance to the Catholic world and Vienna because it was the keystone
in the arch of Habsburg authority over the sprawling multiethnic commonwealth of the Austrian Empire. But whatever their direction of travel,
the rapid transfer of revolutionary signals was possible only, the Danish
historian Claus Møller Jørgensen has suggested, because "transurban
interconnectivities" enabled dissenting urban elites across the continent
to appropriate and exchange "knowledge resources" circulating across
political borders.[13]

One recent discussion of proliferation effects in the revolutions has
attempted to loosen the grip of the diffusion metaphor, which implies

---

[11] Hachtmann, *Berlin 1848*, 170.
[12] Alphonse de Lamartine, *History of the French Revolution of 1848* (London, 1849), 37.
[13] Claus Møller Jørgensen, "Transurban Interconnectivities: An Essay on the
Interpretation of the Revolutions of 1848," *European Review of History* 19 (2012),
201–27.

the scattering or dispersal of a more or less homogeneous substance over a large terrain, and to focus instead on the ways in which actors in dispersed locations understood, selected, and acted on newly available information. Reflecting on the parallels between the revolutions of 1848 and the sequence of 2011 upheavals and uprisings known as the "Arab Spring," Kurt Weyland has proposed that the apparently spontaneous horizontal impulses seen in both cases were driven not by the diffusion of ideas and arguments as such but by collective psychological effects known as "cognitive shortcuts" that induced actors in many locations to draw false inferences from what they learned about events in other theaters of upheaval. Two such shortcuts in particular, Weyland argues, shaped behavior in 1848: the "heuristics of availability" and "the heuristics of representativeness." The first refers to the tendency of actors as individuals and in groups to attach disproportionate weight to dramatic or spectacular events, even if this means downplaying or ignoring other less vivid but equally relevant information. The second refers to the tendency of people to infer excessively firm and general conclusions from very limited information. Taken together, these two mechanisms, whose effect is intensified in situations of collective excitement or panic, help to explain how the example of Paris could trigger emulation, even in settings where the regime was far less fragile and the chances of achieving success were far less good. In short, the diffusion of raw information or ideas in themselves caused little; what mattered was the only partly rational process by which such data were filtered and interpreted.[14]

What is lost from view when we focus on rapid diffusion and horizontal cascades are the prerevolutionary crises already brewing in many locations before the February events of 1848. In Berlin, the summoning of the United Diet in 1847 had heightened expectations of political change and the winter of 1847–48 saw a sharpening of political dissent. In Paris, a massive campaign of liberal banquets – public functions organized to articulate political demands and critique – had already laid the foundations for the events of February 1848. In the German constitutional monarchies, the years 1845–48 were marked by polarization and intensified conflict between legislature and executive. In Wallachia, the *Frăția*, or "Brotherhood," that played a central role in the revolutions of 1848 dated back to 1843. And in Rome, a process of political fermentation had

---

[14] Kurt Weyland, "The Arab Spring: Why the Surprising Similarities with the Revolutionary Wave of 1848?," *Perspectives on Politics* 10 (2012), 917–34; Kurt Weyland, "The Diffusion of Revolution: '1848' in Europe and Latin America," *International Organization* 63, 3 (2009), 391–423. For a study that sets these observations in a larger context, see Kurt Weyland, *Making Waves: Democratic Contention in Europe and Latin America since the Revolutions of 1848* (Cambridge, 2014).

been underway since the election in 1846 of the new pope, Pius IX, whose early behavior in office suggested a readiness to meet liberal demands.

In virtually every theater of revolutionary tumult, then, we can trace chains of local antecedents with highly diverse fields of reference. But investing too heavily in any one of these parochial genealogies risks miring the analysis in the assumed distinctiveness of a plethora of specific national or territorial *Sonderwege*. One potential way around the problem is to de-emphasize the momentary, event-like character of 1848, conceptualize it instead as a transnational process with a deep history, and attend to the forms of interconnectivity that connected civil and political strife across many countries *before* 1848. Robust networks linked Spanish *progresistas* and other Iberian radicals with Italian *carbonari* and activists from the Polish diaspora in Paris. *L'Echo de la fabrique*, organ of the radical silk weavers of Lyon, ran articles on social issues in Britain and published a manifesto addressed "To Our Brothers in England" in 1832.[15] Radical groups in Britain maintained many links with continental radicals and exiles.[16] The liberal Rhenish industrialist David Hansemann, a prominent player in Prussia's 1848, was deeply shaped in both his politics and business practices by Belgian and French models. Hungarian liberals such as Széchenyi, Szemere, and Bölöni Farkas wove observations and readings from France, Britain, the Netherlands, and the German states into their political diagnoses of conditions in Hungary.[17] Both before and after 1848, Italian literary exiles used direct observations of British politics, society, and economic life to stimulate debates about the Italian national question.[18] Europe may not – in objective terms – have been a coherent collective political actor, but the scope of much radical and liberal thinking was emphatically European. "There exists in Europe," Giuseppe Mazzini wrote in an essay published in 1831, "a concord of needs and wishes, a common thought, a universal soul, that drive nations towards the same goal, there exists a European tendency."[19] The fuller our account of these

---

[15] Fabrice Bensimon, "British Workers in France, 1815–1848," *Past and Present* 213, 1 (2011), 147–89, is one of many notable examples.

[16] Iowerth Prothero, "Chartists and Political Refugees," in Freitag (ed.), *Exiles from European Revolutions*, 209–33.

[17] Iván Zoltán Dénes, "The Value Systems of Liberals and Conservatives in Hungary, 1830–1848," *The Historical Journal* 36, 4 (1993), 825–50, here 840.

[18] Maurizio Isabella, "Italian Exiles and British Politics before and after 1848," in Freitag (ed.), *Exiles from European Revolutions*, 59–87.

[19] Ct. in Maurizio Isabella, "Mazzini's Internationalism in Context," in C. A. Bayly and E. F. Biagini (eds.), *Giuseppe Mazzini and the Globalisation of Democratic Nationalism* (Oxford, 2008), 37–58, 42, which refers to G. Mazzini, "D'una letteratura europea," in *Scritti editi ed inediti*, 94 vols. (Imola, 1906–43), vol. I (Imola, 1906), 177–222. On the European frame of Mazzini's radical politics, see also in the same volume Salvo Mastellone, "Mazzini's International League and the Politics of the London

lateral connections becomes, the less urgent the problem of simultaneity begins to appear. If we treat the revolutions as a European event, rather than fetishizing the differences that made each city, each province, village, and nation special, the rapid proliferation of upheavals sheds some of its mystery. After all, even within quite small territories, like the Kingdom of Naples, the intensity and orientation of revolutionary engagement varied starkly from place to place. Why assign the diversity of Europe so much more hermeneutic weight than the diversity of the states and the regions that composed it?

The European International

Historians have always been aware of the connected character of the revolutions. It has always seemed obvious that they spread from country to country like a bush fire or a flu epidemic. But transnationalism in this sense referred to the social and cultural forces of tumult and disorder, rather than to the states in which revolution occurred. *Their* interactions with each other and the impact of these interactions on the revolutions and vice versa have attracted less attention. And one of the consequences of this is that while we have a very nuanced understanding of the dynamics of the revolutions in the cities and the regions and of their meaning for the history of the nation-states – in short, of the revolutions as domestic tumults – we have a relatively underdeveloped sense of the geopolitics of revolution, the place of international, or interstate, relations in their inception, course, and consequences.[20]

Geopolitics mattered for two main reasons. First, geopolitical structures and tensions were implicated in the inception of the revolutions. Second, international interventions (and noninterventions) shaped the revolutions' course, conclusion, and aftermath. The distinction we sometimes draw between domestic tumult and international order made very little sense in a Europe in which constitutional settlements were woven *into* the international order, either because they were its product and instrument, as in the case of the Swiss Federal Treaty signed in 1815 or the German confederal constitution drawn up at Vienna in 1815 and finalized in 1820, or because they were internationally guaranteed, like the constitution of Belgium, itself the consequence of the revolutions of 1830. The European order was a historicizing abstraction. It was usually invoked when there were axes to be ground. Those who appealed to "European" interests often had in mind the interests of their own states.

Democratic Manifestos, 1837–1850," 93–104; and Roland Sarti, "Giuseppe Mazzini and Young Europe," 275–97.

[20] I use the term "geopolitics" here in a doctrinally neutral sense to denote politics, especially international relations, as influenced by geographical factors such as contiguity, proximity, or access to strategically important waterways.

But at this level, too, the level of state interests, geopolitics shaped the inception and early course of the revolutions.

Prussia is a case in point. By the mid-1840s, the Prussian government was under pressure to construct a military railway linking the eastern and western extremities of the state. The Prussian railway network had grown in recent years, from 185 kilometers in 1840 to 1,106 kilometers by 1845. But this growth had been concentrated in areas where private investors stood to make profits; entrepreneurs understandably had little interest in unprofitable major projects geared to macroeconomic and military needs. In the autumn of 1845, news reached Berlin that the French government had embarked upon the construction of a strategic rail network whose eastern terminals would pose a potential threat to the security of the German Confederation. Berlin's calls for a coordinated all-German confederal strategic railway policy were in vain: the Confederation failed to secure a consensus among the member states, even on the question of the appropriate gauge for an integrated network. It was clear that Prussia would have to see to its own needs.

At the center of the program that crystallized during 1846 was the Ostbahn, a railway artery that would link the Rhineland and the French frontier with Brandenburg and East Prussia. The problem was that in order to finance this project, the government needed to borrow a large amount of money. And under the Prussian State Indebtedness Law of 1822, loans on this scale could only be ratified by a united all-Prussian representative assembly. It was this impasse that obliged the Prussian government to convene what became known as the United Diet of 1847. There is no need to go into the details of the role this body played in paving the road to revolution in the following year. Suffice it to say that, not for the first time in European history, an assembly summoned to act as a rubber stamp developed an exalted sense of its own destiny. The first thing the new assembly did in 1847 was to demand that it be transformed into a proper parliament, with a constitution enshrining its rights and powers, with regular sessions and territorial elections. Without these concessions, the deputies declared, there was no question of approving the military railway funds: "Where money is at stake," the liberal Rhenish deputy Hansemann quipped, "geniality has its limits." In this case we can observe with unusual clarity how the pressures exerted by geopolitical tension translated into domestic concessions on the constitutional front that in turn accelerated the radicalization of politics and the readiness of the opposition to form a united front against the government.[21]

---

[21] On the Ostbahn crisis, see Herbert Obenaus, *Anfänge des Parlamentarismus in Preußen bis 1848* (Düsseldorf, 1984), 709–11; Dennis E. Showalter, "Soldiers and Steam. Railways

European geopolitics also impinged on the process of revolution because the revolutionaries themselves thought geopolitically. A euphoric mood suffused the city of Rome in 1846 and 1847 when the new pope, Pius IX, began making what looked like liberal adjustments to the administration of the Papal States. Wherever he went, he was mobbed by cheering crowds. But the enthusiasm for Pius IX soon began to acquire geopolitical connotations. The cry *Viva Pio Nono!* morphed into *Viva Pio Nono, Re d'Italia! Morte ai Tedeschi!* It was one thing to see the streets of Rome choked with masses of people chanting "Long live Pius IX!," "Long live Leopold II!," "Long live the Tuscan civic guard!" It was fun when people converged on the Roman residence of the Minister of Tuscany, Marquese Bargagli, in the middle of the night, forcing the good-natured marquese to illuminate his house. And if things went well, why not repair to the residence of the Piedmontese Minister – he could hardly object to a crowd below his balcony chanting *Viva Carlo Alberto! Viva l'Italia! Long live the union of the Italian princes!* But it was another matter entirely for the crowd to surge down the street and around the corner into the nearby Piazza Venezia, where the Austrian legation was, and to wake the minister and his family with threatening chants, or even to force him to move his family out of the city. It was in response to alarming demonstrations of this kind that the Austrians decided to reinforce the Austrian garrison at Ferrara on the northern border of the Papal States, a move that in turn did much to escalate the upheaval unfolding in the city of Rome.[22] From the very beginning, then, the movement of radical and liberal enthusiasm for reform on the streets of Rome represented a factor in international relations.

We see a similar mechanism in operation in Paris in the summer of 1848. The summer troubles in Paris began with the *journée* of 15 May. On that day, a crowd of demonstrators, led by the Paris radical clubs, broke into the newly elected National Assembly in an effort to influence a scheduled debate on Poland in the direction of a French intervention to support the struggle for independence there. After a few hours of pandemonium, one of the club leaders proclaimed the dissolution of parliament and the crowd marched on the Paris City Hall to set up a revolutionary government. Within one hour the insurgents were

and the Military in Prussia, 1832–1848," *The Historian* 34, 2 (1972), 242–59; Hanna Schissler, "Preussische Finanzpolitik nach 1807: Die Bedeutung der Staatsverschuldung als Faktor der Modernisierung des preussischen Finanzsystems," *Geschichte und Gesellschaft* 8, 3 (1982), 367–85, 385; and Hansemann's remark is cited in Heinrich von Treitschke, *Deutsche Geschichte im neunzehnten Jahrhundert*, 5 vols. (Leipzig, 1879–94), vol. V (Leipzig, 1894), 626.

22 Stefano Tomassini, *Storia avventurosa della rivoluzione romana: Repubblicani, liberali e papalini nella Roma del 48* (Milan, 2008).

dispersed, and their leaders under lock and key. There was no French intervention in support of the Polish struggle. Instead, there was a conservative crackdown that culminated in the decision to shut down the national workshops, brainchild of the radical exponent of the "organisation of labour," Louis Blanc.[23] And the closure of the workshops triggered the far more bloody "June Days" of June 23–26. Here, too, geopolitics helped shape the course of the revolution, though in contradictory ways. Transnational revolutionary solidarity on the left established the Polish Question as a subject of political contestation. At the same time, an increasingly conservative French republican administration refused to intervene in the affairs of a neighboring state.

In the Austrian Empire, the revolutions created a crisis that could only be resolved through intervention by an external power. The Hungarian struggle, first for national autonomy, later for national independence, was perhaps the most complexly structured conflict of the revolutions. It was here that the radical dream of a cosmopolitan nationalism was tested to destruction. The Croats marched against the Hungarians. Volunteers from other nationalities, Transylvanian Romanians, Slovaks, and Serbs also joined the fray against the Hungarian revolution. To them it seemed that the Hungarians had assumed the position "of a nation striving to impose or to continue the yoke upon the necks of their own dependents, instead of labouring to throw off a yoke from their own shoulders."[24] The Poles tended, by contrast, to side with the Hungarian movement, partly because they hoped thereby to counter the efforts of the Ruthenians in Eastern Galicia to claim nationality rights in a region the Poles regarded as part of the Polish heartland. But the Hungarians fought a determined campaign, and by early 1849, it was becoming clear to the Austrians that the conflict could only be brought to a definitive end through Russian intervention.

In the summer of 1849, after some beating about the bush, Emperor Francis Josef formally requested military aid from Tsar Nicholas I. A Russian force of 200,000 men invaded Hungary and the war came to an end on August 13, 1849, when the Hungarians capitulated to the Russians at Világos. Continental geopolitics was deeply woven into this dénouement. Tsar Nicholas I obtained French and British acceptance of Russian intervention only by acquiescing in Napoleon III's counterrevolutionary assault on the Roman Republic – also in summer 1849 – and assuring Viscount Palmerston that Russian troops would stay only briefly in the Principalities (they did not fulfill this promise). But Palmerston also

---

[23] Peter Amann, "A 'Journée' in the Making: May 15 1848," *Journal of Modern History* 42, 1 (1970), 42–69.

[24] Thus the hostile contemporary appraisal by Francis Bowen, "The War of Races in Hungary," *North American Review* 70 (1850), 78–136, 79.

accepted the intervention because he wanted to preserve the Austrian Empire, both as a bulwark against Russia and as a barrier to the German nation-building ambitions of the Prussian king Frederick William IV. For the Russians, who could ill-afford this large operation, there was the additional calculation that if the Hungarian revolutionaries, whose commanders included veterans of the Polish revolution of 1830–31, remained undefeated, the next target would be Russian Poland. Underlying these measures was a hostility to the revolution shared by all the great powers – including France from the summer of 1848 onwards, and even Britain, whose continental envoys were frequently dismissive of the revolutionaries and skeptical of their objectives. The only revolution to occur on "British" soil was the insurrection on the Ionian Islands, which the British authorities repressed with a severity comparable with counterrevolutionary measures elsewhere.[25]

One insight in particular emerges from the chaotic closing phase of the revolutions. And that is that there *was* an international, but it was not revolutionary, as the radicals and liberals had hoped. It was counterrevolutionary. The Prussians intervened against the revolution in Saxony, Baden, and Württemberg. The French intervened in the Papal States against the Roman Republic. The Russians intervened in Hungary. The radicals and liberals were impressively successful in creating *trans*national networks, but these networks were horizontal; they lacked the vertical structures and resources required to wield decisive force. The counterrevolution, by contrast, drew on the combined resources of armies whose loyalty to the traditional powers had never been seriously in question. "Towers" prevailed over "squares." Hierarchies beat networks. Power prevailed over ideas and arguments. The effort to make sense of this is at the center of the intellectual history of the 1850s, from the "blood and iron" of Bismarck, to the *Realpolitik* of Rochau, to the "historical materialism" of Marx and Engels.

---

[25] A process of reform was already underway on the Ionian Islands under governor Seaton, who hoped to introduce a genuinely representative element into the repressive and antiquated constitutional arrangements imposed by the British, but also to remove limitations on the freedom of the press and to increase expenditure on public works. These policies had already reached a degree of maturity before the 1848 revolutions broke out, but the slowness of the British government in ratifying the governor's proposals generated frustration and tension on the Islands, heightening their susceptibility to the revolutionary contagion of 1848. The repressions that followed were severe and aroused widespread criticism. On the background, see Eleni Calligas, "Lord Seaton's Reforms in the Ionian Islands, 1843–8: A Race with Time," *European History Quarterly* 24, 1 (1994), 7–29; David Hannell, "A Case of Bad Publicity: Britain and the Ionian Islands, 1848–1851," *European History Quarterly* 17, 2 (1987), 131–43. Anonymous, *The Ionian Islands under British Protection* (London, 1851) is a tendentious contemporary account defending British measures; on the broader context, see Thomas Gallant, *Experiencing Dominion: Culture, Identity and Power in the British Mediterranean* (London, 2002).

Beyond Europe: The Global 1848

The revolutions of 1848 took place before the age of the transoceanic telegraphs. The announcement that a republic had been proclaimed in France reached New York by the steamship *Cambria* on March 18, 1848, just as the revolution in Berlin was beginning. It took around thirty days for news to get from Paris by packet boat to Martinique. It was not until Monday June 19, 1848, that the citizens of Sydney in the colony of New South Wales could read of the February revolution. Did these exorbitant delays make a difference to how the revolution was received and processed? Longer and more complex routes and conflicting reports from different sources made confusion more likely. In July 1848, the *Sydney Morning Herald* reported that a general European war had broken out (the story was later retracted), and in Jamaica, reports that Queen Victoria had gone to the Isle of Wight mutated into rumors that she had been forced to abdicate.[26] But long distances also transformed the temporal texture of the news, which arrived in large packets of newspapers that might carry a week or a month of editions. And this presumably meant that to readers in Kingston, Capetown, or Auckland, the chronology of the revolutions seemed even more compressed than they did to in situ contemporaries. Distance attenuated the immersive euphoria of the eyewitness, offering instead a clearer view of the historical shape of events.

Yet even across great distances, the report of events in Europe made a deep impression. The news from France, the *New York Herald* declared on March 20, "are on every tongue and palpitating in every bosom of this great metropolis. The excitement during the last two days has been most tremendous and the public feeling has expressed itself in every possible way – celebration, the hanging out of flags, speeches and congratulations of all kinds, have occupied the people for the last forty hours."[27] On May 30, the liberal *El Mercurio* of Valparaíso in Chile was exultant:

The French revolution of 1848, [...] led by enlightenment and sanctioned by religion, will bring to Chile true liberty, and even if the most unheard of forces assemble to contain this spirit and this feeling which has been germinating in the land for so long, it is rising today with such freshness and vigour that nothing will be able to oppose its development.[28]

As the news fanned out from Europe, it was refracted through myriad mechanisms, like a beam of light breaking on the inner facets of a crystal.

---

[26] Miles Taylor, "The 1848 Revolutions and the British Empire," *Past and Present* 166, 1 (2000), 146–80, 172.

[27] Anonymous, "Editorial," *New York Herald* (March 20, 1848).

[28] Ct. in Cristián Gazmuri, *El "48" Chileno: Igualitarios, Reformistas Radicales, Masones y Bomberos* (Santiago de Chile, 1999), 64, which refers to *El Mercurio* (May 30, 1848).

In Martinique and Guadeloupe, colonial possessions of France, the news of the February revolution was read through the lens of the abolition question. When the February revolution broke out in Paris, slavery was still legal in the French Caribbean. In 1845, the July Monarchy had promulgated a bundle of measures known as the Mackau Laws, which envisaged a slow and phased process of emancipation focused on allowing slaves to purchase their own liberty and compensating the slave-owners. But the laws were blocked in the colonies, despite their generous concessions to slave-owners' interests.[29] Only after the February revolution of 1848 did abolitionists in metropolitan France succeed in imposing their agenda on the government.

Yet the narrative of emancipation in the French Caribbean is less linear, less "diffusionist," than one might assume. The news of the fall of the monarchy and the establishment of a republic was read in Martinique as a harbinger of imminent emancipation, even before the Provisional Government had begun to address the slavery question. "Liberty is on its way," declared the *Courrier de la Martinique* on March 27, in an appeal addressed to the plantation owners. "Do not wait for it to dictate its orders to you; prepare yourselves to receive it. Let the whip, the instrument of an expiring order of things, fall under your all-powerful will."[30] Further signals followed: on April 12 the *Journal Officiel de la Martinique* and the *Courrier de la Martinique* both published a decree issued by the provisional government in Paris on March 4. "In view of the fact that there can no longer be slaves on French soil," it stated, a commission had been formed to prepare with the greatest possible haste "an act of emancipation to take effect immediately in all the colonies of the Republic."[31]

The commission announced in Paris on March 4 did eventually produce a decree dated April 27, 1848, announcing the complete, immediate, and general abolition of slavery, but by the time this decree reached Martinique, the slaves had already taken matters into their own hands. In the second half of April, a broad wave of agitation engulfed the island. There were protests and demonstrations, clashes between crowds and troops and mass absconding from the plantations. By May 22 there were major skirmishes in the main city of Saint-Pierre as slaves invaded the town and fought with armed white settlers; the island was in a state of

---

[29] Seymour Drescher, "British Way, French Way: Opinion Building and Revolution in the Second French Slave Emancipation," *American Historical Review* 96, 3 (1991), 709–34, 715–23.

[30] Ct. in Édouard de Lépine, *Dix semaines qui ébranlèrent la Martinique, 25 mars – 4 Juin 1848* (Paris, 1999), 19, which refers to *Courrier de la Martinique* (March 27, 1848).

[31] Lépine, *Dix semaines qui ébranlèrent la Martinique*, 26.

general insurrection. On the afternoon of May 23, with no definitive general emancipation order from Paris yet in hand, Governor Rostoland gave in to pressure from many quarters and signed a local act of emancipation, waiving the two-month transition period envisaged by the government in Paris and appending to the decree an unconditional amnesty for "any political offences committed during the period of movement through which we have just passed."[32] As David Ringoulet-Roze has put it, "the slaves anticipated the application of the decree issued in Paris; indeed, they conquered their liberty for themselves without even waiting for the decree of 27 April to arrive on the island."[33]

Guadeloupe followed suit a few days later, issuing exactly the same proclamation on May 27, 1848, also without metropolitan sanction. And once the slaves of Martinique and Guadeloupe had secured their freedom, it proved impossible to sustain the authority of the slave-owners on the nearby Dutch islands of the Lesser Antilles, St. Martin, St. Eustatius, and Saba. The Dutch slaves simply ceased to behave as slaves, and since their "masters" lacked any means of coercing them, the institution was unilaterally nullified. This was a de facto abolition, not a legal one: only years later would the Dutch government get around to compensating the slave-owners. Something broadly similar happened on Sainte Croix, a Danish possession of the Lesser Antilles: on July 2, 1848, rebels occupied plantation buildings and raised a general alarm. On the following day, eight thousand slaves refused to commence work and gathered instead in the town of Frederiksted to demand their liberation. The Danish governor responded much as Rostoland had done in Martinique, telling the crowd: "Now you are free, you are hereby emancipated."[34]

In the case of Martinique, the outward diffusion of the news of revolution intersected with an autochthonous, self-organized movement powerful enough to preempt metropolitan abolition. But the impact of the upheavals on Martinique and Guadeloupe then passed sideways to the nearby possessions of another empire. Although the Dutch authorities

---

[32] Lépine, *Dix semaines qui ébranlèrent la Martinique*, 34; Tyler Stovall, "The Myth of the Liberatory Republic and the Political Culture of Freedom in Imperial France," *Yale French Studies* 111 (2007), 89–103, here 99.

[33] David Rigoulet-Roze, "À propos d'une commémoration: L'abolition de l'esclavage en 1848," *L'Homme: Revue française d'anthropologie* 145 (1998), 127–36, 133; see also Roger Botte, "L'esclavage africain après l'abolition de 1848: Servitude et droit du sol," *Annales. Histoire, Sciences Sociales* 55, 5 (2000), 1009–37, 1009–11.

[34] Robin Blackburn, *The Overthrow of Colonial Slavery, 1776–1848* (London, 1988), 507–8; Neville A. T. Hall, *Slave Society in the Danish West Indies: St. Thomas, St. John, and St. Croix*, ed. by B. W. Higman (Baltimore, 1992), 208; and Wim Klooster, "Slave Revolts, Royal Justice, and a Ubiquitous Rumor in the Age of Revolutions," *The William and Mary Quarterly* 71, 3 (2014), 401–24.

looked favorably on emancipation in theory, they would not otherwise have freed their Antillean slaves, because they were reluctant to accept the costs of compensating slave-owners: as a result of this calculus, the Dutch possession of Surinam, for example, retained slavery until 1863. On the Dutch Antillean possessions, it was proximity to another theater of political change that triggered events, not signals from the metropolis. And the insurrection on Sainte Croix was sparked not just by the news from Paris but also by rumors to the effect that the King of Denmark was about to issue a decree of emancipation. Spain, another important Caribbean stakeholder, offers a curious contrast: here there was no official decision to emancipate. The uprisings of 1848 in continental Spain were swiftly crushed by the moderado government under Narváez; slavery survived in the Spanish Caribbean. On the other hand, in those Latin American countries – now independent republics – that had once been Spanish colonies, the shock effect of the February revolution in *Paris* sufficed to set in train a cascade of initiatives that by the mid 1850s had abolished what remained of slavery in Peru, Argentina, Ecuador, Colombia, Bolivia, and Venezuela.[35]

The complexity of the "global 1848" is evident, even in the small world of the Antilles. Similarly, fractal cascades of causes and effects can be observed – on a much larger geographical scale – along the periphery of the British Empire. In a landmark essay, Miles Taylor showed how Britain protected itself against upheaval by adopting policies that pacified home populations but heightened tensions on the imperial periphery.[36] The transportation en masse of potential trouble-makers from England and Ireland triggered protests in Australia and the Cape Colony. To keep sugar cheap, the British government abandoned the system of tariff walls known as imperial preference, exposing colonial planters in Jamaica and British Guyana to competition from outside the British Empire and giving rise to protests, riots, and political paralysis. In Ceylon, the introduction of new taxes to cut costs without burdening British middle-class taxpayers triggered the emergence of a protest movement that soon encompassed around sixty thousand men. In the longer term, Taylor argues, disruptions like this across the imperial periphery produced constitutional adjustments that transformed the relationship between Westminster and its colonies.[37]

---

[35] Blackburn, *The Overthrow of Colonial Slavery*, 509.
[36] Taylor, "The 1848 Revolutions and the British Empire," 146–80.
[37] Robert Livingston Schuyler, "The Abolition of British Imperial Preference, 1846–60," *Political Science Quarterly* 33, 1 (1918), 77–92, who suggests that these adjustments "came near to dissolving the British Empire," here at 92.

This franchising out of political contention to the periphery puts paid to the myth that there was no "British 1848."[38] But it also illustrates the great variety of ways in which the potential for conflict could be transmitted and the diversity of responses it could elicit. The constitutional realignments on the imperial periphery that resulted were not, of course, direct consequences or echoes of the events of 1848 in continental Europe, even if the leaders of local tumults drew inspiration from the news from Europe.[39] They were a parallel phenomenon rooted in a policy of British counterrevolutionary prophylaxis.

Nevertheless, in far-off New South Wales, the editors of the *Sydney Morning Herald* were quick to see the link. Why, they asked in October 1848, when they learned (after more than three months) of the bloodshed of the June Days in Paris, had England escaped the bloodshed that had recently disfigured Paris? The answer lay in the fact that England possessed settler *colonies* – "those vast outfields wherein her redundant masses may find the sustenance which they cannot find at home."[40] The drawback of this model was that the very colonial appendages that insulated England against unrest also conducted the spirit of revolt outward, towards the edge of the British world. The paper returned to this theme in 1854, when an uprising broke out on the goldfields around Ballarat in the Australian colony of Victoria. A campaign by the Ballarat Reform League against heavy-handed policing and the high cost of miners' licenses culminated on December 3, 1854, in an encounter between miners and mounted troops at the "Battle of the Eureka Stockade," in which around twenty-seven men perished, most of them miners. The *Sydney Morning Herald* deplored the lawlessness of the Victorian diggers. But it added that upheavals of this kind were inevitable on the periphery of an Empire whose solution to the problem of "loose and disorderly populations" was to throw them at regular intervals "off to its outskirts."[41] Two weeks later, the newspaper developed the point in more depth. It

---

[38] For an analysis that emphasizes the connected character of politics and organized dissent in Britain and continental Europe in 1848, see Roland Quinault, "1848 and Parliamentary Reform," *Historical Journal* 31 (1988), 831–51; for a study that explores these connections in some social depth, see Bensimon, "British Workers in France, 1815–1848."

[39] Taylor points out that the leaders of the tax protesters in Ceylon cited the overthrow of the French monarch Louis Philippe in February 1848 as a model worthy of emulation by those who toiled under the yoke of colonial rule, New Zealand radicals in Wellington held banquets on the French model and Henry Parkes, a campaigner for Australian franchise reform, eulogized the French leader Alphonse de Lamartine, see Taylor, "The 1848 Revolutions and the British Empire," 171.

[40] Anonymous, Leader article, *Sydney Morning Herald* (October 11, 1848).

[41] Anonymous, Leader article, *Sydney Morning Herald* (December 7, 1848).

appeared, the editors noted, "that the bulk of the insurgents were south-ern Irish and foreigners."

The leaders did not understand our British principle of moral force and Constitutional agitation [...]. They adopted the plan with which they were the most familiar, that of revolution and red republicanism. You will observe that the secretary of Mazzini was there, and Vern, the Hanoverian, for whom a reward of £500 is offered, was, it is said, one of the June heroes of Paris.[42]

The "secretary of Mazzini" was Raffaello Carboni, a native of Urbino who had fought for the Roman Republic under Mazzini and Garibaldi in 1849, before fleeing to London and thence to Melbourne. Carboni's chatty, meandering book *The Eureka Stockade*, published in 1855, became the only complete firsthand printed account of the insurrection. "Vern the Hanoverian" was Friedrich Wern, a German radical who had fled continental Europe after the revolutions and had traveled to Victoria as a ship's mate. Wern absconded from the Stockade to avoid capture and ran off into the bush; the Victoria government offered the huge sum of £500 as a reward for his capture; he was eventually hunted down and imprisoned.[43]

There was massive public support for the arrested miners during the subsequent trials and Eureka became a focal point for forces in Australian society seeking constitutional reform. Within two years of the fighting at Ballarat, the governments of Victoria and New South Wales were forced to concede universal male suffrage, the secret ballot, and a reduction in the property qualification for holders of public office. "The mechanisms for future change had been established."[44] But if 1848 was part of the Eureka story, its impact transmitted on this occa-sion through the presence of exiles and transportees, it was only a small part. A movement to secure franchise reform already existed in New South Wales and Victoria, whose intellectual substance had more to do with the rights of "freeborn Englishmen," as expounded by John Lilburne, Richard Overton, John Milton, and John Locke, than with continental radical traditions. The memory of 1848 could only play a role here because it merged temporarily with the efforts of local interests to secure local objectives.

---

[42] "Melbourne (from our own correspondent)," *Sydney Morning Herald* (December 18, 1854).

[43] Volkhard Wehner, "The German-Speaking Community of Victoria between 1850 and 1930: Origin, Progress and Decline" (PhD dissertation, University of Melbourne, 2017), 51.

[44] Jerome O. Steffen, "The Mining Frontiers of California and Australia: A Study in Comparative Political Change and Continuity," *Pacific Historical Review* 52, 4 (1983), 428–40, 434.

As we move away from Europe, "impact" becomes a less pertinent metaphor. When actors in remote locations responded to the tidings of revolution, they did so because they saw in them the vindication of claims they were already making. In the United States, for example, once the initial wave of excitement had subsided, public discussion of the revolution was refracted through American partisan tensions. On March 29, Senator William Allen (Ohio) moved that the Senate formally congratulate the French people "upon their success in their recent efforts to consolidate liberty by imbodying [*sic*] its principles in a republican form of government." There might well have been very wide support for this proposal, but on the following day when debate on Allen's resolution began, Senator John P. Hale (New Hampshire) proposed an amendment in which the French were additionally congratulated for "manifesting the sincerity of their purpose by instituting measures for the immediate emancipation of the slaves of all the colonies of the republic." It was this amendment that brought the pro-slavery Senators into open opposition. Senator John Calhoun (South Carolina) spoke against it, conceding archly that the upheaval was "a wonderful event – the most striking in my opinion, in history" but that the real test of a revolution was whether or not it would continue to "guard against violence and anarchy" and that "the time [had] not yet arrived for congratulation."[45]

The same issue would dog the Hungarian patriot Lajos Kossuth after his arrival in New York on December 5, 1851. Kossuth had come in search of American money and diplomatic support for the now militarily defunct Hungarian cause against the Austrian Empire. He was a superstar, mobbed by jubilant crowds in almost every town he visited; Indiana, Mississippi, and Ohio named towns for him, and his fans could be seen wearing Hungarian-style fur hats and boots in the streets. But when, a few weeks after his arrival, a delegation of African Americans visited him and asked him to say a few words in support of the abolitionist cause, Kossuth refused, fearing that taking sides in such a contentious question might alienate potential high-value donors. The result of this reticence was a famous letter of rebuke in *The Liberator*, penned by its abolitionist editor, William Lloyd Garrison:

It was natural that the uncompromising advocates of impartial liberty should look to you for at least one word of sympathy and approval, – at least an incidental expression of grief and shame at the existence of a bondage so frightful, in a land so

---

[45] Matthew Norman, "Abraham Lincoln, Stephen A. Douglas, the Model Republic and the Right of Revolution, 1848–61," in Daniel McDonough and Kenneth W. Noe (eds.), *Politics and Culture of the Civil War Era: Essays in Honor of Robert W. Johannsen* (Selinsgrove, PA, 2006), 154–77, 158–9.

boastful of its freedom. [...] Deplorable as it is, the relation of your countrymen to the Austrian government is incomparably more hopeful, a million times less appalling, then that of our slave population to the American government; yet you invoke for the Hungarians the sympathy of the civilized world.[46]

Precisely the issue that had aligned abolitionist US senators with the French Republic now drove a wedge between the antislavery movement and the charismatic representative of the failed Hungarian national struggle.[47] Although Kossuth remained a crowd-puller, there was deepening ambivalence about the liberal and revolutionary credentials of the Hungarian cause. A long piece published by Francis Bowen in his *North American Review* in 1850 argued that the Hungarian struggle was not "a republican or independence war" at all but rather "an attempt on the part of the Magyar untitled nobility, 600,000 in number, to preserve the ancient feudal Constitution of the state, which guaranteed their aristocratic privileges and the dominion of their race." This was hardly a program with a legitimate claim upon American sympathies.[48]

The ideas released by the revolutions found many other points of entry too. Indeed, one of the distinctive features of these revolutions is the diffuseness of what was being diffused. The impact of 1848 did not equate to the triumph of a single idea or policy. Rather, the revolutions traveled as a loose constellation of ideas – including counterrevolutionary ones. Bruce Levine and others have shown how the influx of German radical exiles after the collapse of the revolutions had a deep impact on the evolving fabric of mid-century labor organization in the United States.[49] The year 1848 elicited many kinds of response from many parts of the American political landscape, reframing old debates, accelerating processes of political differentiation, and generating effects so diverse and dispersed that summarizing them is difficult, as Timothy Roberts has

---

[46] William Lloyd Garrison, "Letter to Louis Kossuth," *The Liberator* (February 20, 1852).
[47] Timothy M. Roberts and Daniel W. Howe, "The United States and the Revolutions of 1848," in R. J. Evans and Hartmut Pogge von Strandmann (eds.), *The Revolutions in Europe, 1848–1849* (Oxford, 2000), 157–79, 169.
[48] Francis Bowen, "The War of Races in Hungary," *North American Review* 70 (1850), 78–136, 82. The views expressed in this article were not uncontroversial: In the same year (1850) Bowen was blocked by the board of overseers at Harvard from taking up the McLean Professorship in History there on account of them, see Bruce Kuklick, *The Rise of American Philosophy: Cambridge Massachusetts, 1860–1930* (New Haven, CT, 1979), 29; on the impact of Kossuth, see Donald S. Spencer, *Kossuth and Young America: A Study of Sectionalism and Foreign Policy, 1848–1852* (Columbia, MO, 1977); see also Tibor Frank, "Lajos Kossuth and the Hungarian Exiles in London," and Sabine Freitag, "'The Begging Bowl of Revolution': The Fundraising Tours of German and Hungarian Exiles to North America, 1851–1852," both in Freitag (ed.), *Exiles from European Revolutions*, 121–43 and 164–86.
[49] Bruce Levine, *The Spirit of 1848: German Immigrants, Labor Conflict, and the Coming of the Civil War* (Urbana, 1992), esp. 111–45.

shown.[50] And Larry J. Reynolds has followed the impulses of 1848 into mid-century American literature, showing that the key works of the American Renaissance of the 1850s, from *The Scarlet Letter* to *Moby Dick* and *Leaves of Grass*, were in deep dialogue with the recent events across the Atlantic.[51] Senator John Calhoun was more impressed by the German revolutionaries in Frankfurt than by the French revolutionaries in Paris, because he admired the seriousness of their federalism and their interest in states' rights.[52]

In Peru, the news of revolution in Paris resonated with local debates over suffrage: whereas conservatives preferred to retain a tax qualification that prevented the majority from voting, liberals demanded franchise expansion. It was the latter who saw in the European revolutions an incitement to action: "It is not possible to remain stationary when the entire world is moving," declared the liberal *El Comercio* of Lima in January 1849. "In Europe they are tearing down thrones amidst torrents of blood [...]. Should we be sleeping?"[53] Liberal journalists were cheered by the prominence of the press as an agent of political change. "For the first time," the editors of *El Zurriago* declared, the press "was achieving the purpose for which it was destined in this world, namely, to serve as the vehicle for the liberty of the human race."[54] Liberal, radical, and conservative arguments circulated in a Lima public sphere that had greatly increased in density and sophistication since around 1840.[55]

In Santiago de Chile, the ideas of 1848 first arrived in the form of a book. A cult sprang up around Lamartine's epic three-volume *Histoire des Girondins*, which arrived in Valparaíso in February 1848. A group of prominent liberals met in the offices of the newspaper *El Progreso* to read it aloud; early copies were sold for six ounces of gold apiece, enough to buy a small library; Lamartine was venerated as "a demigod, like Moses." His work was an epic account of the *first* French revolution composed in the high romantic style with many fanciful inventions, but it was read as "a

---

[50] Timothy Mason Roberts, *Distant Revolutions: 1848 and the Challenge to American Exceptionalism* (Charlottesville, 2009); see also Richard C. Rohrs, "American Critics of the French Revolution of 1848," *Journal of the Early Republic* 14, 3 (1994), 359–77.

[51] Larry J. Reynolds, *European Revolutions and the American Literary Renaissance* (New Haven, CT, 1988), 15–20.

[52] Roberts and Howe, "The United States and the Revolutions of 1848," 169.

[53] Ct. in Claudia Rosas Lauro and José Ragas Rojas, "Las revoluciones francesas en el Perú: una reinterpretación (1789–1848)," *Bulletin de l'Institut français d'études andines* 36, 1 (2007), 51–65, 59, which refers to *El Comercio* (January 2, 1849).

[54] José Frank Ragas Rojas, "Ciudadanía, cultura política y representación en el Perú: La campaña electoral de 1850" (thesis for the Licenciado en Historia at the Pontificia Universidad Católica del Perú: Lima, 2003), 128.

[55] Claudia Rosas Lauro and José Ragas Rojas, "Las revoluciones francesas en el Perú: una reinterpretación (1789–1848)," *Bulletin de l'Institut français d'études andines* 36, 1 (2007), 51–65, 56.

prophetic book," a key to the present. Prominent members of the liberal and radical intelligentsia adopted the names of his characters as pseudonyms.[56] The extraordinary impact of Lamartine's *Girondins* reminds us that 1848 was available for a historicized contemporary understanding by contemporaries in a way that its great predecessor had not been. It was not just that Madrid could no longer filter the information available to literate Chileans; it was the fact that a mental template existed against which one could anticipate, interpret, and "understand" the mid-century revolutions as a piece of history unfolding in the present.

It is not easy to quantify intellectual excitement, and even harder to measure its impact on events and structures, but the emergence of new associations in Santiago, such as the Club de la Reforma (1849) and the Society of Equality (under the leadership of Francisco Bilbao, who had just returned from Paris) in 1850, and the creation of a new campaigning periodical (*El Amigo del Pueblo*) suggest that the discussions triggered by the news of the continental revolutions concentrated and sharpened Chilean radicalism as a system of "principles, symbols, ideas and images." At the same time, they consolidated a liberal milieu whose members would later occupy the highest public offices of Chilean institutional life. The liberal Chile that emerged in the last three decades of the century was largely conceived and formed in this moment.[57]

One could examine further cases of contagion, influence, and reception across Latin America[58] without greatly sophisticating the picture that has already emerged: charismatic individuals, newspapers, and even printed books carried the drama and ideas of revolution to remote locations, triggering waves of euphoria and enthusiasm. How these played out in the longer term depended upon processes of contestation already underway in the receiving location. And this meant that reception entailed the

---

[56] Lastarria became Brissot; Bilbao became Vergniaud; Domingo Santa María became Louvet and so on. Eusebio Lillo, a poet-musician who would later be the chief writer for the paper *El Amigo del Pueblo*, adopted the pseudonym Rouget de Lisle. Santiago Arcos became Marat – as this selection makes clear, Lamartine's book was not just about the Girondins, see Benjamin Vicuña Mackenna, *The Girondins of Chile: Reminiscences of an Eyewitness*, ed. by Cristián Gazmuri (Oxford, 2003), xxix, xxxviii, x 1 (introduction by Cristián Gazmuri) and 9, which was first published in 1876.

[57] Clara A. Lida, "The Democratic and Social Republic of 1848 and its Repercussions in the Hispanic World," in Guy Thomson (ed.), *The European Revolutions of 1848 and the Americas* (London, 2002), 46–75, 64; and Gazmuri, *El "48" Chileño*, 71 and 205.

[58] There is now an abundance of work on the reverberations of 1848 in Latin America. In addition to the excellent essays assembled in Thomson (ed.), *The European Revolutions of 1848 and the Americas* and the other works cited, see Marcus de Carvalho, "Os Nomes da Revolução: Lideranças Populares na Insurreição Praieira, Recife, 1848–49," *Revista Brasileira de Historia* 23, 45 (2003), 209–38; and Amaro Quintas, *O Sentido Social da Revolução Praieira* (Recife, 1977).

parallel processing of a plurality of liberal, radical, socialist, or even counterrevolutionary strands of the European revolutions, as different groups co-opted the revolutions, or specific readings of them, for their own purposes.

Was there a Global 1848?

If we compare the impact of 1848 worldwide with the transformative power of the transatlantic revolutions of the axial era between the 1770s and the end of the Napoleonic Empire (discussed in the previous chapter by David Bell), then the global balance of the 1848 revolutions appears rather modest. Was this because the world was less interconnected than it had been in the late eighteenth century? Or, was it rather that the world's geopolitical structure had changed? Paul Schröder has suggested that one of the effects of the settlement reached at Vienna in 1815 was to attenuate the geopolitical linkage between Europe and the wider world while heightening the cohesion of Europe itself as a political system.[59] What is perhaps most distinctive about the Atlantic revolutions of the axial era is the close relationship between revolutionary transformation and war. France intervened against Britain in the American War of Independence; Britain joined with the other continental powers in attempting to contain first revolutionary and later Napoleonic France. Across the wider world, many places, from India and the Caribbean to Egypt and Java, were flexed by conflict among the great powers.

The revolutions of 1848 were not born in war. For all their cruelty, the wars sparked by the revolutions (Denmark, Italy, southern Germany, Hungary) were counterrevolutionary police actions that, for the most part, came to an end once "order" had been restored. They tended to shut the revolution down, rather than to diffuse its ideology. A continental revolutionary power capable of projecting and embodying ideology by force of arms in the manner of 1790s France never emerged. And the revolutions were defeated too quickly to become an ordering principle in international relations. This is not to say that the mid-nineteenth century was an era of global tranquility: the opposite is true. As Martin Geyer and Charles Bright have pointed out, this was a period of "endemic worldwide violence played out within global patterns of conflict in which warfare was dispersed, decentered, and mostly of low intensity." What was distinctive about these years, and

---

[59] Paul W. Schroeder, *The Transformation of European Politics 1763–1848* (Oxford, 1994), 635 and passim.

so different from the previous revolutionary wave, was the lack of any "grand design or central nervous system" linking them.[60] We should thus resist the temptation to infer that there must have been a linkage of some kind between the European revolutions of 1848 and the largest single non-European upheaval of that era, the Taiping Rebellion (1850–1864) – a civil war between the Qing Dynasty and the Christian millenarian movement of the Heavenly Kingdom of Peace that cost between twenty and thirty million lives. There was a European (or at least a western) link, mediated through Christian missionary tracts illegally distributed in China, but no direct connection to the mid-century upheavals in the European cities.[61] "There is nothing to suggest," writes Jürgen Osterhammel, "that the Taiping rebels in China had heard a word about the '48 revolution in Europe."[62]

In the absence of revolutionary armies, the good tidings of revolution in 1848 had to travel in civilian clothes. They arrived in the form of books, newspapers, and charismatic personalities; they reverberated in cafés and political clubs, circulating in communicative networks that were denser, socially deeper, and more sophisticated than their late eighteenth-century predecessors. They could do this because the locations and societies we have examined were connected through imperial structures, postcolonial social and cultural ties, migrant diasporas, or through common institutions, such as the Catholic Church, whose importance in shaping patterns of political mobilization in mid-nineteenth-century Europe and Latin America has recently been demonstrated.[63] The architecture of intercontinental communications was much more diverse and robust than at the turn of the century – after all, the revolutions were the first overseas conflict to which several American newspapers sent their own correspondents.[64] If the revolutions failed in most places (the Caribbean was an exception!) to work deep social transformations, this was because in differentiated public spheres the spectacle of revolution tended to trigger responses that were nuanced, selective, and ambivalent. The understanding of revolution that took root in such settings was not necessarily less deep or important; it was

---

[60] Michael Geyer and Charles Bright, "Global Violence and Nationalizing Wars in Eurasia and America: The Geopolitics of War in the Mid-Nineteenth Century," *Comparative Studies in Society and History* 38, 4 (1996), 619–57, 629–30.

[61] Jonathan Spence, *God's Chinese Son: The Taiping Heavenly Kingdom of Hong Xiuquan* (New York, 1996), 30–32.

[62] Osterhammel, *The Transformation of the World*, 547.

[63] On Catholic political activism in the German states, see Wolfram Siemann, *The German Revolution of 1848–1849* (New York, 1998), 101–4; Sperber, *The European Revolutions*, 52; and Eduardo Posada-Carbó, "New Granada and the Revolutions of 1848," in Thomson (ed.), *The European Revolutions of 1848 and the Americas*, 217–40, 223.

[64] Roberts, *Distant Revolutions*, 11.

just more subtle.[65] "The French revolution of 1848 produced a powerful echo in Chile," the contemporary Chilean writer, journalist, historian, and politician Benjamin Vicuña Mackenna wrote in his memoirs, and he added:

For us poor colonials living on the shores of the Pacific Ocean, its predecessor in 1789, so celebrated in history, had been but a flash of light in our darkness. Half a century later, however, its twin had every mark of brilliant radiance. We had seen it coming, we studied it, we understood it, we admired it.[66]

---

[65] José Ragas, "Los 'espejos rotos' de la opinión pública: periodismo y política en el Perú (1845–60)," *Debate y perspectivas*, 3 (2003), 107–25.
[66] Mackenna, *The Girondins of Chile*, 3.

3   The Worlds of the Paris Commune

Quentin Deluermoz

At the height of the struggle of the Paris Commune, as events were unfolding before his eyes, the German revolutionary Karl Marx described the Paris Commune of 1871 as an event of global, even "universal historical importance."[1] Yet in other texts – not only *The Civil War in France*, which assessed the results of the Paris insurgency – the same Marx severely criticized the strategic choices of the Commune or the limitations in its patriotic dimension.[2] These writings may reveal an uncertainty in Marx's analysis, but, most of all, they reflect the persisting uncertainty of the Paris Commune.

The Parisian uprising was indeed one of many paradoxes, in both spatial and temporal terms. How could those seventy-two days in the French capital have resonated so intensively that, still today, it arouses a familiarity across the world?

In contrast to the Atlantic Revolutions, the shockwave of the 1848 revolutions, and the Russian Revolution of 1917, the Commune isn't usually seen as part of a conventional transnational "wave" of uprisings. Even at the national level, the events in Paris had a limited impact. Although it was simultaneously preceded and prolonged by other, so-called provincial, Communes (Lyon, Marseille, Le Creusot, and so on), its echo wasn't as resounding in the rest of the country. Within the framework of the global history of revolutions, the Commune indeed appears as a "local interlude."[3] In this context, its ensuing reverberations would partake of the strength of its symbolism and, above all, of the effect of its communist reinterpretation after 1917, which dispersed knowledge of the Parisian struggle far into the twentieth century, on an unheard-of scale, from China to Latin America.

The recent historiographical developments on the Paris Commune are of no assistance here. The Parisian revolt was the object of many research

---

[1] Ct. in Gareth Stedman Jones, *Karl Marx: Greatness and Illusion* (London, 2016), 505.
[2] Karl Marx, *The Civil War in France* (London, 1871).
[3] Jürgen Osterhammel, *The Transformation of the World: A Global History of the Nineteenth Century* (Princeton, NJ, 2014), 558.

efforts led by Marxist historians or inspired by Marxist frames of interpretation, particularly between the 1950s and the 1970s. The venture was
extremely international, reflected in a literature in French, English,
Spanish, Italian, Russian, Polish, and so on, due to the strategic position-
ing of the Parisian event within the Marxist analysis of the historical
development of revolution. The Commune, according to a famous saying, was at the same time "dawn" and "dusk."[4] Haunted by the specter of
1789–1793, but singular in its working-class governance, it would, simultaneously, mark the end of the French and European revolutions of the
nineteenth century and open the way to the era of modern revolutions,
thought to be more ideologically and organizationally structured, starting
with the 1917 Russian Revolution. Thus, the Commune has been heavily
scrutinized, in its unfolding and its influence, following this hypothesis of
a transitional revolution. Many studies, some detailed, others more
superficial, have examined its relation to the First International and its
impact on the trajectories of workers' movements, be they on the
European, American, or Asian continents. As this Marxist-inspired
research has slowly run out of steam, since the 1980s, historical studies
of the Paris Commune, such as those of Jacques Rougerie and Robert
Tombs, have returned to the event itself and have broken away from the
Marxist theoretical tradition, a historiographical development that was
perhaps also facilitated by the fall of the Soviet bloc.[5] The weight of
circumstances and the general uncertainties of the situation have been
reevaluated, as has the importance of a singular revolutionary republican
culture in an insurgent Paris, stirred by the ideal of a "democratic and
social Republic" in which citizens would immediately hold a stake in
political power and free themselves from economic servitude. This type
of study, at tarmac level, has never ceased, as demonstrated by John
Merriman's recent *Massacre: The Life and Death of the Paris Commune*
(2014).[6] But if recent scholarship has contributed to our understanding
of the complexities of the Parisian experiment, the questions of its echoes
and its relation to other protest movements of the time beyond France
have been relegated to a secondary role.

Following on from my previous research, this chapter seeks to answer
this very question.[7] In so doing, it draws on approaches from transnational,

---

[4] Jacques Rougerie, *Le Procès des communards* (Paris, 1964).
[5] An overview of the historiography on the Commune can be found in Robert Le Quillec,
Bibliographie critique de la Commune de Paris (Paris, 2006); Jacques Rougerie, *La Commune
de 1871* (Paris, 2009); Robert Tombs, *The Paris Commune* (London, 1999); and, for
a revised edition, Idem, *Paris, Bivouac des révolutions* (Paris, 2014).
[6] John Merriman, *Massacre: The Life and Death of the Paris Commune* (New York, 2014).
[7] Quentin Deluermoz, *Commune(s), 1870–1871: Une traversée des mondes au XIXe siècle*
(Paris, 2020).

imperial, and global history. We will consider here both indirect connections, linked to shared external dynamics, which can explain the simultaneity of conflicts in various regions, such as wars, the weakening of a world power, the weight of "imperial societies," development of means of transport and communication, as well as direct connections, which protagonists are usually aware of and which bind these experiences more immediately together, such as the circulation of ideas and actors.[8] To be sure, it is impossible to follow all the links and echoes, and it is a delicate task to define their precise articulations. Thus, this chapter offers, based on research in local and diplomatic archives and on a synthesis of previous work, a view on the global history of the Paris Commune. Four groups of links can be identified, which are at once in resonance and discordance with each other, but they can in this way help uncover what was also the global dimension of the Paris Commune.

The Commune in the Struggles for a "Universal Republic"

The Commune is, first of all, to be understood within the history of the conflicts of the years 1848–1870: socialist and republican struggles as well as national liberation insurrections.

At its root were the military dynamics unleashed by the Franco-Prussian war of 1870–1871, which have increasingly become the starting point for those studies of the Commune that aim to underline the context of slow disintegration in which the Commune emerged: a series of defeats, a regime change (from Empire to Republic), a long-lasting siege in the capital, and later, at the beginning of 1871, following the painful capitulation of France, electoral results in favor of monarchists. But the war also prepared the future transnational reach of the Commune. As early as September, after the fall of the Second Empire, the French cause had become a republican cause and had merged with the common post-1848 idea of a "Universal Republic." In its name, thousands of international volunteers had come to France to fight for freedom against the oppression of a conservative monarchy. They were for the most part Italians, but also Polish, Spanish, Belgium, Irish, Greek, Uruguayans, and citizens of the United States. These men (rarely women) had generally taken part in other great struggles of the time:

---

[8] Richard Drayton and David Motadel, "The Futures of Global History," *Journal of Global History* 13, 1 (2018), 1–21. On "imperial societies," see Christophe Charle, *La Crise des sociétés impériales: Allemagne, France, Grande-Bretagne 1900–1940: Essai d'histoire sociale comparée* (Paris, 2001); and Christophe Charle, "The Crisis of 'Imperial Societies'," in Roland Lardinois and Meenakshi Thapan (eds.), *Reading Pierre Bourdieu in a Dual Context: Essays from India and France* (London, 2006), 56–76.

the Italian Wars of Independence in 1848 and 1859–1860, the Polish conflicts of 1830 and 1848, the Spanish "Glorious Revolution" of 1868, the American Civil War of 1861–1865, Irish Fenianism in the 1850s and the 1860s, and so on. After some hesitation, they were put together with the French volunteers in an army corps called the "Armée des Vosges" (Army of the Vosges), placed under the command of the internationalist revolutionary Giuseppe Garibaldi. Aged, Garibaldi was the romantic republican figure par excellence, possessing an exceptional aura, especially following his activities in Brazil, Uruguay, and Italy. The very presence of these men gave a transnational dimension to the French republican war, which, nonetheless, was not without its difficulties for the leaders of this gestating new regime.[9]

But at the end of the conflict, in early 1871, some left for the capital and, in spring, joined the Paris Commune. Maximilien Rogowski was one of them. A former fighter in the Polish insurrection, he had settled as a costermonger in Marseille before becoming commander in the Polish cavalry in Garibaldi's army. At the end of March he offered his services to the Commune. In practice, with the dissolution of the Army of the Vosges in February and the second siege, the Commune was in some way a relay in the international volunteers' movement. Many had arrived in Paris in September, like Lucien Combatz, a Sardinian telegraph officer who had participated in the Italian wars at the end of the 1850s. Having taken command of the Garibaldian legion in Tyrol in 1866 and then the Argon volunteers in autumn 1869, he found himself in Paris during the Franco-Prussian war and took part in the social and political events in the capital. Under the Commune, he was appointed director of the Commune Telegraphs and later colonel in the Sixth Legion. Many fighters who intervened as "foreigners" in the Commune (which included nationalized legions, such as the Belgian and Italian Legions) were in fact revolutionary refugees who had lived in the capital for several years. The Poles, whose divisions were deployed when the Republic and later the Commune were put in place, exemplified this well. Although some of the Poles who had come to France during the failed insurrections of 1830 and 1848 left Paris, others rallied to the Commune in memory of past struggles and of the hospitality offered by their host country.[10] It is

---

[9] Lucy Riall, *Garibaldi: Invention of a Hero* (New Haven, CT, 2007); Gilles Pécout, "The International Armed Volunteers: Pilgrims of a Transnational Risorgimento," *Journal of Modern Italian Studies* 14, 4 (2009), 413–26; and Mark Lause, *War for the Republic in the Age of Blood and Iron: A Transnational View of Giuseppe Garibaldi's Army of the Vosges and the Transformation of Republicanism, 1870–1871* (forthcoming, 2021).

[10] Mareike König, "Les immigrés allemands à Paris, 1870–1871," *Migrance* 35 (2010), 60–70; and Quentin Deluermoz, "Être étranger sous la Commune, les soubresauts du rêve nationalitaire au XIXᵉ siècle," *Migrance* 35, (2010), 23–33.

difficult to assess with precision the importance of these combatants in the Commune. The study of the composition of the battalions of the National Guard clearly shows that these were formed mainly of Parisians. These foreign combatants were nonetheless highly visible in the insurgent capital as, given their expertise, they were found in the higher ranks of the Commune, particularly among the legion's colonels (three out of twenty-two), war delegates (Gustave Cluseret, Jaroslaw Dombrowski), and within the High Command. And so they gave substance and credit, though not without any tensions, to the frequent calls of the Commune for a "Universal Republic." They were not alone in this, as one is reminded by the trajectory of Léo Fränkel, a Hungarian silversmith and member of the First International, who arrived in France in 1867 and took part in the Labour Commission. When becoming a member, the Commune solemnly declared: "considering that the flag of the Commune is the flag of the universal Republic, that any city has the right to grant citizenship to the foreigners who serve it ... the [electoral] commission is in favour of foreign nationals joining."[11]

This example suggests another relay in the connections between the Commune and republican and social struggles: the existence of workers' and republican organizations, most notably the International Workingmen's Association (IWA). The IWA was founded in London in 1864, following the meeting between French workers and British trade unionists in 1862; and one year later, with the addition of the committee's support for the 1863 Polish January Uprising (an insurrection for independence against Russia). The IWA was acting simultaneously as a union, an international political association, and a place of exchange and discussion of themes such as peoples' freedom and the defense of the proletariat. In London it had set up a general council on which, notably, Karl Marx sat, and it extended its reach via local sections surfacing throughout Great Britain, France, Belgium, and Switzerland.[12] Historians have consistently countered the idea of a Commune organized by the IWA (even if 43 percent of the members of the Commune council were also members of the IWA). Its role as an organization was instead more external. Here again the reaction of the Central Committee, influenced by the mistrust of British trade unionists, was at first cautious

---

[11] François-Louis Parisel, "Rapport de la commission des élections," *Journal Officiel* 1, (March 31, 1871), 1–2. "Considérant que le drapeau de la Commune est celui de la République universelle, que toute cité a le droit de donner le titre de citoyen aux étrangers qui la servent, ... la commission [des élections] est d'avis que les étrangers peuvent être admis."

[12] Marcello Musto, *Workers Unite! The International 150 Years Later* (London, 2014), 68. See also the updated chronology proposed by Fabrice Bensimon, Quentin Deluermoz, and Jeanne Moisand, *"Arise Ye Wretched of the Earth": The First International in a Global Perspective* (Leiden, 2018).

towards a movement that it deemed "very French." It was only on May 23, 1871, that, in its name, Marx declared: "the principles of the Commune are eternal and indestructible; they will present themselves again and again until the working class is liberated."[13]

The event resonated more strongly among national sections. Demonstrations were organized in April in London and Geneva, and later in Brussels and Hamburg. But support also came from other groups linked, loosely or otherwise, to these sections, such as British republicans who organized rallies, or the democratic society of Florence. To be sure, some groups supported while others did not, depending on localized issues. In this regard, the Parisian revolution took place within a multifaceted marquetry of labour, republican, radical, and socialist associations whose complex dynamics and interactions have only just begun to be uncovered.[14] It was sometimes directly associated with local struggles, as was the case of the British section of the IWA in New York, which held a "sympathy meeting" for both the Paris Commune and the locked-out miners of Pennsylvania.[15]

In the end, it is not possible to say that the Commune belonged to a coherent social and political oppositional strand, but it nevertheless appears strongly moored to the post-1848 struggles, be they republican, socialist, or social-economic, in which it crystallized.

The Parisian Uprising as Test of the French Imperial Nation-State

The Commune, or to be more precise the Communes movement, correlated, from an unexpected point of view, with other forms of protests – colonial and global ones. The Parisian event can also be seen as a test moment for the imperial nation-state that France had become in the 1860s. Like other historians, scholars of French history have begun to question nation-centric histories, and with it the supposed exceptionalism (politically speaking in particular) of France, pointing to the complex internal and external connections of French society.[16] The reassuringly

---

[13] Minutes of the General Council, May 30, 1871, published in *Le Conseil général de la première Internationale, 1870–1871* (Moscow, 1975), 174.

[14] Malcolm Chase, *Chartism: A New History* (Manchester, 2007); and Thomas Welskopp, *Das Banner der Brüderlichkeit: Die deutsche Sozialdemokratie vom Vormärz bis zum Sozialistengesetz* (Bonn, 2000), are good case studies on the various movements which shook Great Britain and the German world.

[15] Minutes of the General Council, May 23, 1871, published in *Le conseil général de la première Internationale*, 174.

[16] Sebastian Conrad, *Globalisierung und Nation im Deutschen Kaiserreich* (Munich, 2006); and the contributions to Thomas Bender (ed.), *Rethinking American History in a Global Age* (Berkeley, CA, 2002) are important examples. For France, see the series of Johann Chapoutot (ed.), *Histoire de France contemporaine*, 10 vols. (Paris, 2012–2018);

inevitable historical trajectory, which would have seen the country move toward the liberal Republic of the 1880s, has been substituted by an understanding of France as a heterogeneously mutating imperial nation-state. This is particularly well reflected in the Parisian uprising and its so-called provincial counterparts. Once again, the starting point of the shake-up was the 1870–1871 war. Following a string of defeats, the imperial power's gauges were fluttering, a situation that greatly worried foreign affairs ministers. The repayments of certain loans were suspended (in Haiti and Venezuela, for example), as were technological and expert-ise transfers, as the Egyptian consul soon found out, much to his chagrin, in the case of the preparation of the judiciary reform in which France (with other countries) had been involved and from which, at that moment, it was set apart. In Martinique, more directly, the announce-ment in September of the advent of the Republic in mainland France triggered what is referred to as the "Southern Insurrection," which was the biggest uprising in Martinique since 1848, fed by disappointment over post-abolition politics and by the resurgence of the memory of 1848, as well as that of the Haitian Revolution of 1791–1804. It was more tied to the proclamation of the French Republic on September 4 than to the Commune – even if the latter caused fear of the local authorities at the time of the insurgents' trial in April 1871.[17]

In this context, the eruption of the Commune in March 1871 appeared to many as the last blow in a long series of setbacks. To the French authorities, it was happening at the worst moment, when the country was desperately attempting to reinstate and stabilize the new regime. "The Sublime Porte is in total dismay," reported the consul in Istanbul, "at the persistence of the Parisian events, in that they are postponing the conclusion of the loan" (of 1869).[18] Thus, the eruption of the Parisian revolution was often used either by the elites or by populations under French control (both directly and indirectly) as an opportunity to call into question this imperial power. This was particularly true in the religious domain. In Ottoman Jerusalem, detailed knowledge of the attacks com-mitted by the Commune and republican radicals against churches weak-ened France's position as a protector of the region's Catholics. It stirred local divisions and the critique of competing nations: according to them, "the protection of sacred places must cease to be the responsibility of

and David Todd, "A French Imperial Meridian, 1814–1870," *Past and Present* 210, 1 (2011), 155–86.

[17] Gilbert Pago, *L'insurrection de Martinique 1870–1871* (Paris, 2011).

[18] French Ambassador in Turkey to Minister of Foreign Affairs, March 31, 1871, Constantinople, Centre d'Archives Diplomatic (CAD), La Courneuve, Political Correspondence (Turkey), 133 CP 387.

a nation which no longer shows respect for the principles of religion and authority."[19] In China, these difficulties were used by the authorities to slow down the judicial ruling on a diplomatic affair which had been ongoing for several months (the reparations following the Tientsin massacres in June 1870 against French and Europeans). And shortly after the news of the events in Paris, a "note of religious missions" was published by Beijing, directly threatening their presence in the Chinese countryside.[20]

But the strongest connection, with the most consequential effects, took place in the southern Mediterranean, with the Kabyle insurrection between January and October 1871 – considered as the greatest in nineteenth-century colonial Algeria. The unfolding of the uprising, which involved 800,000 people, is relatively well known. One of its immediate causes was the Franco-Prussian war, which was also an imperial war: by mobilizing "African" troops, it weakened the military positions there, a situation made worse by the establishment of the Republic and the programmed extension of civil territories on Algerian soil. The calls for revolt, monitored and translated by the French military, explicitly stated: "Civil is coming" ("*Le Civil arrive*"). The movement was fueled by deeper social and political forces. Such was the influence of notable aristocrats, sometimes juxtaposed with a resurgence of precolonial expectations on the part of the Regency of Algiers. Muhammad bin al-Haj Ahmad al-Mokrani, first leader of the insurrection, and descendant of a family that ruled the Medjana since the sixteenth century, is a good example of this. An additional factor was the revival of religious brotherhoods in the Muslim world, and particularly North Africa, since the beginning of the nineteenth century, as exemplified by the role of the *rahmaniyya* and with it that of Sheikh al-Haddad, who declared jihad against the French rulers in April 1871. Finally, the rebellion was fueled by the anger of local populations exhausted by dispossession and a series of natural disasters in the years 1866–1869, sometimes referred to as "the Great Famine."

The insurrection was largely driven by non-European dynamics, but its connection to the communalist movements cannot be ignored. There were two levels of connections. The first was through the republican movement, led by deported 1848 veterans, who had taken control, from September 1870, of Algiers and the region's other main cities. The movement had taken on the name of "Commune" relatively early on in the capital, in reference to 1793, under the aegis of, among others, the

---

[19] Commander-in-Chief of Le Levant to French Ambassador in Turkey, Constantinople, June 14, 1871, CAD, Political Correspondence (Turkey), 133 CP 387.
[20] Deluermoz, *Commune(s) 1870–1871*, discusses these echoes.

rebel lawyer Romuald Vuillermoz. It was revived by the outbreak of the Paris Commune, to the extent that the radicals of Algiers sent a letter of congratulations and support to Paris, which was reproduced in the *Journal Officiel* of the Commune.[21] One of those revolutionaries, Alexandre Lambert, former secretary to Georges Sand, was even sent as Algiers delegate to Paris, where he ended up with a position at the Home Affairs ministry, the "bureau du ministère de l'Intérieur." This intensification of republican protest in Algiers was taking place at the same time as the Arab insurrection was spreading. It fired up the Arab insurgents, who understood the threat presented by the autonomy project of the Algiers' Commune, which was driven by the most "colonialist" French fringe. But most of all, it hampered the possibilities of action available to Governor Louis-Henri de Gueydon, whom the inhabitants of Algiers directly opposed. The second level was described in detail by the Algerian military authorities: the troops that could have contained the insurrection in Algiers were being held up in metropolitan France by the uprisings in Paris and other cities. Together, those two conditions encouraged the spread and radicalization of the Arab uprising, and it was only with the end of the Commune in metropolitan France that, in late May, the French were able to take control of the situation once again.[22]

Both insurrections were thus linked, not, as one may sometimes read, in a common wave of opposition against an oppressing power (at least, this remains to be demonstrated) but, rather, through these indirect connections. In any case, historical analysis can only benefit from taking into account the breadth of those ricochets that linked European revolutionary movements and colonial dispute struggles in the nineteenth century. They were the result of complex social and power reconfigurations in multiple places and heterogeneous impulsions, which were not without reverberating effects on either side. The Paris Commune finally made the "legal anomalies," on which the French imperial power was based, more apparent, fueling revolt movements even further.[23] In the end, this imperial dimension also explains why many European (imperial)

---

[21] Alexandre Lambert, Lucien Rabuel, and Louis Calvinhac, "Adresse de la Commune de l'Algérie à la Commune de Paris," *Journal Officiel de la Commune* (March 29, 1871), 1.

[22] Charles-Robert Ageron, *Les Algériens musulmans et la France, 1871–1919* (Paris, 1968); James McDougall, *A History of Algeria* (Cambridge, 2017); M'Hamed Oualdi, "*Une succession d'empires: Comment réinterpréter l'histoire moderne et contemporaine du Maghreb*" (HDR, École des Hautes Études en Sciences Sociales, 2017); and Idir Hachi, *Histoire sociale de l'insurrection de 1872 et du procès de ses chefs (Constantine, 1873)* (PhD Dissertation, Aix-Marseille Université, 2017).

[23] Laura Benton, *A Search for Sovereignty: Law and Geography in European Empires, 1400–1900* (Cambridge, 2010).

countries happened to be directly involved in the resolution of the Parisian revolution.

The Revolution Makes Headlines

Nonetheless, the most structuring phenomenon was undoubtedly the strong and rapid "mediatization" of the Commune, which took place at a moment of great transformation. Great Britain had entered the age of mass media some thirty years before, while in the post–Civil War United States the press was reorganizing itself and included at its peak 5,800 titles. France was experimenting, since the end of the Second Empire, with mass production; *Le Petit Journal*, notably, had a circulation of 500,000 copies daily in 1869. Other countries were concerned to a lesser extent, from German-speaking Europe to Italy, but the years between 1850 and 1860 were also a moment of transnational organizational and technical mutation of the media. The major press agencies (Reuters, Wolff, Havas) were created around the year 1850 and expanded rapidly during the following decades. The consequences of the 1866 transatlantic telegraph cable were also significant; from then on, news could travel from one continent to the other in only a few hours, rather than a few days, modifying relationships to "current affairs."[24] Finally, the sheer scale of attention was sustained by the fact that a revolution was taking place not only in France but also in Paris, the city then viewed as the capital of revolutions and modernity, in particular after its Haussmannization.[25] The Commune revived in many places a rich and manifold imagination, reshaped continuously since the beginning of the century of the French Revolution.

The Commune thus found itself at the center of media attention. A good way of assessing the transcontinental magnitude of an event is to measure the number of words circulating on the Reuters network, the most important media network of the time.[26] Those relating to the Commune, in the week of its instigation, then represented 75 percent of the total number of words – a proportion higher than the news of the assassination of Lincoln in 1865 or that of Alexander II in 1881, and even higher than the great moments of the Franco-Prussian war. Such types of

---

[24] Donald Read, *The Power of News: The History of Reuters* (Oxford, 1992); and Emily S. Rosenberg, "Transnational Currents in a Shrinking World," in Emily S. Rosenberg (ed.), *A World Connecting, 1870–1945*, (Cambridge, MA, 2012), 815–37.

[25] *Walter Benjamin: Selected Writings*, 4 vols. (Cambridge, MA, 2004–2006), vol. 3, *1935–1938*, ed. by Howard Eiland and Michael W. Jennings (Cambridge, MA, 2006).

[26] Gordon Winder, "London's Global Reach? Reuters News and Network 1865, 1881, and 1914," *Journal of World History* 21, 2 (2010), 271–96.

count have always to be taken with caution, but the Commune undoubtedly appears to have been one of the greatest global media events of the century. Thanks to the telegraph, it was followed hour by hour throughout Europe, in India, Australia, and on the American continent. Its media resonances were particularly strong in the United States during the post–Civil War rebuilding era. The uprising, according to Philipp Katz, was even the first "national event" in American history. "No other economic or political theme in the United States, save governmental corruption, has made more headlines in the American press of the 1870s than the Paris Commune," concluded the historian Samuel Bernstein in 1971.[27]

This reception didn't simply involve the diffusion of Communard or anti-Communard ideas (especially as these were often vague) but also phenomena of reappropriations that followed local, regional, or national logics. To take the example of the United States once again, the events were presented differently depending on whether one was a Republican or a Democrat, from the North or the South. Such appropriations can be observed in Latin America. The case of Mexico, still marked by the memory of Napoleon III's expedition and animated in the years 1850–1870 by an intensive democratic and associative life, is particularly significant. The press there followed French events avidly, even translating Communard posters and Versailles telegrams into Spanish. The *Siglo diez y Nueve,* an important liberal newspaper, offered daily coverage of the event, mixing telegrams freshly received from the United States and long "Parisian letters" from its correspondent there, written sometimes two weeks earlier. They make for a very unusual read. The general interpretation oscillated between defense of the republican idea and of the municipal franchise, and critique of the "mad socialist reforms" of the "revolutionary junta."[28] This vacillating reading was even more profound among the radical and associative movement, reflected, for instance, in the young socialist newspaper *El socialista,* which was run by qualified craftsmen. *El socialista* identified a series of innovations in the Commune ("down with the clergy, the Napoleonic nobility ... let's annihilate the landlord"), but it also criticized its excessive violence: "Mexico doesn't possess the same elements of destruction as France; even in the midst of the backwardness we are said to be in, our customs are better."[29]

---

[27] Philipp Katz, *From Appomattox to Montmartre: Americans and the Paris Commune* (Cambridge, MA, 1998); and Samuel Bernstein, *Essays in Political and Intellectual History* (New York, 1955), 169–82#.

[28] Special Correspondent from Paris, "París, 10 de abril," *Siglo diez y Nueve* (May 18, 1871).

[29] Michelet, "La Comuna y el petroleo," *El Socialista* (August 20, 1871).

Although many Mexican newspapers looked at the Commune sympa-
thetically, they were soon disappointed by its violence. These interpretations were typical of the tension, identified by the historian James
Sanders, between what appeared here to be European modernity (characterized by economic development and the strengthening of the State)
and Latin American modernity (based on the ideas of equality, political
freedom, and humanity).[30] In this respect, the Commune was rich in
ideas (communal republicanism, workers' association, federalism) but
proved, in the eyes of these observers, that they were not made for
European soil, scarred by too many years of hierarchical submission and
brutal industrialization. By contrast, they were perceived to be more
adapted to the American context. With its peculiar definitions of "modernity" and "republicanism," this case, which may illustrate other Latin
American appreciations, opened the way to a salutary de-
Europeanization of perspectives and vividly exposed those skewed reappropriations. In their eyes, other types of "communes" could then be
formed, and thus a transnational production of the "Commune" was in
progress, too.

Parisian Re-readings of a Worldwide Event

Had the global multifaceted dimension of the Commune some impact on
the insurgents in Paris?[31] Undeniably, Communards were only partially
aware of it. Their attention was quickly absorbed by the battles taking
place at the ramparts, and, in a besieged city with severed telegraphic
communication, news of the outside world could only reach them via the
rare French and foreign newspapers still in circulation in the capital.

Certain collectives and journals did refer to the global resonance of its
aftershocks. Thus, the *Journal Officiel* listed them in its column "foreign
news," and so did a revolutionary "groupe de citoyennes," as they presented themselves, who incited Parisians to act by taking inspiration from
other struggles, such as the ones in "Germany whose Princely armies were
destroying our country, wishing death upon its democratic and socialist
tendencies, [and which was now] itself shaken and torn by the revolutionary murmur!"[32] Most of the time, however, calls to the world and references to "the Universal" referred to imagined worlds, suggesting the scale
of the transformations they hoped would come. Thus, the socialist Gustave

---

[30] James Sanders, "The Vanguard of the Atlantic World: Contesting Modernity in
   Nineteenth-Century Latin America," *American Research Review* 46, 2 (2011), 104–27.
[31] Jeanne Gaillard, *Communes de province, Commune de Paris 1870–1871* (Paris, 1971).
[32] Un groupe de citoyenne (signed), "Appel aux citoyennes de Paris," *Journal Officiel de la
   Commune* (April 10, 1871), 3.

Lefrançais reminded his audience, at a meeting of the Commune council, that the emancipation it sought was that of "the workers of the whole world."[33] This effect was accentuated by a discontinuity, so typical of moments of this kind, marked by a resurgence of the memories of past revolutionary times and feelings that new futures are ahead. "The current movement," announced the republican alliance of departments on another poster, "is not just a miserable insurrection . . . . It is perhaps – despite some deplorable incidents – the greatest revolution of modern times."[34]

These projections should not obscure other metropolitan spatial horizons. France was the reference point of all the major calls and declarations, starting with the April 19 poster, considered to be the defining text of the Commune, addressed to "the French people." Such a stance is understandable for a revolution which came after the war against Prussia and was greatly shaped by the memories of 1789–1793. Paris itself was another point of reference made even more prominent not only by the encirclement of the city and the Civil War context but also by the circulation of republican and socialist ideas. Notwithstanding their diversity, these ideas highlighted the defense of a "people of Paris" and supported, for some, the principle of municipal autonomy and, for others, the realization of a "true," immediate republic, both democratic and social at the same time.[35] Finally, the number of opponents should not be underestimated, starting with those who attempted to remain neutral, and nor should the wavering flux and reflux of support for the Commune.

These spatial layers did not necessarily contradict each other. Yet the Parisian situation deserves closer examination, as it possessed its own internal rhythm, both connected to and disconnected from entanglements with the outside world. The collision of spatial and temporal horizons here observed shouldn't be underestimated; all the more that it explains why reference to the Commune by other territories later became a relevant factor of universalization.

Legacies of the Communal Idea

The end of the uprising, whose tragic dimension was obvious to everyone, created torsions within the different threads discussed here. The Parisian uprising ended in a blood bath. If the number of casualties is still debated

---

[33] "Commune de Paris. Séance," *Journal Officiel de la Commune* (April 30, 1871), 2.

[34] Poster (April 23, 1871), published in *Murailles politiques françaises depuis le 4 septembre Tome II – Commune* (Paris, 1874), 125.

[35] Jacques Rougerie, "Entre le réel et l'utopie: République démocratique et sociale, Association, commune, Commune," in Laurent Colantonio and Caroline Fayolle (eds.), *Genre et utopie: Avec Michèle Riot-Sarcey* (Saint-Denis, 2014), 273–92.

today (somewhere between 7,000 and 40,000 individuals perished), historians agree that it was the greatest civil massacre in the history of the nineteenth century in France and perhaps Europe.[36] On the Communard side, this concluding chapter is characterized by the massacre of the hostages – around eighty people killed – by the *fédérés*, and by fire outbreaks. Faced with the progress of the Versailles troops, the *fédérés* set alight the city's main buildings, among them the Town Hall, the Tuileries Palace, and the Cour des comptes. The horror that seemed to unfold on the streets of Paris created a shock, drawing even more attention and modifying the reading described earlier, favoring a reduction in the initial diversity of points of view.

In the heat of the moment, circulation of news from one paper to another – and from one language to the other – was more apparent than ever. If one could synthesize, in a single word, the mass of discourses on the Commune, which undoubtedly require further examination, it would be "rejection." The massacres led by the troops of Versailles were mentioned, but the most horrified reactions were provoked by the destruction of buildings, which commentators compared to the great fires that devastated Rome or Moscow. By these actions, it seems that revolutionaries were touching the heart of high "civilization," with which France was associated, demonstrating their "barbarism." *The Times*, on May 25, 1871, set the tone: "the history of the world presents no such national tragedy. It began in vanity and weakness; it ends in crime, in horror, and in despair."[37]

The same tone prevailed in the liberal and republican press, sometimes even in the socialist press. In June, the Commune was unanimously condemned by foreign governments too, yet again in the name of "civilization," though the shockwave in the colonial territories was dissipating. The post-Commune period brought about a series of political measures on extradition, and passport and police exchange, between countries worldwide (Spain, Belgium, Germany, Austria, the United States, and the Ottoman Empire). These were imperfectly enforced, but they were not without results, as is seen in the fate of the IWA, which, after a period of development, collapsed in 1877, even if this collapse was also the result of internal divisions.

This was the moment when myriad commonplaces about the Commune were shaped, some of which would endure for more than a century. The insistence on violence and criminal fires during the

---

[36] Robert Tombs, "How Bloody was *la Semaine sanglante* of 1871? A Revision," *Historical Journal* 55, 3 (2012), 679–704.
[37] Anonymous, "Latest Intelligence: The Destruction of Paris," *The Times* (May 25, 1871).

Bloody Week was inscribed into popular memory, as was the association made between the Commune and the IWA. This perceived collusion was often portrayed as an intrigue in which one would be the evil emanation of the other, a view that would later be reinforced, for other reasons, by Marxist readings. The Commune was thus revealed as an outmoded anachronism symbolizing the dangers that revolution represented for the modern world. Yet a more positive assessment of the Commune also existed, emerging from more diverse trains of thoughts seeking to reevaluate the struggle of those who had quickly become martyrs, a process which intensified all the more since its symbolic weight had come to seem more remarkable.

Different appreciations combined. It was at this moment that Marx, in defending the Parisian uprising, gained an international audience. In June 1871, he published, in the name of the IWA, *The Civil War in France*, copies of which quickly became available in English, German, French, and Spanish. Bakunin, who had until then remained relatively distant, also gave a brief anarchist interpretation of the Commune.[38] Among several outpourings, his most famous was the 1878 reworking by Élisée Reclus of a text then published under the title "The Paris Commune and the Idea of the State," in which the Parisian rebellion is described as the "bold, clearly formulated negation of the State."[39] Historians have pointed out the obvious incongruities of these texts – Marx defending a form of republican federalism and Bakunin arguing sometimes in favor of the Jacobins – but they did expose, too, two different perspectives and two conceptions of the historical process. To sum them up briefly: Marxists considered that the Commune was part of a lineage of revolutions while being an intermediate stage from which lessons could be learnt for future struggles to come; anarchists placed the Commune within the constant struggle of the exploited against the exploiters, following a more organic and germinal definition of the concept of revolution. Together, these views tended to reinforce the idea that the Commune was a decisive moment in the class struggle. In this regard, the hypothesis of the "transition" was not incorrect, but it could only emerge retrospectively. In a more national framework, other protagonists played important roles; such was the case of the German SPD, within which the Marxist perspective slowly prevailed.[40]

---

[38] Mikhail Bakunin, *L'Empire knouto-germanique et la révolution sociale* (Genève, 1871); most of the texts have been published in *Michel Bakounine, œuvres complètes*, ed. by Max Nettlau, 8 vols (Paris, 1973–82).

[39] Mikhail Bakunin and Élisée Reclus, "La Commune de Paris et la notion d'État," *Le Travailleur* (July 1878).

[40] Jürgen Kocka, *Arbeiterleben und Arbeiterkultur: Die Entstehung einer sozialen Klasse* (Bonn, 2015), 406–407.

But that is not all. The variety of the reappropriations within the different above-mentioned republican and socialist currents should also be appraised. The Commune was called upon and used in other struggles of the time, no longer as a locus of discussion but as a vivid reference point giving meaning to ongoing tussles, in the same way that the 1789–1793, 1830, and 1848 revolutions were recaptured by the Commune. Thus, it was mobilized extensively during the Spanish Cantonal rebellion, where it contributed to bringing to life the Spanish federalist spirit and its action at the cantonal level.[41] Needless to say, local dynamics played an essential role, as did other memories of the past, such as the 1868 revolution, the insurrectional liberalism of the 1800s, the French Revolution, and the *fueros* of the Middle Ages. But this revived Commune also allowed the Spanish movement to take on social and international dimensions.

Italian reappropriations could also be observed. While Mazzini, the republican hero, was criticizing the fatal self-dissolution which, so he thought, class struggle would infer, the Commune prompted a rise in membership to the IWA and became aligned to a strand of libertarian socialism. In fact, during the failed rural uprisings of 1874 and 1877, the leaders invoked at once the Cantonal rebellion and the Commune in order to stir up mobilization. Feeding local social and federalist movements, the Commune became a landmark for numerous local anarchist pockets.

Moreover, reference to the Commune and circulation of its ideas spread globally. Thus, the concept of the Commune traveled throughout the Latin American continent, sometimes in association with the cantonalist experience, although not exclusively. This was certainly observable in Argentina, Brazil, Chile, and Bolivia. Once again, Communard exiles played a part in this process. Some six thousand are estimated to have left for Great Britain, Belgium, Switzerland, and the United States, and, to a lesser extent, Spain, Italy, and South America. But local reappropriation was always the dominant factor. In the mid-1870s, several papers named *El Comuna* were established, explicitly referencing the Commune. In Mexico, in June 1874, *El Comuna* became *El Comuna Mexicana*, stating: "As long as there is a man or a woman alive, the Commune will continue to exist, because great principles are immortal . . .. The Commune is alive in France as in Mexico, in the United States as in Germany, in China as in Arabia."[42]

---

[41] Clara Lida, *Anarquismo y revolución en la España del XIX* (Madrid, 1972); see also Jeanne Moisand, "Les exilés de la 'République universell': Français et Espagnols en révolution (1868–1878)," in Delphine Diaz, Jeanne Moisand, Romy Sanchez, and Juan Luis Simal (eds.), *Exils entre les deux mondes. Migrations et espaces politiques atlantiques au XIXe siècle* (Mordelles, 2015), 161–87.

[42] Bruno Bosteels, "The Mexican Commune," in Shannon Brincat (ed.) *Communism in the Twenty-First Century* (Santa Barbara, CA, 2013), 161–89, 169, which refers to *La Comuna* (June 28, 1874).

The idea of the Commune found other relays; thus, the Greek tailor and translator of Proudhon Plotino Rhodakanati argued in several articles published in *El Combate* that a Commune could even happen in Mexico.[43] Again, the significance of these traces should not be exaggerated, as they were often nothing more than shattered fragments, not necessarily supported by all. But they do indicate the powerful assimilation of the Commune into the revolutionary struggles of other countries. In the case of Mexico, the Commune was later able to seep into anarcho-syndicalism, socialism, agrarian communism, and indigenous communalism, following polymorphous lines of thoughts.

Just as knowledge of the main protagonists and their heroic deeds was traveling abroad, the Commune could take on different guises. In the United States, for instance, despite the overwhelming rejection it faced there in the 1870s, including during the most important strike movements of 1877, the memory of the Commune slowly settled among the emerging radical culture.[44] From 1880 onwards, commemorative festivals were established, melding speeches, concerts, and balls, such as "Strike for the universal Commune," organized that same year in New York. In this way, the Commune could be turned into an active past, fertile in its critical reflection on the present. Various nationalities, among them French, Germans, Spanish, Cubans, and Venezuelans, gathered together, as did political groups, such as socialists, radicals, feminists, and free-thinkers. There, internationalism took on a very different meaning from, say, the one it held within the German Social Democratic Party. In other words, in the decade between 1870 and 1880, it was not so much a diffusion that took place but rather a sort of multicentered layering of appropriations, some important, others more minor, that could resurface at a later date. To use a visual metaphor, we were faced with a rhizomatic development that engendered several other histories, simultaneously connected yet differentiated from one another.[45]

Later on, the Marxist interpretation of the end of the century and, most importantly, of the interwar years, following the advent of the USSR, introduced another torsion to this complex history of reception, while allowing reference to the Commune to reach other spaces, notably Asia and Africa. In turn, the present demonstration explains why, at the time, this interpretation was able to reach such a large global audience, and why the so-called "orthodox" Marxist reading never imposed itself as such:

[43] Plotino Rhodakanati, "La Comuna Americana," *El Combate* (August 1877).
[44] Michelle Coghlan, *Sensational Internationalism: The Paris Commune and the Remapping of American Memory in the Long Nineteenth Century* (Edinburgh, 2016).
[45] Gilles Deleuze and Felix Guattari, *Mille plateaux* (Paris, 1980).

the Commune had a global resonance earlier and was already the object of different local re-readings and appropriations. The history of the Commune after the Commune is thus less transparent and linear than previously envisaged.

Concluding Thoughts

A local phenomenon, the Paris Commune, and with it the provincial Communes, resonated on a global scale. First, the Parisian uprising was part of an international and imperial war that laid the basis of surrounding contexts, while the unexpectedness of its outbreak made a deep impression at a time when the cycle of revolutions was supposed to be a thing of the past. Second, it should be remembered that it took place in the capital of the second most important imperial power of the time, one blessed with solid symbolic and cultural wealth. Third, the Commune happened during the globalization years of the 1860s and 1870s, marked by changes in transport and communication, echoing a vast and multiform space of debate on a large scale, at least within the Atlantic and Mediterranean ambits. Finally, the sheer creative force of the event, producing those unfinished "Communes," is striking. Overall, there was what one could call a heterogeneous and polycentric "Commune moment."

Undeniably, these sometimes-discordant reverberations were less transformative in their socio-political force than were the Atlantic Revolutions and the 1848 People's Spring. If we were to follow Theda Skocpol's well-argued idea, one of the most visible effects of the Commune could almost be the semi-liberal, semi-authoritarian reinforcement of the states involved.[46] That said, this brutally interrupted revolutionary movement, whose protagonists were elevated to the ranks of either demons or martyrs, turned out to be subject to a breadth of possible reinvestments. In the context of the years 1880–1900, it participated in the formalization of the idea of an international working class; it also provided an emotive force for other protest, intellectual, and rebellious movements, in particular within insurgent cities. Finally, by connecting different social or political movements – republican, socialist, mutual-help, associationist, and so on – and different territories, sometimes ignorant of one other, or at least not always in agreement, the Commune contributed, possibly in an important way, to

---

[46] Theda Skocpol, *States and Social Revolutions: A Comparative Analysis of France, Russia and China* (Cambridge, 1979); on these trends, see also Christopher Clark, "After 1848: The European Revolution in Government," *Transactions of the Royal Historical Society* 22 (2012), 171–97.

what the historian Ilham Khuri-Makdisi has called the "global radicalism" of the 1860s and 1870s.[47]

The event, therefore, was global, and it was so in a particular way. This raises a question which, to conclude, is perhaps a matter of debate for the history of revolutions in general – the question of time, and in particular of revolutionary historicity, with the unique reshuffling of past, present, and future threads that it generates. Some of its most surprising aspects, perhaps because it was so short-lived, are these misaligned eruptions and the connections between them, which correspond to as many qualitative changes of time and to a discontinuous relation to it.[48] Thus, in addition to conditions of possibility, to circulations, and to the richness of local contexts, the shock of temporal and historical regimes must also be considered in order to provide a finer understanding of spatial interrelations. This analytical path draws a more abundant and more difficult history, one that crosses several planes at the same time. But it can probably allow us to understand the modes of upsurge that are also typical of these insurrectional and revolutionary moments. On the smoking ruins of the capital, the Commune was compared to a "sphynx," both by its supporters, like Marx, and by its opponents, like the painter Gustave Doré, who famously depicted it in his 1871 painting "The Enigma" ("L'Énigme"). Almost 150 years later, it continues to provoke questioning interpretations, including those of historians.

---

[47] Ilham Khuri-Makdisi, *The Eastern Mediterranean and the Making of Global Radicalism, 1860–1914* (Berkeley, CA, 2013).

[48] Reinhart Koselleck, *Futures Past: On the Semantics of Historical Time* (New York, 2004); and, for revolutionary situations, Haim Burstin, *Révolutionnaires: Pour une anthropologie politique de la Révolution française* (Paris, 2013); and Claudia Moatti, Michèle Rios-Sarcey (ed.), *Pourquoi se référer au passé?* (Paris, 2018).

4   The Global Wave of Constitutional Revolutions, 1905–1915

Charles Kurzman

On Monday, October 30, 1905, late in the afternoon, Tsar Nicholas II of Russia signed a one-page document promising to respect civil rights, share power with a parliament, and hold free elections. "There was no other way out than to cross oneself and give what everyone was asking for," Nicholas wrote to his mother two days later. General strikes gripped the major cities of his realm; his government's finances were a shambles; his sole candidate to lead a hard-line crackdown had refused the job that very morning, threatening to kill himself in the tsar's presence if reforms were not granted.[1]

This was the first revolution covered "live" by international telegraph services, and by midnight, the news was all over Europe. Strikes had shut the St. Petersburg–Berlin telegraph lines, but telegrams were re-routed via Scandinavia and some European papers were able to include notice of the tsar's manifesto on Tuesday morning, October 31. "Only a few thousand people throughout Russia as yet know the glad news," wrote the correspondent of *The Times* of London. *The Dawn* (*L'Aurore*) of Paris, longtime supporter of the Russian liberal movement, put the manifesto on its front page.[2]

Radiating from London, international telegraph services carried the tsar's manifesto around the world. In Portugal, the newspaper *The World* (*O Mundo*) published its first comment on Wednesday, cautiously worrying about the tsar's real intent: "Hopefully a bloody deception will not follow [the Russian people's] generous hopes!" On Friday, the *North-China Herald* in Shanghai called the event "remarkable." The chief Iranian constitutionalist newspaper, *The Strong Bond* (*Habl al-Matin*), published in Calcutta, India, mentioned the manifesto the following Monday. In mid-November, a pro-democracy socialist in Hong Kong

---

[1] E. J. Bing, *The Secret Letters of the Last Tsar* (New York, 1938), 185; Andrew M. Verner, *The Crisis of Russian Autocracy* (Princeton, NJ, 1990), 241; A. A. Mosolov, *At the Court of the Last Tsar* (London, 1935), 90; and Sergei Iulevich Witte, *The Memoirs of Count Witte* (Armonk, NY, 1990), 486.

[2] James H. Billington, *Fire in the Minds of Men* (New York, 1980), 507; *The Times* (London) (October 31, 1905), 5; and *L'Aurore* (Paris) (October 31, 1905), 1.

Figure 4.1 Japanese lithograph by T. Miyano showing women organized in military units during the revolutionary attack on Nanjing in 1911. (Wellcome Library, No. 581222i)

commented, "the great ferment of the Russian Revolution has affected the entire globe like a clap of thunder." An Ottoman constitutionalist paper, resuming publication in December in Cairo after a long absence, fulfilled its "duty, as staunch liberals, to send a fraternal salute to the champions of liberalism who are even now struggling in the vast Russian empire in the name of the Rights of Man and Citizen."[3]

Thus began a global wave of constitutional revolutions, consuming more than a quarter of the world's population by the First World War. After Russia's revolution in 1905, mass sit-ins in Iran forced a constitution on the shah in 1906. Military rebellions compelled the Ottoman sultan to reintroduce a long-dormant constitution in 1908 and ended the Portuguese monarchy in 1910. Armed uprisings led to the ouster of a resurgent shah of Iran in 1909, the resignation of the autocratic president of Mexico in 1911, and the removal of the Chinese monarchy in early 1912 (Figure 4.1).

---

[3] *O Mundo* (Lisbon) (November 1, 1905), 2; *North-China Herald* (Shanghai) (November 3, 1905), 237; *Habl al-Matin* (Calcutta) (November 6, 1905), 23; Robert A. Scalapino and Harold Schiffrin, "Early Socialist Currents in the Chinese Revolutionary Movement," *Journal of Asian Studies* 18 (1959), 312–42, 327; and *Ijtihd* (Cairo) (December 1905), 142.

Though later upstaged by socialist, fascist, nationalist, and other movements, the pre–First World War wave of constitutional revolutions marked a turning point in the history of all of the countries it affected, on a scale equivalent to the wave of revolutions sparked by the French Revolution of 1789, the uprisings of 1848, anticolonial movements after the First and Second World Wars, and democratic movements of the late twentieth century.

These constitutional revolutions followed parallel trajectories. In each, an opposition movement unseated a long-standing autocracy with startling speed. The nascent constitutional regime held competitive elections – most with limited suffrage – convened parliaments, and allowed freedom of the press and freedom of association. Considerable disorders accompanied these transitions, and the constitutional regimes failed in numerous instances to uphold the rights and freedoms that they proclaimed. Coups d'état soon undermined the constitutional experiments in every case but one, Portugal, where the new regime survived an attempted coup d'état in 1915 and lingered until 1926. A rough tabular chronology is as follows (Iran went through this cycle twice):

Table 4.1 *Evolutions of the Constitutional Revolutions*

	Russia	Iran	Ottoman	Iran	Portugal	Mexico	China
Movement takeoff	1905	1905	1908	1908	1910	1910	1911
Constitutional revolution	1905	1906	1908	1909	1910	1911	1912
Parliamentary elections	1906	1907	1908	1910	1911	1911	1913
Parliament convenes	1906	1907	1908	1910	1911	1912	1913
Parliament subjugated	1907	1908	1909	1911	1926	1913	1913

Naturally, each case has its own unique history. Yet the shared aspects of the trajectory distinguished the constitutional revolutions of 1905–1912 from other movements of the same period: reformist democratizations, such as Austria in 1907, Sweden in 1909, Colombia in 1909–1910, Monaco in 1910, Greece in 1909–1912, Siam in 1912, and Argentina and Italy in 1912; failed democracy movements, such as the Young Afghans, Young Bukharans, Young Khivans, and the Radical Civic Union's uprising in Argentina in 1905; anticolonial movements such as the Herero and Maji-Maji rebellions in southern Africa, Swadeshi in India, Sarekat Islam in Indonesia, Irish nationalism, Korean resistance to Japanese rule, the Watchtower movement in Malawi, and Shaykh Ma al-ʾAynayn's defense of the Sahara; and peasant uprisings in Moldavia and Burma. Many of these movements also drew on intellectual identities, constitutionalist ideals, and anti-imperial ideologies, but they did not combine all three elements in the way that distinguished the constitutional revolutions of the period.

International observers at the time noted the flurry of constitutional revolutions. V. I. Lenin lumped several of these events together as "bourgeois-democratic revolutions." James Bryce, the British liberal, called them misguided attempts to "set a child to drive a motor car." British positivists noted that positivism played "so great a part" in them.[4] *The Journal of Despotism (Majallah-yi Istibdad)*, a satirical journal in Iran, ran an article written by fourteenth-month-old "Democracy" to its half-brother "Parliament" in Russia likening various constitutionalist movements around the world to siblings:

My father [is] Justice-of-the-State, and my mother Iran-of-All-Lands. My father married a woman in every country that he visited; his first wife he married in England . . .. Now – praise be to God – I have 47 brothers[,] the majority of whose names I don't know, but I know [this much] that we all look alike except maybe with just a little difference in appearance . . . Another thing that I've heard is that from India Justice-of-the-State intends to go to China, [and] I don't know where he will go first, the Ottoman country or China, undoubtedly he will not stay [put] in India; I know my father, where ever he goes he takes a wife and as soon as his wife becomes pregnant he leaves that country. [So] if you [happen to] know where he is going after India [please] write to me.[5]

As it happened, Justice-of-the-State appears to have visited the Ottoman Empire first and then China several years later. I attempted to bring the global scale of these events into focus in my book *Democracy Denied, 1905–1915*, from which this chapter is drawn.[6]

The Dreyfusard Moment

Participants and observers of the constitutional revolutions of the early twentieth century consistently identified these events with a single social group: the emerging global class of modern intellectuals. The term "intellectuals," as

---

[4] Vladimir I. Lenin, "The Right of Nations to Self-Determination" (St. Petersburg, 1914), in Robert C. Tucker (ed.), *The Lenin Anthology* (New York, 1975), 153–80, 162; James Bryce, *Modern Democracies* (New York, 1922), 501–02; and Anonymous, Untitled, *The Positivist Review* (London) (December 1, 1911), 387.

[5] Ali Gheissari, "Despots of the World Unite! Satire in the Iranian Constitutional Press: The Majalleh-ye Estebdad, 1907–1908," *Comparative Studies of South Asia, Africa and the Middle East* 25, 2 (2005), 360–76, 367–69.

[6] Charles Kurzman, *Democracy Denied, 1905–1915: Intellectuals and the Fate of Democracy* (Cambridge, MA, 2008). A more recent treatment of the same period can be found in Nader Sohrabi, *Revolution and Constitutionalism in the Ottoman Empire and Iran* (Cambridge, MA, 2011).

a collective self-identification, had recently gained international popularity through the Dreyfus Affair in France in 1898, in which a movement of French writers and academics contested and eventually overturned the conviction of a Jewish military officer imprisoned for treason. Intellectuals around the world followed news of the campaign intently. Thousands wrote letters of support to Dreyfus and his family. A decade later, an Iranian newspaper reporting on a momentous political trial in Iran could still comment, "Of course, the Dreyfus Affair is implanted in [our] memories." In the Ottoman Empire, the sultan was reportedly concerned that the scandal might encourage the Ottoman opposition. Indeed, many educated people, drawing inspiration from the mobilization of their French comrades, adopted the activist identity of "intellectuals." In Egypt, a leading Islamic modernist reported on the difficulties of the French *'uqala*, an Arabic term for rational intellectuals, as contrasted with religious scholars. In Iran, the terms *danishmandan* (knowledgeable ones) and later *munavvaran al-fikr* (people of enlightened thought), borrowed from Ottoman Turkish, became popular terms of self-identification among those with a modern education, as did the term *ziyalilar* (enlightened ones) in Central Asia. In Russia, the older term *intelligentsia*, previously used to refer to alienated, radical youths, changed in meaning to encompass the broader meaning of "intellectuals." China, by contrast, lacked a specific term for intellectuals at this time, as evidenced by the use of the descriptive phrase "people of education and knowledge" (*you jiaoyu zhishi zhe*) to translate the Russian word *intelligentsia* in 1906. Only in the late 1910s was the term *zhishi jieji* (knowledge class) adapted from Japanese.[7]

In country after country, intellectuals aspired to state power in an almost messianic combination of positivist elitism and democratic populism. "We learn that in chemistry," wrote Abdullah Cevdet, a leading pro-democracy figure in the Ottoman Empire, "two particular elements mix and transform

---

[7] *Habl al-Matin* (Tehran) (June 22, 1907), 2; Mustafa Refik, "Abdülhamid ve Dreyfüs Meselesi," *Osmanlı Mecmuası* (September 1, 1899), 2; Rashid Rida, "Al-Yahud fi Faransa wa fi Misr," *al-Manar* (March 18, 1898), 53–55, 55; Charles Kurzman, "Mashrutiyat, Meşrutiyet, and Beyond," in Houchang Chehabi and Vanessa Martin (eds.), *Iran's Constitutional Revolution* (London, 2010), 277–90, 285–89; Ali Gheissari, *Iranian Intellectuals in the 20th Century* (Austin, TX, 1998), 15–16; Yahya Daulatabadi, *Hayat-i Yahya*, 4 vols. (Tehran, 1992), vol. 2, 86; Mahmud Khoja Behbudiy, "Padarkush" (1911), translated in Edward A. Allworth, "Murder as Metaphor in the First Central Asian Drama," *Ural-Altaischer Jahrbücher/Ural-Altaic Yearbook* 58 (1986), 72–83, 74–76, 81; Cholpan, "Dokhtur Muhammadyor" (1914), ed. by Sirojiddin Ahmad and Ulughbek Dolimov, *Sharq Yulduzi* 1 (1992), 132–38, 136; Michael Confino, "On Intellectuals and Intellectual Traditions in Eighteenth- and Nineteenth-Century Russia," *Daedalus* 101 (1972), 117–49, 138; *Min Bao* (Tokyo) (April 3, 1906), 1 (I thank Mei Zhou for translation and transliteration); Wolfgang Lippert, *Entstehung und Funktion einiger chinesischer marxistischer Termini* (Wiesbaden, 1979), 316; and Vera Schwarcz, *The Chinese Enlightenment: Intellectuals and the Legacy of the May Fourth Movement of 1919* (Berkeley, CA, 1986), 186.

into a novel, valuable compound. Let us [intellectuals] all unite to form such an immense power. Then let us attack and destroy, with our own hands, this bastion of the castle of despotism established against us." Intellectuals provided the leadership and much of the early membership of the Constitutional Democratic Party in Russia, claiming to represent "a new era of history." In Iran, a constitutionalist organization proposed that "the wisest of the country, the nation's intellectuals and graduates," should replace the "ignorant and vulgar men" who were currently "in charge of all the important things and make fun of science." In Portugal, constitutionalist leader Bernardino Machado stated: "If the thinkers do not govern, the interests and passions will govern without the bridle of reason." In Mexico, constitutionalist leader Francisco Madero demanded that "intellectual element" should "lead the country." In China, constitutionalist leader Sun Yat-Sen proposed that all government officials, including democratically elected ones, be tested through a positivist examination system to prevent "foolish and ignorant people" from holding office.[8] By themselves, this tiny class of elitist intellectuals was incapable of toppling autocratic regimes. But in some countries, the intellectuals were not by themselves.

General Strikes: Russia and Iran

The first mass mobilization to line up behind the leadership of the intellectuals involved the Russian working class, which itself had emerged rather suddenly in the 1890s when the monarchy embarked on a policy of rapid industrialization. The Assembly of Mill and Factory Workers of St. Petersburg adopted a resolution for political and social reforms that "several intellectual Liberals" had helped to craft. On January 9, 1905, thousands of union members carried these demands to the tsar's palace in a massive demonstration. The tsar was not there to receive them; instead, the military blocked the protestors' path and then fired on them, killing hundreds. The event known as "Bloody Sunday" ignited activism across Imperial Russia. Although the constitutionalist movement and the workers' movement traveled separate paths during 1905, they reunited during the general strike in October, a strike triggered by the railway workers' union, one of the few working-class unions that had a significant white-collar

---

[8] Fatma Müge Göçek, *Rise of the Bourgeoisie, Demise of Empire: Ottoman Westernization and Social Change* (New York, 1996), 76; Shmuel Galai, *The Liberation Movement in Russia, 1900–1905* (Cambridge, 1973), 173; Daulatabadi, *Hayat-i Yahya*, vol. 2, 42; Angelo Vaz, *Bernardino Machado: Sentimentos, Ideias e Factos do seu Tempo* (Oporto, 1950), 80; Francisco I. Madero, *The Presidential Succession of 1910* (New York, 1990), 210, which was first published as Idem, *La Sucesión Presidencial en 1910* (San Padre, 1908); Sun Yat-Sen, *Prescriptions for Saving China: Selected Writings of Sun Yat-sen*, ed. by Julie Lee Wei, Ramon H. Myers, and Donald G. Gillin (Stanford, CA, 1994), 49.

membership and a largely constitutionalist ideology. Other working-class organizations and leftist parties followed suit, generally adopting constitutionalist demands along with socialist demands. "The extent of such sentiments is difficult to judge," according to one major study, "but there can be no doubt that demands for civil liberties and for a constitutional system of government had the support of a great many workers during the final months of 1905."[9]

The October Manifesto shattered the alliance between workers and the intellectuals' constitutionalist movement. Many workers were dissatisfied with the semi-democratic promises of the October Manifesto. Some of this sentiment may have been linked to the workers' resentment of intellectuals, for whom political rights took precedence over the improvement of economic conditions. After the October Manifesto, as intellectuals prepared to participate in parliament, workers in the south argued that political freedom was useful only for socialists and "the well-educated." "For what do we need a constitution?" they shouted. The intellectuals' Constitutional Democratic Party, commonly known as the Kadets, scored an impressive victory in the breakthrough parliamentary election of early 1906, with socialists refusing to stand for office and the more radical workers refusing to vote. But in the second parliamentary elections, in January 1907, leftist candidates fared better than the Kadets. Leftist participation in parliament was not intended, and did not serve, to prolong the constitutional experiment. Rather, leftists sought to use parliament as an organizational center for a revolutionary uprising. While the Kadets tried to "protect the duma" through conciliation and moderation, the leftists were outspoken and provocative. They booed government ministers, proposed legislation that would have brought about an immediate dissolution of parliament, and made speeches calling for armed revolution. Ironically, given this record, the monarchists resorted to fabricated evidence in order to charge the socialist parliamentary bloc with subversion, the charge that served as pretext for dissolution of the second parliament in early June 1907. The Kadets' last-ditch negotiations to save the parliament warned of the specter of unrest, but workers failed to rise in defense of constitutionalism. When the constitutionalists were suppressed, so were working-class organizations. The Russian monarchy held two more parliamentary elections before it was overthrown during the First World War, but it rewrote election and labor laws to ensure that it would not face serious constitutionalist challenges.[10]

---

[9] Henry Reichman, *Railwaymen and Revolution: Russia, 1905* (Berkeley, CA, 1987); and Victoria E. Bonnell, *Roots of Rebellion: Workers' Politics and Organizations in St. Petersburg and Moscow, 1900–1914* (Berkeley, CA, 1983), 170.

[10] Charters Wynn, *Workers, Strikes, and Pogroms: The Donbass-Dnepr Bend in Late Imperial Russia, 1870–1905* (Princeton, NJ, 1992), 222; Abraham Ascher, *The Revolution of 1905,*

Intellectuals in Iran, to Russia's south, took heart from Russia's constitutional revolution. According to a British diplomat in Tehran, "the Russian Revolution [of 1905] has had a most astounding effect here. Events in Russia have been watched with great attention, and a new spirit would seem to have come over the people. They are tired of their rulers, and, taking example of Russia, have come to think that it is possible to have another and better form of government." Iranian intellectuals drew on their long-standing ties with colleagues in the Russian Caucasus as they began to mobilize their own revolutionary movement. Unlike Russia, however, Iran had virtually no modern working class in the early twentieth century. The country's first electrical plant had begun operation only in 1904; Iran had two railways, which totaled only eight miles. When the intellectuals of the constitutionalist movement looked for mass allies, they looked instead to the traditional guild associations of the bazaar. In December 1905, an intellectual from one of the two main constitutionalist organizations instigated a crisis that led to the public beating of two leading merchants by the governor of Tehran. During the protest that followed, the merchants' demands were delivered to the government of Muzaffar al-Din Shah by a member of the other constitutionalist organization, who added constitutionalist language to the list of demands.[11]

In the summer of 1906, the guilds of Tehran held a massive sit-in held on the British legation grounds, the equivalent of a general strike, as a protest against recent arbitrary oppressive actions of the monarchy. It acquired its constitutionalist character when a delegation of teachers, graduates, and students from modern schools joined the sit-in and commandeered it. Setting up their own tent alongside those of the guilds, these modern intellectuals lectured on constitutionalism, teaching that

2 vols. (Stanford, CA, 1988–1992), vol. 2 (*Authority Restored*) (Stanford, CA, 1992), 284 and 349; Alfred Levin, *The Second Duma: A Study of the Social-Democratic Party and the Russian Constitutional Experiment* (New Haven, CT, 1940), 67; Abraham Ascher, *P. A. Stolypin: The Search for Stability in Late Imperial Russia* (Stanford, CA, 2001), 199; and Geoffrey Swain, *Russian Social Democracy and the Legal Labour Movement, 1906–14* (London, 1983), 31.

[11] Seyyed Hassan Taqizadeh, "The Background of the Constitutional Movement in Azerbaijan," *Middle East Journal* 14, 4 (1960), 456–65; Houri Berberian, *Armenians and the Iranian Constitutional Revolution of 1905–1911* (Boulder, CO, 2001); Edward G. Browne, *The Persian Revolution of 1905–1909* (Washington, DC, 1995), 120, which was first published in 1910; Anne Enayat, "Amin al-Zarb," in Ehsan Yarshater (ed.), *Encyclopaedia Iranica*, 15 vols. (London, 1985–2011), vol. 1 (London, 1985), 953–54, 953; Ervand Abrahamian, *Iran Between Two Revolutions* (Princeton, NJ, 1982), 87; Julian Bharier, *Economic Development in Iran* (Oxford, 1971), 15; Charles Issawi, *The Economic History of Iran, 1800–1914* (Chicago, IL, 1971), 155–59; Mangol Bayat, *Iran's First Revolution: Shi'ism and the Constitutional Revolution of 1905–1909* (New York, 1991), 110; and Muhammad Nazim al-Islam Kirmani, *Tarikh-i Bidari-yi Iranian*, ed. by Sa'idi Sirjani, 2 vols. (Tehran, 1968), vol. 1, 119.

"when the nation no longer wants a shah he is not recognized" and turning the sit-in into "one vast open-air school of political science." "Since those who took refuge in the Embassy had absolutely no concept as to what a constitution was or what it required, a special group kept them informed and instilled in them its own ideas," according to Haydar Khan, a socialist constitutionalist. Intellectuals dominated the sit-in's negotiating committee and inserted a constitution and elected parliament among the protest's demands. They convinced various groups not to leave the sit-in as negotiations continued over these demands.[12]

After a month, the shah agreed to a constitution, a parliament, and elections, which were held in early 1907. Intellectuals dominated the new parliament, passing legislation to expand modern education, the modern judicial system, the modern medical profession, and modern accounting systems, all of which threatened the position of the monarchy and traditional authorities. The guilds soon turned against parliament. By the spring of 1908, Hajj Muhammad Husayn Amin al-Zarb, a supporter of constitutionalism and perhaps the leading Iranian businessman of the period, considered himself almost entirely isolated among his merchant friends. The guilds of Tehran did not defend constitutionalism when Muhammad 'Ali Shah's Cossack Brigade, led by a Russian military officer, shelled the parliament building and disbanded the elected body. The Russian monarchy, fighting constitutionalism at home, sought to retain its dominant position in northern Iran by suppressing constitutionalism in Iran as well.[13]

The Iranian constitutionalist movement survived in several provinces, where it mobilized militias that marched on Tehran and ousted Muhammad 'Ali Shah, who had inherited the throne from his late father, Muzaffar al-Din Shah, installing his eleven-year-old son on the throne. New elections were held, and a second parliament met in 1909, but the guilds and other business leaders continued to be critical of the disorderliness of the new democracy. Party debates were "ruining our house ..... Until we throw this talk out of parliament, we will never achieve our goals," said 'Ali-Quli Khan Sardar As'ad, a Bakhtiyari tribal leader turned

---

[12] Ahmad Tafrishi-Husayni, *Ruznamah-yi Akhbar-i Mashrutiyat*, ed. by Iraj Afshar (Tehran, 1973), 41–42; Vanessa A. Martin, *Islam and Modernism: The Iranian Revolution of 1906* (London, 1989), 93–96; Abrahamian, *Iran Between Two Revolutions*, 84–85; Reza Sheikholeslami and Dunning Wilson, "The Memoirs of Haydar Khan 'Amu Ughlu'," *Iranian Studies* 6, 1 (1973), 21–51, 37; Ervand Abrahamian, "The Crowd in the Persian Revolution," *Iranian Studies* 2, 4 (1969), 128–50, 134; Bayat, *Iran's First Revolution*, 135; and Browne, *The Persian Revolution*, 122.

[13] Daulatabadi, *Hayat-i Yahya*, vol. 2, 303 On the Russian government's role in the Iranian Constitutional Revolution, see Moritz Deutschmann, *Iran and Russian Imperialism* (London, 2015), 153–210.

businessman – he leased land to a British oil company operating in Bakhtiyari territory and subcontracted tribesmen as security teams – who had helped to found a constitutionalist organization and convinced his fellow Bakhtiyaris to restore the constitutional regime in 1909. When the new regime attempted to increase tax income, "the wealthier businessmen," as well as landowners and clergy, objected, according to a German diplomatic report. They "are all sick and tired of the ruling parliamentary demagoguery, primarily because this now begins to question even their traditional prerogatives and their most sacred possession: their freedom to steal and their freedom from taxes." Meanwhile, Russia had invaded northern Iran and threatened to conquer Tehran if parliament did not offer it massive concessions. Parliament refused, and the Bakhtiyari leaders cut a deal with Russia, with British approval, in which parliament was dissolved for a second time. Elections were postponed until 1914, by which time the great powers' military maneuvers in the First World War had reduced the Iranian government to virtual colonial status.[14]

Regional Revolts: Mexico and China

The only constitutional revolution of the early twentieth century to garner significant rural support was in Mexico, where large-scale commercial estates, *haciendas*, had accumulated millions of hectares over the past half-century, exploiting peasants' lack of written title and taking advantage of their debts. The *haciendas* faced organized opposition in some regions from peasant communities that had retained their customs and limited autonomy. One such community in the central state of Morelos led a rural revolt in support of the democracy movement. Known by the name of its leader, Emiliano Zapata, the Zapatista revolt sought and received accreditation from constitutionalist leader Francisco Madero and considered itself the official constitutionalist movement in Morelos. It was especially interested in the portion of the constitutionalist platform that promised to return unlawfully taken lands to their rightful owners – a limited but important land reform proposal.

This platform was drawn up by young intellectuals who self-consciously formed "the nucleus of the democratic resurgence of 1909," as one participant later commented: schoolteachers who helped to mobilize rural areas; graduates, engineers, and journalists who

---

[14] Isma'il Amirkhayzi, *Qiyam-i Azarbayjan* (Tabriz, 1960), 488; Mansoureh Ettehadieh (Nezam Mafi), "Origin and Development of Political Parties in Persia, 1906-1911" (PhD dissertation, University of Edinburgh, 1979), 395; and Robert A. McDaniel, *The Shuster Mission and the Persian Constitutional Revolution* (Minneapolis, MN, 1974), 190.

corresponded profusely with Madero; youths who were "possessed of the absurd belief that the world ought to be governed by college students or professional men still in the infantile stages of their intellectual development." These young intellectuals challenged the older generation of educated men, known as *Científicos*, who had allied themselves with long-time dictator Porfirio Díaz. In Madero's vision, the "intellectual element … would lead the country." The "illiterate masses," he argued, are "not an obstacle that should deprive us of democratic practices," just as they had not prevented Russia and the Ottoman Empire from attempting to dislodge "absolute power" in recent years.[15]

Díaz had Madero thrown in jail for contesting his reelection in 1910. When Díaz announced his fraudulent victory, rebellions broke out around the country, coalescing around Madero's armed campaign from Texas, where he had fled after escaping from prison. Díaz was forced to resign in May 1911, after thirty-five years in power. Elections brought Madero to power, along with young intellectuals who "picked up the plums of office, while the real captains of the revolution" – the nonintellectuals who had fought the dictator's army – "were fobbed off with, at best, lowly commissions in the *rurales* [gendarmes]." In Morelos, Zapata was not named to high office. Instead, Madero's assistants appointed the landowners' candidates in Morelos.[16]

The constitutional regime was slow to implement even the limited, legalistic rural reforms that it had promised. While the government moved ahead with educational reform and other plans, Madero called for peasants to await the results of "a series of studies." The radical wing of the constitutionalist movement proffered land reform proposals in parliament, the most famous being Luis Cabrera's plan to restore peasants' communal ownership rights, but in practice the government ruled in cooperation with large landowners. Peasant movements that had contributed to the victory of constitutionalism now continued their struggle against the constitutional regime; the largest of these, the Zapatistas, threatened the capital city itself.[17]

In February 1913, the elected government faced an attempted coup d'état. Madero's newly appointed chief of staff, Victoriano Huerta,

---

[15] Arnaldo Córdova, *La Ideología de la Revolución Mexicana* (Mexico City, 1973), 142; James D. Cockcroft, "El Maestro de Primaria en la Revolución Mexicana," *História Mexicana* 16 (1967), 565–87; Francisco Bulnes, *The Whole Truth About Mexico* (New York, 1916), 138; and Madero, *The Presidential Succession of 1910*, 210 and 123.

[16] Alan Knight, *The Mexican Revolution*, 2 vols. (Cambridge, 1986), vol. 1 (*Porfirians, Liberals and Peasants*), 166–67; and John Womack, *Zapata and the Mexican Revolution* (New York, 1968).

[17] Córdova, *La Ideología de la Revolución Mexicana*, 190 and 138; and Knight, *The Mexican Revolution*, vol. 1, 274–351.

launched a fake attack on the rebel stronghold, sending loyal constitutionalist troops to be trapped and slaughtered. After ten days, Huerta took Madero captive, with the support of the US ambassador, then had him assassinated. Zapata and other rural movements refused to come to the aid of the elected government. Mexico dissolved into civil war.[18]

China, too, fell into civil war after its brief constitutional government was toppled in a coup. Constitutionalist intellectuals in China had taken inspiration from Japan's military defeat of Russia in Manchuria in 1905, months before the constitutionalist revolution in Russia. As one newspaper crowed: "Isn't it Heaven's will that the way forward – constitutionalism – has been shown to China! This is not the defeat of Russia by Japan but the defeat of an autocratic country by a constitutional country." The following year a leading constitutionalist intellectual translated the new Russian constitution into Chinese, along with the constitutions of several other countries.[19]

The Revolutionary Alliance in China, searching for allies in its constitutionalist struggle against the Qing monarchy, sought the support of "secret societies" – semi-criminal, often lower-class organizations that served as informal representatives of popular aspirations, as idealized in the Chinese saying: "The officials draw their power from the law; the people, from the secret societies." These groups were not inherently sympathetic to the constitutionalist movement, but Sun Yat-Sen and his fellow intellectuals were able to convert individual secret-society leaders to the cause, in part by emphasizing ethnic Han hostility toward the ethnically Manchu dynasty. In Zhejiang, the secret societies were brought into revolutionary plans for 1907, but premature uprisings ruined the scheme and the intellectuals' liaisons with the secret societies were aborted. In Guangdong, intellectual revolutionaries arranged repeated plots involving secret societies from 1905 through early 1911, all of which came to naught. In Hunan and Guizhou, the revolutionaries had somewhat more success in maintaining alliances with rural secret societies, which adopted the platform of the Revolutionary Alliance and contributed significantly to the 1911 revolution.[20]

---

[18] Rosa E. King, *Tempest Over Mexico: A Personal Chronicle* (Boston, MA, 1935), 111; and Womack, *Zapata and the Mexican Revolution*, 161.

[19] Li Shu, "A Re-Assessment of Some Questions Concerning the 1911 Revolution," in Hu Sheng, Liu Dania, Hu Sheng, Liu Dania, et al., *The 1911 Revolution* (Beijing, 1983), 67–127, 73; and K.S. Liew, *Struggle for Democracy: Sung Chiao-jen and the 1911 Chinese Revolution* (Berkeley, CA, 1971), 60–61.

[20] Fei-Ling Davis, *Primitive Revolutionaries of China: A Study of Secret Societies in the Late Nineteenth Century* (Honolulu, 1971), 3; Prasenjit Duara, *Rescuing History from the Nation: Questioning Narratives of Modern China* (Chicago, IL, 1995), 115–46; John Lust, "Secret Societies, Popular Movements, and the 1911 Revolution," in Jean Chesneaux (ed.), *Popular Movements and Secret Societies in China, 1840–1950* (Stanford, CA, 1972), 165–200, 177–84; Dian H. Murray, in collaboration with

The alliance in Hunan triggered the revolution by taking over the provincial capital in October 1911. As in Mexico, multiple revolts broke out around the country. Within a month, the imperial government had resigned in favor of General Yuan Shikai, who became the provisional president of the new republic. Constitutionalist intellectuals soon disbanded the revolutionary armies. The thousands of poor Chinese who had joined military regiments in the fall of 1911 were now seen as a drain on the treasury and a threat to public order. Song Jiaoren, one of the theorists of the pro-democracy movement, had worried about this possibility just weeks before the outbreak of the revolution in fall 1911; he praised the recent constitutional revolution in Portugal for sticking with professional troops. Disbanding these troops proved to be tricky, since the soldiers naturally wanted to be paid their back wages, plus a severance bonus. Given the financial difficulties of the new government, these demands were not always met. Some of the troops rioted and looted to earn their pay, thereby fulfilling the fears and prejudices of the intellectuals.[21]

Elections in early 1913, won by the constitutional movement's new party, populated the bicameral legislature with young intellectuals, more than half of whom had studied abroad. Parliament, however, was undermined before it could get started. In its first days of deliberation, as parliament sought to establish control over the executive branch through oversight of General, now President, Yuan Shikai's budget and cabinet, Yuan stepped up negotiations with various European banking consortiums for a significant loan without parliamentary approval, contrary to the provisional constitution. The evening that the loan was concluded, parliamentary leaders searched Beijing for the location of the signing ceremony. They found it, managed to gain entrance, and made a small speech on the unconstitutionality of the loan – all in vain. Within months, Yuan used the funds from the loan to send troops to subdue the pro-constitution provinces; to reorganize the police force, which he used to

Qin Baoqi, *The Origins of the Tiandihui: The Chinese Triads in Legend and History* (Stanford, CA, 1994), 118–19; Mary Backus Rankin, *Early Chinese Revolutionaries: Radical Intellectuals in Shanghai and Chekiang, 1902–1911* (Cambridge, MA, 1971), 173–185; Edward J. M. Rhoads, *China's Republican Revolution: The Case of Kwangtung, 1895–1913* (Cambridge, MA, 1975), 110–21, 188–89; Jean Chesneaux, *Secret Societies in China* (Ann Arbor, MI, 1971), 135–59; Joseph W. Esherick, *Reform and Revolution in China: The 1911 Revolution in Hunan and Hubei* (Berkeley, CA, 1976); and Shimizu Minoru, "The 1911 Revolution in Hunan and the Popular Movement," in Eto Shinkichi and Harold Z. Schiffrin (eds.), *The 1911 Revolution in China: Interpretive Essays* (Tokyo, 1984), 193–208.
[21] Noriko Tamada, "Sung Chiao-jen and the 1911 Revolution," *Papers on China* 21 (1968), 184–229, 200; and Edmund S. K. Fung, *The Military Dimension of the Chinese Revolution: The New Army and Its Role in the Revolution of 1911* (Vancouver, 1980), 237.

arrest the constitutionalist members of parliament in the fall of 1913; and to dismiss the parliament entirely in early 1914. A new assembly was elected in 1914, but only the very wealthy were allowed to vote.[22]

Few popular organizations assisted the elected government when it came into conflict with Yuan Shikai in mid-1913. In Guangdong, the constitutionalist forces' appeals for aid went unanswered. In Shanghai, promises of high wages and opportunities for looting attracted some poor people into a reconstituted revolutionary army, but not enough to counter the greater paychecks and prospects for victory offered by Yuan's government and its foreign backers. By and large, the secret societies that had helped usher in constitutionalism sat out the civil war as it was destroyed, just as the Zapatistas had in Mexico. These popular organizations were ultimately not as invested in constitutionalism as their intellectual allies had been.[23]

Military Mutinies: Ottoman Empire and Portugal

The intellectuals' constitutionalist movement in the Ottoman Empire was opposed to mass mobilization. Ottomans followed events in Russia with "extra-ordinary interest," according to a Russian correspondent, reading newspapers smuggled from Europe and the Caucasus. Constitutionalist intellectuals urged Ottomans to learn from the Russian example, while debating the risk that strikes and other mass actions might encourage secessionism and European military intervention in the Ottoman Empire. Preventing the disintegration of Ottoman lands was a primary concern of Ottoman intellectuals, who supported constitutionalism in large part because they hoped liberty and justice would instill Ottoman national sentiment, in keeping with the positivist sociological theories that many Ottoman intellectuals adopted while in exile in Europe. The constitutionalist movement focused its recruitment almost entirely among educated elites, including modern-educated military officers. These officers were scornful of old-style commanders lacking modern training, whom they blamed for the weakness of the Ottoman national defense. When the constitutionalists decided to mobilize

---

[22] P'eng-Yüan Chang, "Political Participation and Political Elites in Early Republican China: The Parliament of 1913–1914," *Journal of Asian Studies* 37, 2 (1978), 293–313, 303–12 ; Samuel Yale Kupper, "Revolution in China: Kiangsi Province, 1905–1913" (PhD dissertation, University of Michigan, 1973), 374–90; Fernand Farjenel, *Through the Chinese Revolution* (London, 1915), 302–05; and Jerome Ch'en, *Yuan Shih-k'ai* (Stanford, CA, 1972), 178–79, which was originally published in 1961.

[23] Rhoads, *China's Republican Revolution*, 261–63; and St. Piero Rudinger, *The Second Revolution in China, 1913: My Adventures of the Fighting Around Shanghai, the Arsenal, Woosung Forts* (Shanghai, 1914), 23–24 and 118.

a revolutionary movement in 1907, they renewed efforts to recruit military officers, especially junior officers in the Third Army, which was stationed in the Ottoman Empire's European provinces.[24]

The constitutional revolution followed directly from the linkages forged between military officers and civilian intellectuals. In June 1908, military members of the Society for Union and Progress attempted to assassinate an Ottoman officer in Salonica who had been investigating the opposition movement. As a result, a number of constitutionalist officers in the Third Army came under suspicion and were transferred from Macedonia to Istanbul for investigation and possible court-martial. Instead of obeying, one officer, Ahmed Niyazi, fled into the countryside with a group of supporters. Another Society member assassinated the general who had been ordered to pursue Niyazi. Several days later, with several more military members of the Society roaming the hills of Macedonia, the Society began to issue demands for the reinstatement of the constitution. The sultan quickly acquiesced, announcing elections and limits on royal authority.[25]

The restoration of the constitution prompted massive public celebrations. Arabs, Armenians, Greeks, Jews, Macedonians, and other groups who would soon demand independent homelands celebrated democratization alongside Turks and others. In Ottoman Jerusalem, for example, a crowd estimated at 40,000 – larger than the permanent population of the city – gathered for a public proclamation by the governor, who wrote to Istanbul: "The voices of joy in the city of Jerusalem, which has no equal in the world to the contrast of religions, sects, and races in it, were raised to the heavens in a thousand languages and styles. Speeches were given. Hands were shaken. Pleasant tunes were played. In short, the proper things were expressed for the honor of liberty."[26]

Elections were held in the fall of 1908, and parliament convened in early 1909, with representatives from many minority communities. Immediately, however, the alliance between constitutionalist intellectuals and their military allies frayed. In February 1909, dozens of officers made

---

[24] Sohrabi, *Revolution and Constitutionalism in the Ottoman Empire and Iran*, 79–81; Şerif Arif Mardin, *Jön Türklerin Siyasî Fikirleri, 1895–1908* (Ankara, 1964); Ahmet Rıza, "L'Inaction des Jeunes-Turcs," *Revue Occidentale*, series 2, 27 (1903), 91–98; M. Şükrü Hanioğlu, *Preparation for a Revolution: The Young Turks, 1902–1908* (New York, 2001), 224 and 219–21; İsmet İnönü, *Hatıralar*, ed. by Sabahattin Selek (Ankara, 1985), 48 and 56; and Handan Nazir-Akmeşe, *The Birth of Modern Turkey: The Ottoman Military and the March to World War I* (London, 2005), 51–53.

[25] Hanioğlu, *Preparation for a Revolution*, 266–75.

[26] Michelle Campos, "A 'Shared Homeland' and its Boundaries: Empire, Citizenship and the Origins of Sectarianism in Late Ottoman Palestine, 1908–1913" (PhD dissertation, Stanford University, 2003), 40 and 42.

a show of force in parliament to demand the removal of recently appointed ministers of the navy and army, and then the dismissal of the prime minister. Parliament acquiesced. When a mutiny led by anti-democratic religious leaders erupted in April 1909, the military used the occasion to subdue parliament as well. The military government declared martial law, placed a pliable sultan on the throne, and forced parliament to pass a series of laws limiting constitutional freedoms. The regime maintained a charade of constitutional rule. But for the next several decades, governments in the Ottoman Empire and almost all of its successor states would be decided by military intervention.

In Portugal, constitutionalist intellectuals mobilized both working-class supporters and educated elites, including military officers. As in the Ottoman Empire, intellectuals sought to reinstate and reform a constitution that had been promulgated decades earlier but had been undermined by the monarchy. The constitutionalists espoused a positivist ideology that saw popular sovereignty and intellectual expertise as natural allies in the struggle against despotism. "Science tells us that monarchies have no raison d'être," wrote Teófilo Braga, a university professor, a leader of the constitutionalist movement, and the first president of Portugal after the revolution of 1910. "All the evils which our national organism suffers are derived from the monarchical institution; let us extirpate this cancer which will impoverish us, with the same impassiveness and experimental knowledge that the surgeon attacks a morbid degeneration." As in the Ottoman Empire, the constitutional revolution was triggered by a military uprising in October 1910. Working-class organizations joined the fray in large numbers, and the king left for exile within forty-eight hours. But it was intellectuals who dominated the new government. Almost every cabinet member, and more than three quarters of parliament, had some higher education, in a country that was 70 percent illiterate (the lowest level of all these constitutional revolutions of this period).[27]

The new regime appointed military officials who were deemed sympathetic to constitutional oversight, in particular a group of officers known as the "Young Turks," who began a purge of monarchists in the military. The results were chaotic. Older officers resented the quick promotion of constitutionalist junior officers; radical enlisted men resented the

---

[27] Aubrey F. G. Bell, *Portugal of the Portuguese* (New York, 1915), 98; Joel Serrão, *Antologia do Pensamento Político Português: Liberalismo, Socialismo e Republicanismo* (Oporto, 1970), 319; A. H. de Oliveira Marques *et alia*, *Parlamentares e Ministros da 1a República (1910–1926)* (Lisbon, 2000); Vasco Pulido Valente, *O Poder e o Povo: A Revolução de 1910* (Lisbon, 1976), 223; and Luis Vidigal, *Cidadania, Caciquismo e Poder em Portugal, 1890–1916* (Lisbon, 1988), 77.

continued employment of the older officers. Discipline deteriorated to the point where even staunchly constitutionalist officers labeled the situation "chaos" and implored soldiers to behave with "uniformity, decency, and composure." Moreover, the fighting ability of the military sank to near zero. A British naval attaché reported that the Portuguese navy, once the pride of this sea-faring nation, was no longer seaworthy. The army was so little respected by Portugal's allies Britain and France that when the First World War broke out, they insulted Portugal by requesting weapons but no troops.[28]

Their pride wounded, a number of officers resigned their commissions in early 1915 as a political protest against the constitutional government, pledging their allegiance instead to an elderly general and military-school instructor, Joaquim Pimenta de Castro. In a legal coup d'état, the president selected Pimenta as the new prime minister. Pimenta had "lost faith in the Republic," according to his wife's cousin, another army general. Once in office, Pimenta moved to consolidate power, refusing to allow parliament to meet, dissolving local elected governments, postponing new elections, and giving every impression of creating a dictatorship.[29]

After less than five months in office, however, Pimenta was ousted by constitutionalist military officers, along with a popular uprising, restoring the constitutionalist forces to power. The result was a stalemate: both the constitutionalist forces and their rivals in the Portuguese military had the power to disrupt, even to overturn governments they did not favor – a dictatorial government was installed for a time in 1918–19 as well – but neither had the power to maintain governments they favored. Only in 1926 did the anti-democratic forces in the military gain the upper hand decisively, installing a fascist regime that lasted until 1974. In both the Ottoman Empire and Portugal, the constitutionalists' reliance on military officers came to haunt them.

Collapse and Legacy

Intellectuals plunged into despair, and themes of hopeless bleakness emerged in the literatures of all of these countries in the wake of failed constitutional experiments. A constitutionalist poet in Iran lamented, "This ruined graveyard is not Iran. This desolate place is not Iran;

---

[28] [Francisco] Cunha Leal, *As Minhas Memórias: Romance duma Época, duma Família e duma Vida de 1888 a 1917* (Lisbon, 1966), 226; Valente, *O Poder e o Povo*, 217; and A. H. Kelly (British naval attaché in Paris) to Arthur Hardinge (British ambassador in Lisbon), June 5, 1913, Great Britain, The National Archives, London, FO 371/1740.

[29] Gonçalo Pereira Pimenta de Castro, *As Minhas Memórias*, 3 vols. (Porto, 1947–1950), vol. 1 (Porto, n.d. [1947]), 406.

where is Iran?" An Ottoman author opined: "My friend, sometimes the environment is like a bad omen, like a graveyard. What intelligence, what wisdom, what talent can survive there?" A well-known Mexican novelist came to the "basic conviction that the fight is a hopeless one and a thorough waste." In Portugal, the journal *School Federation* (*A federação escolar*) warned that "Black days await us. Days of hunger threaten us. Days of slavery await us." In Russia, a leading poet worried: "Already, as in a nightmare or a frightening dream, we can imagine that the darkness overhanging us is the shaggy chest of the shaft-horse, and that in another moment the heavy hoofs will descend."[30]

A Chinese writer offered this extreme metaphor for the futility of intellectuals' constitutionalist activism:

Imagine an iron house having not a single window, and virtually indestructible, with all its inmates sound asleep and about to die of suffocation. Dying in their sleep, they won't feel the pain of death. Now if you raise a shout to awake a few of the light sleepers, making these unfortunate few suffer the agony of irrevocable death, do you really think you are doing them a good turn?[31]

With their class mobilization in ruins, intellectuals began to criticize the collective identity of "intellectual." In Russia, a widely noted book of essays berated the intellectuals' class mobilization. In the Ottoman Empire, a popular pamphlet denounced constitutionalist intellectuals for aping the West. In Iran, constitutionalist intellectuals were mocked as "national goody-goodies." In China, leftist intellectuals adopted the slogan "Down with the intellectual class." Ironically, it was at this time that a handful of activists, recognizing that "the class of intellectuals" had become "disinherited," tried to establish an international organization to promote their identity and represent their interests.[32]

---

[30] Sorour Soroudi, "Poet and Revolution: The Impact of Iran's Constitutional Revolution on the Social and Literary Outlook of the Time," *Iranian Studies* 12, 1–2 (1979), 239–73, 258; Tarik Z. Tunaya, *Hürriyet İlanı: İkinci Meşrutiyetin Siyasî Hayatına Bakışlar* (Istanbul, 1959), 64; John Rutherford, *Mexican Society during the Revolution: A Literary Approach* (Oxford, 1971), 89; Maria Filomena Mónica, *Educação e Sociedade no Portugal de Salazar* (Lisbon, 1978), 179; and Alexander Blok, "The People and the Intelligentsia," in Marc Raeff (ed.), *Russian Intellectual History: An Anthology* (n.p. [Atlantic Highlands, NJ], 1966), 359–63, 363, an essay that was first published in Russia in 1908.

[31] Schwarcz, *The Chinese Enlightenment*, 13.

[32] Christopher Read, *Religion, Revolution and the Russian Intelligentsia, 1900–1912: The Vekhi Debate and its Intellectual Background* (New York, 1979); the essays in Marshall S. Shatz and Judith E. Zimmerman (eds.), *Vekhi (Landmarks): A Collection of Articles about the Russian Intelligentsia* (Armonk, NY, 1994), which were first published in 1909; Sarah G. Moment Atis, "Turkish Literature," in John L. Esposito (ed.), *Oxford Encyclopedia of the Modern Islamic World*, 4 vols. (New York, 1995), vol. 4, 245–54, 250–52; Homa Katouzian, "Nationalist Trends in Iran, 1921–1926," *International Journal of Middle East Studies* 10, 4 (1979), 533–51, 544; Schwarcz, *The Chinese Enlightenment*, 186; and Roger Lévy, *Intellectuels, Unissez-Vous!* (Paris, 1931), 6.

The decline of the intellectuals' collective identity during this period corresponded with their reluctance to pursue constitutionalist movements. In place of collective mobilization for constitutionalism, intellectuals scattered, "looking for new gods."[33] If some intellectuals served in interwar governments, they no longer ruled in their own name but rather in the name of the socialist working class, the nationalist bourgeoisie, or the fascist fatherland, which replaced constitutionalism as prominent themes in the global flow of ideas after the First World War.

Still, some of the achievements of the constitutional revolutions of 1905–1915 endured. Many of the institutions established or expanded as part of the intellectuals' brief tenure remained, including educational reforms, judicial offices, and medical and public health initiatives. In addition, the elections held during this period stood as a reminder in each country that constitutional government was possible – an ideal that broad sectors of the population sought to recover in democratic uprisings later in the twentieth century.

---

[33] Teodor Shanin, *Russia, 1905–07: Revolution as a Moment of Truth* (New York, 1986), 208.

5   The Global Red Revolution

Rachel G. Hoffman

On the evening of September 7, 1920, in his closing speech to the Congress of the Peoples of the East convened in Baku, the chairman of the seventh and final session, Grigorii Zinoviev, proposed a revision to the *Communist Manifesto*. In their tract, published in London in 1848 as revolutions broke out across Europe, Marx and Engels had called, "Workers of all lands, unite!" Now, however, according to Zinoviev, head of the Communist International (Comintern) and one of the seven members of the first Politburo, the global winds of change necessitated a reformation of this political vision. The new doctrine he exclaimed was "Workers of all lands *and oppressed peoples of the whole word, unite!*" Zinoviev's declaration was greeted with "tumultuous applause" and the eruption of the *Internationale* (performed for the sixth though not the last time during the proceedings that day).[1]

Although dominated by speeches from members of the Russian Communist Party, the week-long assembly ostensibly celebrated and united the hopes of the nearly two thousand attendees who represented more than two dozen ethnic backgrounds gathered from across Asia, America, and Europe. An extension of the Comintern, founded in 1919 with the objective of encouraging world revolution, and shortly following the Second Congress of the International, held in Moscow in July and August 1920, the meeting at Baku sought to tie revolutionary radical labor and anti-imperialist movements to the momentum of 1917. The program relayed a declaration of opposition to imperialism and laid the foundations for a united organized global resistance, adopting a "Manifesto of the Congress to the Peoples of the East" and an "Appeal from the Congress of the Peoples of the East to the Workers of Europe, America and Japan."

---

[1] *Congress of the Peoples of the East: Baku, September 1920 (Stenographic Report)* (London, 1977), 145–61 (Seventh Session, September 7), 161, which was first published in Russian in 1920. On the congress, see Stephen White, "Communism and the East: The Baku Congress, 1920," *Slavic Review* 33, 3 (1974), 492–514; John Riddell, *To See the Dawn: Baku, 1920-First Congress of the Peoples of the East* (New York, 1993); and John Sexton, *Alliance of Adversaries: The Congress of the Toilers of the Far East* (Leiden, 2018).

The Russian Revolution of 1917 sent shockwaves across the globe. Stirred by the social, political, and economic turmoil of the First World War, and inspired by the events unfolding in St. Petersburg, revolutionaries across the world took up pens and arms in an effort to overthrow the existing order. At one time or another between 1917 and 1924, the Red flag flew from Glasgow to Budapest, from Berlin, Munich, and Rome to Gilan in North Persia, from the Tuvan People's Republic in southern Siberia to Ulan Bator in Mongolia, and across much of Finland and the Netherlands. As workers and peasants, soldiers and sailors, philosophers and politicians revolted and national communist parties gained in strength and number, Lenin offered encouragement and guidance to their leaders. In fact, Moscow increasingly sought to coordinate this wave of revolutions through the Third International. Still, the socialist upheavals outside the new Soviet state rarely took the form and course that Bolshevik ideologues had envisioned, and most of them were short-lived.

Historians have long shown an interest in the uprisings that occurred in the midst and immediate aftermath of the First World War.[2] They have thereby predominantly examined these revolts within the framework of the nation-states or empires in which they took place. The upheavals have thus for the most part been treated in isolation, as national and imperial historical episodes and explained by peculiar domestic social, political, and economic tensions. Moreover, scholars have explored the uprisings from the perspective of shifting geopolitical conditions. More recently, however, historians, inspired by the rise of transnational and transimperial history, have begun to push beyond the bounds of national and imperial frameworks, and have examined these revolts in the transnational and transimperial context of a regional, largely European, postwar moment. The global history of 1917, however, remains unwritten.

A second historiographical line that has touched upon these revolutions runs through the scholarship on global communism more broadly.[3] Since the 1970s, there has been a sustained interest in Moscow's efforts to help unfurl the Red flag outside the Soviet Union after 1917. Studies have

[2] Robert Gerwarth, *The Vanquished: Why the First World War Failed to End, 1917–1923* (London, 2016) is the most important work in this field. The chapters in Stefan Rinke and Michael Wildt (eds.), *Revolutions and Counter-Revolutions: 1917 and its Aftermath from a Global Perspective* (Frankfurt, 2017) provide a geographically broad account. Jean-François Fayet, "1919," in Stephen A. Smith (ed.), *The Oxford Handbook of the History of Communism* (Oxford, 2014), 109–24, offers a concise overview.

[3] Robert Service, *Comrades: A History of World Communism* (London, 2007), 85–96; David Priestland, *The Red Flag: A History of Communism* (London, 2009), 103–31; and Silvio Pons, *The Global Revolution: A History of International Communism, 1917–1991* (Oxford, 2014), 43–101, provide excellent general accounts.

examined the official Soviet state-funded and state-sanctioned organizations tasked with this venture, most significantly, from 1919 to 1943, the Comintern and, from 1947 to 1956, the Cominform (Information Bureau of the Communist and Workers' Parties). They have also explored the emergence and evolution of communist movements and organizations outside the Soviet Union which were often heavily influenced or even controlled by Moscow. Moreover, historians have looked at the biographies of cosmopolitan, colonial revolutionary figures such as Willi Münzenberg, M. N. Roy, and Ho Chi Minh.[4] Scholarship has focused more and more on the ways in which the activities of these institutions and individuals were limited, restricted not only by the stipulations of diplomatic and trade agreements upon which historians of earlier decades have focused but also by social and political conditions on the ground. We are beginning, more than ever before, to have a more balanced view of the hopes and dreams of the Bolshevik Revolution as well as of the realities and constraints it operated under not only in Europe but also across the globe.

This chapter draws a broader picture of the Red revolutions that took place during and after the First World War. First, taking a comparative perspective, it explores the similarities and differences of these various uprisings. It shows that they were not limited to the shattered empires of Europe but erupted across the colonial world and indeed the globe, arguing that this wave of revolutions can be seen not only through the lens of national or regional conflict, for example a European civil war, but as part of a global struggle and – what's more – as a historical phenomenon, or moment, in its own right (Part I). Second, it examines the connections between these Red revolts. Global structural transformations and events, significantly the First World War and its ramifications, including the dissolution of most major European empires, produced a global power vacuum and led to volatilities and revolutionary situations in various countries at the same time (Part II). Yet it was not just these indirect connections that linked those uprisings: the revolts spilled over

---

[4] Babette Gross, *Willi Münzenberg: A Political Biography* (East Lansing, MI, 1974); Sean McMeekin, *The Red Millionaire: A Political Biography of Willi Münzenberg, Moscow's Secret Propaganda Tsar in the West, 1917–1940* (New Haven, CT, 2004); and, John Green, *Willi Münzenberg: Fighter against Fascism and Stalinism* (London, 2019), on Münzenberg; John Patrick Haithcox, *Communism and Nationalism in India; M. N. Roy and Comintern Policy, 1920–1939* (Princeton, NJ, 1971); S. M. Ganguly, *Leftism in India: M. N. Roy and Indian Politics, 1920–1948* (Columbia, MO, 1984); Samaren Roy, *M. N. Roy: A Political Biography* (New Delhi, 1997); and Kris Manjapra, *M. N. Roy: Marxism and Colonial Cosmopolitanism* (Delhi, 2010), on Roy; and Jean Lacouture, *Ho Chi Minh: A Political Biography* (New York, 1968); William J. Duiker, *Ho Chi Minh: A Life* (New York, 2000); and, most importantly in this context, Sophie Quinn-Judge, *Ho Chi Minh: The Missing Years* (London, 2003), on Ho Chi Minh.

and shaped one another. The third section of the chapter scrutinizes these direct connections. It traces the spread of ideas and the movements of revolutionary actors across state borders, following the Red philosophies and the itinerant revolutionaries who tried to mobilize people across the globe. It shows that insurgents borrowed ideas from the Russian Revolution to justify and popularize their actions but that their campaigns differed from and at times clashed with those of their Bolshevik comrades in Russia. Finally, the chapter reflects on the efforts made by the nascent Soviet institutions and representatives to spread revolution, whether through material or non-material support (Part III). To be sure, while looking at these broader global realities of the revolutions, it is crucial not to ignore that preexisting imperial, national, and local conditions were crucial in shaping the development and form of the individual revolutionary situations. Ultimately, however, no matter how vigorous and victorious these uprisings appeared, counterrevolutionary movements rapidly repressed these revolts. In the end, the Red revolutionary moment was fleeting and far more fragmented than Moscow had hoped.

Landscapes of Revolt

In March 1917, exhausted by the war and disillusioned with the tsar, the army garrisoned at St. Petersburg joined striking workers to force Nicholas II from his throne and pull the empire out of the conflict. Tsarist Russia descended into a state of chaos. While the Provisional Government occupied the vacant seat of power and continued to fight on the Entente side, the German Kaiser, hoping to destabilize the Central Powers' Eastern adversary, helped to smuggle the exiled Bolshevik doctrinaire and agitator Vladimir Lenin back into St. Petersburg, from Switzerland via Germany and Finland.[5] Lenin arrived in disguise, fearing arrest, and stayed incognito in the outskirts of the city. In the following months, the split between the revolutionaries – Mensheviks and Bolsheviks – grew wider. The situation was chaotic. A provisional government struggled to maintain order. On October 25, 1917, the Bolsheviks, led by Trotsky, staged a coup. Soldiers who had joined the city's Soviet took over major buildings, including the train station, telegraph bureaus, and government offices. The poorly defended Winter

---

[5] On the Russian Revolution, see William H. Chamberlin, *The Russian Revolution*, 2 vols. (London, 1935); Sheila Fitzpatrick, *The Russian Revolution* (Oxford, 1982); and Orlando Figes, *A People's Tragedy: The Russian Revolution: 1891–1924* (London, 1996). Catherine Merridale, *Lenin on the Train* (London, 2006), provides a fascinating account of Lenin's return.

Palace was surrounded and then seized. Around 10 o'clock in the morning, Lenin proclaimed the overthrow of the Provisional Government. Moderate socialists, most importantly the Mensheviks, were quickly sidelined, and Lenin swiftly announced a new government. It was a coup within a popular revolution. The ensuing civil war would engulf Russia and its borderlands for years to come.[6] Despite Allied intervention on the side of the loyalist White Armies against the Bolshevik Reds, the collapse of the monarchists in European Russia in 1919/1920 and in Siberia in 1920/1922 marked Lenin's triumph. Moreover, by then the First World War had ended. Great Britain, the Allied nation most heavily involved in giving direct and material assistance to the Whites, had expanded its intervention operations from 1918 to 1919 but liquidated its support in spring 1920.[7] Even though Winston Churchill, then Secretary of State for War, declared to his constituents in Dundee as late as February 1920 that the parliamentary campaign against the Reds continued directly on from the war with Germany, "to crush the Bolshevist peril at its centre," wartime support was now defunct, even as concern over long-term British–Russian rivalry in the Great Game continued.[8]

The events that transpired in Russia in 1917 vibrated across the globe. The red flame cast by Lenin did not go unnoticed: Lenin, as Churchill later reflected, was the "plague bacillus" that had been injected into the Russian body politic at precisely the moment it could do the most harm. The Russian Revolution was followed by a growing number of protests across Europe. Many, often soldiers and workers, started to call for an end to the war, spurred on by the successes of the ongoing experiment in the former Russian Empire.

As the war dragged on, with the situation on the Western Front remaining deadlocked and conditions in the trenches consistently abject, the

---

[6] On Azerbaijan, as an example, see Tadeusz Swietochowski, *Russia and Azerbaijan: A Borderland in Transition* (New York, 1995); Tadeusz Swietochowski, *Russian Azerbaijan, 1905–1920: The Shaping of a National Identity in a Muslim Community* (Cambridge, 2004); Touraj Atabaki, *Azerbaijan: Ethnicity and the Struggle for Power in Iran* (London, 2000); Hovann H. Simonian, *Troubled Waters: The Geopolitics of the Caspian Region* (London, 2003); and Michael G. Smith, "Anatomy of a Rumour: Murder Scandal, the Musavat Party and Narratives of the Russian Revolution in Baku, 1917-20," *Journal of Contemporary History* 36, 2 (2001), 211–40.

[7] James Ramsey Ullman, *Anglo-Soviet Relations, 1917–1921*, 3 vols. (Princeton, NJ, 1968–1972); Stephen White, *Britain and the Bolshevik Revolution: A Study in the Politics of Diplomacy, 1920–1924* (New York, 1979); and Christine A. White, *British and American Commercial Relations with Soviet Russia* (Chapel Hill, NC, 1992).

[8] Churchill to Dundee constituents February 14, 1920, reported in *The Times* (February 16, 1920). John Howes Gleason, *The Genesis of Russophobia in Great Britain. A Study of the Interaction of Policy and Opinion* (London, 1950), provides the context.

situation in the German Empire became increasingly unstable.[9] In the autumn of 1918, workers and sailors went on strike. In Kiel, on November 3, a major mutiny by the sailors of the German High Seas Fleet broke out. Workers' and soldiers' councils were proclaimed. On November 9, 1918, as Kaiser Wilhelm II fled his tottering throne, fearing for his life, protestors flooded the streets of Berlin. Amidst the uprisings now spreading across the continent, governments were reluctant to allow the Kaiser's request for asylum. In the end, Queen Wilhelmina of the Netherlands, a relation of Wilhelm II, reluctantly allowed him entry, though she remained extremely cool toward him throughout his exile. Leftist factions twice proclaimed Germany a republic: Just after 2 o'clock in the afternoon of November 9, the moderate Social Democrat leader Philipp Scheidemann declared a democratic republic from one of the parliament's balconies. Two hours later, speaking from a lorry in the Lustgarten in front of Berlin Palace, the radical revolutionary lawyer Karl Liebknecht, who advocated a communist revolution, declared a soviet republic: "The day of the revolution has come."[10] After his followers had stormed the palace, he addressed the people again, referring to his Russian comrades in solidarity. "The revolution of the German proletariat has begun," Liebknecht cabled the Kremlin.[11] "This revolution will save the Russian revolution from all attack and will sweep away all the foundations of the imperialist world." The Social Democrats formed a new, moderate left-wing, provisional government under Friedrich Ebert. The communists, led by Liebknecht and his Polish comrade Rosa Luxemburg, "Red Rosa," and her partner Leo Jogiches, rallied their followers, organized in the "Spartacus League."[12] Its members met on December 29, 1918, to found the German Communist Party (KPD). Three days later, on January 1, 1919, mass demonstrations

[9] On the German Revolution, see Sebastian Haffner, *Failure of a Revolution: Germany, 1918–19* (New York, 1973); Richard Grunberger, *Red Rising in Bavaria* (London, 1973); Ulrich Kluge, *Die deutsche Revolution 1918/1919* (Frankfurt, 1985); Mark Jones, *Founding Weimar: Violence and the German Revolution of 1918–19* (Cambridge, 2016); and Volker Ulrich, *Die Revolution von 1918/19* (Munich, 2018). On the factory councils, see Peter von Oertzen, *Betriebsräte in der Novemberrevolution* (Bonn, 1976); and Eberhard Kolb, *Die Arbeiterräte in der deutschen Innenpolitik 1918 bis 1919* (Düsseldorf, 1962). On the broader context, see Eric D. Weitz, *Creating German Communism, 1890–1990: From Popular Protests to Socialist State* (Princeton, NJ, 1997).

[10] Harry Schumann, *Karl Liebknecht: Ein unpolitisches Bild seiner Persönlichkeit* (Dresden, 1919), 59.

[11] Ct. in Service, *Comrades*, 86.

[12] On Liebknecht and Luxemburg, see J. P. Nettle, *Rosa Luxemburg*, 2 vols. (Oxford, 1966), which remains the classic on Luxemburg; and Harry Schumann, *Karl Liebknecht: Ein unpolitisches Bild seiner Persönlichkeit* (Dresden, 1919); Heinz Wohlgemuth, *Karl Liebknecht* (Berlin, 1975); and Helmut Trotnow, *Karl Liebknecht, 1871–1919: A Political Biography* (Hamden, CT, 1984), on Liebknecht.

erupted against the Provisional Government in Berlin. The new state reacted ruthlessly. Liebknecht and Luxemburg were captured and killed by right-wing Freikorps militias, and their bodies were dumped near the Zoological Gardens. Jogiches was killed a few months later. In the end, Friedrich Ebert allied with right-wing Freikorps groups against the communist movement.

Around the same time, revolutionaries in Munich began to organize themselves, leading strikes, protest marches, and workers' councils.[13] In early 1919, when a right-wing assassin killed the socialist intellectual and political leader Kurt Eisner, head of the Independent German Social Democratic Party in Bavaria, Munich was engulfed in chaos. On April 7, 1919, led by Max Levien, Munich's communists, who were already organized into workers' councils, announced the founding of the Bavarian Soviet Republic. The Munich revolutionaries were also in contact with their comrades in the Soviet Union. After the establishment of the new republic, Lenin cabled his congratulations. The Munich communists tried from the outset to forge close connections with both Kun's Soviet Hungary and Lenin's Soviet Union. In the end, just like their comrades in Berlin, the Munich revolutionaries were swiftly suppressed by right-wing militias. Many were killed. Levien fled via Vienna to Moscow.

Inspired by events in Russia and Germany, from November 9 to 14, 1918, in the Netherlands socialists initiated a revolt in the so-called "Red Week" or "De Roode Week," also known as "Troelstra's mistake" or "Vergissing van Troelstra," an unsuccessful attempt to start a socialist revolution under the leadership of the Dutch socialist Pieter Jelles Troelstra.

The shattered Habsburg Empire experienced a Red Wave at the same time. In Hungary, where independence was declared on October 17, 1918, the Provisional Government under Count Mihály Károlyi was soon challenged by communist revolutionaries.[14] On March 21, 1919, led by the radical journalist Béla Kun, the revolutionaries seized control.

---

[13] On the Munich Socialist Republic, see Allan Mitchell, *Revolution in Bavaria, 1918–1919: The Eisner Regime and the Soviet Republic* (Princeton, NJ, 1965); Richard Grunberger, *Red Rising in Bavaria* (London 1973); Rosa Leviné-Meyer, *Leviné the Spartacist* (London, 1978); and Michael Seligmann, *Aufstand der Räte: Die erste bayerische Räterepublik vom 7. April 1919*, 2 vols. (Grafenau-Döffingen, 1989). Unique insights are provided by the contributions to Tankred Dorst (ed.), *Die Münchner Räterepublik: Zeugnisse und Kommentar* (Frankfurt, 1966); Karl Bosl (ed.), *Bayern im Umbruch. Die Revolution von 1918, ihre Voraussetzungen, ihr Verlauf und ihre Folgen* (Munich, 1969); and Gerhard Schmolze (ed.), *Revolution und Räterepublik in München 1918/19 in Augenzeugenberichten* (Düsseldorf, 1969).

[14] On the Hungarian Soviet Republic, see Rudolf L. Tokes, *Béla Kun and the Hungarian Soviet Republic: The Origins and Role of the Communist Party of Hungary in the Revolutions of*

The Red flag was hoisted above Budapest's Imperial Palace. As a soldier in the First World War, Béla Kun had been captured by the tsarist army in 1916. Following the October Revolution, he began working with the Bolsheviks and was put in charge of a group of Hungarian communist prisoners of war which was to sow the seeds of revolution in Hungary. One month after the Russian Revolution, they convened in Moscow's Hotel Dresden to found the Hungarian Communist Party. Shortly after, the revolutionaries moved back to Hungary. Once in power, Béla Kun unleashed a wave of repression. The Hungarian communists thereby kept in close contact with Moscow. The Hungarian Soviet Republic was, however, short-lived. In spring 1919, Romanian and Czech forces invaded the country. Kun's Red Army, however, pushed the Czech troops back into Slovakia and soon, in June 1919, declared the Slovak Soviet Republic.[15] (A similar plan to establish a soviet regime in Vienna failed.) The war against Romania was less successful. That summer, Romanian troops occupied Budapest. Across the Hungarian countryside and in the cities unrest broke out. Famine spread. The Red Republic, after only 133 days of existence, was toppled. Kun escaped via Austria to the Soviet Union. Many communists were killed by Romanian troops and by Hungary's new right-wing forces, led by Admiral Miklós Horthy.

In Italy, simmering popular discontent surfaced in violent fashion directly after the war.[16] Widespread hostility toward the government, which had entered the war without the backing of the majority of the country and which, during the conflict, failed to alleviate poor living and working conditions – conditions which further deteriorated as a result of rapid wartime industrialization – erupted in the so-called "Biennio Rosso" or "two Red years" of 1919–1920. The months were characterized by mass strikes and factory occupations, the formation of factory councils, and the expansion of the membership of the trade unions. Its epicenter was northern Italy. But protests extended from the industrialized towns of

---

1918–1919 (New York, 1967); Sándor Szilassy, *Revolutionary Hungary, 1918–1921* (Astor Park, FL, 1971); Tibor Hajdu, *The Hungarian Soviet Republic* (Budapest, 1979); Molnár Miklós, *From Béla Kun to János Kádár: Seventy Years of Hungarian Communism* (New York, 1990); and György Borsányi, *The Life of a Communist Revolutionary, Béla Kun* (Boulder, CO, 1993).

[15] On the Slovak Soviet Republic, see Peter A. Toma, "The Slovak Soviet Republic of 1919," *American Slavic and East European Review* 17, 2 (1958), 203–15.

[16] On communist unrest in Italy, see Stefano Caretti, *La rivoluzione russa e il socialismo italiano (1917–1921)* (Pisa, 1974); Giuseppe Maione, *Il biennio rosso: Autonomia e spontaneità operaia nel 1919–1920* (Bologna, 1975); Roberto Bianchi, *Pace, pane, terra: Il 1919 in Italia* (Rome, 2006); and Fabio Fabbri, *Le origini della guerra civile: L'Italia dalla Grande Guerra al Fascismo, 1918–1921* (Turin, 2009); and Nives Banin, *Il biennio rosso 1919–1920* (Arezzo, 2013). Giovanna Procacci, "Popular Protest and Labour Conflict in Italy, 1915-18," *Social History* 14, 1 (1989), 31–58, on the roots.

Turin and Milan to the agricultural plains of Padan, where armed skirmishes between peasants and landlords, and left- and right-wing militias, regularly took place. At the forefront of the movement was the Sardinian revolutionary Antonio Gramsci, who edited the Turin paper *L'Ordine Nuovo* (*The New Order*) and hoped that the factory councils would merge into a new soviet state.[17] Yet they were too disorganized to form a strong centralized movement. Right-wing militias soon gained the upper hand; a socialist republic was never declared. The situation was similar in the "Trieno Bolchevista" in Spain.[18]

A revolutionary situation had already emerged before the end of the war in Ireland, from 1917 to 1923. Suffering from economic want and let down by the British Empire, the working class went on the offensive, with an average of 200 strikes and lockouts each year; landless laborers and small farmers followed the lead of workers.[19] On April 15, 1919, revolutionaries declared the Limerick Soviet, which existed for less than two weeks.

So too in Scotland, where widespread abject poverty and poor working conditions had regularly been expressed in labor and later antiwar rallies led by leftist radicals since the 1910s, with these events referred to in the popular press as the activities of the "Red Clydeside."[20] At the close of the war, the combination of mass unemployment, the discharge of soldiers, and the dismantling of the formerly busy shipbuilding yards at Glasgow, brought feelings to breaking point. Notoriously, at the height of the disturbances, activists spilled onto George Square in Glasgow's city center to clash with troops and tanks sent from England, with newspapers

---

[17] On Gramsci, see Giuseppe Fiori, *Vita di Antonio Gramsci* (Bari, 1966); John McKay Cammett, *Antonio Gramsci and the Origins of Italian Communism* (Stanford, 1967); James Joll, *Antonio Gramsci* (New York, 1977); and Alastair Davidson, *Antonio Gramsci: Towards an Intellectual Biography* (London, 1977). On his thoughts about the factory councils, see Antonio Gramsci, "Unions and Councils," *L'Ordine Nuovo* (25 October 1919), in Antonio Gramsci, *Selections from the Prison Notebooks of Antonio Gramsci* (London, 1971), 98–108.

[18] Ángeles Barrio Alonso, *La modernización de España (1917–1939): Política y sociedad* (Madrid, 2004).

[19] On revolutionary Ireland and the Limerick Soviet, see Conor Kostick, *Revolution in Ireland: Popular Militancy 1917 to 1923* (Cork, 2009); and Liam Cahill, *Forgotten Revolution: Limerick Soviet 1919: A Threat To British Power in Ireland* (Dublin, 1990).

[20] On revolutionary Scotland, see Ian MacLean, *The Legend of Red Clydeside* (Edinburgh, 1983); Joseph Melling, "Whatever Happened to Red Clydeside?," *International Review of Social History* 35, 1 (1990), 3–32; and Jacqueline Jenkinson, "Black Sailors on Red Clydeside: Rioting, Reactionary Trade Unionism and Conflicting Notions of 'Britishness' following the First World War," *Twentieth Century British History* 19, 1 (2008), 29–60, as well as the contributions to Robert Duncan and Arthur McIvor (eds.), *Militant Workers: Labour and Class Conflict on the Clyde 1900–1950* (Edinburgh, 1992). An insightful primary source is William Gallacher, *Revolt on the Clyde: An Autobiography* (London, 1936).

capturing the images of disgruntled citizens waving the Red flag on high. Among the revolutionaries were workers and demobilized soldiers in the Red Clydeside who reacted to intransigent government and industrial policies. On January 21, 1919, tens of thousands gathered in a massive rally, organized by the trade unions, which took place in George Square. Though the uprisings that broke out at the beginning of 1919 enjoyed no material support from Moscow, the ideological connections were clear to everyone. "It is," declared Robert Munro, Secretary of State for Scotland, "a misnomer to call the situation in Glasgow a Strike – this is a Bolshevist uprising."[21]

In the case of Finland, the 1917 Revolution in Russia opened a power vacuum and made space for claims to independence for the lands which had long been ruled first by the Swedes and later by the Russians.[22] The decades of "Russification" had provoked deep-seated anti-Russian attitudes and – when the Tsarist Empire collapsed – helped to fuel the nationalist White Finns in their struggle for national independence against the minority of Reds who favored Soviet annexation. While Finland had declared its independence from the Grand Duchy rule of Tsarist Russia as early as 1917, the engagement of Red troops in the civil war in Russia helped the Whites to gain the upper hand during the spring of 1918, and finally victory in the form of independence.

Elsewhere on the borderlands of the decaying Tsarist Empire, in Mongolia, the revolution in Russia seemed to offer the potential for the final purge of Chinese rule.[23] In fact, it was the Tsarist Empire that the Mongolians had called upon only a few years earlier, in 1911, to exorcise Chinese control completely. In the summer of 1924, the Red Army occupied Mongolia, and the Mongolian People's Republic was declared, an oppressive satellite state.

In Persia, just when the country seemed to have wiggled its way out from under the twin thumbs of Tsarist Russia and imperial Britain, the setbacks of the recent constitutional gains of the early 1900s appeared to collapse under the Anglo-Persian Treaty of 1919, which fueled

---

[21] Ct. in Jenkinson, *Black 1919: Riots, Racism and Resistance in Imperial Britain* (Liverpool, 2009), 42.

[22] On the Finnish civil war, see Anthony F. Upton, *The Finnish Revolution 1917–1918* (Minneapolis, 1980); Risto Alapuro, *State and Revolution in Finland* (Berkeley, CA,1988); and Pertti Haapala and Marko Tikka, "Revolution, Civil War and Terror in Finland in 1918," in Robert Gerwarth and John Horne (eds.), *War in Peace: Paramilitary Violence in Europe after the Great War* (Oxford, 2013),72–84; as well as the contributions in Tuomas Tepora and Aapo Roselius (eds.), *The Finnish Civil War 1918: History, Memory, Legacy* (Leiden, 2014).

[23] On the Mongolian People's Republic, see George G. S. Murphy, *Soviet Mongolia: A Study of the Oldest Political Satellite* (Berkeley, CA, 1966).

revolutionary activism.[24] The fleeting Persian Socialist Soviet Republic in Gilan, which lasted from June 1920 to September 1921, was an attempt to establish socialist modernity in the country. Its leader, the charismatic revolutionary Mirza Kuchik Khan, had already rallied his Jungle Movement (*Nehzat-i Jangal*) at the beginning of the First World War. The rebels made ample use of Bolshevik ideals and symbols. The short-lived victory of the revolutionaries is often explained by the fact that they had relied upon Anglo-Soviet antagonism in exchange for support from Russia; when this antagonism ceased in 1921 with the Anglo-Russian Trade Agreement and an informal "truce" in the region, Gilan fell. Soon, however, government forces under Reza Khan, who would become the first Pahlavi shah of Iran, smashed the movement.

In London, British politicians considered a possible Allied intervention in the Russian Civil War in the context of the longer-term Anglo-Russian rivalry in the Middle East and South Asia. The revolution, it was feared, could spread from Armenia, Turkestan, and Persia to Afghanistan and India. Even when the war turned in favor of the Whites in 1919, with General Denikin's successes, the fact that Bolshevik emissaries from Afghanistan and Bukhara entered into negotiations with Lenin in Moscow provoked British concerns about the stability in Central Asia. British interests in ensuring that the Soviets did not interfere in India or Afghanistan were spelled out unambiguously in the 1921 Anglo-Soviet Trade Agreement that prohibited propaganda outside of national territories and identified specific regions by name as off-limits.[25]

Still, the Russian Revolution was also felt in the colonial world. Throughout the early 1920s, anticolonial revolutionaries from West Africa to Southeast Asia turned to the Soviet Union as a model. Among them was the Indochinese rebel Nguyen Tat Thanh, later known as Ho Chi Minh ("He Who Enlightens"), who had initially put his hopes in Wilsonian liberalism but after the disappointments of Versailles had turned to Lenin and founded the Indochinese Communist Party in

---

[24] On the Soviet Republic of Iran, see Schapour Ravasani, *Sowjetrepublik Gilan: Die sozialistische Bewegung im Iran seit Ende des 19. Jh. bis 1922* (Berlin, 1973); Ibrahim Fakhrayi, *Sardar-i Jangal (The Commander of the Jungle)* (Tehran, 1362 [1983]); and Cosroe Chaqueri, *The Soviet Socialist Republic of Iran, 1920–21* (Pittsburgh, PA, 1994); and Oliver Bast, "Duping the British and Outwitting the Russians? Iran's Foreign Policy, the 'Bolshevik Threat', and the Genesis of the Soviet-Iranian Treaty of 1921" in Stephanie Cronin (ed.), *Iranian-Russian Encounters: Empires and Revolutions since 1800* (London, 2013), 261–297. For the Russian side, see Mikhail Volodarsky, *The Soviet Union and Its Southern Neighbours: Iran and Afghanistan, 1917–1933* (London, 1994), 32–52.

[25] James Ramsey Ullman, *Anglo-Soviet Relations, 1917–1921*, 3 vols. (Princeton, NJ, 1968–1972), vol. 3 (*The Anglo-Soviet Accord*), 474–8, provides the text.

1930.[26] Impressed by Lenin's *Theses on National and Colonial Questions* of 1920, he believed that socialism and national independence could be achieved in the same fight.[27]

Further east, in China, the May Fourth Movement, which swept across the country in the aftermath of the First World War, as protestors demanded an end to foreign intrusion, became the cradle of China's communist movement.[28] Also disillusioned with Woodrow Wilson's liberal promises of national self-determination, which had initially sparked hope, Chinese revolutionaries turned to the Soviet Union as a model. Among them were Chen Duxiu, head of humanities at Peking University, and Li Dazhao, librarian at Peking University, who in the summer of 1921 founded the Chinese Communist Party in Shanghai and received practical help from Lenin's Comintern official Grigorii Voitinskii.[29] Li in particular significantly influenced the young Mao Zedong, who in 1918 became his assistant librarian. Mao, who felt betrayed by the postwar settlement, pleaded in summer 1919, in an article in his *Xiang River Review*, to follow the model of the "Russian extremist party."[30]

Outside Europe, even in the United States the repercussions of the revolutionary wave were felt.[31] In 1919, the Communist Party of America and the Communist Labor Party were established, both of them pro-Soviet. Yet Washington ruthlessly persecuted these radicals during these years of the "Red Scare."[32] It soon became clear that America was not about to turn communist.

[26] Lacouture, *Ho Chi Minh*; Duiker, *Ho Chi Minh*; and Quinn-Judge, *Ho Chi Minh*.

[27] Ho Chi Minh, *On Revolution: Selected Writings 1920–1966* (London, 1967), 5.

[28] Erez Manela's chapter in this volume provides the context. On the May Fourth Movement, see Tse-Tsung Chow, *The May Fourth Movement: Intellectual Revolution in Modern China* (Cambridge, MA, 1960); Vera Schwarcz, *The Chinese Enlightenment: Intellectuals and the Legacy of the May Fourth Movement of 1919* (Berkeley, CA, 1986).

[29] Lee Feigon, *Chen Duxiu: Founder of the Chinese Communist Party* (Princeton, NJ, 1983); Maurice Meisner, *Li Ta-Chao and the Origins of Chinese Marxism* (New York, 1970); and Philip Short, *Mao: A Life* (London, 1999).

[30] Mao Zedong, "Study the Extremist Party" (July 14, 1919), cited in Stuart R. Schram (ed.), *Mao's Road to Power: Revolutionary Writings, 1912–1949*, 10 vols. (Armonk, NY, 1992–), vol. 1 (*The Pre-Marxist Period, 1912–1920*), 332.

[31] On communism in the United States, see Theodore Draper, *The Roots of American Communism* (New York, 1957); Theodore Draper, *American Communism and Soviet Russia: The Formative Period* (New York, 1960); Irving Howe and Lewis Coser, *The American Communist Party: A Critical History* (Boston, 1957); Harvey E. Klehr, *Communist Cadre: The Social Background of the American Communist Party Elite* (Stanford, 1978); Harvey Klehr and John Earl Haynes, *The American Communist Movement: Storming Heaven Itself* (New York, 1992); Harvey Klehr, John Earl Haynes, and Fridrikh Igorevich Firsov, *The Secret World of American Communism* (New Haven, CT, 1995); and Jacob A. Zumoff, *The Communist International and US Communism, 1919–1929* (Leiden, 2014).

[32] William Preston, *Aliens and Dissenters: Federal Suppression of Radicals, 1903–1933* (Cambridge, MA, 1963), 118–50.

Aside from occurring around about the same time, what did these events have in common, and what were the differences? Geographically, they broke out on the Soviet Union's borders and within Russia's traditional spheres of influence – in Finland, northern Persia, southern Siberia, and Mongolia – as well as further afield in Scotland, the Netherlands, Italy, and in the former German and Austro-Hungarian empires. Each local uprising had its own local "Lenin," as it were, to lead the revolution: Mirza Kuchik Khan in Persia, Bogd Khan in Mongolia, Béla Kun in Hungary, and so on.

The revolts were also shaped by each country's specific social, economic, and political circumstances. In all cases, political and socioeconomic grievances were thereby interwoven. In Ireland, from 1917 to 1923 the Irish working class went on the offensive, while landless laborers and small farmers followed their lead. In Scotland, poverty and poor working conditions combined with unemployment, exacerbated by the demobilization of soldiers and the decline of the formerly busy shipbuilding yards at Glasgow. In Persia, the uprising followed the setbacks of the recent constitutional gains of the early 1900s; and just when the country seemed to have struggled free from the influence of Tsarist Russia and imperial Britain, the final blow came in the form of the Anglo-Persian Treaty of 1919, fueling revolutionary activism. In Mongolia, the revolution in Russia appeared to signal the potential for the final purge of Chinese rule – it was the rulers in Russia on whom the Mongolians had called only a few years earlier (in 1911) to get rid of the Chinese. In Italy, inflation and unemployment were aggravated by mass demobilization, while trade union activism helped to swell the numbers of the anarchist movements. In Finland, the collapse of the Tsarist Empire provided a space for national hopes to be realized.

There were, however, significant differences between these movements. Those in Hungary and Germany, for instance, were smashed by strong, right-wing paramilitary forces. In Italy, on the other hand, communists did not manage to take over state organs. Those in Persia and Mongolia were similar to one another in that they were united by antagonism to domestic rule and imperial forces: In Persia, the authoritarianism of the shah as well as British and tsarist influence mixed with postwar anarchy and a power vacuum; in Mongolia, there was the potential return of Chinese occupation. These factors helped to unify resistance fighters and groups in Persia and Mongolia, with some success. Yet this success was dependent on the direct intervention of Russia and unity among the revolutionaries: The Soviet Republic in Gilan fell when the Soviets weighed up their potential material losses with regard to trade agreements with Britain against the gains of ideological victory in Persia. There was also a lack of cohesion among the Gilan revolutionaries, split as they were by the question about the part that religion should play in the new republic, the socioeconomic role of feudalism, and their inability to decide on common goals. In contrast, Mongolia was united by Buddhism and against China – it was the era of Bogd Khan.

Global Revolutionary Volatilities

The revolutionary situations in these different parts of the world were the result of global structural transformations, predominantly wars and the fall of empires, which resulted in volatile political situations that destabilized different parts of the world in a similar way.

The most important destabilizing event that lay behind all of these revolutionary situations was the First World War. The wartime burdens resulted in social and political discontent, particularly as a consequence of the depressed economic conditions that the demobilized troops faced when they returned home. Moreover, the last years of the First World War witnessed the dramatic collapse of the social, economic, and political orders around the world.

Equally important, the war left the continental European empires shattered and Europe's colonial overseas possessions destabilized. With the exception of imperial rivalries and minor skirmishes, the world of the nineteenth century, dominated by the European empires, had been relatively peaceful. However, under the pressures of the Great War, these empires now came crashing down. The dissolution of existing imperial landscapes created political volatility across the European continent and beyond.

Moreover, the events of the October Revolution itself had an impact on revolutionaries around the world. The collapse of the Tsarist Empire shook surrounding regions, leaving massive power vacuums. And soon, the apparent successes of the experiment in Russia further invigorated socialist movements beyond the new Soviet Union's borders.

Finally, all revolutions were connected by a global shift in the political zeitgeist. Though leftist political radicals had rallied from the 1910s, political militancy peaked between 1917 and 1921. Over the previous decades since the nineteenth-century Restoration, socialist ideas had increasingly gained traction in Europe and beyond. They were fueled by growing poverty, an expanding working class, and pressing social injustice. This led, despite the lack of ideological cohesion, to a vast transnational intellectual current which lay behind the Red revolutionary wave of 1917–1921. At the same time, ironically, this had led to a Red scare, in which rulers and politicians frequently envisioned a red column, connecting and imagining the uprisings as a single, unified surge. State and police officials, politicians, journalists, and political writers, and the public in general, had frequently explained events by focusing on their potential to spread, often using metaphors of contagion.

At the same time, the authoritarian monarchist style of rule had gradually been declining since the late seventeenth and eighteenth centuries, while popular political movements had challenged the old political foundations of the relationship between state and society, rulers and ruled, for decades. Inspired by ideas of popular sovereignty, social change, and mass political participation, fueled by local grievances, and given substantive content by modern ideologies such as liberalism, nationalism, socialism, anarchism, and religious revivalism, these groups had challenged the existing social and political order. As the nineteenth century progressed, these movements spread, equipped with the technological innovation of mass printing and rising rates of literacy, and spurred on by the effects of the dismantling of the institution of serfdom and education, warfare, mobility, urbanization, and industrialization. The individuals and the groups they represented, as well as the ideas and principles they advocated and promulgated, matured and pollinated, crossing villages and oceans, nation-states, and empires. Across the global political landscape, mass popular politics was born.

Revolutionary Connections

The direct links that connected these revolts were manifold. The spread of ideas was vital. Revolutionaries and ordinary people caught in the crosshairs of social, political, and economic pressures across the globe borrowed ideas from the Russian Revolution to justify and popularize their actions, even though the campaigns differed from and at times clashed with those endorsed by Moscow. To be sure, in the revolutionary situations themselves it was often rhetoric and slogans, rather than bodies of thought, that were crucial. Yet, most of the revolutionary leaders were influenced by Lenin's political slogans and strategies, which seemed to succeed. More generally, socialist ideas, originating in Western Europe, had since the second half of the nineteenth century spread across the continent and beyond. Crucial here were often radical exile communities of intellectuals and political dissidents. The global socialist revolutionary discourse had, in fact, from the outset been transnational and transimperial.

Moreover, roaming itinerant Bolsheviks, on the other side, drove and propagated Red revolutions across borders. Some of them were truly global figures. Among them was Indian radical Narendra Nath

Bhattacharya, who became world famous as M. N. Roy.[33] Roy had joined
an anticolonial resistance group in Bengal before the First World War. In
1915 he was forced to escape India, moving via the Dutch East Indies,
Japan, and China to the United States. He then moved on to Mexico,
where he saw from afar the Russian October Revolution. It was this
momentum that turned him into a socialist, influenced by the Russian
Comintern internationalist Mikhail Borodin. In Mexico, in late 1917, he
cofounded the Mexican Communist Party. He then moved back to
revolutionary Europe in 1919. In Berlin he witnessed the collapse of the
revolution. With his hopes for a communist Europe shattered, he concentrated on exporting it into the colonial world. Roy went to Moscow,
where he met Lenin and became a key figure in the new regime's schemes
to export the revolution. Lenin entrusted Roy to prepare Asia – especially
India – for revolution. In October 1920 he formed the Communist Party
of India, seeking to sway contemporaries who were deciding between
radicalism and Gandhi's program. In 1922, when in Moscow, he published his major political reflections, *India in Transition*, which was almost
simultaneously translated into numerous languages and spread across the
globe. Roy's role in global revolution continued later on, too, in his
capacity as a delegate to the congresses of the Communist International
and as the Soviet Union's aide to China.

Another prominent example is Ho Chi Minh. Having traveled abroad
to France, the United States, and the United Kingdom, at Versailles he
helped to petition for recognition of the civil rights of the Vietnamese
people in French Indochina, and thereafter became a symbol of the anticolonial movement in Vietnam.[34] Delivering fiery speeches on the prospects of
Bolshevism in Asia, he went on to become a representative to the Congress of
Tours of the Socialist Party of France and was a founding member of the
French Communist Party. He used his communist connections in France to
draw his comrades' attention toward the oppressed people in the French
colonies, including Indochina, and wrote journal articles and short
stories to spread the word. In 1921, he left Paris for Moscow, where
he was employed by the Comintern, studied at the Communist
University of the Toilers of the East, and participated in the Fifth
Comintern Congress in June 1924, later organizing "Youth
Education Classes" in Vietnam. When Chiang Kai-shek's 1927 anti-
sommunist coup came, Ho Chi Minh fled Canton for Moscow and
later went on to lead the Vietnamese independence movement.

[33] Haithcox, *Communism and Nationalism in India*; Ganguly, *Leftism in India*; Roy, *M. N. Roy*; and Manjapra, *M. N. Roy*. For his own account, see M. N. Roy, *Memoirs* (Bombay, 1964).
[34] Lacouture, *Ho Chi Minh*; Duiker, *Ho Chi Minh*; and Quinn-Judge, *Ho Chi Minh*.

Another legendary itinerant revolutionary of the time was known as "Williams," or "Mikhailov," among other names. In 1922 Moscow had despatched him to Berlin to support revolutionary activities there.[35] A year later he was in Hamburg during the failed uprising. In 1924 he moved to Paris to foment a revolution there, and in 1926 traveled to Great Britain, before returning to Germany. He then left Europe for India to stir up an anticolonial revolution but was briefly imprisoned by the British authorities. In 1930 he went to Latin America, engaging in subversive activities in Argentina and Chile. "Williams" later became the press officer of the Soviet embassy in Paris. These three itinerant revolutionaries had one thing in common – their connection to Moscow.

The most important power connecting these revolutionary movements was the newly founded Soviet Union. The new rulers in Moscow from the beginning made efforts on exporting the revolution, spreading ideas and slogans across the world, sending advisors, weapons, and money into revolutionary hotbeds abroad, and convening international congresses to bring together the revolutionaries of the world. They sent advisors, literature, and cash to places as far away as Germany and Gilan. Communist leaders like Béla Kun in Budapest, Max Levien in Munich, and Karl Liebknecht in Berlin were in close contact.

At the heart of this network was the Third "Communist" International – the Comintern – formed in Moscow in spring 1919.[36] Its headquarters in central Moscow, an impressive building designed by Vladimir Tatlin, became a hub of international revolutionary activism. Its aim was to support the foundation of communist parties around the world and to export violent revolution. The Comintern was inaugurated at a congress in March 1919, bringing together fifty-two delegates from twenty-five countries. "Comrades, our gathering has great historic significance," Lenin declared in his opening remarks: "It testifies to the collapse of all the illusions cherished by bourgeois democrats. Not only in Russia, but in the most developed capitalist countries of Europe, Germany for example, civil war is a fact."[37] The second Comintern congress, convened in the summer of 1920, would establish a stricter framework of international revolutionary communism controlled by Moscow, adopting "Twenty-One Conditions," which all parties had to fulfill (Figure 5.1).

---

[35] Service, *Comrades*, 110–11.

[36] On the Comintern, see Pons, *The Global Revolution*, 43–101. Steven G. Marks, *How Russia Shaped the Modern World* (Princeton, NJ, 2002), 275–332, provides a brilliant more general overview of the Russian revolutionaries' influences on the world.

[37] Ct. in John Riddell (ed.), *Founding the Communist International: Proceedings and Documents of the First Congress, March 1919* (New York, 1987), 47–50 ("Opening Remarks"), 47.

Figure 5.1 Cover of the English-language edition of *The Communist International*, October 1919. (Public Domain)

The Comintern's major aim was spreading the revolution in Europe. The supply of agents, money, and materiel to Europe's revolutionary hotbeds became an important part of its activities. Often its emissaries used jewelry and diamonds, rather than paper money, which were easier to smuggle across borders, and sold them in the country of destination, receiving cash in the local currency.[38] Soon, revolutionaries from across Europe flocked to the world's new communist capital to receive training and instructions. Many stayed at the legendary (and legendarily run-down) Hotel Lux in central Moscow.[39] It housed some of the greatest radicals of the time, such as Yugoslavia's Tito, Bulgaria's Georgi Dimitrov, Germany's Walter Ulbricht, Italy's Palmiro Togliatti, and America's Earl Browder. Later, Moscow would also train foreign European revolutionaries at its International Lenin School for Western Communists, which was established in 1926.[40] The Comintern's Willi Münzenberg, a German revolutionary who had worked with Lenin since their time in Swiss exile during the First World War, was despatched to Europe to support revolutionary movements across the continent.

Beyond Europe, the Comintern soon also targeted the colonial world.[41] In 1920, as discussed in the beginning of this chapter, it convened the Congress of the Peoples of the East in Baku, bringing together revolutionaries of thirty-seven nationalities.[42] In his introductory address, the organization's head, Grigorii Zinoviev, explained clearly why the Russian revolutionaries recognized that their struggle was only a small part of a wider effort and that the Russian Revolution could not succeed unless it was part of a much broader movement: "We want to put an end to the rule of capital everywhere in the world. And this will become possible only when we have lit the fire of revolution not merely in Europe and America but throughout the world, and when all the working people of Asia and Africa march with us."[43] Tom Quelch, representing the British Socialist Party, referred to Karl Marx's statement that the British proletariat would only be free when Britain's colonial subjects

---

[38] Service, *Comrades*, 110.

[39] Ruth von Mayenburg, *Hotel Lux* (Munich, 1978); and, for a fascinating primary source, Waltraut Schälike, "Ich wollte keine Deutsche sein': Berlin-Wedding – Hotel Lux" (Berlin, 2006).

[40] Branko Lazitch, "Les Écoles de Cadres du Comintern," in Jacques Freymond (ed.), *Contributions à l'histoire du Comintern* (Geneva, 1965), 233–57; Leonid Babitschenko, "Die Kaderschulung der Komintern," *Jahrbuch für historische Kommunismusforschung* (1993), 37–59.

[41] On the Comintern's activities in the colonial world, see Stephen White, "Colonial Revolution and the Communist International, 1919–1924," *Science and Society* 40, 2 (1976), 173–93; Stephen White, "Soviet Russia and the Asian Revolution, 1917-1924," *Review of International Studies* 10, 3 (1984), 219–32; Ronald Grigor Suny, "'Don't Paint Nationalism Red': Nationalist Revolution and Socialist Anti-Imperialism," in Prasenjit Duara (ed.), *Decolonization: Perspectives from Now and Then* (New York, 2003), 176–98; Frederik Petersson, "Imperialism and the Communist International," *Journal of Labor and Society* 20, 1 (2017), 23–42; and Oleksa Drachewych, *The Communist International, Anti-Imperialism and Racial Equality in British Dominions* (London, 2018).

[42] On the Baku congress, see White, "Communism and the East"; Riddell, *To See the Dawn*; and Sexton, *Alliance of Adversaries*.

[43] Ct. in Riddell, *To See the Dawn*, 50.

were free and that, therefore, the enemy of the British working class, the British capitalists, was the enemy of the oppressed peoples of the East.[44] Revolution in the colonial world, it was believed, would not only bring freedom and socialism to the working peoples of these countries but also destabilize the European imperial centers. Conflict within the anticolonial international emerged about whether the communists should forge a temporary alliance with bourgeois anticolonial nationalists. Soon, the Bolsheviks also opened an educational institution, the Communist University of the Toilers of the East, in Moscow, which enrolled student cohorts of 1,500–2,000, among them were Ho Chi Minh and Deng Xiaoping. In the end, however, it took a few more years before serious communist movements emerged across the colonial world. Overall, the Comintern's structures would persist and expand long after the revolutionary wave of 1917–1921 had ebbed.

In each case, revolutionaries across the world sought to take advantage of the unfolding situation, domestically and internationally, by allying their movements with Lenin and Trotsky's call for global revolution. At the same time, Lenin and his Soviet comrades attempted to manipulate the situation to the advantage of the new Soviet state, seeking material gains (in the form of trade agreements, for instance), as well as "soft" power and influence. These efforts were made to ensure formal and informal recognition of communist parties and revolutionary gains abroad – recognition that at the same time cemented and celebrated the new Soviet state as the leader of a political and ideological revolution. There was also a knock-on effect, so to say, among revolutions outside of the Soviet Union. So, for example, when the Tuvan People's Republic declared itself an independent Communist entity, it was the Soviet Union and the newly founded Mongolian People's Republic that officially recognized it. In the end, however, Soviet Russia's role in supporting some revolutions with arms and others with rhetoric drastically shaped events.

Concluding Thoughts

In the end, the revolutionary waves were met with strong resistance. The bloodshed was worst in Russia itself. In the civil war between royalists and communists, between seven and twelve million lost their lives. Many soldiers and civilians – estimates range between one and one and a half million – were forced to flee the country, scattered around the globe, from Berlin to Belgrade, from Paris to Riga, from New York City

---

[44] Ct. in Riddell, *To See the Dawn*, 116.

to Prague, from São Paulo to Shanghai, from Constantinople to Warsaw, from Tunis to London.[45]

Outside Russia, communist movements were soon quashed by right-wing paramilitary surges. In Hungary, Béla Kun's state was eliminated in the summer of 1919. On November 16, 1919, the victorious Miklós Horthy entered Budapest, establishing a conservative right-wing regime. In Germany, from Berlin to Bavaria, the right-wing paramilitary Freikorps, endorsed by the government, used massive violence to put down the revolt. In Italy, the Red years ended with the takeover by Benito Mussolini's fascists. In Iran, too, the revolutionaries were soon suppressed by the newly established regime of Reza Shah. Across the colonial world, the nascent communist movements stood little chance against the military might of the European empires. In the end, outside Russia, communists failed to secure power permanently in the years of upheaval between 1917 and 1921. The reasons for the ebbing of the revolutionary wave were manifold. Repression by right-wing militants was crucial. Yet, there were other reasons, including the sectarianism within the communist movements in each country and their failure to pragmatically organize revolts and new regimes. Finally, in the early 1920s, as the Soviet Union sought to build relationships with countries across Europe, from Britain to Poland, Lenin became less and less enthusiastic about exporting revolution.[46]

This chapter has provided a sketch of what we might view as the global moment of the Russian Revolution: a series of uprisings, shaped by domestic social and political conditions, but nevertheless influenced by common intellectual, social, political, economic, and geopolitical experiences and exchanges. These uprisings were not limited to the vanquished or the collapsed empires of Europe, but they were affected by their relationship with the international realm, the great balance of power regionally and globally: with Mongolia, the split between China to the East and Russia to the West; with Persia, between the British and the

---

[45] M. Osharov, "To Alien Shores: The 1922 Expulsion of Intellectuals from the Soviet Union," *Russian Review* 32, 3 (1973), 294–98; Marc Raeff, *Russia Abroad: A Cultural History of the Russian Emigration, 1919–1939* (Oxford, 1990); James E. Hassell, "Russian Refugees in France and the United States between the World Wars," *Transactions of the American Philosophical Society* 81, 7 (1991), 1–96; Zdeněk Sládek, "Prag: Das 'russische Oxford'," in Karl Schlögel (ed.), *Der große Exodus: Die russische Emigration und ihre Zentren 1917 bis 1941* (Munich, 1994), 218–33; Lesley Chamberlain, *The Philosophy Steamer: Lenin and the Exile of the Intelligentsia* (London, 2006); and Rachel G. Hoffman, Russian Émigrés in London, 1917–1928 (MPhil dissertation, University of Cambridge, 2008), provide accounts of these refugee streams.

[46] Ullman, *Anglo-Soviet Relations, 1917–1921*; White, *Britain and the Bolshevik Revolution*; and White, *British and American Commercial Relations with Soviet Russia*.

Russians. Other territories were directly affected by their borders with the Soviet Union.

The revolutions were structurally connected through the global political, social, and economic instability which undermined states and societies in the aftermath of the First World War and through the shattering of Europe's vast continental empires. It was these general, global shocks which, often together with preexisting domestic circumstances, led to – and connected – the outbreak of unrest. Moreover, the communist uprisings that followed the First World War were directly linked, through "spill-over" effects, both physically – in terms of connections among each other and direct Soviet military support – and ideologically. Revolutionaries around the world borrowed ideas from the Russian Revolution to justify and popularize their actions; but their campaigns also differed from and at times clashed with those endorsed by Moscow. The Bolsheviks appeared to be successful in the years after 1917. Further research will help us to disentangle this turn to the revolutionary left. It was a turn to something new, something that went against the old order, something that fought – from afar – against the Tsarist White Armies and the capitalist great European powers that supported them – this may make some sense. This moment of transition appears to have been a global political one that placed its bets on the novel, the Bolshevik. This was Lenin's moment.

6 The Wilsonian Uprisings of 1919

Erez Manela

Among the hundreds of petitions and memoranda submitted before the Paris Peace Conference in 1919 was a fifteen-page document entitled *Memorandum on the Claims of the Kurd People*. Its author, Sherif Pasha, had been a high-ranking Ottoman diplomat, serving for a time as Istanbul's ambassador to Sweden, but he later broke with the Young Turks, criticized the wartime killings of Armenians by Ottoman forces, and by the war's end had joined the Society for the Rise of Kurdistan, a Kurdish nationalist organization dedicated to the establishment of an independent Kurdish state in eastern Anatolia. Addressed to the world leaders in Paris who had taken on "the task of remapping the globe on the basis of nationality," the memorandum delineated in great detail the geographic boundaries and demographic character of the territories it claimed for the future Kurdish state and cited Western scholarly authorities on the history and ethnography of the region to support its assertions. It concluded that by "virtue of the Wilsonian principale [*sic*] everything pleads in favour of the Kurds for the creation of a Kurd state, entirely free and independent." The Turkish government having accepted President Wilson's Fourteen Points, they could not deny Kurds that right.[1]

The year 1919 is now remembered primarily as the year in which peace was restored to Europe following the cataclysm of the Great War. But the peace, as recent scholarship has emphasized, was only partial, and major fighting continued in much of Europe and the Middle East well into the 1920s. The Bolshevik revolutionaries in Russia, fighting for the survival of their regime against opposition from within and without, inspired numerous uprisings in East and Central Europe, notably in Germany and Hungary. Across the territories of the collapsed empires of the Habsburgs, Romanovs, Hohenzollerns, and Ottomans, competing

---

[1] Sherif Pasha, *Memorandum on the Claims of the Kurd People* (Paris, 1919). To the arguments from demography and history Sherif added an economic one, noting the "national wealth of the Kurds being almost entirely derived from cattle-raising which requires, on account of the climate, Winter and Summer pastures, we urgently request that these pastures shall not remain outside the frontiers assigned to Kurdistan."

claimants struggled for power, legitimacy, and recognition through a combination of diplomatic negotiations centered on Paris and bloody military clashes on the ground.[2] Out of the ashes of these fallen empires, new nation-states were emerging to stake their claim to sovereignty and self-determination.[3]

The upheavals of this era, however, were not limited to Europe or Anatolia, even if it was in those places that they were the bloodiest. In North Africa, Egyptians rose in revolt against British control and Tunisian protesters demanded the restoration of the constitution from their French overlords. Indians, too, rose up against British rule, launching a concerted campaign that year for Indian self-determination. Across East and Southeast Asia, in China, Korea, Indochina, and the Dutch East Indies, growing opposition to imperialism transformed polities and societies. Africans and people of African descent also mobilized, with the first Pan-African Congress convening in Paris with fifty-seven delegates from fifteen countries in February of that year and Marcus Garvey's Universal Negro Improvement Association reaching some two million members.[4] Thus, 1919 marked the outbreak of a global revolt against an imperial world order, one that would see, in the ensuing decades, nation-states replace empires as the dominant political formation, not only in Europe but across the globe.

Peoples living under authoritarian or alien regimes had, of course, often resisted such rule throughout recorded history. The revolution of 1919, however, was not simply about resisting specific rulers or tyrannies; rather, it was an uprising against imperialism per se as a long-established global principle of legitimacy and order. This revolution, like others, involved violent clashes across vast parts of the world, from Berlin, Budapest, and Anatolia to Cairo, Amritsar, Beijing, and Seoul. At its heart, however, was a revolution in discourse, challenging the legitimacy of imperial rule even more than it did its material power by placing the principle of self-determination at the center of the debate over the postwar order. Although the principle of national self-determination was introduced into the international debate over Allied war aims by the Russian Bolsheviks and taken up by major statesmen, such as British prime minister David Lloyd

---

[2] On fighting beyond the Armistice, see Robert Gerwarth and Erez Manela (eds.), *Empires at War, 1911–1923* (Oxford, 2014); and Robert Gerwarth, *The Vanquished: Why the First World War Failed to End* (New York, 2016).

[3] On the origins of this new language of diplomacy, see the classic account by Arno Mayer, *Political Origins of the New Diplomacy, 1917–1918* (New Haven, CT, 1959).

[4] Sarah Claire Dunstan, "Conflicts of Interest: The 1919 Pan-African Congress and the Wilsonian Moment," *Callaloo* 39, 1 (2016), 133–50; and Adam Ewing, *The Age of Garvey: How a Jamaican Activist Created a Mass Movement and Changed Global Black Politics* (Princeton, NJ, 2014).

George, it was US President Woodrow Wilson, widely seen by the war's end as the preeminent figure in the international arena, who brought it into the center of global attention after incorporating it into his wartime rhetoric. It was, therefore, Wilson who became closely associated in many minds with expectations for the "remapping [of] the globe on the basis on nationality." To the extent that Wilson's adoption of that rhetoric was belated, ambivalent, and, to a significant extent, misconstrued by unintended audiences, the role of what I have elsewhere called the "Wilsonian moment" of 1919 in galvanizing movements against empire must count as one of the great ironies of the Great War.[5]

At the peace table itself, most of the discussion about remapping was focused on the territories of the defeated empires in East-Central Europe and Western Asia. It was here that the peacemakers constructed what Tomáš Masaryk, the first president of Czechoslovakia, called a "laboratory over a vast cemetery."[6] In this laboratory, they devised and tested various instruments for determining and managing post-imperial sovereignty, instruments such as successor states, plebiscites, and population transfers, all designed to ensure a better fit between nations and states or (as in the case of minority treaties) to manage situations where such a fit proved impossible to achieve. Of course, the peace negotiators in their laboratory weighed the principle of self-determination against numerous other interests – military, political, economic – and thus honored it in the breach as much as in the observance even in Europe. Moreover, for the territories that lay outside of Europe a different instrument was invented, that of the League of Nations Mandate, which was intended more to extend empire than to transcend it. Still, in the end this instrument, like those implemented within Europe, served to facilitate the transition from empires to nation-states.[7] All told, the process led to the birth of numerous such states, many of which remain, in one form or another, on the map today.

The revolutions of 1919 encompassed a broad mobilization in the name of self-determination, one that went far beyond the territories officially discussed in Paris or the peoples formally represented at the peace table there. Among the authors of the hundreds of petitions and memoranda that flooded into Paris, whether official or not, recognized or not, were Chinese, Koreans, and Indians, Armenians, Assyrians, and

---

[5] Erez Manela, *The Wilsonian Moment: Self-Determination and the International Origins of Anticolonial Nationalism* (New York, 2007). This essay draws substantially on that volume.

[6] This quote is borrowed from Leonard V. Smith, *Sovereignty at the Paris Peace Conference of 1919* (New York, 2018), 13.

[7] Susan Pedersen, *The Guardians: The League of Nations and the Crisis of Empire* (New York, 2015).

Kurds, Arabs and Jews, Egyptians and Tunisians, Catalans, Basques, and Irish, and many others.[8] Although in each of these cases there were specific forces – political, economic, social, cultural – that were reflected in these mobilizations, they were all also tied to expectations for the "remapping of the globe" in the aftermath of the war and all relied, to one extent or another, on an appeal to the principle of self-determination to demand a greater measure of self-rule. It was the first time in history, though not the last, that this principle was invoked by numerous claimants in disparate parts of the globe to challenge a world order based on imperial formations. Although its invocation to restructure international order during the era of decolonization from the late 1940s to the early 1970s would see far more dramatic successes, after the Wilsonian Revolution of 1919 the imperial world order never regained the stability and legitimacy that it had once possessed.

Revolution Articulated: The Rise of Self-Determination

The notion of a right to national self-determination was introduced into the international debate over war aims by the Russian Bolsheviks in mid-1917. The term had long been current in internal debates among socialists, though it was controversial: Marx himself had shown only intermittent support for nationalist movements in Europe during his lifetime, his interest fluctuating depending on how he perceived their relationship to the interests of the proletariat. During the Great War the Bolsheviks remained divided on the issue, with one camp, notably represented by Rosa Luxemburg, viewing nationalism as a dangerous, irrational force in conflict with the goal of international proletarian solidarity. Lenin, however, viewed Bolshevik support for national self-determination, defined as a right of secession from imperial rule, as a useful tool for undermining imperial regimes in Russia and elsewhere and gaining the support of subject peoples for the revolution.[9] In March 1917, therefore, even before the Bolshevik seizure of power, Lenin declared that when the Bolsheviks ruled Russia their peace plan would include "the liberation of all colonies; the liberation of all dependent, oppressed, and non-sovereign

---

[8] Many of these appeals are discussed, often quite briefly, in Margaret MacMillan, *Paris 1919: Six Months That Changed the World* (New York, 2002). In addition, on the Kurds, see B. Destani (ed.), *Minorities in the Middle East: Kurdish Communities, 1918–1974*, 4 vols. (Slough, 2006), vol. 1; and, on the Assyrians, Bīth Shamū'īl, *al-Āshūriyūn fī Mu'tamar al-Ṣulḥ, Bārīs 1919* (Dahūk, 2000).

[9] V. I. Lenin, "The Socialist Revolution and the Right of Nations to Self-Determination," in Idem, *Collected Works*, 45 vols. (Moscow, 1960–72), vol. 22 (Moscow, 1964), 143–56, which was first published in October 1916; see also Jeremy Smith, *The Bolsheviks and the National Question, 1917–1923* (London, 1999), 8–20; and Jean-François Fayet, "1919," in Stephen A. Smith (ed.), *The Oxford Handbook of the History of Communism* (Oxford, 2014), 109–24.

peoples."[10] That spring, the Russian Provisional Government, under pressure from the Bolshevik-controlled Petrograd Soviet, became the first among the belligerent governments to call for a peace settlement based on a right of "self-determination of peoples."[11]

The Bolshevik call for a settlement based on national self-determination, though phrased in universal terms, was initially aimed at the left in Europe, especially in Britain, France, and Germany, where Lenin hoped to help spark a revolution.[12] It was in this context, the battle for European opinion, that the British prime minister David Lloyd George first incorporated the term "self-determination" into the rhetoric of the Western allies. President Wilson had already advocated for a postwar settlement based on "the consent of the governed" – long a favorite phrase of his, taken from a tradition of American political rhetoric going back to the Declaration of Independence. Lloyd George, worried that the enthusiasm of the left in Britain and other Allied countries for the rhetoric of both Wilson and Lenin would undermine the war effort, moved to redefine British war aims in line with it, in the process conflating the rhetoric of Lenin with that of Wilson. The peace, he announced in an address on January 5, 1918, must be based "on the right of self-determination or the consent of the governed."[13] Thus merging Lenin's call for self-determination to Wilson's faith in the "consent of the governed," the prime minister obfuscated the distinction between the revolutionary agenda of the former and the gradualist, liberal reformism implied in the latter.

Wilson and Lenin each came from very different political contexts and had in mind two very different things when they spoke of self-determination. Wilson, who saw autocracy and militarism as the main causes of the war, envisioned a stable peace as one based on the long-standing republican principle of government by consent. Lenin, whose immediate concern was toppling the Russian Empire and gaining the support of its subject peoples as well as undermining the German and Austrian crowns, defined national self-determination as a right of secession from a multinational empire.[14] Thus, the Bolshevik declarations invariably spoke of the right to "national" self-determination, a characterization that reflected the term's origins in Marxist theory as

---

[10] Mayer, *Political Origins of the New Diplomacy*, 248 and 298–303.   [11] Ibid., 74–76.
[12] Ibid., 385–87.
[13] Thomas J. Knock, *To End All Wars: Woodrow Wilson and the Quest for a New World Order* (New York, 1992), 143; see also George W. Egerton, *Great Britain and the Creation of the League of Nations: Strategy, Politics, and International Organization, 1914–1919* (Chapel Hill, NC, 1978), 57–59. The full text of the address is in David Lloyd George, *British War Aims: Statement by the Prime Minister, the Right Honourable David Lloyd George, on January 5, 1918* (London, 1918).
[14] Borislav Chernev, "The Brest-Litovsk Moment: Self-Determination Discourse in Eastern Europe before Wilsonianism," *Diplomacy and Statecraft* 22, 3 (2011), 369–87.

distinct from other forms of self-determination – individual, proletarian, and so on. As part of the Bolshevik revolutionary strategy, it served as a call for the overthrow of imperial rule through an appeal to the national sentiments of subject peoples, even if the ultimate goal of the revolution remained the institution of a worldwide communist system based on class solidarity, one in which national distinctions would be secondary. Wilson, on the other hand, seldom if ever described the right to self-determination as specifically "national." Instead, he understood it as akin to the sort of Enlightenment notions of popular sovereignty and government by consent that underlay the American Revolution and US political traditions, and like many political thinkers in the West at the time, he also saw it as related to stages of political development. So while in his wartime speeches he couched the phrase in universal terms, he also saw it as immediately applicable only to "advanced" (i.e., European) peoples. Over time other societies might reach that stage of political development, but it would be through a gradual process of tutelage and reform, such as the one he had initiated in the US colonial administration of the Philippines.[15]

The divergent meanings and intentions behind the invocations of the principle of self-determination, however, were not readily apparent to most observers at the time; indeed, the flexibility of the term and its interpretation was then, and has continued to be, one of its primary attractions. As it was, in the final year of the war Wilson himself adopted the phrase "self-determination" as his own with growing fervor and emphasis. Despite a common belief to the contrary, the term itself was nowhere to be found in the Fourteen Points Address of January 8, 1918, though several of the points there – the resurrection of Poland, the evacuation of Belgium, and the call for the "autonomous development" of the peoples of the Ottoman and Habsburg empires – implied that he had this principle in mind.[16] Wilson's first public, explicit use of the term "self-determination" came the following month, in February 1918, when he addressed Congress again to outline the US peace plan. In the coming settlement, he said, "national aspirations must be respected; people may now be dominated and governed only by their own consent." He continued, even more emphatically: "'Self-determination' is not a mere phrase. It is an imperative principle of action, which statesmen will henceforth ignore at their peril."[17] It is

---

[15] Lloyd E. Ambrosius, *Wilsonianism: Woodrow Wilson and His Legacy in American Foreign Relations* (New York, 2002), 125–43; and N. Gordon Levin, *Woodrow Wilson and World Politics: America's Response to War and Revolution* (New York, 1968), 247–51.

[16] Address to a joint session of Congress, January 8, 1918, *The Papers of Woodrow Wilson* (hereafter *PWW*), ed. Arthur S. Link et al., 69 vols. (Princeton, NJ, 1966–94), vol. 45 (Princeton, NJ, 1984), 534–39.

[17] Address to Congress, February 11, 1918, *PWW*, vol. 46 (Princeton, NJ, 1984), 321.

significant to note that in his draft of the address – he composed his speeches himself, no speechwriters were employed in the White House back then – Wilson had placed the phrase "self-determination" within quotes, suggesting that he was conscious of incorporating a novel term into his lexicon.

Thereafter, calls for a peace based on self-determination would recur regularly, alongside references to the "consent of the governed," in Wilson's wartime rhetorical arsenal.[18] This was no accident. As with Lloyd George's earlier use of the term, it was designed to co-opt Bolshevik rhetoric in order to neutralize its appeal within the European Left. The new term may not have changed the essence of Wilson's vision in his own mind, but it did lend his pronouncements a more radical tone, amplifying their impact as his words echoed around the world. For Wilson, the consent of the governed would be crucial to the stability and legitimacy of the postwar order. If that meant remapping the globe, or some parts of it, on the basis of nationality, he was willing to abide.[19]

Thus, though neither Wilson and Lloyd George nor Lenin and Trotsky saw the subject peoples of the Global South as the primary audience for their declarations in support of self-determination, their rhetoric nevertheless echoed far beyond the European audiences it was intended for. By the time of the armistice in November 1918, nationalists across the world had adopted the language of self-determination, adapted it to their own needs and circumstances, and mobilized to bring their claims to the peace conference and the world leaders assembled there, Wilson foremost among them. By late 1918, the notion that the postwar settlement would be based on "President Wilson's principle of self-determination" had become commonplace in political discourse across much of the world and Wilson himself was lionized in print as the harbinger of a new era in international affairs. One Indian observer, who noted the rapturous reception Wilson encountered upon his arrival in Europe in December 1918, wrote: "Imagination fails to picture the wild delirium of joy with which he would have been welcomed in Asiatic capitals. It would have been as though one of the great teachers of humanity, Christ or Buddha, had come back to his

---

[18] For a longer perspective on the US deployment of the rhetoric of self-determination, see Brad Simpson, "The United States and the Curious History of Self-Determination," *Diplomatic History* 36, 4 (2012), 675–94.

[19] Trygve Throntveit, "The Fable of the Fourteen Points: Woodrow Wilson and National Self-Determination," *Diplomatic History* 35, 3 (2011), 445–81; Michla Pomerance, "The United States and Self-Determination: Perspectives on the Wilsonian Conception," *American Journal of International Law* 70, 1 (1976), 1–27; and Allen Lynch, "Woodrow Wilson and the Principle of 'National Self-Determination': A Reconsideration," *Review of International Studies*, 28, 2 (2002), 419–36. For more on the origins of Wilson's international thought, see Throntveit, *Power without Victory: Woodrow Wilson and the American Internationalist Experiment* (Chicago, 2017).

HERE ARE THE OPPRESSED NATIONS OF THE WORLD; WHAT WILL THE PEACE CONFERENCE DO FOR THEM?

1. Dependencies.

2. Nominally independent. Really dependent.

3. Nominally republics. Whites free: natives dependent.

4. Freed by Russian, German, Austrian Revolutions.

5. Protectorates.

6. Old Turkey. Fate undecided.

7. Independent.

Figure 6.1 Map published in *Young India*, the journal of the India Home Rule League of America, 1919. (Public Domain)

home."[20] Though Wilson limited his travels to Europe, the global ubiquity of his wartime rhetoric made it easy to imagine him in Asia.[21]

The full geographic scope of the task of "remapping the globe" in the wake of the war was illustrated in a world map featured the following month in *Young India*, the recently established publication of the India Home Rule League of America (Figure 6.1). The map was captioned "Here Are the Oppressed Nations of the World; What Will the Peace Conference Do for Them?" On this map, the parts of the world labeled "independent," including the Americas, Western Europe, Australasia, Russia, and Japan, were left

[20] Ct. in D. V. Gundappa, "Liberalism in India," *Confluence* 5, 3 (1956), 216–28, 217, which refers to V. S. Srinivasa Sastri's introduction to an Indian edition of Wilson's selected speeches.

[21] Erez Manela, "Imagining Woodrow Wilson in Asia: Dreams of East-West Harmony and the Revolt against Empire in 1919," *American Historical Review* 111, 5 (2006), 1327–51.

unshaded. Everywhere else – the "Oppressed Nations" – was shaded in one way or another. Some territories, including most of Africa, South Asia, and Southeast Asia, were labeled "Dependencies." Others, including China, Iran, and Afghanistan, were described as "Nominally independent. Really dependent." Southern Africa was listed as "Nominally republics; Whites free, natives dependent," while the territories of the recently defeated Ottoman Empire were described as "Fate undecided." Finally, and tellingly, the smallest bit of shaded territory on the map was a strip running along East-Central Europe designated as "Freed by Russian, German, Austrian Revolutions."[22]

The message of the map and the accompanying text could not be clearer, but should anyone miss it, every issue of *Young India* also included the motto, "Europe is not the only place that is to be made safe for democracy," echoing Wilson's own famous call for the world to be "made safe for democracy." If the postwar settlement was really to be based on the principle of self-determination, as the Allies' wartime rhetoric had seemed to suggest, then that principle should apply equally to the lands of empires both vanquished and victorious, to territories both within and outside the borders of Europe. Neither Wilson nor Lenin, after all, had explicitly limited the application of that principle to only one continent or to only one type of empire.

Within a few months it would become evident that the victors – the British and French empires accounted for the vast majority of the "dependent" territories marked on the map – had no intention of applying that principle to their own possessions and that, even with the territories of the defeated empires, those lying outside Europe would move toward self-determination only at a glacial pace, if at all, under the aegis of the League's Mandate System. But in early 1919 those outcomes still lay in the future. Besides, *Young India* noted, even if the world outside Europe was not on Wilson's mind when he spoke of self-determination, "ideas have a knack of rubbing off all geographical limitations" and his words would therefore be "the war cry of all small and subject and oppressed nationalities in the world."[23] The principle, then, could be detached from its source and deployed in ways that he had neither necessarily intended nor anticipated; the significance of Wilson's rhetoric, in this reading, was to be found less in what he said or in what he meant but rather in how it was disseminated, received, interpreted, and mobilized.

Revolution Disseminated: Communications and Propaganda in 1919

The rapid spread of news about the war and the declarations of wartime leaders around the world depended on the rapid expansion in

---

[22] Anonymous, Untitled, *Young India* 2, 1 (1919), 2.   [23] Ibid., 3.

communication technologies, namely the telegraph and mass print media, across much of the globe by the turn of the twentieth century. By the time of the war, India, for example, had hundreds of newspapers in English and vernacular languages that reached millions of subscribers. In China, a political press that first appeared in coastal cities in the 1890s had burgeoned in the first decades of the twentieth century with the expansion of literacy.[24] Across much of the Middle East and North Africa, modern newspapers had developed and spread by the time of the First World War, with dailies and magazines that published news about international affairs. European papers, too, were often available in major urban centers to those who could read European languages.[25] Even on the Korean peninsula, where Japanese censorship was severe, news about the outside world was smuggled in by activists from abroad. By 1918, all of these places had seen the emergence of broad, politically aware publics who were interested in and informed about national and international developments.

These new publics and new venues of mass communications were also often the targets of wartime US propaganda efforts aimed at spreading the Wilsonian message, efforts that were carried out during the war by the Committee on Public Information (CPI). This committee, established by Woodrow Wilson's executive order in April, 1917, was headed by the longtime muckraking journalist George Creel. Creel, who was fiercely loyal to the president and his proclaimed ideals, saw in the CPI an opportunity to spread the Wilsonian gospel of progressivism and democracy on a global scale. The goal of the CPI propaganda efforts abroad, Creel wrote, was "to drive home the absolute justice of America's cause, the absolute selflessness of America's aims."[26] Creel made creative use of the recent advances in communication and media technologies, such as the wireless communications and the moving picture, in his campaign to advertise America's war aims and peace plans at home and abroad: "The printed word, the spoken word, the motion picture, the poster, the signboard – all these were used in our campaign," he boasted.[27] The

---

[24] Leo Lee and Andrew J. Nathan, "The Beginnings of Mass Culture," in David Johnson, Andrew J. Nathan, and Evelyn S. Rawski (eds.), *Popular Culture in Late Imperial China* (Berkeley, CA, 1985), 368–78; and Joan Judge, *Print and Politics: "Shibao" and the Culture of Reform in Late Qing China* (Stanford, CA, 1996).

[25] Ami Ayalon, *The Press in the Arab Middle East: A History* (New York, 1995). On the rise of a modern press in Egypt specifically, see also P. J. Vatikiotis, *The History of Modern Egypt: From Muhammad Ali to Mubarak* (Baltimore, MD, 1991), 179–88, which was first published in 1969.

[26] George Creel, *Complete Report of the Chairman of the Committee on Public Information* (Washington, DC, 1920), 1. Scholarship on the CPI's operations outside the United States has been thin, but see Alan Axelrod, *Selling the Great War: The Making of American Propaganda* (New York, 2009), 189–209.

[27] Creel, *Complete Report of the Chairman of the Committee on Public Information*, 2.

CPI produced and distributed innumerable texts and images that celebrated the successes of the American war effort and also, more generally, the purported ideals and advantages of American society. These were distributed widely both within the United States and in many places abroad, most especially in Latin America and East Asia.[28]

Unsurprisingly, Wilson's own wartime pronouncements and declarations, and most especially the text of the Fourteen Points Address, became linchpins of CPI propaganda, particularly in its international operations. Already in mid-1917, more than a year before the CPI opened an office in China, American missionary volunteers were translating Wilson's speeches into Chinese and having these translations distributed free of charge to the Chinese-language press or published in pamphlet form. In the fall of 1918, around the time of the armistice, a volume containing the full text of Wilson's wartime speeches in Chinese translation was published in China to considerable fanfare, becoming a bestseller and going through several printings.[29] Carl Crow, the Missouri-born journalist, ad-man, and "China hand" who headed the CPI operation in the country, later testified that he received thousands of letters from Chinese citizens expressing "an air of confidence in the future, a faith in the idea that President Wilson's words would prevail and that China, as well as all other oppressed nations, would be liberated."[30] A bilingual edition of Wilson's speeches, with the original English text side by side with the Chinese translation, circulated in Chinese schools as a textbook for English instruction, and soon more than a few Chinese students could recite the Fourteen Points by heart.[31] Crow also ordered 20,000 large photographs of Wilson to be distributed among students at missionary schools, as well as buttons and engravings carrying the president's image.[32]

It is hard to measure the precise impact of CPI propaganda efforts in China or elsewhere, and other major belligerents, including the British, French, and Germans, also had extensive international propaganda operations.[33] It is clear, however, that by the time of the armistice

---

[28] Ibid., 4.

[29] George Creel, *How We Advertised America: The First Telling of the Amazing Story of the Committee on Public Information That Carried the Gospel of Americanism to Every Corner of the Globe* (New York, 1920), 362; and Hans Schmidt, "Democracy for China: American Propaganda and the May Fourth Movement," *Diplomatic History* 22, 1 (1998), 1–28.

[30] Carl Crow, *China Takes Her Place* (New York, 1944), 113–15; also Idem, *I Speak for the Chinese* (New York, 1937), 27–29.

[31] Creel, *How We Advertised America*, 362.

[32] Schmidt, "Democracy for China," 11–12.

[33] For a recent reconsideration of this topic, see the essays in Troy Paddock (ed.), *World War I and Propaganda* (Leiden, 2014).

enthusiasm for the new world order that President Wilson appeared to promise ran high among many in China as it did in Europe and elsewhere around the world. For Chinese at the time, who saw their country's relations with the outside world since the mid-nineteenth century as a litany of humiliations, the prospect of an international order predicated on the principle of self-determination held the promise of respect and equal status for China in international society.[34] Animated by the widespread expectation that a new era was ready to dawn in international affairs and, no less importantly, by indications suggesting that the United States would support Beijing's claims at the peace table, the Chinese delegates in Paris, as well as politically aware Chinese at home and abroad, hoped to claim their rightful place among nations.[35]

While Washington's wartime propaganda played a role in fomenting such expectations, Wilson's fame also spread in regions of little interest to US policymakers. Across the Middle East and North Africa, where the CPI was not directly active, Wilson's rhetoric nevertheless echoed widely, reportedly causing a stir "even in the remotest villages."[36] The recent spread of telegraph technology in the region and the ubiquity of Reuters News dispatches meant that readers in the region remained well-informed about the US role in the war, and the texts of Wilson's wartime speeches, including the Fourteen Points, were widely available in Arabic translation.[37] By mid-1918, therefore, the expectation that the emerging postwar order would reflect Wilson's wartime rhetoric was widespread in that region as well. Throughout North Africa, across the Fertile Crescent to Persia, and into the Arabian Peninsula, demands for self-determination were on the rise.[38]

In India, too, the press often reported on Wilson's utterances and his vision for a new era in world affairs despite the absence of CPI

---

[34] See, for example, Tang Zhenchang, *Cai Yuanpei zhuan* (Shanghai, 1985), 159. Cai was the president of Peking University at the time.

[35] Koo to Lansing, November 25, 1918, Waijiaobu (Foreign Ministry) Archives, Academia Sinica, Taipei, Taiwan, Record Group (RG) 03–12 (Archives of Chinese Embassy in Washington), Box 8, Fol. 2, 477.

[36] Ronald Wingate, *Wingate of the Sudan* (London, 1955), 228 and 232.

[37] James D. Startt, "American Propaganda in Britain during World War I," *Prologue* 28, 1 (1996), 17–33; and Peter Buitenhuis, "Selling the Great War," *Canadian Review of American Studies* 7, 2 (1976), 139–50.

[38] 'Abd al-Rahman Rafi'i, *Thawrat sanat 1919: Tarikh misr al-qawmi min sanat 1914 ila sanat 1921* (Cairo, 1968), 57; and 'Abd al-Khaliq Lashin, *Sa'd Zaghlul wa-dawruhu fi al-siyasah al-Misriyyah* (Beirut, 1975), 126–27. On Tunisia, see Stuart Schaar, "President Woodrow Wilson and the Young Tunisians," *The Maghreb Review* 31, 1–2 (2006), 129–44. On Algeria in 1919, Jeffrey James Byrne, *Mecca of Revolution: Algeria, Decolonization, and the Third World Order* (New York, 2016), 20–22. On Iran, Oliver Bast, "Putting the Record Straight: Vosuq al-Dowleh's Foreign Policy in 1918/19," in Erik Jan Zurcher and Touraj Atabaki (eds.), *Men of Order: Authoritarian Modernization under Atatürk and Reza Shah* (London, 2004), 260–81.

activities.[39] In one episode that resonated all the way to the British Parliament, a retired Indian judge and prominent campaigner for Indian home rule wrote an open letter to Wilson after his war speech to the Senate in April 1917, expressing the hope that the US president would convert the British government, too, to his "ideals of world liberation."[40] The veteran Indian home rule activist Lala Lajpat Rai, founder of the India Home Rule League of America and publisher of *Young India* who was living in wartime exile in the United States, published an editorial that thanked the president for his Fourteen Points, which, he said, were bound to "thrill the millions of the world's 'subject races'."[41] Many other Indians shared the sense that the world was on the cusp of a new era. If Wilson's principles were to be the basis for the peace conference, numerous editorials noted, then the British, even despite themselves, would at the very least have to reform the Government of India in line with those principles.[42]

Not everyone, of course, saw things this way, and there were those who did not believe that President Wilson would be of much help to colonial peoples in their struggle for self-determination. One example is the Bengali revolutionary M. N. Roy, who would become a leading figure in the Comintern in the 1920s and play a major role in turning Lenin's attention toward the colonial world. Roy, who spent much of the war years in exile in Mexico, could not miss the hostility of his hosts to their overweening northern neighbor. Wilson himself, after all, had ordered a months-long US military occupation of the Mexican port city of Vera Cruz in 1914 and as well the then-ongoing US military interventions in Nicaragua, Haiti, and the Dominican Republic, and Roy therefore remained skeptical of the president's commitment to the implementation of self-determination outside of Europe.[43] In Beijing Li Dazhao, the soon-to-be cofounder of the Chinese Communist Party,

---

[39] S. Natarajan, *A History of the Press in India* (Bombay, 1962), 183.

[40] Subramanya Aiyar to Woodrow Wilson, June 24, 1917, National Archives of India, New Delhi (hereafter NAI), Home Department (Political Branch), Deposit File, February 1918, File No. 36, "Action taken in regard to a letter sent by Sir Subramanya Aiyar to the President of the United States of America invoking his aid in obtaining Home Rule for India," 3–6; see also Hunter Committee Report (7:3), n.d., India Office Library, London (hereafter IOL), V/26/262/9.

[41] Anonymous, "Editorials," *Young India*, 1, 3 (March 1918), 1–3.

[42] Editorials to this effect appeared, for example, in *Mahrátta* (October 6, 1918); "Bombay Press Abstract, 1918," IOL, L/R/5/174, 19; *Tribune* (Lahore) (December 20, 1918); Anonymous, Report ("Punjab Press Abstract, 1919"), 1919, IOL, L/R/5/201, 3; *Hindi Brahmin Samachar* (November 25, 1918); and *Kesari* (Poona), n.d., IOL, L/R/5/ 200, 596.

[43] Roy to Wilson, n.d. (late 1917), in *Selected Works of M. N. Roy*, ed. by Sibnarayan Ray, 4 vols. (Delhi, 1987–1997), vol. 1 (Delhi, 1987), 67–83; see also Kris Manjapra, *M. N. Roy: Marxism and Colonial Cosmopolitanism* (London, 2010), 33–35. On Latin

noted the distinction between Lenin's call for world revolution and Wilson's notions of international reform and concluded that China should celebrate Lenin, not Wilson, since it was the defeat of militarism by socialism that was the true harbinger of the new "dawn of humankind."[44]

Still, in the initial months after the armistice even many who thought Wilson's pronouncements insufficient or doubted his true commitment to them nevertheless borrowed his rhetoric as they sought to advance their claims of self-determination. The peace conference gathering in Paris seemed to be poised to reshape international order, and the US president, whatever his deficiencies, appeared to be the most powerful advocate for a new order present at the table. The Russian Bolsheviks, after all, were excluded from Paris and mired in civil war, and the other major victors – Britain, France, Italy, and Japan – were clamoring for the retrenchment and expansion of the imperial world order.[45] Wilson remained, at least until the late spring of 1919, the leading world figure who seemed committed to a settlement that would promote an international order based on, or at least attentive to, the principle of self-determination.

Revolution Mobilized: Challenging the Imperial Order

In the months after the armistice, therefore, those who wished to advance their case for self-determination mobilized to influence the peacemaking process underway in Paris. In December 1918, when the Indian National Congress (INC) convened in Delhi for its annual session, it resolved to demand the application of the principle of self-determination to India and urged that India be represented at the peace table by elected delegates, rather than ones appointed by the colonial government. It nominated three men to serve in that position: the veteran home-rule activist Bal Gangadhar Tilak, who had been dubbed "the father of Indian unrest," the Muslim Congress leader Syed Hasan Imam, and Mohandas Gandhi,

---

Americans at the Paris Peace Conference, see Alan McPherson, "Anti-Imperialism and the Failure of the League of Nations," in Alan McPherson and Yannick Wehrli (eds.), *Beyond Geopolitics: New Histories of Latin America at the League of Nations* (Albuquerque, NM, 2015), 20–32. On the impact of the war in Latin America more generally, see Stefan H. Rinke, *Latin America and the First World War* (New York, 2017).

[44] Li Dazhao, "*Wei-er-xun yu pinghe*," (February 11, 1917), in *Li Dazhao wenji*, 5 vols (Beijing, 1999), vol. 1, 271; and Li Dazhao, "Bolshevism de shengli," *Xin Qingnian* (November 1918).

[45] On the discussions surrounding the possibility of including the Bolsheviks in the peace conference, see David W. McFadden, *Alternative Paths: Soviets and Americans, 1917–1920* (New York, 1993), esp. chapters 8 and 9.

who had returned from South Africa not long before and was then just beginning his rise on the Indian political scene.[46] In a coordinated campaign, dozens of local "self-rule leagues" that sprouted up throughout India also sent petitions to the peace conference asking that India be granted self-determination.[47]

The British government, however, summarily rejected the INC demand that it be allowed to nominate India's delegates to the peace conference, instead populating the delegation with supporters of British rule on the subcontinent. Nevertheless, Tilak, a scholar and journalist who was already widely known across India for his long-standing advocacy for home rule, traveled to London and launched a campaign for Indian self-determination which was aimed squarely at "world opinion" and the gathering peace conference in the hope that an international campaign of this sort would put pressure on London to bend to Wilsonian principles.[48] Confident that the peace conference would have to take up "the question of India," it was up to Indians themselves "to see that the decision is in our favour."[49] He also appealed directly to Wilson, writing him that "the world's hope for peace and justice is centered in you as the author of the great principle of self-determination."[50] For Tilak, Wilson may not have been an ideal ally, but he seemed to offer the best chance of putting Indian demands for self-determination on the peacemakers' agenda.

Unlike India, recognized in Paris only as a constituent part of the British Empire, China was represented there as a sovereign state, even if its sovereignty was circumscribed by a battery of unequal treaties signed decades earlier with the major powers that, among other things, compromised Chinese control over the tariffs levied at its ports and the foreigners living within its borders. Having declared war on Germany in August 1917 in order to secure a seat at the peace table, Chinese at home and abroad felt that the time was ripe to demand real equality for China in the international arena, that is, the abrogation of the unequal treaties and the restoration of full Chinese sovereignty over its territory.[51] Chinese activists, including intellectuals, students, merchants, and others both in

---

[46] Anonymous, Thirty-third INC session, December 1918, Delhi, Nehru Memorial Museum and Library, New Delhi (hereafter NMML), All-India Congress Committee, File 1, Part 2, 347.

[47] Numerous such documents are found in the British National Archives, Kew (hereafter TNA), FO 608/211, Fol. 126–36.

[48] Anonymous, Memorandum, December 11, 1918, London, enclosed to Tilak to Khaparde, December 18, 1918, NAI, G. S. Khaparde Papers, File 1, 1–2.

[49] Tilak to D. W. Gokhale, January 23, 1919, London, NAI, Khaparde Papers, File 1, 4–7.

[50] Ct. in T. V. Parvate, *Bal Gangadhar Tilak* (Ahmedabad, 1958), 463, referring to a letter from Close to Tilak, January 14, 1919.

[51] On China's wartime policy and experience, see Xu Guoqi, *China and the Great War: China's Pursuit of a New National Identity and Internationalization* (Cambridge, 2005).

China and abroad, produced a veritable avalanche of petitions and memoranda calling for a new international order based on Wilson's wartime messages and demanding the application to China of the principles of self-determination and the equality of nations.[52] When it soon became clear that the peace conference would not consider treaties that long predated the war, the Chinese focused on the status of the German concession territories in Shandong Province, which Japan had occupied during the war and was now claiming the right to keep. The Shandong Question, as it was known, became the crucial litmus test for what the postwar order would mean for China.

The members of the Chinese delegation in Paris – and it was largely they, rather than the weak and divided government in Beijing, who guided Chinese policy in Paris – believed that the United States would side with China at the conference.[53] The two most prominent among them were both educated in the United States – V. K. Wellington Koo (Gu Weijun) held a doctoral degree from Columbia University and C. T. Wang (Wang Zhengting) was a graduate of Yale. They wanted to see China emerge from its state of weakness, disunity, and humiliation to take its rightful place among nations, and they saw in Wilson's stated principles their best chance to achieve that goal. In a coauthored pamphlet, they compared what they described as President Wilson's vision of international harmony to that of the Chinese sage Confucius: "Confucius saw, just as the illustrious author of the present League of Nations has seen, the danger to civilization and humanity involved in the continued existence of such a sad plight [of constant war]" and therefore worked to create and preserve "a new order of things which would ensure universal peace."[54] The Wilsonian project of fashioning a more harmonious international order, they suggested, was the culmination of thousands of years of Confucian teachings, and the establishment of a League of Nations would fulfill the Confucian ideal. In retrospect, it seems a rather fanciful take, but it fit in well with the spirit of the moment.

Koreans, too, mobilized to seize the moment. As a colony of Japan, Korea had no formal representation at the peace table, and an unofficial delegation to Paris sent by exiled activists arrived late, remained unrecognized, and achieved little. But a manifesto posted along the

---

[52] Reinsch to Lansing, November 8, 1918, US National Archives and Records Administration (hereafter USNA), RG 256, 893.01/1; see also excerpts from the *Peking Leader*, November 3–5, 1919, enclosed in USNA, RG 256, 893.00/5; and Foreign Minister of Canton Government to Lansing, January 23, 1919, UNSA, RG 256, 893.00/18.

[53] Wunsz King, *China at the Peace Conference in 1919* (Jamaica, NY, 1961), 3.

[54] V. K. Wellington Koo and Cheng-ting T. Wang, *China and the League of Nations* (London, 1919).

main street of Seoul in the early dawn hours of March 1, 1919, by a group of students reflected the spirit of the time. After describing at some length the suffering of the Korean people under Japanese rule, it concluded: "Since the American President proclaimed the Fourteen Points, the voice of national self-determination has swept the world . . . . How could we, the people of the great Korean nation, miss this opportunity?"[55] The same morning, a Korean "Declaration of Independence," which adopted Wilsonian language to assert Korea's right to liberty and equality within the world of nations and was signed by thirty-three prominent religious leaders, was read aloud at Pagoda Park in downtown Seoul in front of hundreds of cheering students. When the reading ended, those gathered streamed into the streets of the city calling: "long live an independent Korea." Over the following months, more than a million people participated in demonstrations and protests across the peninsula – the Japanese colonial police reported disturbances in all but seven of its 218 provinces. The March First Movement, as it came to be known, was the first mass uprising in the history of modern Korean nationalism, involving men and women of every province, faith, and class on the peninsula and marking a watershed in the evolution of Korean nationalism.[56]

The arc of upheaval that emerged in the Wilsonian revolution of 1919, then, which in Europe famously stretched from the Baltics to the Balkans, spanned a much greater distance outside the continent, reaching from the Pacific to the Mediterranean and beyond. Thus, even as events in Korea were unfolding, a group of prominent men in Egypt, a British protectorate, launched into action, forming a delegation and demanding to head for Paris to stake a claim there for self-determination. When the group, headed by veteran politician Sa'd Zaghlul, later celebrated by Egyptians as the "father of the nation," was refused permission to travel, it mobilized protests in the streets and launched an international propaganda campaign for its cause. The usually sleepy US diplomatic office in Cairo was deluged with petitions protesting the British position and demanding that the United States support Egyptian self-determination.[57] Zaghlul also wrote to Wilson himself, expressing the joy of the Egyptian people at "the birth of a new era" in international affairs and asking the president to help free

---

[55] Cited in Chong-sik Lee, *The Politics of Korean Nationalism* (Berkeley, CA, 1963), 112.

[56] Chong-Sik Lee, *The Politics of Korean Nationalism* (Berkeley, CA, 1963), 113–18; see also Carter J. Eckert, Ki-baik Lee, Young Ick Lew, Michael Robinson, and Edward W. Wagner, *Korea Old and New: A History* (Cambridge, MA, 1990), 278.

[57] A few examples among many include a petition from Leon S. Farhj, an official at the Egyptian Ministry of Agriculture, December 11, 1918, and a petition from members of the "Egyptian National Delegation," December 12, 1918, enclosed to Gary to Secretary of State, December 30, 1918, USNA, RG 256, 883.00/4 and FW 883.00/30.

Egypt from foreign domination.[58] Here, too, a flood of petitions rose from a broad cross-section of Egyptian elites – legislators, government officials, local politicians, merchants, lawyers, physicians, and army officers – all calling for the support of the US president for their bid for self-rule.[59]

By early March, as protest filled the streets of Cairo as it did in Seoul, the anxious British authorities decided to move against its leadership. They arrested Zaghlul and three of his colleagues and deported them to the British-controlled Mediterranean island of Malta to be interned there.[60] According to one biographer, one item found on Zaghlul's person when he was arrested and searched was a clipping from the newspaper *Daily Express* enumerating President Wilson's Fourteen Points.[61] The arrests, however, failed to calm the streets, instead sparking a massive wave of strikes and demonstrations across Egypt and precipitating a period of violent clashes that came to be known as the "1919 Revolution." As elsewhere, here too the uprising included men and women from all walks of life: students and urban workers, professionals and rural residents. Members of religious and ethnic minorities – Christians, Jews, Greeks – expressed solidarity with the movement, and women took to the streets with unprecedented numbers and visibility (Figure 6.2). As violent clashes proliferated and railway and telegraph lines were sabotaged, London countered with martial law. Over the next months some eight hundred Egyptians were killed in clashes and many more wounded, and sixty British soldiers and civilians also died.[62] The 1919 Revolution marked a watershed in the Egyptian struggle against British rule, and the violence unleashed during this period cast a long shadow over the subsequent history of the region.[63]

The British response to the Indian campaign for self-determination followed the same two-pronged playbook as in Egypt, working to prevent any discussion of the issue in Paris while suppressing protests on the ground. Thus, when Tilak, citing his appointment by the INC as its

---

[58] Zaghlul to Wilson, December 14, 1918, December 27, 1918, and January 3, 1919, for example. For telegrams from Zaghlul to Wilson, see George E. Noble, "The Voice of Egypt," *Nation* (January 3, 1920), 861–64.

[59] See examples enclosed to Gary to Secretary of State, December 30, 1918, USNA, RG 256, 883.00/4; and Gary to US Department of State, December 19, 1918, USNA, RG 256, 883.00/3.

[60] Isma'il Ṣidqi, *Mudhakkirati* (Cairo, 1991), 46–49; and Gary to Secretary of State, March 10, 1919, USNA, RG 256, 883.00/37.

[61] Lashin, *Sa'd Zaghlul wa-dawruhu fi al-siyasah al-Misriyyah*, 128.

[62] PID reports in TNA, FO 371/4373, 35, 51; see also Gary to Secretary of State, 10, 11, and March 16, 1919, USNA, RG 256, 883.00/37, 41 and 53.

[63] Rafi'i, *Thawrat sanat 1919*, 5. Tahrir (or Liberation) Square in Cairo, which stood at the heart of the "Arab Spring" protests of 2011, first acquired its name as a result of the upheaval of 1919, when it also served as a center for protests; see the chapter by James L. Gelvin in this volume.

Figure 6.2 Photograph of a woman making a public speech during the 1919 revolution in Egypt. (Public Domain)

delegate to the peace conference, applied for a passport to travel to Paris, his application was denied, and at the same time the Imperial Legislative Council in Delhi passed the "Anarchical and Revolutionary Crimes Act," commonly known as the Rowlatt Act, extending the government's wartime powers of internment without trial.[64] Indian activists, who had expected the war to be followed by an immediate push toward self-government, were incensed. Gandhi, who during the war had campaigned to recruit Indians for the imperial war effort, now emerged as a leader of the movement to oppose these "Black Acts," calling for civil disobedience and a nationwide strike.[65] The colonial authorities responded to the mounting protests with violence, most infamously with the killing on April 13, 1919, of some four hundred unarmed

---

[64] Tilak to D. W. Gokhale, February 6, 1919, NAI, Khaparde Papers, File 1, 8–10; Tilak to D. W. Gokhale, London, January 23, 1919, NAI, Khaparde Papers, file 1, 4–7; and Unsigned memorandum titled "How We Get On II," enclosed to Tilak's letter, March 20, 1919, London, NAI, Khaparde Papers, File 1, 13–14.

[65] Gandhi to Chelmsford, February 24, 1919, and March 11, 1919, NMML, Chelmsford Papers, Roll 10.

civilians gathered in Jallianwala Bagh, in the Punjab city of Amritsar. Two days later, martial law was imposed in the region, public floggings proliferated, and, by the end of year, eighteen men had been publicly hanged as part of the authorities' effort to suppress the upheaval.[66] The Amritsar Massacre, as it soon became known, came to epitomize the oppressive nature of British rule in India and augured a new era in the evolution of Indian resistance to the empire.

In Korea, too, the Japanese colonial authorities engaged through the spring and summer of 1919 in a campaign of suppression that left thousands of casualties.[67] They also, along with the Japanese press, saw US influence behind the events, and most specifically that of American Protestant missionaries: more than half of the thirty-three signatories to the Declaration of Independence, after all, were Korean Christians.[68] The missionaries, charged the authorities, spread subversive Wilsonian propaganda in Korea, encouraging revolt. They even suspected President Wilson of direct complicity: according to a Japanese police report, an American missionary, one Shannon McCune, had traveled to the United States in October 1918 and met with President Wilson, reached an understanding with him about the future of Korea, and upon his return encouraged Koreans to revolt in order to demonstrate to foreign countries that they rejected Japanese rule and thus bring their case before the peace conference. Such, concluded the colonial police, "was the secret viewpoint of the 'mystical president'."[69] There is no evidence that such a meeting occurred; still, the Japanese inclination to assign Wilson such power over events in Korea is a further reflection of his global stature at that moment.

By that time, however, it was becoming clear that the Paris Peace Conference, rather than constructing a new world order based on self-determination, was largely aiming to restore the old imperial one, at least outside of Europe. In early May, it emerged that, in order to secure

---

[66] Derek Sayer, "British Reaction to the Amritsar Massacre, 1919–1920," *Past and Present* 131, 1 (1991), 130–64.

[67] Report from British Consulate-General in Seoul, May 13, 1919, TNA, FO 262/1406, F. 158–60; see also Eckert, Lee, Lew, Robinson, and Wagner, *Korea Old and New*, 279; and Lee, *The Politics of Korean Nationalism*, 122–23.

[68] US Mission in Tokyo to Secretary of State, March 8, 1919, USNA, RG 59, 895.00/587; and Morris to Secretary of State, March 15, 1919, USNA, RG 59, 895.00/572; see also news report in TNA, FO 262/1406, F. 414.

[69] Ct. in Lee, *The Politics of Korean Nationalism*, 107; see also Timothy L. Savage, "The American Response to the Korean Independence Movement, 1910-1945," *Korean Studies* 20 (1996), 189–231, 195. George Shannon McCune was an educator and known to the US government as an expert in Eastern affairs, see Anonymous, "Rev. Dr. G. M'Cune Expert On Orient," *New York Times* (December 6, 1941), 17, but *PWW* shows no record that he met with Wilson.

Japanese membership in his League of Nations, Wilson had agreed to award Japan the former German concessions in Shandong. On 4 May, after students in Beijing learned of this decision, they took to the streets in violent protest. The students, who not long before had filled the streets to chant their admiration for President Wilson, now saw the American president as a liar, his promise of a new world exposed as a mere illusion. Street protests and strikes spread throughout the country over the next weeks, with merchants and workers soon joining the students in protest. A contemporary pamphlet summed up the prevailing sentiments: "Throughout the world like the voice of a prophet has gone the word of Woodrow Wilson strengthening the weak and giving courage to the struggling. And the Chinese people . . . looked for the dawn of this new Messiah; but no sun rose for China." One student recalled that they now "awoke to the fact that foreign nations . . . were all great liars . . . We could no longer depend upon the principle of any so-called great leader like Woodrow Wilson . . . we couldn't help feel that we must struggle!"[70] Like the other upheavals across the colonial world in the spring of 1919, the May Fourth Movement galvanized hitherto inchoate strands of political, social, and cultural discontent and marked a defining moment in the evolution of resistance to the imperialist world order.

Concluding Thoughts

Just like the news of the war and of wartime proclamations, news of the upheavals that followed it circulated worldwide.[71] In the summer of 1919, in the provincial city of Changsha, a twenty-five-year-old budding Chinese nationalist surveyed the recent developments in the international arena and noted that China was not alone in having entertained high hopes for a new era only to be disappointed. "India," he wrote, "has earned herself a clown wearing a flaming red turban as representative to the Peace Conference" – this was the Maharaja of Bikanir, selected by the British to represent the Indian princely states – but "the demands of the Indian people have not been granted . . . So much for national self-determination!"[72] In India itself, a twenty-nine-year-old Cambridge-educated Brahmin lamented that the

---

[70] Schmidt, "Democracy for China," 16; and Chow Tse-tsung, *The May Fourth Movement: Intellectual Revolution in Modern China* (Cambridge, MA, 1960), 92–93.

[71] See, for example, *Shibao* (April, 23–26 and 29 1919), for numerous reports of "riots" and "chaos" in India, as well as in Egypt and Korea. In India, see, for example, *Mahratta* (October 19, 1919), which reports on "President Wilson's Betrayals" of numerous nations, including Korea, Ireland, and Egypt.

[72] Mao Zedong, "Afghanistan Picks Up the Sword" and "So Much for National Self-Determination!," *Xiangjiang pinglun* (July 14, 1919), in Stuart R. Schram (ed.), *Mao's Road to Power: Revolutionary Writings, 1912–1949*, 8 vols. (Armonk, NY, 1992–2015),

war, which "was to have revolutionized the fabric of human affairs," had "ended without bringing any solace or hope of permanent peace or betterment ... The 'fourteen points,' where are they?"[73]

But as President Wilson and his principles stood defeated, the two young writers, Mao Zedong and Jawaharlal Nehru, detected another force rising to rally the newly mobilized peoples of Asia. Russian Bolshevism, Mao wrote, was making headway in Asia, and Chinese must now take its ideas seriously if they were to make progress toward liberation. Nehru, too, noted that with the decline of Wilson, "the spectre of communism" now appeared on the horizon in Asia.[74] For both Mao and Nehru, as for countless other nationalists across the colonial world then and later, the interest in Lenin and his message, as in Wilson, was centrally informed by their desire to find a path toward self-determination for their nations.

Though the peace settlement of 1919 allowed the victorious empires, the British and French in particular, to expand their domains as never before, it also marked the beginning of the end for the imperial world order. After 1919, empire as a principle of international order and legitimacy faced a series of challenges of unprecedented scope and intensity. The League of Nations Mandate System, with all its limitations, entrenched for the first time in international society the principle that progress toward self-determination should be the goal of colonial rule and the yardstick against which it should be measured. Within this new international framework, Egyptians, who continued to resist British rule, won partial sovereignty in 1922 and Iraq followed a decade later, joining the League of Nations. The Shandong concessions, whose transfer to Japan at Versailles launched the May Fourth Movement, were restored to China at the Washington Conference in 1922, and throughout the 1920s and 1930s the Chinese government chipped away at the unequal treaties that circumscribed its sovereignty. In India, resistance to British rule entered a new era, posing a challenge to the legitimacy of empire far more radical than any that came before the war, and in 1929 the Indian National Congress asserted, for the first time, the goal of complete independence, one that would sever India's connection to Britain entirely.

vol. 1 (Armound, NY, 1992), 335 and 337; see also Mao Zedong, "Poor Wilson," *Xiangjiang pinglun* (July 14, 1919), in Schram, *Mao's Road to Power*, vol. 1, 338.

[73] Incomplete and unpublished review of Bertrand Russell, *Roads to Freedom: Socialism, Anarchism, and Syndicalism* (London, 1918), undated but written sometime in the summer of 1919; and the documents in NMML, Jawaharlal Nehru Papers, Writings and Speeches, Serial No. 21.

[74] Ibid; and Mao Zedong, "Study of the Extremist Party," *Xiangjiang pinglun* (July 14, 1919), reprinted in Schram, *Mao's Road to Power*, vol. 1, 332.

The global revolution against the imperial world order continued to spread and strengthen through depression and war, culminating with the radical restructuring of international society in the waves of decolonization that came in the decades after the Second World War. By then, the illegitimacy of imperial formations, which had not long before served as the pillars of international order, had become an iron principle of international relations. The revolutionary idea that Wilson had come to symbolize in 1919, that of an international order predicated on formally equal, self-determining nation-states, was modeled in his League of Nations and then codified in the structure of the United Nations, when the nation-state decisively displaced the multi-national empire as the dominant state form in international society. Power, of course, remains at the center of international relations and power relationships in the international arena remained anything but equal. But the remapping of a world of empires into one of nation-states over the course of the past century has transformed its territorial configurations, modes of operation, and discourses of legitimacy in far-reaching ways.

7   The Third World Revolutions

Odd Arne Westad

The world we live in today was created by the rebellions against colonialism and Western control in the twentieth century. Before the First World War, the globe consisted mainly of empires, European and other, with Western expansionism having gone through a particularly virulent phase since the 1870s. Non-imperial sovereignty was weak, even among the European and Latin American countries that constituted most of the world's independent states. Now, a hundred years later, the empires are gone (with a possible exception for the United States, China, and Russia) and the number of sovereign countries has more than quadrupled. Behind this transformation was a set of revolutions that insisted on the right of colonized peoples to construct states with the same forms of sovereignty and authority as empires had had in the past. In this metamorphosis lies both a nominal democratization of interstate affairs and the origins of many of our present troubles.

But before we get to current conditions, let us concentrate on the past. This chapter will set forth two main positions. The first is that the anticolonial revolutions of the twentieth century cannot be understood without reference to European and American revolutions of the previous 150 years. For far too long decolonization has had a history that has been mainly untouched by the historiographies of revolution elsewhere and at other times. It is almost as if the leadership of these revolutions by non-Europeans inherently has put them in a category of their own. Instead, this chapter will argue, the links to 1776, 1789, and 1848, as well as to the Latin American revolutions from 1803 to 1822, form fundamental and integral parts of the history of revolts against colonialism in the twentieth century.[1]

I am grateful to Thomas Field and Vanessa Freije for their comments on draft versions of this chapter.

[1] I am of course not the first to make this point: For a comparative overview, see Jack A. Goldstone, *Revolutions: Theoretical, Comparative, and Historical Studies* (Belmont, CA, 2008), which was originally published in 1986; and Keith Michael Baker and Dan Edelstein (eds.), *Scripting Revolution: A Historical Approach to the Comparative Study of Revolutions* (Stanford, CA, 2015); see also Wim Klooster, *Revolutions in the Atlantic World: A Comparative History* (New York, 2009); Martin Malia, *History's Locomotives:*

My second position is that all anticolonial revolutions in the twentieth century, from India and China to Namibia and Eritrea, took place in the shadow of the Russian Revolution and were in some form directly inspired by it and its effects. This is true even in those cases when the leaders of independence movements had no intention of becoming political allies of the Soviet Union or emulating the intemperances of Bolshevism. In every single case the use of the instruments of state power for social and economic planning, for mass education, and for control of resources was influenced by the Soviet experience. The Leninist concept of a vanguard political organization was also key to many of these revolutions, and, of course, for some of them, direct links with the Soviet Union or the Comintern were of critical importance, though the main argument here is not about organizational links as much as about political and intellectual inspiration across time and continents.[2]

What Were Third World Revolutions?

The anticolonial revolutions of the mid-twentieth century were the fourth major wave of modern political revolutions, following the Atlantic Revolutions of 1776–1822, the European and Asian nationalist

---

Revolutions and the Making of the Modern World (New Haven, CT, 2006); and the classics Theda Skocpol, States and Social Revolutions: A Comparative Analysis of France, Russia, and China (Cambridge, 1979); and Michael Mann, The Sources of Social Power, 3 vols. (Cambridge 2012), especially vol. 3 (Global Empires and Revolution, 1890–1945). For more specific discussions of the effects of the American and French Revolutions, see David Armitage, The Declaration of Independence: A Global History (Cambridge, MA, 2007); Jonathan Israel, The Expanding Blaze: How the American Revolution Ignited the World, 1775–1848 (Princeton, NJ, 2017); Michel Vovelle, La découverte de la politique: géopolitique de la Révolution française (Paris, 1993); and the contributions to Suzanne Desan, Lynn Hunt, and William Max Nelson (eds.), The French Revolution in Global Perspective (Ithaca, NY, 2013).

[2] Again, the point has of course been made before, even though the more specialized literature is very limited. For two good overviews of international communism that include the non-European world, see Silvio Pons, The Global Revolution: A History of International Communism 1917–1991 (Oxford, 2014) and David Priestland, The Red Flag: Communism and the Making of the Modern World (London, 2009). On the Bolshevik revolution and its effects in Asia, Africa, and Latin America, see the chapters by Sobhanlal Gupta, Serge Wolikow, and Andrea Graziosi in The Cambridge History of Communism, 3 vols. (Cambridge 2017), vol. 1 (Silvio Pons and Stephen A. Smith (eds.), World Revolution and Socialism in One Country, 1917–1941); by Andreas Hilger, Sara Lorenzini, and Victor Figueroa Clark in Silvio Pons, Norman Naimark, and Sophie Quinn-Judge (eds.), The Cambridge History of Communism, vol. 2; and by Artemy Kalinovsky and Piero Gleijeses in Silvio Pons, Juliane Fürst, and Mark Selden (eds.), The Cambridge History of Communism, vol. 3; see also the contributions to Leslie James and Elisabeth Leake (eds.), Decolonization and the Cold War: Negotiating Independence (London, 2015).

revolutions after 1848 and 1905 respectively, and the socialist and Wilsonian revolutions after the First World War.[3] Their aim was to defeat foreign imperial control and build indigenous states that could deliver social and racial justice as well as economic progress and transnational solidarity. For a while the more radical anticolonial revolutionary projects took pride in the somewhat ahistorical concept of the Third World, a catch-term created by the French geographer Alfred Sauvy in 1952 as a riff on France's revolutionary Third Estate of 1789; "this Third World, ignored, exploited, despised like the Third Estate, also wants to be something," Sauvy wrote.[4] Although only a few anticolonial revolutionaries would make use of the term emblematically, the Third World is still a useful marker for some of these revolutions, since it encompassed a few specific political aims of revolutionary movements and new states in the 1950s and 1960s, when the decolonization process was at its peak.

The best way of approaching a definition of what we mean by Third World revolutions is by singling out movements and states that aimed for a radical redistribution of political and economic power both within their own countries and on a global scale, as well as prioritized support for countries or regions that were still under colonial rule. Algeria and Indonesia are instances of militant nationalist anticolonial revolutions with radical aims. Both new states had regimes that saw themselves as vanguards of anticolonial revolutions globally and that refused to be defined by Cold War strategic dichotomies. They were in a way archetypes of Third World revolutions.[5] The rebellions against Portuguese rule in Angola, Mozambique, and Guinea Bissau were also victorious after long periods of armed struggle, though the new regimes they engendered soon transformed themselves into ruling Marxist-Leninist parties, more communist than Afro-Marxist. They were Third World revolutions of a slightly different kind, still oriented toward anticolonial solidarity, but more Soviet in their practices. Kenya, on the other hand, is perhaps the best example of a struggle against colonial violence that did not produce a radical regime. Neither was it particularly internationalist (except in a regional, east African setting). It makes little sense to see Jomo Kenyatta's Kenya as a Third World revolution, even though it was definitely an anticolonial project

---

[3] Mark Katz, *Revolutions and Revolutionary Waves* (New York, 1997); and Charles Tilly, *European Revolutions, 1492–1992* (Oxford, 1995).
[4] Alfred Sauvy, "Trois Mondes, Une Planète," *L'Observateur* (August 14, 1952), 14.
[5] Jeffrey James Byrne, *Mecca of Revolution: Algeria, Decolonization, and the Third World Order* (Oxford, 2016), provides important insights into the Algerian case.

ending in a postcolonial state that declared its adherence to "democratic African Socialism."[6]

Some Third World revolutions took place as struggles against colonial settler regimes. Zimbabwe and Namibia are good examples. In South Africa the struggle was against an ethnic minority regime that put in place a racist form of societal organization. The Cuban revolution, which had great significance for transnational revolutionary solidarity throughout the latter phase of the Cold War, was a rebellion against domestic class oppression and informal but strong US dominance and control. All of them seem to belong within a concept of Third World revolutions because of their aims of radical social transformation and internationalism.

Is it meaningful to count China and India among these revolutions? The first was a nationalist revolution against imperialist control (though not always and everywhere imperialist occupation), which then was superseded by a socialist revolution from within. The second was a long anticolonial resistance, which contributed to the decision of the imperial power to withdraw. In both cases the concepts of rights for people native to the country, of social and political equality, and of international solidarity played significant roles, probably enough to characterize them as Third World revolutions, even though India's promise of equality never materialized and postcolonial China went through a lengthy trajectory away from Third World cooperation – first as an ally of the Soviet Union, then Cultural Revolution isolation, and finally, at the end of the Cold War, as a de facto ally of the United States. Both countries are today among the most unequal places on the planet.[7]

In many cases, Third World regimes emerged within states set up as a result of colonial withdrawal rather than through revolutionary overthrows of imperial control. These were "instituted revolutions" rather than anticolonial movements. In spite of vast differences among them, states that moved in a radical direction post-decolonization would encompass Ghana, Guinea, Congo-Brazzaville, Benin, Somalia, South Yemen, Tanzania, Egypt, Iraq, Libya, Syria, Mali, and Burkina Faso. These countries may not have gone through revolutions against colonial control but, as states, still became part of the revolutionary framework we know as the Third World.

---

[6] Republic of Kenya, *African Socialism and Its Application to Planning in Kenya* (Nairobi, 1965), 2.

[7] Mao Zedong's version of "The Third World" was very different from Sauvy's. Mao divided all countries into three "worlds": the first was the Cold War Superpowers, the second was the other industrialized countries, and the third was the rest of the world (led by China), see Record of Conversation, Mao Zedong-Kenneth Kaunda, February 22, 1974, in Zhonggong zhongyang wenxian yanjiushi (ed.), *Mao Zedong waijiao wenxuan* (*Selected Foreign Affairs Manuscripts of Mao Zedong*) (Beijing, 1994), 600–01.

Given the trouble we have had with terminologies for twentieth-century revolutions, and how politicized this issue still is, one may ask whether there is a need to distinguish between Third World revolutions and decolonization in general. Do not all decolonizations imply a form of revolution? And is it right, analytically, to differentiate between, say, Kenya and Tanzania, in terms of whether or not they should be encompassed by the term "Third World"? For our purposes here, such distinctions do make sense. Far too often the Third World has been seen as a region rather than as a set of loosely connected political projects. For us to discuss these revolutions in a historically comparative manner, we are dependent on broad but workable definitions of the phenomena under review. Therefore this attempt at situating the Third World in political terms – we will get back to whether the concept should be placed in time as well as in scope.

Third World Revolutions and the Trajectory from 1789

Before the middle part of the twentieth century, most of the world's population still lived within empires. But, for at least 150 years, these empires had been challenged, first and foremost in Europe, by other forms of organizing principles for the state, such as nation or class. During the nineteenth century, such ideals sometimes cohabited, often awkwardly: In France, where the revolutionary concept of an all-encompassing, democratic nation was pioneered, Bonaparte quickly transformed the revolutionary state into an empire, which throughout the century competed with other empires for overseas dominions. In Britain, in the mid-nineteenth century, expanding democracy led to an intensification of the quest for overseas control. In Germany and Italy, the national revolutions led to new states that democratized while searching for foreign expansion.

These tensions coming out of European revolutions of the late eighteenth and nineteenth centuries strongly influenced the Third World revolutions of the twentieth century. It makes sense to try to understand such influences through a set of key concepts that Third World revolutionaries inherited from the European past. But let it first be noted that these transmissions did not simply go in one direction. Sometimes, ideas became revolutionary through their encounters with politics and social practices outside of Europe – think of how collective ownership influenced concepts of property or how racial equality influenced concepts of democracy (or the nation, for that matter). Neither did these concepts remain static after they had been taken up by anticolonial activists. They developed along with the political trajectories of the anticolonial struggle. In some cases, as we will see later, they returned to Europe thoroughly transformed through implementation elsewhere. Think of "solidarity" and "justice," for instance, as used globally since the 1960s. But, first, let us look at four key concepts of European nineteenth-century revolution and state-building that came to be of crucial importance to Third World revolutionaries: nation, equality, sovereignty, and centralization.

Nation is a term first used constitutionally during the French Revolution and later picked up by all aspiring state-building revolutionaries. Diderot's *Encyclopedie*, published in 1765, had defined nation as "a considerable number of people, who live in a specific area of land, within specific boundaries, and obey the same government."[8] It is, as could be expected, a rationalist definition, in which the state is part of the term but culture and language are not. In many ways it fits postcolonial (and especially Third World) approaches to the concept of nation better than the revolutionary definitions that developed out of the European century that followed the *encyclopedistes*. Jacob Grimm's 1846 definition of a people, which became built into so many European national projects, is very different: "A people is the essence of all those who speak the same language."[9] The tension between these definitions came to color very significant aspects both of anticolonial resistance and Third World state-building.

Just as their counterparts in Europe in the nineteenth century, African and Asian revolutionaries in the twentieth century had to mobilize a concept of nation both to oppose empires and to define their project. The right to self-determination had to be based on the idea of a preexisting community of ancient origins and not just on colonial borders drawn by Europeans less than 100 years ago. This was hard to do, of course, since almost all new nation projects had to include many different groups, beliefs, and identities. The solution for Third World revolutionaries was often to develop a romantic concept of how different entities had become one nation through the anticolonial struggle. The argument is, of course, not unlike those of a Mazzini, when he told the Italians (a group he helped define) that only through an Italian national state could any dreams of social transformation be realized, in a nation "which will give them a name, education, work, and fair wages, together with the self-respect and purpose of men."[10]

---

[8] *Encyclopédie, ou dictionnaire raisonné des sciences, des arts et des métiers, etc.*, ed. by Denis Diderot and Jean le Rond d'Alembert, 28 vols. (Paris, 1751–1772), vol. 11 (Paris, 1765), 36("Nation").

[9] Jürgen Habermas, *The Postnational Constellation: Political Essays* (Cambridge, MA, 2001), 6, provides a good discussion.

[10] Mazzini, *Doveri del'Uomo* (Rome, 1873 [1860]).

Mazzini's critique of empire is very similar to that of Third World leaders such as Sékou Touré, Amilcar Cabral, or, for that matter, Sukarno. The problem with empire, as they saw it, is that it cannot, by its very design, deliver for those who are peripheral or of a different ethnicity, race, or religion than the elite at the imperial center. It is not the institutions of the empire or its claim to modernity and civilization that there is something wrong with. It is that the empire will not deliver for the colonized. Only a nation constituted as a sovereign state can produce the desired political, social, and economic outcomes. As Touré put it in 1958, when rejecting a future integration into a reformed French Union: "The overseas territories no longer demand latitudes and generosities from the hand of a 'humane' colonial regime, but the freedom for their movement, which implies their enjoyment of the right to choose for themselves, the natural right of all people to independence and self-determination. All forms of subjugation, all manifestations of paternalism or charity towards us will cause severe injury to our collective dignity and offend our African consciousness."[11] In Third World nationalisms, just as in nineteenth-century Europe (or, as we shall see later, Latin America), the nation as a narrative had woven into it a set of promises of transformation that could only be delivered through independence and separate statehood. This does of course not imply that the nation was the *only* possible critique of empire. Leaders who had grown up within an empire often started out by appealing to its institutions and laws in order to achieve the improvements that they sought, and it took a long time before all roads toward new forms of integrated communities within the framework of the old empires were cut off.[12]

This brings us to another key concept transmitted from nineteenth-century revolutions, that of *equality*. For Mazzini, or for Polish nationalists such as Adam Mickiewicz or countless others across Europe, equality between peoples and among people could only be established if the subservience imposed by foreign imperial elites was brought to an end. The struggle for liberation made true equality possible. In language reminiscent of Frantz Fanon or Aimé Césaire, nineteenth-century

---

[11] *Discours prononcé par Monsieur Sékou Touré, président du conseil de gouvernement a l'ouverture de la session extraordinaire de l'assemblée territoriale, le 28 juillet 1958* (Conakry, 1958), 13.

[12] Fred Cooper put it well: "The world in 1945 was still a world of empires – in the immediate aftermath of the defeat of two of the most aggressive in recent history – and nation-states existed among colonies, protectorates, mandated territories, dominions, federations, and national republics. The route out of empire did not necessarily, as far as anybody at the time knew, lead to the independent, sovereign, territorial nation-state," see Frederick Cooper, *Africa in the World: Capitalism, Empire, Nation-State* (Cambridge, MA, 2014), 91.

European nationalists outlined how the nations they had defined could only find redemption through struggle, and that community and authenticity were only achievable through personal as well as national liberation. Just as in Asia, Africa, and the Caribbean in the twentieth century, European anti-imperial rebels of the previous century were divided on how their aims could best be achieved, and many of them went through a long process of radicalization. Open rebellions against imperial institutions often came because empires did not live up to their stated ideals on matters such as equality.

While ethnic discrimination was always an element of imperial oppression, the increased emphasis on concepts of race within European overseas empires augmented tensions from the late nineteenth century on. While Gandhi could still appeal to British authorities for his and his community's rights as British subjects in South Africa at the very start of the twentieth century, time for postulating empires as moving toward increasing equality for all its inhabitants was running out. With ideas of modernization, improvement, and reform within European empires came also a stronger emphasis on racial hierarchies and divisions. Pseudo-Darwinian concepts of racial differences and capabilities increased distances between rulers and ruled, conveying a clear message to Western-educated elites in the colonies that the imperial institutions were for Europeans only. By the aftermath of the First World War, imperial centers had had time to prove themselves unwilling to share power or to create an international order in which non-Europeans had a say. The postwar "Wilsonian moment," to borrow Erez Manela's phrase, was therefore the Third World's 1848, out of which nationalist alternatives to empire grew.[13]

In addition to race, capital was key to the changes empires went through in the late nineteenth century, and which inspired anticolonial rebellion. As industrialization took hold in parts of Europe, colonies came to serve primarily as raw material producers for the metropole. The rampant exploitation of colonial resources, the ecological destruction, and the transformation into foreign-owned capital increased conflict in the colonies and forced indigenous elites to organize on behalf of their communities. The late nineteenth-century globalization of capitalism therefore both deepened inequality within empires and gave rise to resistance.[14]

---

[13] Erez Manela, *The Wilsonian Moment: Self-Determination and the International Origins of Anticolonial Nationalism* (Oxford, 2007). For a slightly different argument, stressing the 1905–1911 revolutions in Asia, see Charles Kurzman, *Democracy Denied, 1905–1915: Intellectuals and the Fate of Democracy* (Cambridge, MA, 2008).
[14] Sven Beckert's argument, that the "frontiers of capitalism are often to be found in the world's countryside" and "that the global countryside should be at the center of our

But if early globalization increased inner imperial tension, then economic instability in the 1920s and the Great Depression that followed contributed to making empire unviable. With much of the immediate economic benefit of empire eroded, the metropoles were increasingly forced to exploit colonial revenue for metropolitan purposes. These distended extractive practices were feeble, at best, because the administrative efforts of empires were increasingly concentrated on the metropolitan areas. But they did further increase radicalism in the colonies. Already caught between anticolonial resistance, economic pressures, and ideological commitment to liberty and self-determination in fighting the Second World War, the irrelevance of empire to reconstruction at home tipped the metropolitan political balance toward decolonization from the mid-1940s on.

The third concept that links the Third World to earlier revolutions is therefore *sovereignty*. In the European tradition, up to the nineteenth century, sovereignty belonged primarily in empires, because the emperor claimed a God-given right to rule over whoever he ruled. There had of course been exceptions and limitations, but the overall picture was clear: Sovereignty resided in the sovereign. The years 1776 and then 1789 blew up all that. The idea that sovereignty belonged to the people, which connected the American and French Revolutions, made it very difficult for empires to keep their hegemony in Europe. And the turn toward modernization and improvement as imperial purposes in the later nineteenth century came too late to save empire in the Americas, where the Latin American rebellions in the 1820s created new states based on popular sovereignty. In these new countries the very definition of territorial sovereignty was based on the reach of popular organizations. These "state-nations," as Jeremy Adelman rightly calls them, reinvented sovereignty as a tool of the postcolonial state. Very much as in the case of twentieth-century decolonization, the revolutions that produced the Latin American states out of the wreckage of Iberian empires were, as Adelman astutely observes, "the consequence, not the cause, of the end of imperial sovereignty."[15]

Another challenge to European empires in terms of sovereignty was the retreat of God. For centuries the justification for European overseas

thinking about the origins of the modern world" makes great sense in this context, see Sven Beckert, *Empire of Cotton: A Global History* (New York, 2014), 441. On dependence on the colonies, see Sven Beckert, "American Danger: United States Empire, Eurafrica, and the Territorialization of Industrial Capitalism, 1870-1950," *American Historical Review* 122, 4 (2017), 1137-70.

[15] Jeremy Adelman, *Sovereignty and Revolution in the Iberian Atlantic* (Princeton, NJ, 2009), 395; see also Jeremy Adelman, "Mimesis and Rivalry: European Empires and Global Regimes," *Journal of Global History* 10, 1 (2015), 77-98.

expansion had been to convert the heathen. Imperialism could be construed as a form of mission: Just as the emperor received his authority from God, empires received their justification from doing God's work. When imperial modernizers in the late nineteenth century tried to replace God with "progress," the results were at best mixed. Seeley's argument, in *The Expansion of England*, that the "dominion of England in India is rather the empire of the modern world over the medieval," made the whole imperial project dependent on modernity.[16] But the idea that imperial authority emanates from the emperor (or empress in Seeley's case) was very hard to square with modern concepts of governance, at least when the twentieth century began and governance *within* the metropole was so clearly connected to some idea of democracy. Moreover, designs for "modern" government were spread globally, as Amanda Behm points out, within networks that between the 1880s and the 1920s "trafficked in a shared political idiom of liberty, rights, and constitutional development."[17]

The claims to sovereignty that Third World revolutionaries put forward grew out of the receding competence and purview of empires. Their claims were contested and, sometimes, diffuse but centered on a revolutionary state representing the people.[18] Just as in the 1848 revolutions in Europe and (even more) the early nineteenth-century revolutions in Latin America, Third World leaders added statements about the natural direction of world history and about transnational solidarity against empires as part of their legitimacy. The biggest challenge against them (and against their claims) was not attempts at recolonization or the existence within their borders of settler minorities but the international economic and political system that they had to operate within. The new states of the 1950s and 1960s had reason to question whether real sovereignty was possible within a capitalist world economy that was centered on Western Europe and North America. While Third World states attempted to regulate their interaction with the world economy, the Cold War forced them into patterns of international allegiances that served neither their political nor economic interests. Attempts at developing extensive South–South exchanges of trade, technologies, and expertise failed almost at the first hurdle. And calls for multilateral changes to the world economy to better serve the needs of new states went largely unheeded, such as in the UN Declaration on the Granting of

---

[16] John R. Seeley, *The Expansion of England: Two Courses of Lectures* (London, 1883), 282.
[17] Amanda Behm, "Settler Historicism and Anticolonial Rebuttal in the British World, 1880-1920," *Journal of World History* 26, 4 (2015), 785–813, 788.
[18] David Armitage and Sanjay Subrahmanyam (eds.), *The Age of Revolutions in Global Context, c. 1760–1840* (New York, 2010), provides comparative perspectives.

Independence to Colonial Countries and Peoples, passed by the General Assembly in 1960, which noted that "peoples may, for their own ends, freely dispose of their natural wealth and resources without prejudice to any obligations arising out of international economic cooperation."[19] The New International Economic Order, passed by the General Assembly a decade and a half later, fared little better.[20]

The fourth key concept with echoes of older revolutions in the Third World discourse was the perceived need for centralization and integration. Just as in the French Revolution, which emphasized the strengthening of the nation through national integration, the Latin American revolutions had called for building the nation through specific programs: Regulation, education, infrastructure, and banks were all created in the service of national ideals. In Latin America there was also a need to create laws and institutions that separated the "indigenous" Spanish or Portuguese from those of the same origin who had simply been there to serve the empires (and who should be excluded from the "nation"). Difficult as this process was, it was further complicated by the need to integrate, through assimilation, the non-European indigenous population of the Americas. The term *indigenismo*, when applied to nineteenth-century Latin America, was, primarily, an attempt not at improving the conditions of the pre-Columbian population but at separating "native" Europeans from "imperial" Europeans. Along with the romantic image of the Indian as symbol for the new states went the subjugation of Africans and the extermination of the actual indigenous peoples who were deemed too uncivilized to be part of the new nation.

These concepts (and the problems that went with them) were found in many radical Third World states after independence. Centralization and integration were, it was believed, the only means by which industrial development could be created and the new state-nation could be defended (including against challenges from within). Just as in Latin America a century earlier, there were strong divisions between anticolonial Europeanized elites, wedded to programs of modernist social and economic transformation, and the communities over which they ruled, for whom the new nation was, at best, an abstraction. There were, in the Third World revolutions, deep fears that alternative (or hybrid) identities could compete with the new national identities that state leaders wanted to create. Local solidarities and beliefs were therefore often defined as being against the state-nation: Values connected to lineage, caste, tribe, or

---

[19] UN General Assembly Resolution 1514 (XV), December 14, 1960. 89 countries voted in favor, nine abstained: Australia, Belgium, the Dominican Republic, France, Portugal, Spain, South Africa, Britain, and the United States.
[20] UN General Assembly Resolution 3201 (S-VI), Declaration on the Establishment of a New International Economic Order, May 1, 1974.

religion should be struck out through centralization and integration. Just as Spanish and Portuguese had become the languages of integration in the new Latin American republics, all over the decolonized world colonial languages came to symbolize the new nations. Except in a few countries, where an indigenous minority language became the new standard, and regions where Arabic was already established, almost all new states chose to converse (and enforce) in English, French, or Portuguese.[21]

Third World Revolutions and the Trajectory from 1917

While it would be entirely wrong to set the Russian Revolution aside from the overall trajectory of European revolutions since 1789, the Bolshevik takeover did imply a new direction in the purpose to which revolutionary change could be put. The key innovation of the 1917 revolution was of course the rule of a new social class through a vanguard party. While similar ideas had existed among European revolutionaries at least since the French Revolution, Lenin and his followers were the first ones to put them into practice on a large scale and thereby create a revolutionary state of great power and ambition. The year 1917 is therefore a dividing line in the history of modern revolutions, not because it stands aside from older trends, but because of the communists' categorical claim to be the fulfillment of everything that had gone before.

The impact of the Bolshevik Revolution on Third World radicals was intense and direct. Some of this was due to its timing, some of it to its character. It was of course not accidental that revolution in Russia, itself a major European empire, happened as a result of the same great war that weakened other empires. What the Bolsheviks took over was a colonial empire, which they then tried to form into a multinational socialist state, a union of Soviet republics. But, in spite of the USSR's global assertions, there were only limited causal relationships between endeavors by the Soviet state and anticolonial rebellions and decolonizations, except, perhaps, in China, where the Soviets at first shaped the revolutionary movement, and possibly in Iran.[22] The Russian Revolution and the communist-led state that followed was a strong inspiration and, at times, aid to revolutions that had their own geneses, although their contemporaneousness ensured that many Third World revolutionaries would move toward, and sometimes through, the Soviet experience while setting up their own states.

---

[21] Some of the most populous countries are exceptions in choosing an indigenous minority language: China, India, Pakistan, and Indonesia.

[22] Jean-François Fayet, "1919," in S. A. Smith (ed.), *The Oxford Handbook of the History of Communism* (Oxford, 2014), 109–24.

Throughout its existence, the Soviet Union insisted that part of its purpose was to assist in the liberation of colonies. Such liberation had several objectives from a Soviet perspective: It was in line with the Soviet dedication to international justice (as defined by Moscow); it was part of a necessary and unavoidable historical process; and it would prevent access for capitalist countries to resources they depended upon. The latter perspective was particularly important after 1941, when the Soviet Union itself went from being a peripheral to a central actor in world affairs. But throughout its existence the USSR helped shelter, train, educate, and supply Third World radicals, some of whom (but in no way all) became founders of communist parties in their home countries. Already in December 1919 the Comintern had set up a Department of the East, which was intended to coordinate these initiatives. The following year the first Congress of the Peoples of the East was held in Baku, outlining a communist policy on national liberation. Programs of education, such as the Communist University of the Toilers of the East (1921) and Patrice Lumumba University (1961), were set up in Moscow for students from Asia and Africa. Anticolonial activists received organizational and military training in the USSR, and the Soviets supplied civilian aid and weapons to liberation movements across the globe.[23]

One of the main contributions the Soviets made to anticolonial movements was their role in establishing international networks. Although many of these efforts were intended simply to supplement Comintern and Soviet policy (and in some cases provide much-needed intelligence for the USSR), they had a much broader importance for the participants. The League against Imperialism, set up by agents secretly working for the Comintern in Berlin in 1926, came to connect a large number of anticolonial activists from different continents. Many of them were not communists (such as Jawaharlal Nehru, Mohammad Hatta, or the Algerian nationalist Ahmed Ben Messali Hadj – all prominent participants at the League's Brussels conference in 1927). A number of the concepts of international solidarity, organization, and state formation that became integral to Third World revolutions came out of networks set up and often staffed by communists.

---

[23] Sauvy, in postulating the Third World concept, feared that the Soviets would end up dominating the project, especially since he lamented, like many Frenchmen of his generation, that the Americans were "neophytes of domination, mystics of free enterprise to the point of conceiving it as an end, [who] have not yet clearly perceived that the underdeveloped country of the feudal type could pass much more easily to a Communist regime than to democratic capitalism," see Sauvy, "Trois Mondes, Une Planète."

One key concept that links these revolutions to the Soviet experiment was the large-scale expropriation of land that many postcolonial states carried out, ostensibly on behalf of the peasants who were the overwhelming majority of inhabitants in the new countries. Revolutionaries had of course carried out land expropriations before the 1917 revolution, but what the Bolsheviks did was on an entirely different scale, by, in effect, declaring that all land in the country was owned by the state as a representative of its citizens. For the new states, as for the Bolsheviks, the physical control of rural areas that expropriations were intended to produce also meant that the surplus of the peasants' labor would be available to fund large-scale and rapid industrialization. Even those who did not carry out complete nationalizations à la communist states came to understand that the only major domestic contribution toward "development" would come, in some form or another, from controlling access to the agricultural surplus.

Another major concept to which the Soviets made a strong contribution was central economic planning. Just as with expropriations of land, planning was not exclusively a Bolshevik game; some of the new European and Latin American states of the nineteenth century had tried their hand at the pooling of national resources, and state planning had become a major tool of all warring countries in the First World War. But it was the Soviet communists who elevated central planning to a dogma of development. And with what was seen as their rapid economic progress in the 1930s, during the otherwise global Great Depression, and with the Soviet victory against Nazi Germany in the Second World War, Moscow-style planning became a favored instrument in Third World states. Even in a country such as India, where Nehru was intent on setting up a new state as a Third World alternative to communism, the new government's economists concentrated on the Soviet experience when they drew up their country's first five-year plans in the 1950s.[24]

A third, and even more specific, connection between the Russian Revolution and Third World revolutions was the concept of one-party rule as an alternative to a multi-party system. Ideas about centralization coming out of the European nineteenth century contributed to this trend (as they did to the Bolsheviks' own notion of "the dictatorship of the proletariat," a concept they had taken over from Marx and especially Engels).[25] But the

---

[24] David C. Engerman, *The Price of Aid: The Economic Cold War in India* (Cambridge, MA, 2018).

[25] The concept of the dictatorship of the proletariat was first mooted in January 1852 by the immigrant Marxist Joseph Wedemeyer in the New York *Turn-Zeitung* (a German-language journal promoting gymnastics as self-improvement). Wedemeyer later became a US Army officer, serving as a colonel in the Civil War.

key to its success was the notion that rule by a vanguard party would help promote rapid industrial development through efficiency and single-minded determination. Instead, what often happened was that the failings of the regime were hidden by a dictatorship that was more personal than class-based. After the first postcolonial era, most one-party states in Africa and Asia collapsed and were replaced by more pluralistic or democratic systems. The exception is of course the world's remaining Marxist-Leninist states: China, Vietnam, North Korea, and Cuba.

As with the fall of one-party states, the end of the Third World as a project is intimately connected with the end of the Cold War and the collapse of the Soviet Union. Again, the causes are more simultaneous than sequential: The second phase of intense capitalist globalization from the 1970s placed increased pressure on Third World regimes as on the Soviet Union to make their peace with the West. The choices made, both individually and collectively, by most Third World countries to prioritize economic demands over political principles or cooperation contributed to the collapse of the Third World project roughly during the same phase as the Soviet Union itself got into trouble. By the late 1980s there was little left both of Third World solidarity and of the Soviet alternative to global capitalism.[26]

Soviet hopes to influence and, eventually, lead radical Third World movements and states toward a more established socialism failed for three main reasons. The complicated relationship Western European communist parties had with radical nationalist movements in the colonies made many Third World leaders suspicious of where Soviet loyalties lay. To them, it seemed as if the Soviets always prioritized the support of the European parties and that those parties were more preoccupied with their electoral support in the metropolitan countries than with anticolonial principles.[27] The Soviet Union may have been an ideal in some respects, but it was also a very white country, led by older European men. The second challenge for Soviet claims to leadership was embedded in its Marxist political theory. Marxism (especially in its Stalinist form) saw development toward a vanguard party, a socialist revolution, and the building of a socialist state as a very long-term process for countries in which industrialization was barely beginning. In spite of attempts at developing new theories for social change as Soviet involvement in Asia and

---

[26] The chapters in Artemy Kalinovsky and Sergey Radchenko (eds.), *The End of the Cold War and The Third World: New Perspectives on Regional Conflict* (London, 2011) provide a very useful introduction.

[27] The French Communist Party is the best example; for a critique, see Aimé Césaire, "Letter to Maurice Thorez," *Social Text* 28, 2 (2010), 145–52.

Africa grew in the 1960s, Soviet Marxism's insistence that only the proletariat could build a communist party and a socialist state meant that many Third World leaders suspected that Moscow looked down upon them and did not regard them as "true" revolutionaries. Finally, there was the problem of the Soviet state itself remaining, in shape at least, remarkably similar to that of the Russian empire. The Soviets of course insisted, and often got away with, the notion that they had taken an empire and transformed it into a voluntary union of socialist republics. But all Africans and Asians who had spent time in the USSR knew that the reality was very different. Europeans controlled non-Europeans in the Soviet Union, in ways that were sometimes menacingly similar to those former colonial subjects had experienced in their own countries.

Anticolonial Revolutions Compared

Understanding Third World revolutions through a comparative historical framework makes a lot of sense. It helps us better differentiate among various strands and voices within these revolutions, but first and foremost it assists us in recovering the long-term trajectories that most anticolonial revolutionaries themselves saw so clearly. Concepts such as sovereignty and nation linked them to processes of political change that were global and long term, and that have direct connections to our own time. Even though the crescendo of anticolonial rebellion has died down, most of the issues that liberation movements and postcolonial states attempted to address are still with us: Massive global inequality, destruction of common resources, and international instability and conflict are not just mid-twentieth-century phenomena.

This chapter has argued that one way in which the comparative approach is helpful is through overcoming false distinctions in terms of concepts and their relationships. Linking the European past to events in Africa and Asia in the twentieth century makes it possible to see continuities and potentialities across state or national borders. The continental separations themselves should be queried: Seen from an immediate post-imperial angle, the notion that all of "Europe" naturally belonged together in a union for common advantage, while countries across the world that for centuries were part of the same empire did not, was unconvincing. As we have seen in the 2015–2016 refugee crisis, both Europe and the United States sometimes act as if decolonization removed any immediate responsibility for the rest of the world. It is easy to see why the Senegalese leader Léopold Senghor in 1953 argued that Africa did not want to be the dowry France paid to Germany as part of the marriage contract of the two former enemies.[28] But the idea that long-term imperial connections, say between France and Mali or between Portugal and Mozambique, count for less than the relationship between each of these European Union countries and, say Finland or Croatia, is in historical terms puzzling.

The chapter has also argued that the comparative approach helps critique some of the culturally based separations that have been created by treating revolutionary change as inherently national or regional. Looking at how the colonial world collapsed through World Wars and global capitalist crises helps us understand how transnational anticolonial resistance came from the nature of empires themselves. Very often fixed concepts of race and religion were secondary in the political part of these struggles, though they grew in importance as new states established themselves. So too the concept of nation was transformed, until some postcolonial states started behaving as if they in substance were empires in the making, either domestically and internationally, or both – think Ba'athist Iraq (for both) or Myanmar (in the treatment of minorities).

Finally, there is the issue of what happened to international affairs as a result of the break-up of empires. Avoiding global imperial clashes or the inevitable suppression on behalf of the center that empires produced are undoubtedly good things, even though many of these imperial ills were replicated through the Cold War. But recognizing all independent states as having equal sovereignty, in theory if not in practice, has led to an odd form of democratization of world politics, in which the rights of states have been prioritized over almost everything else that societies and communities possess. As we move toward an era in international affairs that may see more multi-polarity than any time since the early imperial epoch, it is worth reminding ourselves that, in spite of their own claims to perfect representation, states are not people and that sometimes concepts, ideas, and practices spread in ways that neither state-nations nor empires can fully comprehend.

---

[28] Ct. in Cooper, *Africa in the World*, 95. Senghor had good reasons not wanting to be part of the dowry for such a marriage. During the Second World War he had spent two years in a German Stalag camp as a French prisoner of war.

8 The Global Islamic Revolution

Abbas Amanat

The last years of the 1970s and early 1980s witnessed an unprecedented growth of radical Islamic movements throughout the greater Middle East and North Africa from Pakistan to the Sudan. The climax of this process, and its most consequential trajectory, was no doubt the 1978–1979 Iranian Revolution and the emergence of the Islamic Republic of Iran. It was a revolution in the classic sense with instantaneous and vast popular support and with an Islamic ideological core that throughout the 1980s gradually evolved into a theocratic doctrine.

The Islamic Revolution was by no means the only Islamist upheaval of the period that changed the sociopolitical climate of the region. Other movements of dissent in the Sunni world shared with Shi'i Iran the desire to transform their societies, cultures, and political orders with the presumed desire of returning to the paradigm of "pristine" Islam. They widely differed from the Iranian case in their doctrinal objectives, organizational format, radical intensity, and mass appeal. In the half century prior to the Iranian revolution of 1979, Islamist movements ranging from the Society of Muslim Brothers in Egypt to the Jama'at-i Islami in Pakistan came to contribute, at times even more then the Islamic Revolution in Iran, to the rise of a defiant Islamic awareness. At this juncture, it may be argued, the societies of the Muslim world offered a perfect example of "connected histories," made possible through the press and other forms of mass media.[1]

Between 1978 and 1983 there emerged at least seven proto-revolutionary trends throughout the region promoting a shari'a-based Islamic order in one form or another. The anti-Ba'athist uprising in Syria, the siege of the Holy Mosque in Mecca, the storming of the US Embassy in Islamabad, the Shi'i unrest in southern Iraq, and pro-

---

[1] David Motadel, "Islamic Revolutionaries and the End of Empire," in Martin Thomas and Andrew S. Thompson (eds.), *The Oxford Handbook of the End of Empires* (Oxford, 2018), 555–79, discusses this longer trajectory of Islamic revolutionary movements. For "connected histories," albeit in early modern times, see Sanjay Subrahmanyam, *Explorations in Connected History: Mughals and Franks* (Oxford, 2012).

Khomeini rallies from Jakarta to West Africa are but few examples. By the end of 1980s, the face of the greater Middle East substantially differed from that of the mid-1970s. In most cases these Islamic movements of dissent – often in the guise of Salafi Islam – compelled some Sunni regimes in power to adopt explicit Islamic postures, such as legislating the shari'a into the constitution and the civil law. Yet they often did not intend to directly take over political power and when they did, they categorically failed.

The Changing Face of the Lands of Islam

The core of these new radical trends, and by far the most successful, was the Islamic Revolution in Iran that culminated in the overthrow of the Pahlavi dynasty in February 1979 and soon after the establishment of the Islamic Republic of Iran. In a short timespan mass rallies which brought hundreds of thousands into the streets, sit-ins, strikes, and clashes with security forces evolved into a tumultuous movement with diverse ideological objectives and with equally diverse aspirations for the establishment of an almost utopian order. With Ayatollah Khomeini increasingly its de facto leader, however, the Islamist trend gained momentum. His arrival from exile and the victory of the revolution soon after continued with a referendum in favor of an Islamic republic, an Islamic constitution, and the election of the first president and the first Islamic *majlis* (parliament). In a record period, perhaps unprecedented for any revolutionary movement in modern times, the Islamic revolution succeeded to wipe out nearly all alternative trends, including the liberal nationalists, the Marxists, and the Marxist-Islamist Mujahidin-i Khalq. Moreover, it managed to dismantle the Iranian secularized elite and remove the greater part of the secularized middle classes from virtually all positions of privilege and power. At the same time the revolutionary regime in Iran was waging a bloody war of attrition against the invading armies of neighboring Iraq that lasted more than eight years, and was engaging in a reckless diplomatic crisis whereby a number of American diplomats and staff of the embassy were held hostage by a breakaway revolutionary faction for more than a year (Figure 8.1).[2]

Yet Iran was not the first case of Islamist activism in the region. As early as July 1977, the fall of Zulfikar Ali Butto, the prime minister of Pakistan, in a military coup that brought to power General Muhammad Zia' ul-Haqq

---

[2] Abbas Amanat, *Iran: A Modern History* (New Haven, CT, 2017), 703–867, provides an overview; see also below for further references.

Figure 8.1 Photograph of armed militants demonstrating in support of a revolutionary cause, Tehran, Iran, 1979. (Abbas, Magnum)

displayed a shift toward radical Islamist discourse through the machinery of the state rather than revolutionary overthrow of the government. Zia' ul-Haqq's decade-long rule (1977–1988) in effect catered, at least initially, for increasingly vociferous trends such as Jama'at-i Islami and its founder, Abu A'la Mawdudi.[3] Pakistani Islamists and their cohorts in power soon found a new ground to preach their brand of radicalism to the Mujahidin resistance movement in the neighboring land.

In Afghanistan following the fall of the Davud Khan regime in 1978, the ensuing rivalry between the two wings of the communist party eventually paved the way for a decade-long Soviet occupation of the country starting in December 1979. The Soviet military intervention, the first since the 1968 invasion of Czechoslovakia, was viewed by the United States and its Cold War allies as a major setback in the region's fragile geopolitics, especially coming in the wake of the Iranian revolution and its anti-American postures. The Pakistani army and security services, traditionally close allies of the United States, thus came to serve as a conduit for funneling US logistical support to the emerging Afghan resistance, which soon came to be known as the Mujahidin.

CIA operatives oversaw a grand Islamist collision against Soviet occupation. With its self-assumed stance as the bastion of "true" Islam, Saudi Arabia soon became a willing partner on Washington's side. It financially backed the Mujahidin and dispatched volunteers to fight along with the Afghans against the heathen communists. Yet the outcome of Soviet invasion proved to be more complex than what the Soviet leadership and its Afghan allies bargained for. Support for the Mujahidin, too, proved to be more complex and costly than the over-confident but naïve US policymakers and advisors first anticipated, both in the Carter and Reagan administrations. The decade-long Soviet occupation not only proved to be a political and military disaster, but it ushered a period of instability and conflict that in turn triggered further Salafi radicalism and contributed to factional and ethnic tensions in the region.[4]

The Soviet withdrawal from Afghanistan in early 1989 was followed by a devastating civil war in which many factions vying for power seriously damaged the very fabric of Afghan society and economy, its feeble urban middle class, and eventually gave rise to the Taliban in 1994. Narrow-minded and intolerant, the establishment of the Taliban regime in Kabul in 1996 was the end product of a disastrous civil war that further dimmed Afghanistan's prospects for civil liberties, secular education, women's advancement, and communal coexistence. The Taliban regime moreover came to harbor a legion of Islamist volunteers, mostly from the Arab world, who were eager to spread a message of global jihad under the aegis of a terrorist organization that eventually came to consolidate as al-Qa'ida.[5]

Aside from the tumultuous events in Iran, Pakistan, and Afghanistan at the close of the 1970s, in Saudi Arabia, too, the short-lived but symbolically significant seizure of the Grand Mosque of Mecca on November 20, 1979 by a group of Wahhabi extremists who harbored messianic aspirations shook the oil-rich Saudi kingdom and its complacent princely class.[6] Up to then the Saudi kingdom had managed to present itself to

---

[4] Steve Coll, *Ghost Wars: The Secret History of the CIA, Afghanistan, and Bin Laden, from the Soviet Invasion to September 10, 2001* (New York, 2005).

[5] Abbas Amanat, "Empowered Through Violence: The Reinventing of Islamic Extremism," in Strobe Talbott and Nayan Chanda (eds.), *The Age of Terror* (New York, 2001), 23–52; and, more generally, Ahmed Rashid, *Taliban: Militant Islam, Oil and Fundamentalism in Central Asia* (New Haven, CT, 2000); Lawrence Wright, *The Looming Tower: Al-Qaeda and the Road to 9/11* (New York, 2006); and Thomas H. Johnson, *Taliban Narratives: The Use and Power of Stories in the Afghanistan Conflict* (Oxford, 2018).

[6] Thomas Hegghammer, "Rejectionist Islamism in Saudi Arabia: The Story of Juhayman Al-Utaybi Revisited," *International Journal of Middle East Studies* 39, 1 (2007), 103–22.

its own people and the outside world as a land of harmonious coexistence between a conservative religious establishment that enforced a strict Hanbali-Wahhabi shari'a and a privileged Saudi elite. To check the existential threat to Saudi survival and to uphold its self-assumed status as the custodian of the holy shrines of Islam, and to buttress its bruised Islamic credentials within and outside the Muslim world, it became imperative upon the Saudi regime to embark on a worldwide Wahhabi-Salafi propaganda campaign throughout the 1980s and beyond.[7]

At the time the siege of the Grand Mosque provoked anti-American reaction elsewhere. In Pakistan, after a radio broadcast on November 21, 1979 alleged that the US had bombed the Grand Mosque, the Jama'at-i Islami and their allies provoked the angry crowd to attack the American embassy in Islamabad and burn the building down to the ground. After some commotion the staff of the embassy was rescued but the incident helped in belittling the US image abroad. Coming soon after the hostage crisis in Iran, Khomeini was quick to allege that Washington was behind the seizure of the Grand Mosque, hence fueling anti-American conspiratorial sentiments. Shortly thereafter, on 2 December 1979, the US embassy in Tripoli, Libya, was also burnt down by a crowd incited by the Libyan regime, even though at the time the embassy staff had already been reduced to the bare minimum.[8]

Beyond a halfhearted effort to dampen radicalization at home, the Saudi kingdom for the greater part was concerned with the challenge of the Islamic Revolution in Iran that had captured the Muslim imaginations worldwide.[9] The long-term repercussions of a Shi'i revolution in neighboring Iran was bound to trigger a Saudi-sponsored program of Wahhabicization of Sunni communities from Pakistan to the Balkans and from the Caucasus to Southeast Asia. The Saudi initiative proved to be truly transformative. Saudi-trained and Saudi-financed preachers and missionaries, with anti-secular, anti-Shi'i and anti-Sufi agendas,

---

[7] Thomas Hegghammer, "Jihad, Yes, But Not Revolution: Explaining the Extraversion of Islamist Violence in Saudi Arabia," *British Journal of Middle Eastern Studies* 36, 3 (2009), 395–416; and Michel G. Nehme, "Saudi Development Plans Between Capitalist and Islamic Values," *Middle Eastern Studies* 30, 3 (1994), 632–45. Yaroslav Trofimov, *The Siege of Mecca* (New York, 2007), provides a good account of the Mecca uprising. At the time Khomeini allegedly claimed that the Meccan incident was an attack orchestrated by the West.

[8] Coll, *Ghost War*, on the events in Pakistan.

[9] Fred R. Von Der Mehden, "Indonesia," in John L. Esposito (ed.), *The Oxford Encyclopedia of the Modern Islamic World* (Oxford, 1995); Uta Lehmann, "The Impact of the Iranian Revolution on Muslim Organizations in South Africa during the Struggle against Apartheid," *Journal for the Study of Religion* 19, 1 (2006), 23–39; and, more generally, Vali Nasr, *The Shia Revival: How Conflicts within Islam Will Shape the Future* (New York, 2007), esp. 155–56.

infiltrated not only the Mujahidin ranks in Afghanistan but the madrasas from Pakistan to Yemen and throughout the African continent. The physical representation of the new brand of Salafi Islam was particularly visible in the construction and maintenance of Saudi-sponsored mosques and religious madrasas all over the Muslim world. Remarkably their message of ultra conservative, and yet potentially revolutionary, Salafi Islam carried a kernel of anti-Westernism. What is characterized as radical Islamism, and the terrorist impulses that later aimed at secular societies or at traditional forms of Islamic practices were largely influenced by Salafi motives. To this day these nodes of Islamism were nurtured and financed in a Wahhabi-inspired environment.[10]

Another important turning point in the calendar of Islamic militancy, but somewhat independent from the Iranian Revolution or Saudi-inspired Wahhabi radicalism, came with the assassination of President Anwar al-Sadat of Egypt on 6 October 1981. The conclusion of the peace treaty between Egypt and Israel in March 1979, which stirred much anger and frustration among Arab nationalists and in the Muslim world at large, revealed a fissure in the Arab leadership primarily with regards to the fate of the Palestinians. The peace accord was seen by many as proof of Egypt's (or rather Sadat's) betrayal of the Arab cause. It was a bitter reality that revealed disempowerment and defeat in the thirty-five-year struggle against Zionism, occupation of the Palestinian territories, and the calamity of the 1967 defeat in the Six-Day War with Israel.

Sadat's assassination was carried out by the military wing of a splinter group of Egypt's Islamic Jihad (*Al-Jihad al-Islami al-Masri*), which predictably also laid claim to the liberation of the holy sites in Palestine. The attack on the spectators' stand, where Sadat was observing a military parade, displayed a remarkable shift in ideology, since frustration with Zionism and Israel was expressed not through the predominant prism of Arab nationalism and its largely secular perspective, but through a radical Islamist ideology directed towards a Muslim head of state.[11] Sadat was declared not merely a traitor to the Egyptian people but an infidel to the cause of Islam. This was ironic given the fact that Sadat displayed a greater degree of religiosity than any of his predecessors – even calling himself the "believer president," proudly wearing his prayer mark on his forehead, and letting many Muslim Brothers (*Jama'a al-Ikhwan al-Muslimin*) out of prison.

---

[10] Thomas Hegghammer, *Jihad in Saudi Arabia: Violence and Pan-Islamism Since 1979* (Cambridge, 2010).
[11] Emmanuel Sivan, *Radical Islam: Medieval Theology and Modern Politics* (New Haven, CT, 1990), 83–129; and Henry Munson, *Islam and Revolution in the Middle East* (New Haven, CT, 1989).

As much as the assassination of Sadat symbolized a greater shift toward Islamic militancy, it did not trigger a revolution or even put a permanent dent in the political and economic sway of the Egyptian military establishment over the country.[12] The Egyptian army, which had remained at the political helm since 1952, maintained its grip over Egypt for decades to come and with little interruption up to the present day. Nor did the tumultuous events of the period in Egypt or in Iran, Saudi Arabia, Pakistan, or Afghanistan profoundly alter the behavior of other Arab military or paramilitary regimes in the region. The paradigm of military rule, which was rooted in the late Ottoman era and grew into a predominant mode of governance among the nascent postcolonial Arab states, proved durable once it partially adopted Islamic symbols and legal measures, as for instance in Zia' ul-Haqq's Pakistan after 1978 and Ja'far Nimairy's Sudan after 1981. Mindful of their own survival in the face of a vociferous conservative Islamist camp, both military leaders were obliged to enforce a strict shari'a-based Islamist regime.

Soon after 1979 the Islamists in Syria, too, rose to rebellion. When in early 1982 President al-Assad faced an uprising in Hama headed by the Syrian branch of the Muslim Brothers, his security forces in less than a month massacred at least ten thousand members and sympathizers. The impetus was successfully curbed.[13] This was no doubt the most serious suppression of an Islamist revolt throughout the period. It consolidated the Syrian Ba'athist regime in power, which soon became a tactical ally and long-term partner of the Islamic Republic of Iran largely in opposition to the rival Ba'athist regime in Iraq under Saddam Hussein.[14]

Inspired by the success of the Iranian revolution, the Da'wa Party of Iraq, led by Muhammad Baqir Sadr and other members of his camp, stepped up its efforts aiming in long run at the overthrow of the Iraqi regime. Yet Sadr, a noted clerical scholar who had written on Shi'i law and theology from a modernist perspective, was inclined more toward an Islamic government led by the "community" (umma), rather than by the "guardianship of the jurist" (vilayat-i faqih) as championed by Ayatollah Khomeini and his supporters as the core ideology of the Islamic Republic

---

[12] It did, however, provide the newly-established Islamic Republic of Iran with another propaganda tool. The full coverage of the assassination in the Iranian media, which wholly vindicated Khalid Islamboli, was followed by the renaming of a major Tehran street in the assassin's honor. No doubt the grudge against Sadat was nursed by his welcoming reception of the shah of Iran in exile. The latter had died in a Cairo military hospital in July 1980.

[13] Brynjar Lia, "The Islamist Uprising in Syria, 1976–82: The History and Legacy of a Failed Revolt," British Journal of Middle Eastern Studies 43, 4 (2016), 541–59.

[14] Raphaël Lefèvre, Ashes of Hama: The Muslim Brotherhood in Syria (Oxford, 2013), 81–136.

of Iran.[15] On the eve of the Iraq-Iran war (1980–1988), Sadr and his family paid with their lives at the hands of Saddam's regime on the charge of advocating an Islamic revolution on the Iranian model.

Throughout the war with Iran, the Ba'athist regime in Iraq systematically clamped down on the Shi'is in the south, and more pointedly on the Supreme Council for the Islamic Revolution in Iraq (al-Majlis al-A'la al-Thawra Islamiyya al-'Iraqi) founded in the early 1980s, which was closely associated with revolutionary Iran. The anti-Shi'i crackdown culminated during the Shi'i rebellion in March and April 1991, when at the conclusion of the Persian Gulf War the Shi'i opposition in the south was convinced by what turned out to be a misleading signal by the United States that it was time to rise against Baghdad.[16] In the north the Kurds, who had already suffered the harshest treatment at the hands of Baghdad during the *Anfal* operation, experienced even greater destruction of their towns and villages, displacement, and mass execution of civilians.

On another front, the Islamic Revolution was a great source of inspiration for the underprivileged Shi'i community in southern Lebanon, in the Bekaa Valley, and in west Beirut. It helped solidify Shi'i resolve in the face of sectarian strife during the Lebanese Civil War (1975 to 1990), and especially the devastating Israeli invasion of Lebanon in 1982.[17] In the politically charged environment of the Civil War, the Israeli massacre of the Palestinians in Sabra and Shatila refugee camps in September 1982 (in collaboration with their allies, the Maronite Phalange militias), impacted the Shi'i community and helped in reorienting its sympathies toward revolutionary Iran. The secret murder of the charismatic Iranian-Lebanese Shi'i leader Imam Musa Sadr, presumably at the hands of Colonel Mu'ammar Qadhdhafi of Libya, only added to the Lebanese militancy. The shortcomings of the Amal Movement, the parliamentary wing of the Shi'i movement, moreover, set the ground for the rise of a new militia organization, that came to be known as the Hizb Allah (Party of Allah) of Lebanon.[18]

Deeply motivated, and financially and militarily backed by elements within the Islamic Republic of Iran anxious to "export" the Islamic revolution, and in particular by the Islamic Revolutionary Guards' extra-territorial wing, which came to be known as the Quds Force (*Sipah-i Quds*), by 1985 the Hizb Allah of Lebanon emerged as a force to reckon

---

[15] Joyce N. Willey, *The Islamic Movement of Iraqi Shi'as* (Boulder, CO, 1992), 125–37.

[16] Sarah Graham-Brown, *Sanctioning Saddam: The Politics of Intervention in Iraq* (London, 1999), 17–24.

[17] Yusri Hazran, "Re-Confessionalising the Shi'is and the Druzes: The Failure of Secularism in Lebanon," *British Journal of Middle Eastern Studies* 40, 2 (2013), 162–82.

[18] Augustus Richard Norton, *Hezbollah: A Short History* (Princeton, NJ, 2007), 14–46.

with within the Lebanese complex of power politics and beyond. Yet under Sheikh Muhammad Hussein Fadlallah, the Hizb Allah's costly confrontations with Israel gradually readjusted its perspective on the realities of Lebanese multi-confessional politics and the dire consequences of encounters with the militarily superior Israel.[19]

Support for the Iraqi Da'wa and for the Hizb Allah of Lebanon, as well as tactical alliance with Assad in Syria, were examples of how the Iranian regime candidly encouraged the export of the Islamic revolution to neighboring countries with substantial Shi'i populations. Khomeini's unapologetic call for globalizing the Islamic revolution galvanized dormant Islamist trends, including activists among the Shi'i minority in the oil-rich Eastern Province of Saudi Arabia. In the early 1980s during the annual hajj droves of Iranian pilgrims publicly demonstrated in support of Khomeini's Islamic revolution and against the Saudi regime, which was readily labeled as corrupt and tyrannical. Denial of Saudi sovereignty over the holy shrines of Mecca and Medina and calls for a global Islamic revolution led to deadly clashes with the Saudi authorities, which in turn prompted Khomeini to temporarily ban the hajj pilgrimage, one of Islam's obligatory duties.

From the early days of the revolution, and throughout the years of war with Iraq, Khomeini repeatedly defined in his speeches how he wished the Islamic revolution to be exported. "When we say we wish to export our revolution all over the world," he declared in a speech in March 1983, "this should not give the wrong impression that we wish to conquer other countries":

Though we consider all Islamic countries our own, all countries should stay within their own borders. What we wish to see, however, is what occurred in Iran: an awakening that made Iranians distance themselves from superpowers and cut off their hands from Iran's (natural) resources. This must happen in all nations and by all governments. This is our aspiration ... They must liberate themselves ... and rescue themselves from the state of poverty to which they have fallen.[20]

Further defining the export of the revolution with specific reference to Saudi Arabia, he stressed expansion not by military act but by propagation:

We wish to present an Islamic model to the world, even if our model is (still) incomplete, so that all the thinkers in the world, except those innate criminals, and all the oppressed people of the world can understand what Islam offers and what it can do in the world. How Islam can save the deprived, the oppressed and the

---

[19] Amal Saad-Ghorayeb, *Hizbu'llah: Politics and Religion* (London, 2002), is a seminal study of Hizb Allah's structure and its interaction with various political developments.

[20] Ruhollah Khomeini, *Sahifa-yi Imam*, 22 vols. (Tehran, 1999), vol. 18, 364.

enslaved. You the countries in the (Persian) Gulf and outside the Gulf would like to see that our Islam never steps out of Iran! Yet despite your ill will, it has and it will step out (of Iran).[21]

Khomeini's words proved particularly poignant when applied to the Palestinian struggle. Indeed the Islamification of dissent in the whole of the Middle East was closely affected by the Palestinians' plight under Israel's prolonged occupation and its expansionist ambitions, especially by means of establishing Jewish settlements in the West Bank and the Gaza Strip.[22] The rise of Hamas, and later the Islamic Jihad and other splinter groups, in the late 1980s can be attributed to the same Islamist trends that were ultimately motivated by the success of the Islamic Revolution in Iran. They were consequences of a shift toward an Islamic alternative, a process fostered as much by disillusionment with Arab nationalism and by Israel's oppressive policies toward the Palestinians.[23]

Somewhat outside the arena of Islamic radicalism in the region, but of great relevance to the future of political Islam in Turkey, was the political influx of the late 1970s and early 1980s and its long-term consequences. In a period of intense bickering, primarily between the Kemalist Republican People's Party (*Cumhuriyet Halk Partisi*) and the Justice Party (*Adalet Partsi*), lurked the Islamist National Salvation Party (*Milli Selamet Partisi*) headed by Nacmittin Erbakan. The political quagmire eventually offered the pretext for the ever-present army officer corps to stage a military coup in September 1980. Under the predictable rubric of restoring order and safeguarding the foundation of the republic, General Kenan Evren and his associates banned all major political parties and detained their leadership, suspended civil rights, and ruled by decree over Turkey for three years. Evren's predictable promise to restore the democratic process, once peace and stability were secured, came with an ominous precondition of reshaping the country's seemingly chaotic party politics.

Yet ironically in the shadow of the military junta that aimed to preserve Atatürk's laic legacy, there emerged on Turkey's political horizon as early as 1983 the Welfare Party (*Refah Partisi*). It relied on a newly urbanized lower middle class to advance a moderately-framed Islamist agenda. Rooted in the National Salvation Party of earlier times, the Welfare Party called for return

---

[21] Ibid., 157–58.

[22] Rashid Khalidi, *The Iron Cage: The Story of the Palestinian Struggle for Statehood* (Oxford, 2006); Benny Morris, *Righteous Victims: A History of the Zionist-Arab Conflict, 1881–1998* (New York, 2011); and Bshir Saade, *Hizbullah and the Politics of Remembrance: Writing the Lebanese Nation* (Cambridge, 2016).

[23] Beverley Milton-Edwards and Stephen Farrell, *Hamas: The Islamic Resistance Movement* (Cambridge, 2010), 91–95, 132–33, and 223–25; and Zaki Chehab, *Inside Hamas: The Untold Story of the Militant Islamic Movement* (New York, 2007).

to a mild version of Islamism and traditional values. Like its predecessor, the Welfare Party was able to mobilize support among a new generation of urbanites who were discontent with Turkey's long-established secular course and its secular institutions. Even though Refah resisted collaborating with the junta, the near-purge of Turkey's secular parties allowed it, between 1982 and 1991, to effectively fill the yawning political vacuum. This was a quiet revolution of the sort that, as it turned out, changed the face of secularism in Turkey and introduced a new Islamist ethos.

The remarkable course of the upheavals sketched above cannot be a mere coincidence, even though the ensuing circumstances that led to Islamist prevalence substantially differed from one place to another. Pakistan, Palestine, and Turkey were as much different in their appeal to Islamic loyalties as the predominantly Shi'i Iran was from the Salafi-Wahhabi Saudi Arabia. Yet a discourse of Islamic activism, and a quest for an Islamic alternative to secularism, ran across the region irrespective of national and sectarian bounds. That in a short span of five years, 1977 to 1982, the political morphology of nearly the whole region substantially changed cannot be underestimated. The timeline below illustrates this phase of political outbursts throughout the region.

Table 8.1 *Chronological Table of Middle East Political Upheavals, 1977–1982*

July 5, 1977	Military coup in Pakistan and rise of the pro-Islamist regime of General Zia' ul-Haqq
October 1977	Earliest popular demonstrations leading to the Islamic Revolution in Iran
April 28, 1978	Assassination of Davud Khan and the communist struggle for power in Afghanistan
February 11, 1979	Collapse of the Pahlavi state, triumph of the Islamic Revolution, and establishment of the Islamic Republic of Iran
July 16, 1979	Saddam Hussein becomes president of Ba'athist Iraq
November 4, 1979	Beginning of the Hostage Crisis in Iran (until January 20, 1981)
November 20, 1979	Siege of the Grand Mosque of Mecca (until December 4, 1979)
November 21, 1979	The US embassy in Islamabad, Pakistan, is burned to the ground
December 24, 1979	Soviet invasion of Afghanistan and beginning of the Afghan Mujahidin resistance movement
September 12, 1980	Military coup in Turkey and the rise of General Evren
September 22, 1980	Iraqi invasion of Iran and start of the Iraq-Iran War
October 6, 1981	Assassination of President Anwar Sadat of Egypt by the extremists *Takfir wa'l Hijra*
February 7, 1982	Suppression of the Islamist uprisings in Hama, Syria
June 6, 1982	Israeli invasion of Lebanon (until June 1985) and the emergence of the Hizb Allah of Lebanon

The Socioeconomic and Political Roots

To appreciate the undercurrents that allowed these potentially revolutionary trends to emerge, we may turn our attention to a host of socioeconomic
and demographic processes. The growth in population, a prevalent feature
throughout the 1960s to the 1980s, can truly be defined as a demographic
revolution. The table below demonstrates growth among select countries
of the region in the second half of the twentieth century:

Table 8.2 *Population Growth in the Middle East*

Country	Population, m.				
	1950s	1960s	1970s	1980s	1990s
Egypt	18.9 ('47)	30 ('66)	36.6 ('76)	48.2 ('86)	59.3 ('96)
Iran	19 ('56)	25.7 ('65)	33.7 ('76)	49.4 ('86)	60 ('96)
Iraq	6.5 ('55)	8.3 ('65)	11.6 ('75)	15.5 ('85)	20.2 ('95)
Pakistan	41.1 ('55)	51.9 ('65)	68.4 ('75)	95.5 ('85)	127.3 ('95)
Syria	3.2 ('50)	4.5 ('60)	6.3 ('70)	8.7 ('80)	12.1 ('90)
Saudi Arabia	3.1 ('50)	4 ('60)	5.7 ('70)	9.8 ('80)	16.1 ('90)
Turkey	20.9 ('50)	27.7 ('60)	35.6 ('70)	44.7 ('80)	56.4 ('90)

By the mid to the late 1970s, the population of the greater Middle East
stood in excess of 160 million, with Iran, Egypt, and Turkey in the lead. With
almost double the population of the region in the 1950s, most if not all of the
Middle East experienced a steady income growth even in the lower strata of
society. Relatively improved health and sanitary conditions, especially in the
villages and smaller cities, and better access to lifesaving medications elevated
birth rates, reduced mortality in all age groups, and increased life expectancy.
By the turn of the twenty-first century the Middle East and North Africa
together multiplied their population by 3.7 times compared to 1950, the
highest in the world. In 1980 the birth rate stood at 3 percent annually,
which also was the highest in the world. During the 1970s and 1980s in
nearly all these countries the median age of the population was extremely
young. In Iran alone the population grew from a mere 19 million in 1956 to
nearly 50 million in 1986, an average annual growth rate of 5.4 percent.[24]

Rapid population growth invariably brought greater urbanization. A range
of factors – land reform, better communications, and expectation for better
standard of living – lured many, especially the younger generations, from the

[24] Amanat, *Iran*, 871–73; see also Farzaneh Roudi-Fahimi, "Population trends and challenges in the Middle East and North Africa," *Population Reference Bureau* (December 1,
2001), Online.

countryside to the sprawling cities. Absorbing waves of new immigrants from the rural regions, megacities such as Karachi, Lahore, Tehran, Istanbul, and Cairo appeared on the horizon. In due course they often caved under pressures to provide housing, urban amenities, infrastructure, and education to the newly urbanized multitudes. Poor neighborhoods on the edges of the cities, where the newcomers and their extended families were to find shelter, were eyesores in contrast to the prosperous neighborhoods that housed the privileged middle and upper middle classes.[25] In Iran, for example, the demographics dramatically reversed in favor of urbanization. While in the 1950s nearly 70 percent of the population resided in the countryside, by the late 1970s the rural and nomadic population was reduced to about 45 percent. As the traditional units of agricultural production and the village economy as a whole were unable to sustain the surplus population, the move to the cities was the only realistic alternative. Throughout the 1960s the land reform program, and other state-enforced reform measures known as the White Revolution, which included the Literacy Corp (*Sipah-i Danish*), essentially dismantled the old agrarian regime and paved the way for urban migration.

The mass movement from the countryside to the cities further accelerated throughout the 1970s because of greater demand for labor force, especially in the service sector, in most urban centers in the region. A rapid price rise in oil markets in a short period of time, from $2.29 per barrel in 1972 to $12.9 in 1974, generated massive new revenues for the oil-producing countries of the Persian Gulf: Saudi Arabia, Iran, Iraq, not to mention the sparsely populated Arab Emirates, Kuwait, Oman, and Bahrain. Other members of the OPEC – Nigeria, Algeria, and Indonesia – were too recipients of higher oil revenues, though perhaps with less disruptive effects. Yet by degrees they were all subjected to heavily centralized and poorly implemented modernization programs. Egypt, Syria, Iraq, Turkey, and to a lesser degree Pakistan shared these features with Iran. New populist policies in these countries weakened the dominant economic classes, such as large landowners, while failing to fulfill promises of prosperity to newly emerging working and lower middle classes in the cities.[26]

In the Arab states of the Persian Gulf in particular, the much higher oil revenues throughout the 1970s generated new demands for labor in Saudi

---

[25] Jerzy Zdanowski, *Middle Eastern Societies in the 20th Century* (Newcastle, 2014), for a detailed account though with sparse footnotes; and Khalid Ikam, *The Egyptian Economy 1952–2000* (London, 2006); and Feroz Ahmad, *The Making of Modern Turkey* (London, 1993).

[26] Raymond A. Hinnebusch, "State and Civil Society in Syria," *Middle East Journal* 47, 2 (1993), 243–57, 243; and Fred H. Lawson, "Social Bases for the Hamah Revolt," *MERIP Reports* 110 (1982), 24–28.

Arabia, the United Arab Emirates, and Kuwait. They were fulfilled by skilled and unskilled guest workers from Egypt, Syria, and Jordan as well as from Pakistan, Bangladesh, Malaysia, Indonesia, the Philippines, and soon after, from Afghanistan. Yet by the early to mid-1980s, these petro-economies displayed serious signs of inefficiency largely because of a sharp drop in the price of oil but also because of wishful economic projections, corruption, and mismanagement.

As the surplus workers returned home and the remittance payments from guest workers who stayed behind ebbed, unemployment and pressure on social services in countries such as Jordan and Syria increased. The liberalization programs, which by virtue of privatization and contracting out social services to the private sector tried to remedy economic pressure on the state, instead helped increase unemployment among the young middle classes. The statist education policies in most of these countries, moreover, had already produced a generation of well-educated young men, substantially from the lower middle classes. These waves of educated youth often found themselves jobless and disillusioned not only because of the yawning cultural gap with the political ideologies of the ruling regimes but because of their frustrated economic ambitions.[27]

In nearly all the countries of the region, perhaps with the exception of Turkey, the third quarter of the twentieth century witnessed the greater impacts of policies implemented by authoritarian regimes. Headed by royal autocrats, military officers or paramilitary party leaders in control of one-party systems, these regimes were rife with political repression, abusive security measures, violation of human rights, press censorship, flawed elections, rubberstamp legislation, and intolerance of nearly all forms of criticism and dissent. In effect they managed to close most, if not all, public conduits essential for the survival of a stable polity capable of exercising a modicum of political agency. Monopolizing mass media for ideological ends and to adulate the "beloved" leader, greater exposure to state propaganda engendered among ordinary people cynicism and raw anger but also conspiratorial schemes.

Yet the above factors, often stressed by structuralist theories of revolution, cannot be considered as the only forces behind a successful revolution. [28]

---

[27] Onn Winckler, "The Demographic Dilemma of the Arab World: The Employment Aspect," *Journal of Contemporary History* 37, 4 (2002), 617–36.

[28] Theda Skocpol and Ellen Kay Trimberger, "Revolutions and the World-Historical Development of Capitalism," *Berkeley Journal of Sociology* 22 (1978), 101–13; Theda Skocpol, *States and Social Revolutions: A Comparative Analysis of France, Russia and China* (Cambridge, 1979) ; Shmuel Eisenstadt, *Revolution and the Transformation of Societies: A Comparative Study of Civilizations* (New York, 1978); Jack Goldstone, *Revolution and Rebellion in the Early Modern World* (Berkeley, CA, 1991); and Said

Population growth, rapid urbanization, a rise in the state revenue, economic modernization projects, state monopoly of resources, a repressive machinery of control, rising expectations, and a sense of relative deprivation, it may be argued, were common not only in the greater Middle East, but in Latin America, Southeast Asia, and in sub-Saharan Africa. Attributing one or several of the above factors as the sole cause, or causes, of a revolutionary process militates against the very complexity of revolutions. Any mechanical presupposition of how revolutions often come about have proven to be incomplete, if not unconvincing, a fact reflected in the recent turn towards holistic understanding of revolution whereby cultural contexts and discourses of opposition are as crucial as infrastructural factors.[29] Although "the anatomy of revolution," to borrow from Crane Brinton's seminal study, can convincingly be employed to explain the actual revolutionary process, it is much less convincing to establish a causal theory of revolution.[30] Iran's 1979 revolution is the case in point.

Iran's 1979 Revolution

It is remarkable that in the whole region and among all Islamist trends of the period only Iran gave birth to an enduring Islamic Revolution, with all-embracing ideological and sociopolitical consequences whose shockwaves are still tangible decades later. Iran's Islamic Revolution, the subject of much scholarly debate, especially in the 1980s, cannot be seen as a spontaneous upheaval driven by sheer economic or political factors. Rather, it had roots in a historical process that went back to such an axial moment as the 1501 establishment of Twelver Shi'ism as the official creed of the Safavid Empire.

The complex interaction between the Iranian state and the Shi'i clerical establishment as well as the messianic aspiration ingrained in the Shi'i belief system no doubt contributed to a seemingly theocratic revolution unprecedented in modern and even pre-modern times. The 1979 revolution brought to power, for the first time in the history of the Muslim world, a radical clerical clique that legitimized its monopoly of power by

---

Arjomand, Revolution: Structure and Meaning in World History (Chicago, 2019), are notable examples of work within this structuralist tradition.

[29] John Foran, *Taking Power: On the Origins of Third World Revolutions* (Cambridge, 2005); Charles Tilly, *Contentious Performances* (Cambridge, 2008); as well as Jack A. Goldstone, "Ideology, Cultural Frameworks, and the Process of Revolution," *Theory and Society* 20, 4 (1991), 405–53; and Colin. J. Beck, "The World-Cultural Origins of Revolutionary Waves: Five Centuries of European Contention," *Social Science History* 35, 2 (2011), 167–207.

[30] Crane Brinton, *The Anatomy of Revolution* (New York, 1965), 3–26, which was originally published in 1938.

claiming the "authority of the jurist" (*vilayat-e faqih*) over all affairs of the state and the society.

The Islamic Revolution, moreover, should be seen as the end process of a historical experience that since the turn of the twentieth century exposed Iran first to a liberal democratic revolution – the Constitutional Revolution of 1906–1911 – and later to an intense period of political activity in the postwar era and the shaping of the National Movement between 1945 and 1953. A general sense of frustration with the "failures" of both these episodes, which led to authoritarian Pahlavi rule first under Riza Shah from the early 1920s and then under Muhammad Riza Shah from the 1950s, remained part and parcel of the 1979 revolution and its fast-Islamicized rhetoric and ideals. In its gestation the Islamic Revolution absorbed a wide range of ideas and perspectives, both traditional and modern, that included conservative Shi'i legalism, manifestations of the popular Shi'i messianic cult, the revolutionary Third Worldism of the 1960s, Islamist radical trends then in vogue, and select features of nonpolitical modernity. It denounced the Pahlavi secular autocracy and aimed to make right what went wrong with the secular Constitutional Revolution and with the National Movement under Muhammad Musaddiq.

Among the major oil-producing countries of the region Iran was the only one with a sizeable population no longer engaged in agriculture that firmly bound people to the land. The quadruple increase in oil prices, as it has been often argued, opened new economic and development opportunities, mostly planned and implemented by the Pahlavi state. In a short span of time the Iranian economy had to absorb massive new investment in infrastructure, industrialization, and the service sector. Large injections of capital from oil revenues inevitably generated inflationary pressures, as part of the trend that since the oil price hike of 1974 had plagued economies worldwide. Massive growth of the economy also exposed Iran to inefficiency and wastage, mismanagement, and rampant corruption in the higher echelons of the state and within the economic pyramid.[31] The uneven trickling of the new benefits through networks of nepotism and influence-peddling further sharpened income discrepancies between the privileged elites loyal to the Pahlavi state and what may be called the traditional sectors of the economy. The bazaar and the smalltime businesses associated with it proved to be the net losers. In a booming economy that relied on large-scale industrialization and on access to state

---

[31] Misagh Parsa, *Social Origins of the Iranian Revolution* (New Brunswick, NJ, 1989), 62–86, provides a detailed account of the White Revolution and its outcomes.

resources, the bazaar found few opportunities to excel, at least not at the rapid rate of the new economy of the street. Likewise, the growing sector of fixed-salaried employees, teachers, health workers, and the lower echelons of the service industry were left out, or more likely were not speedily compensated for the value of their services. They too increasingly felt deprived and discriminated against as rising inflation diminished their purchasing abilities while expectations of a better lifestyle were rising.[32]

The sense of relative deprivation was no less strong among the lower middle classes, urban migrants, and their children. Though the White Revolution in the 1960s and the early 1970s was the prime mover of Iran's demographic growth and contributed to improved health and public education, it failed to fulfill at the same rate the growing expectations for better living standards and a larger share of the country's growing economy. The ostentatious wealth and prosperity among the upper middle classes of the late Pahlavi era seemed particularly glaring, and inaccessible, to urban migrants in Tehran's poor neighborhoods and major provincial centers.[33]

The closing of political horizons took a turn for worse throughout the 1970s. The shah's heavy-handed reliance on the security apparatus, the dreaded SAVAK, bred a climate of fear and cynicism first among intellectuals of the left and soon after among other dissidents. In the absence of any genuine political parties or democratic representation, even at local level, or the absence of any conduit for sincere expression of benign criticism of state-enforced policies, the chasm between the state and the general public widened. In the eyes of the ordinary people all that went wrong with state policies was to be squarely placed on the shah's whims and wishes and the image that he nurtured for himself as the nation's savior. The introduction of a single-party system, the Rastakhiz (resurrection) Party, in 1975 by the shah and his technocrats, badly failed to generate any moral and political support for the Pahlavi enterprise.

These trends greatly contributed to the mass movement that rapidly acquired an Islamic ideology. The Islamist ingredient came from more than one source and flavor, often in competition with ideologies ranging from radical left to liberal nationalism. At its core the Qum-based clergy in Ayatollah Khomeini's camp was in part shaped by a century-old political Islam rooted in Sayyid Jamal al-Din Asadabadi (better known as al-Afghani) and his advocacy of pan-Islamism. His ideological successor,

---

[32] Amanat, *Iran*, 577–87; and Nikkie R. Keddie, *Modern Iran: Roots and Results of Revolution*, (New Haven, CT, 2006), 158–69.

[33] Amanat, *Iran*, 617–22 and 654–56; Ervand Abrahamian, *Iran Between Two Revolutions* (Princeton, NJ, 1982), 446–49; and also Farhad Kazemi, *Poverty and Revolution in Iran: The Migrant Poor, Urban Marginality, and Politics* (New York, 1980).

Rashid Rida, had also articulated a notion of Islamic government presided by jurists equipped with *ijtihad* (qualified legal opinion based on the Qur'an, the sacred "traditions" and limited use of logic). Also of some importance in the formation of Iranian revolutionary Islamists was the Muslim Brotherhood in Egypt and its ideological counterpart in Iran known as the Fada'iyan-i Islam (Islamic devotees), a terrorist organization active from the late 1940s to the early 1960s.

Also influential in the shaping of the Islamist revolutionary discourse was the Mujahidin-i Khalq (also known as People's Mujahidin), an urban guerrilla organization that offered an admix of a revolutionary reading of the Qur'an, a violent take on the Shi'i martyrdom narrative, and a superficial reading of Marxism (or more accurately Marxist-Stalinism). With growing cadres and a considerable grassroots support, the Mujahidin offered the largest challenge to clerical radicalism. Matching its fascination for revolution with vengeance and violence, the Mujahidin was motivated by populist romantics such as 'Ali Shari'ati.

In the same vein 'Ali Shari'ati advocated a conjured-up brand of revolutionary Shi'ism as a socio-religious remedy that promised an egalitarian utopia through a so-called 'Alid Shi'i red revolution. A motivational lay speaker and religious pamphleteer, he was an odd byproduct of a postcolonial milieu that in the 1950s and 1960s witnessed the Algerian revolution and the decolonization of Africa. In particular, the socialist Third World discourse articulated by the likes of the popular West-Indian philosopher Frantz Fanon and his concept of the "wretched of the earth" found sympathetic resonance. As portrayed by Shari'ati, the Qur'anic "disinherited of the earth" (*mustad'afin fi'l-ard*), as the "oppressed masses," were eventually to rise up not only against the forces of pagan modernity but the compromising clerical obscurantists.

Likewise, the nativist discourse of "authenticity," as represented since the early 1960s by Jalal Al-i Ahmad, a social critic and a public intellectual, demanded a return to "pristine" Shi'i values. This was a worldview, known as Westoxification (*gharbzadagi*), inimical to a demonized and hegemonic West and rooted in a conspiratorial theory of history. Finding a huge following in the 1970s among Iranian intellectuals and university students, Westoxification depicted the recent course of Muslim history, and Iran in particular, as a regrettable mistake, and worse, as an evil conspiracy hatched by Westernizers and their colonial masters to defame Islam and enslave Muslims. The Manichean worldview of victimized Muslims versus hegemonic Christians offered the groundwork for the anti-Western narrative that bloomed during the Islamic Revolution and became one of its most potent ideological weapons.

What was new in the Islamic Revolution, however, was the rise of a leader confident in his own "mission." It may be argued that the ascent of Ayatollah Khomeini, a "prophet-like" (*payghambar-gunah*) figure in the revolutionary discourse of the time, proved to be essential for binding together diverse ideologies in the proto-revolutionary environment of Iran of the late 1970s. Likewise, he fused the demographic, political, economic, and cultural trends. Several factors worked to his advantage, factors that clearly were lacking elsewhere in the region. He was a consistent voice of opposition to the Pahlavi regime following the 1963 unrest and his subsequent exile to Najaf. His critique of the Pahlavi reform project, and what he characterized as the shah's sellout to the United States, was often regressive, indeed reactionary. Later on his opposition to the 1975 Family Law (*qanun-i khanivadah*), which offered women greater legal rights and protection on issues of marriage and divorce, polygamy, and legal age of marriage, was a case in point.

More importantly, Khomeini was able to preserve throughout his years of exile a fairly robust network of "followers" (*muqallids*), who abided by his legal opinions (*fatwas*) and paid their religious alms and other dues to his clerical and lay agents. Both the followers and the clerical supporters among the "seminarians" (*talabah*) were beneficiaries of the allowances distributed by Khomeini. They provided the groundwork for an increasingly politicized, active, and dedicated powerbase in the late 1970s and after.

The most crucial factor, however, that differentiated Khomeini from other radical leaders of his time, secular and lay, whether within Iran or elsewhere, was his almost unique mystico-philosophical leanings, a combination that soon, and perhaps inadvertently, elevated him to that of a messianic savior. A number of factors contributed to Khomeini's rise to a momentary eminence. For one, he belonged to a generation of Shi'i 'ulama who bore the brunt of the state-enforced Pahlavi modernity. Since the early twentieth century they were deprived of much of their judicial, educational, and other public functions and their status was substantially diminished in the modernized social hierarchy.

Modernity nevertheless penetrated the madrasa milieu if not through new approaches to the shari'a, but by absorbing and internalizing the message of radical Islam. Increasingly in the marketplace of ideas the message of political Islam, as understood and advocated by Khomeini and his cohorts, came to compete with secular or semi-secular lay revolutionary trends that were rife in the milieu of the 1960s and 1970s. Al-i Ahmad's Westoxification thesis along with the 'red 'Alawi' Shi'ism and the plight of the "disinherited of the earth," made fashionable by Shari'ati, gradually entered the sermons of clerical preachers who by the

late 1970s occupied the pulpits of many mosques in the poorer neighborhoods of the capital and the major cities.

As with Khomeini himself, many of the clerical Islamists picked up in
rhetoric and in substance the Third World Islamism of the period as
much as the homebrew socialist themes that were then in vogue. The
"pristine Muhammadan Islam" that the self-assumed "militant clergy"
were advocating claimed to be "neither from the East nor from the West"
but only embedded in the message of the Islamic Republic. Here the
"selfless Islamic community" was urged to withstand the forces of "global
arrogance" (*istikbar-i jahani*), a reference to the two superpowers of the
time. Soon after the "martyr-nurturing community" was encouraged to
combat the mischiefs and temptations of the "Great Satan" (*shaytan-i
buzurg*), a reference to the United States with apocalyptic undertones.

Khomeini relied on this revolutionary rhetoric to publicize his unprecedented theory of the *vilayat-i faqih*. As early as 1970, he argued, in
a series of lectures delivered in Najaf (later revised and published in Beirut
and clandestinely in Iran), that in the absence of the Lord of the Age
(*Sahib al-Zaman*, or the *Mahdi*), it was incumbent upon the Shi'i jurist to
strive for an Islamic government (*hukumat-i Islami*). Such view was in
sharp contrast to an almost unanimous view held by the jurists that they
must not entertain political ambitions, avoid partaking in the affairs of the
state, and solely concern themselves with study of jurisprudence and with
the issuing of legal opinions (*fatwas*) in matters of the shari'a. In
Khomeini's view, however, not only were the jurists responsible for the
nonpolitical affairs of the community, but by the virtue of their legal
training and their presumed austerity and detachment from material
greed, they were qualified to take the reins of power from secular rulers,
whom he labeled as corrupt, treasonous, and detrimental to the best
interest of the community.

Khomeini's was a revolutionary departure in the history of Shi'ism,
moving away from the conventional conception of the "authority of the
jurists." Virtually devoid of any political connotations in the past, it had
now turned into a radical theory of political power that aimed to subvert
the secular state and replace it with an Islamic government. It is likely that
beyond the legal definition in Shi'i jurisprudence, Khomeini was
impressed by the mystical-messianic connotations of *vilayat* long embedded in speculative Sufism in the Muslim world.

The merger between the legal and mystical dimensions of *vilayat*, as
formulated by Khomeini especially in the early 1970s, was facilitated by
greater politicization of Shi'ism. It was as if a range of issues, including
greater secularization of Iranian society, the repressive policies of the
Pahlavi era and effective closure of all avenues of independent political

expression, a nostalgia for the loss of a Shi'i sacred past, the isolation of traditional classes behind the walls of the madrasa and within the confines of the bazaar, and the gravitation of a younger generation of Shi'i clergy toward ideologies of the radical left and toward the nativist anti-Westernism, contributed to the shaping of the revolution.[34]

The events following the victory of February 1979 not only reaffirmed the messianic spirit of the revolution but the monopoly of Khomeini's Islamist supporters. The Hostage Crisis of November 1979 to January 1981 moreover offered Khomeini and his followers the much-needed external nemesis to consolidate their popular base and quickly and violently eliminate their domestic rivals. The labeling of the United States as the "Great Satan" proved emblematic for the messianic demonology that Khomeinists employed to dominate the revolutionary process. This was a blessing in disguise in the early volatile years and while between 1980 and 1988 the war with neighboring Iraq was raging. The battle between the "forces of the good versus the evil," as the prolonged war with Iraq was depicted in the Islamic Republic's propaganda narrative, increasingly came to be viewed as the third stage of a "sacred defense" that was meant to vanquish the demonic forces of "global arrogance" by means of reenacting the drama of Karbala, the Shi'i foundation paradigm.

Concluding Thoughts

Diverse developments of the early 1970s in many ways set the stage for a revolutionary climate throughout the Middle East and some Muslim-majority countries. Yet the results were significantly diverse. Sharp shifts in demographics, greater urbanization, new social demands, rises in oil income, and discrepancies in wealth, when combined with greater and more repressive instruments of state control, corruption, and favoritism, brewed a potent proto-revolutionary admixture. Expressions of political Islam, though in gestation at least since the end of the First World War, reemerged in the 1960s and 1970s and supplanted brands of nationalism and socialism at a time when loyalty to Western ideologies was in decline. State appropriation of nationalism, as a propaganda tool for legitimizing autocracy, dampened public enthusiasm for glorification of pre-Islamic past, for official Arab, Iranian, and Turkish nationalism, and for the positivist cult of modernity and secularism. General disillusionment with the Marxist-Leninist brand, as apparent for instance in a critical reaction to the 1968 Soviet invasion of Czechoslovakia, only helped divert forces of dissent toward alternative revolutionary expressions.

[34] Amanat, *Iran*, 773–867.

Radical Islamism, as it evolved in this period in competition with Marxist revolutionarily models, also dreamed of a utopian society to be achieved through mass revolution. Either inspired by Maoist Marxism or else by indigenous resistance movements such as the Algerian War of Independence, Latin American guerrilla movements, the Palestinian Liberation Organization, and the Viet Cong, the Islamists explored new radical readings of Islam. A sense of Islamic solidarity, a narrative of resistance and sacrifice, especially in Shi'i history, and a return to what was viewed as an "authentic" form of pristine Islam and Islamic shari'a loomed large. The nostalgic yearning for an Islamic alternative was further sharpened by the alienating experience of Western modernity which came about through mindless denial of the Islamic past, its core values, and its rites and rituals. The Islamists condemned Westoxification for robbing the Islamic community of its precious identity and agency and subscribed to critiques of Orientalism for unraveling misrepresentations of Islamic "authenticity."

Why, of all the Islamist radical trends of the 1970s that experienced modernity went awry, was it the Iranian case that turned into a full-blown revolution in the classical sense? As argued above, the Shi'i clergy and their associated groups in the bazaar in particular who felt the long-term alienating impact of Pahlavi modernity may offer one answer. The loss of traditional functions in society and diminished prestige had the adverse effect of diverting clerical attention from serious examination of Islamic law and Islamic norms toward political activism and eventually a revolutionary path. To many this was a realistic alternative to the quietist brand of Islam and its noninterventionist past. That the Pahlavi regime left little incentive for clerical participation in its modernizing project while eliminating alternative political voices, even the moderate trends, contributed to the growth of radical Islamism.

In the Sunni world, on the other hand, Islamism largely opted for a Wahhabi and Salafi ideology that aimed to counter the threatening impact of Iran's call for "exporting the revolution." The Salafi message, backed by vast financial resources offered by the Saudis and their regional allies in the Persian Gulf and by the West's implicit goodwill, managed to spread itself through popular literature, dispatching of missionaries, building mosques and madrasas, and normalizing Wahhabism as a purist and devout interpretation of Islam rather than a heresy, as it was generally treated up to the 1960s. The process of "Wahhabicization" of the Muslim world was well evident, for example in Pakistan, Indonesia, Central Asia, and sub-Saharan Africa. But it had the secondary effect, largely unaccounted for, of viewing other conflicts in the region, such as the plight of the Palestinians in the occupied territories, as religious affronts inflicted by the pagan West on Islam and Muslim communities. Similarly, the Soviet occupation of Afghanistan was seen as an act of aggression to be dealt with by a violent response. Militant Islamist movements that since the 1980s resorted to terrorism were offshoots of this Salafi past.

All defiant impulses and disruptive agitation aside, after nearly half a century of Islamic "revolutionism," one can barely discern traces of political pluralism, social toleration, or a semblance of intellectual novelty. Instead, the Islamic regimes in power and Islamist communities in opposition remained invariably loyal to an incoherent and mostly regressive reading of the past, what they often brandish as "authentic Islam." Marred with intolerance, violence and misogyny, these Islamic states or counter-states survive on a selective dose of globalized, albeit least desirable, aspects of modernity. What is left of the revolutionary momentum in Iran is the Islamic Republic's repression, paranoia, mismanagement, and corruption. Elsewhere it is the narco-terrorism of the Taliban in Afghanistan, Salafi obscurantism in Pakistan, corrupt and coercive Wahhabism in Saudi Arabia, a bitter memory of the Arab Spring pummeled by dictators, a shadow of Islamist authoritarianism casting over Turkey, and ISIS's murderous Caliphate enterprise that further ruined Syria and Iraq. Whether these aftershocks are of a painful postcolonial experience or undeniable consequences of Western aggression, revolutionary Islamism seems to be still a "work in progress."

9   The Anticommunist Revolts of 1989

John Connelly

If we associate revolutions with mass mobilization and violent regime change, then what happened in Eastern Europe in 1989 was hardly revolutionary. The avant-gardes of transformation – Poland and Hungary – showed little commotion beyond peaceful manifestations, the most important being the reburial of Imre Nagy that June. Suddenly hundreds of thousands of Hungarians appeared in central Budapest to witness the laying to rest of Nagy and other martyrs whose bones had been buried in unmarked graves after their executions in 1958. The police stood by, quiet witnesses to a last solemn act in the exit of a Party that had ruled since 1948. It was crushed in elections the following spring. In Poland, regime and opposition had spent the early months of 1989 negotiating an exit from single-party rule around a huge round table in Warsaw, and on June 4 millions of citizens lined up before polling places, sweeping the communists out of office in a few hours of voting. If we limit our view of 1989 to these places, the old regime appears to have voluntarily self-destructed with little direct challenge from the streets.

Yet look to Romania, and you see a different challenge to the notion of revolution: people indeed filling the streets, but regime change that was questionable. In December, a violent upheaval shook Bucharest and hundreds were killed. Just before Christmas supposed revolutionaries executed the husband and wife dictators on live television, but then one group of communist functionaries succeeded the other. In East Germany the best-known revolutionary event was a functionary's slip of tongue. In a live television conference on November 9, Politburo member Günter Schabowski said that new travel regulations went into effect immediately rather than the following day. Without this "fake news" East Germans would have lined up for passports at police offices on November 10 and perhaps continued the revolutionary changes that had been happening from early October, when demonstrations in Leipzig prompted the resignation of Erich Honecker. Instead, the sudden wall opening was a fortuitous rupture and the demonstrations lost urgency as East Germans increasingly looked to the west for solutions. The transition was marked in a shift in the chants of Leipzig demonstrators in November from "We are the people," to the nationalist "we are one people." People remarked here and in neighboring Czechoslovakia how completely and suddenly the regime collapsed, as if a brittle structure with nothing to sustain it.

The election campaigns of 1990 then contributed to "demobilization" as a growing caste of professionals took over the political process.[1] Ensuing shock therapy caused economies to contract and the ranks of the unemployed to multiply and was possible only because democratic structures were poorly developed. The transition to post-communism was achieved by employing methods and tools that few would have demonstrated for in 1989.

This brief meditation on a word we use to depict the events of 1989 opens our minds to a problem: Regime change in Eastern Europe did not happen in one year but grew out of earlier mobilizations and upheavals, which themselves derived from deeper structural problems. If little revolutionary energy was evident in Poland and Hungary in 1989, that was because decisive upheavals had occurred years earlier. And if the regime collapsed suddenly in East Germany, or, in direct contrast, failed to do so in Romania or Bulgaria, that had to do with circumstances dating from earlier decades. Despite central planning and single-party rule, each Soviet satellite had a peculiar style, sometimes called "national communism," reflecting not only the persistence of local traditions but also the importance of contingent factors, like outbursts of dissent at particular junctures, or political personality.[2]

Hungary's outburst of dissent over three decades earlier, in the fall of 1956, had brought into office the pragmatist János Kádár, whose mission became ensuring similar disruption did not recur. From the early 1960s he instituted economic reforms that made Hungary the envy of other socialist states, and stepped down in early 1989, having brought his country to the edge of transition. In a sense, the revolutionary events of the late 1980s were a final logical step of the destalinizing reforms.

The tumult of 1956 not only had brought Poland to the brink of war with the Soviet Union but also left it with a new leader, Władysław Gomułka. In contrast to Kádár, Gomułka was hardly a reformer, and that explains why his country was shaken by mass dissent at regular intervals: in Warsaw in 1968, the Baltic Coast in 1970, Radom and Warsaw in 1976, and then virtually all of Poland in the summer of 1980, when the working class held the party hostage through massive strikes. The result was the trade union Solidarity, revolutionary in its own

---

[1] Philipp Ther, *Europe Since 1989* (Princeton, NJ, 2016), 290–92.
[2] Peter Zwick, *National Communism* (Boulder, CO, 1983).

right because for the first time the totalitarian regime revealed that its legitimacy was far from total. About a third of Polish adults joined the independent trade union.

Yet when General Wojciech Jaruzelski used the army to crush Solidarity in December 1981 and impose martial law, this was no reversion to the preexisting state. Aside from the fact that few, even in the party, still accepted the Marxist-Leninist credo, Poles had lost the fear that was essential to maintaining communist control. Like Kádár, Jaruzelski proved a reformer whose major task was to assure that upheaval did not recur. Though he appeared stiff and inflexible, his rule involved compromise; for example, the de facto acceptance of a massive underground, including state-of-the-art publishing and intermittent radio broadcasts, relatively open borders to the west, through which thousands emigrated, and economic reform. By the late 1980s the Polish leadership included "liberals" arguing that all strata of society had to be drawn to participation in politics. But, very different from the situation in 1956 or 1980, they found an ally in Moscow in the party's First Secretary, Mikhail Gorbachev.

By contrast, the East German, Bulgarian, Czechoslovak, and Romanian leaderships were hostile to Gorbachev. The first two had seen no exchange of top cadres from the Stalinist 1950s; there had been shakeups at the top in Czechoslovakia and Romania, but by the 1970s, they had produced a neo-Stalinist elite in the former – installed after the Soviet invasion of 1968 – and a hardline neo-Stalinist nationalist in the person of Nicolae Ceaușescu in the latter, who used chauvinist arguments in an effort to maintain legitimacy.

This brief discussion of places of unrest and quiescence in the East Bloc features classic elements of historical explanation: structure and event, that is, deep causes, above all of the dysfunctional economy, but also more proximate ones, of leaders' personalities; and the acts of crowds at particular moments, like the students of Budapest on October 23, 1956, or workers of Radom on June 25, 1976. The trick in writing about 1989 is to relate these levels to each other while avoiding extremes; for example, saying that the economy was decrepit and a reformer *like* Mikhail Gorbachev was inevitable, or, by contrast, claiming that Gorbachev acted as a *deus ex machina*. Gorbachev was both a response to enduring crisis and a special leader with his own visions. But he did not make 1989 in Berlin or Prague inevitable. Without the acts in prior decades of millions of Hungarians and Poles, the ground would not have been prepared; and without the acts in the fall of 1989 of thousands of East Germans, Czechs, Romanians, and others, the regimes might have lasted.

Ultimately an underproductive command economy produced the upheaval and dissent we trace to the 1950s. At various points, Hungarian,

Polish, East German, and Czech workers took to the streets to protest cuts in wages or increases in the price of food. Workers in East Berlin's Stalinallee went on strike in June 1953 after they were told they had to work ten percent more for the same wage. And in the summer of 1980 the higher prices of a few cuts of meat caused Poland to shut down. By the end of that decade, even the relatively well-off Czechs and East Germans knew that living standards were declining, but Poles had endured rationing of basic foodstuffs since 1976. The Romanian regime did not even bother to placate its citizenry, arguing that foreign dangers made sacrifice necessary, and feeling impregnable in an autarchic state where fear silenced all dissent.

But when did the socialist economy become dysfunctional? Were its problems embedded in the original notion of scientific planning and the abolishment of the market in the 1920s Soviet Union? State socialist regimes may have had problems in providing consumer goods, but their achievements were also indisputable. Without Stalin's five-year plans of the 1930s the Red Army could not have survived the assaults of 1941 and Europe might have succumbed to Nazism for decades; and without the six- and five-year plans of the early 1950s Poland, Bulgaria, and Romania might have remained "backward" agrarian societies with pockets of illiteracy and villages with unpaved roads and no electricity. The socialist states built and rebuilt cities, educated legions of engineers and physicians, gave manual laborers chances their class had never enjoyed, and in an economic sense brought the region closer to Western Europe even though the continent was politically divided.

But in the 1960s growth slowed and socialist states became more involved in the international economy, exposing themselves to the perils of global trade and competition.[3] Planned economies had once industrialized by massing labor and raw materials while controlling food prices, but after the initial spurts of growth, they gave few incentives to produce above and beyond plan fulfillment, and they proved unable to respond adequately to consumer demand. Planners could not anticipate demand from their own societies, let alone unruly global markets. The "second" industrial revolution of automation and cybernetics caught communists off-guard.

Economists throughout the Bloc worked out reform programs that exploited "market mechanisms" – for example, differentiations in pay and small-scale entrepreneurship – but the uncompetitive heavy industrial

---

[3] Ivan T. Berend, *From the Soviet Bloc to the European Union: The Economic and Social Transformation of Central and Eastern Europe since 1973* (Cambridge, 2009).

sector remained a drain on economic productivity. The Czechoslovak reformers of the 1968 Prague Spring tried to decentralize decision-making in order to encourage greater responsibility and initiative among factory managers. The intervention of Warsaw Pact forces in August 1968 all but smothered such efforts outside of Hungary. The following year Leonid Brezhnev enunciated his eponymous doctrine: no state that had advanced to socialism could revert "backward" to capitalism.

The Unanticipated Reformer

Through the 1970s the Soviet Bloc registered moderate growth, but fell further and further behind the West. Greater efficiencies were achieved, but from mid-decade state socialist economies experienced lags, especially in electronics and computers. The most spectacular signs of trouble came from Poland. Boosted by credits from Western banks holding petro-dollars, Poland's GNP grew by 10 percent from 1972 to 1974, but because of poor investments, and an inability to compete on world markets, it then fell by 2.3 percent in 1979.[4] An extensive industrial policy – shipbuilding, coal, and steel – had absorbed billions of dollars of loans, which the state socialist economy could not repay. The cost of producing steel or ships in Poland was more than what could be earned for these products on international markets. Debts to Western banks had reached over $40 billion and kept growing. In an attempt to restore equilibrium in the domestic market and boost exports, the Polish state raised prices on a few grades of choice meats in July 1980. Protests followed almost imme-diately, and within weeks Poland faced the closest thing to a general strike ever seen in East-Central Europe.

When General Jaruzelski suppressed Solidarity in December 1981, a misleading impression of the Bloc's stability was strengthened, but foreign observers could not help noting an absence of élan in the latter years of Brezhnev's rule, with the average age of Politburo members just under seventy, and the country's appeal as a model for Third World nations steeply declining. According to CIA figures the average rate of growth of GNP declined from 5.1 percent in 1961–65 to 1.9 percent in 1981–85. More recent work suggests the rate was probably negative.

---

[4] This is according to official data. This was the first time GNP had declined in the postwar period. Andrzej Paczkowski, *Pół wieku dziejów Polski 1939–1989* (Warsaw, 1998), 400–04. The GDP (in constant dollars) went up over 30 percent from 1972 to 1974, (from $1,044 to $1,365) and dropped between 1979 and 1980 by over 20 percent (from $2,180 to $1,663), see United Nations Statistics Division, Per capita GDP at current prices – US dollars for Poland, Undata, Online.

Contemporaries knew that the problem lay in the entrenched bureaucratic system where corruption was anecdotal but undeniable and reflected elites' cynical disregard for the population.[5]

The advent of Ronald Reagan's trillion-dollar rearmament program injected a sense of panic into the Soviet cadres; the defense share of the Soviet GNP was 18 percent, and further increases threatened to send the struggling economy into a tailspin. The relation to Eastern Europe made the pressures for reform across the Bloc more urgent.[6] Because of a practice of selling energy resources at below global market prices, the Soviet Union was subsidizing East European economies to the tune of $18 billion per year by the early 1980s.[7]

Brezhnev died in 1983 and the most enduring legacy of his successor – Yuri Andropov, a security official who had overseen the defeat of Hungary's revolution – lay in an acquaintance made on holiday in Stavropol: the energetic young Mikhail Gorbachev, who struck him as the prototype of cadre needed to get Soviet society going again.

What bothered Gorbachev was how the system stifled citizens' independent initiative. He envisioned a pluralism of opinions that retained Leninism's eschatological certainty that state socialism led toward a utopian future while violating Lenin's prohibition on factions; in the meantime Gorbachev's insistence that state socialism urgently needed fixing energized reformers in Eastern Europe. Yet the Soviet leader also confused people. His program of lifting of censorship and increasing use of open elections inside the party seemed indistinguishable from what reform communists had attempted in Prague before stopped by the Soviet invasion of August 1968. If his goal was socialism with a human face, what were the tanks still doing in Czechoslovakia?[8]

As early as Konstantin Chernenko's funeral in March 1985, the freshly elected Soviet leader implied that the invasion had been unjust; he told East European leaders that they would bear responsibility for developments in their countries, and, he added a year later, Moscow would not rescue them with military intervention if they lost the trust of their own

---

[5] John Burns, "The Emergence of Andropov," *New York Times* (February 27, 1983); and, for an analysis, Archie Brown, *The Gorbachev Factor* (Oxford, 1996), 134.

[6] Noel E. Firth and James H. Noren, *Soviet Defense Spending: A History of CIA Estimates, 1950–1990* (College Station, TX, 1998), 136–37. The US could maintain equivalent military strength by spending 5.5 to 7 percent GNP, see Andrew C. Janos, *East Central Europe in the Modern World: The Politics of the Borderlands from Pre- to Postcommunism* (Stanford, CA, 2000), 337.

[7] This through the practice of selling oil and other commodities at below market value, see Jacques Lévesque, *The Enigma of 1989: The USSR and the Liberation of Eastern Europe* (Berkeley, CA, 1997), 88.

[8] Daniel Shanahan, "20 Years Too Late for Czechs: In Time of Glasnost, Restraint Still the Rule," *Los Angeles Times* (August 13, 1988).

citizenries.[9] In December 1988 Gorbachev announced at an address to the United Nations that "force or the threat of force neither can nor should be instruments of foreign policy ... To deny a nation the freedom of choice, regardless of the pretext or the verbal guise in which it is cloaked, is to upset the unstable balance that has been achieved ... "[10] But freedom of choice also meant that Gorbachev could not impose reform.

By 1987 his ideas of openness (glasnost) were triggering discussions in the communist parties about what "activating" the citizenry might mean, but civil society groups were also putting the kleptocracies of Prague or East Berlin, on the defensive with arguments translated from Russian about the need for fundamental changes to socialism. East European citizenries became saturated with knowledge of changes in the Soviet Union, but more importantly, about the Western states with which state socialism competed. The Romanian government attempted to counter this problem by forbidding citizens from keeping foreign guests in their homes, and compelling them to report all contact with noncitizens.[11]

The problem was not only people's possession of basic data that made them envious, but also irrefutable knowledge that signaled the West's superiority. In contrast to the 1950s, there was no longer talk of advancing to a better future, making an ideology based in avant-garde ideas evidently bankrupt. State socialism spelled uniformity, lack of selection, shoddy quality, and an inability to produce original styles or product lines; "socialist consumerism" was at best a shabby imitation of the West, where states cleverly called themselves not "capitalist" but social welfare states, often ruled by the communists' Marxist cousins, the Social Democrats. Everyone knew that the socialist countries were falling behind. The technologically simple Sony Walkman came onto markets in 1979, but not until 1988 did the GDR release its own version, costing over 300 East German marks (the average monthly salary for workers with higher education at that point was 1,477 marks[12]) – if one had the luck to find one in a store.[13] From the 1960s East Bloc states kept up in

[9] Archie Brown, "The Gorbachev Era," in Ronald Suny (ed.), *The Cambridge History of Russia*, 3 vols (Cambridge, 2006), vol. 3, 316–51, 336. In public he still spoke of the paramount need for the unity of the socialist Bloc, see Mark Kramer, "The Demise of the Soviet Bloc," in Vladimir Tismaneanu and Bogdan Iacob (eds.), *The End of the Beginning: the Revolutions of 1989 and the Resurgence of History* (Budapest, 2012), 171–256, 181.
[10] Martin Walker, *The Cold War: A History* (New York, 1994), 309.
[11] Janos, *East Central Europe in the Modern World*, 351.
[12] Helga Stephan and Eberhard Wiedemann, "Lohnstruktur und Lohndifferenzierung in der DDR," *Mitteilungen aus der Arbeitsmarkt- und Berufsforschung* 32, 4 (1990), 550–62, 552.
[13] Bernd Stöver, *Der Kalte Krieg, 1947–1991: Geschichte eines radikalen Zeitalters* (Munich, 2007), 304.

computer technology by pirating Western designs, a fact their citizens learned from Western television stations.[14] The imports and credits allowing Eastern Europe to simulate Western consumerism left the Bloc a debt of some $117 billion by the late 1980s.[15]

In 1988 changes that had been creeping along for years in Poland got a boost when the communist regime invited opposition groups to join in ruling, leading to a gradual transfer of power and self-dissolution. The changes dated to the Solidarity episode of 1980–81, when Poles enjoyed fifteen months of freedom, learning self-organization, shedding fear, insisting on speaking openly, and taking affairs into their own hands. After imposing martial law General Jaruzelski tolerated a growing under-ground and floated reform ideas while Poland's economy sank ever deeper, and hundreds of thousands exploited a liberal travel regime to escape to the West. Near default, and desperate to arrange a repayment of interest on loans, the government held a referendum in November 1987 on "radical" economic reform demanding a "difficult 2–3 year period of rapid changes"; over 50 percent of citizens followed a call from the underground to reject it. But the population was politically indifferent, supporting neither the government, nor the underground Solidarity trade union.[16]

As was true in 1956 or 1968, the first "move" to propel events forward came from below: waves of strikes in April and August 1988 following price hikes. By this point a new, more desperate generation of workers had come of age, who could not even dream of an apartment and had lived their entire adult lives under rationing. Though the workers were not led by Solidarity, among their demands was the union's re-legalization.[17] In late August Interior Minister General Kiszczak met with Union leader Lech Wałęsa and promised a "round table" for negotiations. In exchange, Wałęsa traveled about Poland, enduring boos and whistles, but getting the strikes under control.[18]

On November 30 Wałęsa debated Alfred Miodowicz, head of the country's "official" trade union on live television. The risks were enor-mous. If Wałęsa had turned himself into a laughing stock, as some

---

[14] Stöver, *Der Kalte Krieg*, 303–04.

[15] Janos, *East Central Europe in the Modern World*, 357.

[16] At end of 1987 Poland was mired in 40 billion dollars of debt, which had increased by 6 billion over that year, see Jacek Kuron and Jacek Zakowski, *PRL dla poczatkujacych* (Wroclaw, 1996), 258–59; and Stefani Sonntag, "Poland," in Detlev Pollack and Jan Wielgohs (eds.), *Dissent and Opposition in Communist Eastern Europe* (Burlington, VT, 2004), 3–28, 12.

[17] Artur Kubaj, *Zarestrujcie nam Solidarnosc: strajk sierpnowy 1988 r. w Szczecinie* (Szczecin, 2009), 53, 148.

[18] Kuron and Zakowski, *PRL dla poczatkujacych*, 261.

intellectuals feared, he could have compromised the opposition's chances. Instead he made a mockery of his opponent while gently poking fun at the regime. With reference to political decentralization in Hungary, Miodowicz asked: "But don't you see, Mr. Wałęsa, that we are going in that direction?" Wałęsa responded, "I know we are going, but as I have said, you are going by foot, and the rest of the world is driving by car." If Poland continued at that rate, "we'll have the effects in 200 or 300 years."[19] In effect he was saying that even the Hungarian reformers, a model for Mikhail Gorbachev, were moving too slowly.

Negotiations between government and opposition commenced in February 1989 around a large round table in today's Presidential Palace in Warsaw, also including members of official organizations like the non-communist parties and trade unions, as well as the Catholic Church. By April they agreed on elections in which Solidarity could compete for all of the seats in the parliament's upper house, and 35 percent of those in its lower house. The Communists would be assured the Presidency. Solidarity published a daily, the first free newspaper in 40 years, and prepared for elections on June 4. A little-noticed fine point was that the remaining 65 percent of the lower house did not automatically fall to the Communists. In fact, as noted dryly in the Soviet daily *Izvestia*, Communists would not have a majority. Rather, the seats would be divided by a key according to which 38 percent went to them, but the rest to existing small parties, which had tamely supported the Communists for decades, but now rose to new life.[20]

No other country went as far and the sudden disjuncture of Poland from the still-orthodox Leninist regimes within the Bloc was breathtaking. Moscow's press featured an interview with Wałęsa and complimented the Polish Catholic Church for finding compromises, but East Germany's government would not allow even Russian editions of reports on Poland to cross its borders. Yet even Solidarity's boldest leaders believed they would share rule with the Communists, with fully free elections to transpire four years in the future.[21] Poles casting their ballots that June did not believe in radical change. A reporter overheard some saying that "economic miracles are for Germany and Japan, not us."[22]

---

[19] John Tagliabue, "Wałęsa, in Debate on Unions, Urges End to Remnants of Stalinism," *New York Times* (1 December 1988).

[20] Francis X. Clines, "Isvestia Reports Poland's Changes In Detail and Straightforwardly," *New York Times* (April 7, 1989).

[21] Thus the reminiscences of opposition politician Krzysztof Kozłowski, in Anna Machcewicz, "Historia sentymentalna," *Więź* 37, 7 (1995), 134–52, 135.

[22] John Tagliabue, "For Many the Accords Seem a Non-Event," *New York Times* (April 7, 1989). The underground had done a poll showing that 85 percent of workers wanted fully free elections.

Yet when the polls closed the Communists had lost every seat that was contested, and found themselves unable to form a government. After weeks of talks a compromise emerged by which a Solidarity candidate became prime minister and formed a government of Solidarity politicians plus members of non-communist parties. Thus on August 24, 1989, the first non-communist head of government in postwar Eastern Europe, the Catholic intellectual Tadeusz Mazowiecki, came to power.

What followed was "shock therapy": state subsidies fell, prices rose seeking market levels, stock market and banking systems were introduced, and capitalism returned, in a European guise involving protections for the unemployed. This, as we know, but Gorbachev and Jaruzelski did not, was what happened when one attempted to make a socialist economy operate competitively. Without Gorbachev's belief that democracy would strengthen and not abolish socialism, the rupture would have been impossible.

The world watched Poland with fascination, but only Hungary was traveling in the same direction. Like Poland, but unlike East Germany, Czechoslovakia, or the South-East European states, it featured a strong opposition movement, as well as a solid reform faction in the Communist Party, which by early 1988 had pushed through a law permitting freedom of assembly and association. Though not under such direct pressure from "society" as in Poland (that is, from striking workers), the Hungarian party had been gradually recognizing the legitimacy of independent political groups for over a year. In June 1989 the Hungarian leadership approved its own "national round table" to discuss questions of transition.

The relative social calm was due to Kádár's pacifying of the population with decent living standards and minimal ideological pressure. Yet by the late 1980s the dynamic had run out of energy with a stalled economy and seventy percent of the state's hard currency reserves servicing debt. The government attempted "capitalist" concessions, like allowing private firms up to five hundred employees, as well as joint ventures with Western companies, yet the reforms produced "capitalist" problems like inflation, which ran at seventeen percent in 1987. Salaries and pensions could not keep up, and gradually evil side-effects of a bygone time reappeared: 20 percent of the population lived at the subsistence level. Though the shop windows and cafes were full, Hungarians often worked two jobs to make ends meet.[23] Was this still socialism? If not, what was the justification of the total rule of a socialist party?

---

[23] Lévesque, *The Enigma of 1989*, 65; George Barany, "Epilogue," in Peter Sugar, Péter Hanák, and Tibor Frank (eds.), *History of Hungary* (Bloomington, IN, 1990), 401–04.

The Hungarian opposition, in contrast to the Polish, came almost entirely from the intellectual classes, and now gradually emerged from the shadows of illegal and semi-conspiratorial activity which covered the political spectrum through leftist, liberal, and national forces. Much larger than the opposition groups of Czechoslovakia or East Germany, it dated from the late 1970s, when hundreds of intellectuals and artists expressed support for Czechoslovakia's Charter 77. The émigré George Soros set up an Open Society Foundation in 1979 (with scholarships for students from South Africa) and moved to Hungary in the early 1980s, cooperating with the Academy of Sciences and offering technical equipment (copiers), stipends, and contacts with Western civil society organizations.[24] Even before communism's collapse Hungary was thus "networked" with pro-democracy NGOs, and young underground activists formed peace and environmental movements. A major rallying point was a dam project on the Danube that would have endangered the ecological balance in much of the northwest of the country.

In contrast to Poland, party reformers themselves decided that the emergence of democratic opposition was necessary, and help formed it. They thought in terms of a logical sequence: true reform required a market economy, and market economics required the institutional framework of a multi-party democracy. By the end of 1987 Hungary featured two autonomous political organizations: the conservative Hungarian Democratic Forum (MDF) and the Alliance of Free Democrats (SzDSz), with some 10,000 members. They offered umbrellas to protect other new movements – for example, independent trade unions and old parties like the Smallholders or Social Democrats that were reconstituting themselves.[25] By the spring of 1988, students had challenged the official youth organization by founding FIDESZ (Alliance of Young Democrats).[26] One of its leaders was Victor Orbán, a law student of a modest provincial background, who had authored a thesis on Solidarity and was supported by George Soros.

Because he had presided over decades of gradual, pragmatic reform (now studied carefully in Moscow), János Kádár enjoyed respect in Hungary and had he been put up for election early in the decade he might have won. But now he feared that probing questions would destroy rather than strengthen socialism. In the spring of 1988 Kádár yielded to pressures from Moscow, accepting the symbolic function of "Party

---

[24] Máté Szabó, "Hungary" in Pollack and Wielgohs (eds.), Dissent, 51–72, 51 and 62–63.
[25] Mark Pittaway, Eastern Europe 1939–2000 (London, 2004), 189.
[26] By December there were twenty-one new political associations. Rudolf L. Tőkés, Hungary's Negotiated Revolution: Economic Reform, Social Change, and Political Succession, 1957–1990 (New York, 1996), 308.

President," and more "technocratic" figures streamed into the Central Committee.[27]

Soon, "radicals" dominated the party leadership, and Kádár's successor as General Secretary, Károly Grósz, found he was already behind the times. In November 1988, he lifted censorship, and transferred most privileges incumbent upon the party to the government. The Central Committee accepted a multi-party political system.[28] Like Poland at the same time, Hungary faced a stalemate. On the one hand the regime opened spaces for limited representation of "society," but on the other, society – as represented by the new groupings– hesitated to assume the responsibilities of power.[29] Reforms would confront citizens with price hikes of foodstuffs that had been subsidized for generations. What would they say to unemployment?

In February 1989 the Party's Central Committee approved multi-party elections and renounced its role as the leading force in the country. Historical events not mentioned publicly for decades moved to center stage when Prime Minister Miklós Németh admitted that over one million peasants had been arrested or punished during the collectivization campaigns of 1945 to 1962.[30] Then came the bombshell. For a quarter century no official voice in the Soviet Bloc had called the Hungarian events of 1956 anything but a counterrevolution, but now Imre Pozsgay said they were in fact a "popular uprising."[31] The traitorous culprit of 1956 was not Imre Nagy but the Soviets and their Hungarian allies, *including János Kádár.*[32] Now all who came to power under Kádár had to admit that their careers were built on the ashes of a popular revolution. Complicit were not only Party General Secretary Grósz but also his close associates János Berecz and György Fejti, the former of whom had just published the volume – in English! – *1956 Counter-Revolution in Hungary: Words and Weapons.*[33]

And the problem was not just Stalinism: Kádár was perhaps the Bloc's foremost destalinizer. The source of the crimes lay in the Leninist idea that a tiny unelected, unchecked group could know what was best for a society. Now Hungarian reformers abjured Lenin's "democratic

---

[27] M. S. Gorbachev, *Memoirs* (New York, 1996), 468; and, for an analysis, Roger Gough, *A Good Comrade: János Kádár, Communism, and Hungary*, (London, 2006), 239.

[28] Nigel Swain, "Negotiated Revolution in Poland and Hungary, 1989," in Kevin McDermott and Matthew Stibbe (eds.), *Revolution and Resistance in Eastern Europe: Challenges to Communist Rule* (New York, 2006), 139–56, 147.

[29] David Stark and Laszlo Bruszt, "Remaking the Political Field in Hungary," in Ivo Banac (ed.), *Eastern Europe in Revolution* (Ithaca, NY, 1991), 13–55, 26.

[30] Barany, "Epilogue," 402.   [31] Pittaway, *Eastern Europe*, 190.

[32] This was May 1989, see Tökés, *Hungary's Negotiated Revolution*, 329.

[33] János Berecz, *1956 Counter-Revolution in Hungary: Words and Weapons* (Budapest, 1987).

centralism," and created their own branch of the party in late 1988. This was a return to native traditions of Social Democracy cut off in the 1940s. The following summer the leadership oversaw a transition of the party from a Bolshevik "organizational weapon" to a broad political movement, and by September up to 200,000 party members had turned in their party books as the party retreated from positions where it had exerted power for decades, whether in the workplace, military, or police.[34]

Precisely because it was more open the party was put on the defensive. In June, thirty-one years after their executions, the remains of Imre Nagy and four others who died with him, along with an empty sixth casket representing all victims of the 1956 revolution – including teenagers hanged under Kádár – were reburied in a public spectacle that brought a quarter million people to central Budapest. Communist reformers such as Pozsgay and Németh acted as pallbearers, signaling a plea for reconciliation, while one of Nagy's codefendants, Miklós Vasarhelyi, took the podium, invoking historic justice, national unity, and the opportunity Hungarians now had for "peaceful transition to a free and democratic society."[35] On July 6 Nagy was officially rehabilitated. That same day, Kádár, seemingly haunted by questions of his guilt for the executions, finally succumbed to an extended illness.[36]

In the national roundtable the regime's negotiators committed themselves to a transition "from one-party to representative democracy," and seemed eager to face elections in order to divest themselves of the consequences of failed economic policies.[37] Voters swept them from power, first in November 1989, when they rejected the party's plan to hold presidential elections before parliamentary elections, and then in March and April 1990, when they threw out leaders of the post-communist successor party.[38] The Hungarian Democratic Forum, supported by 43 percent of the votes, constituted a new government, joined by the liberal Alliance of Free Democrats (who attained 24 percent).

The Breaching of the Iron Curtain and the GDR

In the midst of these dizzying changes Hungarian leaders did something inadvertently that proved even more destabilizing for state socialism than

---

[34] Tökés, *Hungary's Negotiated Revolution*, 296 and 332.   [35] Ibid., 330.
[36] See a record of his rambling speech during a final appearance at the Central Committee on April 12, 1989 in Karl Benzinger, *Imre Nagy: Martyr of the Nation* (New York, 2008), 114; and Gough, *A Good Comrade*, 246–47.
[37] Tökés, *Hungary's Negotiated Revolution*, 334.
[38] Milton Goldman, *Revolution and Change in Central and Eastern Europe* (Armonk, NY, 1997), 192.

free elections. Early in the year they learned it was time for renovating the border fortifications, that is, for replacing rusty sections of fence and updating mines past their guaranteed explosion date. But money was tight and people asked: why bother? Hungarians could travel to Austria as often as they liked and the barbed wire served no purpose. In May Hungarian and Austrian officials presided over a snipping ceremony meant to please Western TV audiences. Unfortunately for Erich Honecker, the Hungarian comrades had not contemplated the consequences for the GDR.

One of the decisive acts for the East Bloc was thus more happenstance than decision. We now move to a radical shift in direction for four regimes that had resisted reform, saying that Gorbachev's ideas were irrelevant. If Hungary and Poland registered desultory reforms dating back to the rupture of 1956, for East Germany, Czechoslovakia, Romania, and Bulgaria, 1989 was the break from Stalinism; first in East Berlin and then in domino effect to Prague, Bucharest, and Sofia. The opening of the Hungarian-Austrian frontier undid the calculus by which East Germans made their lives. They had made peace with repression assuming that there was no escape. By contrast Poles like Hungarians could travel westward on a regular basis; those who did not "voice" dissatisfaction could exit.[39] The closest parallel to the GDR was Czechoslovakia, where the neo-Stalinist regime collapsed almost as rapidly, and citizens lived under severe restrictions of speech and movement. But even there many citizens routinely traveled to the west.

Contrary to its leaders' hubristic claims, the need for change was as great in East Germany as anywhere. The country was buttressed by credits from the FRG and open access to markets in the European Union, but the debt crisis, as well as a gradual decline in living standards, environmental devastation and an energy crisis, as well as perennial unrest among creative intellectuals and artists, all pointed to reform. Yet the leadership portrayed the GDR's forty years, including Stalinism, as an unbroken success story, with no need to question the fantastic centralization of power at the top. While Mikhail Gorbachev opened East Germans' paths of imagination, the country's chief ideologue Kurt Hager provoked the Soviets by asking whether one puts on new wallpaper just because one's neighbor is doing so. Though they made protests to Hungary over the border opening, East Germany's aged leaders had become so divorced from reality that they hardly noticed

---

[39] Thus Albert O. Hirschman's influential thesis regarding behavior in organizations, see his "Exit, Voice, and the Fate of the German Democratic Republic: An Essay in Conceptual History," *World Politics* 45, 2 (1993), 173–202.

swelling numbers of their subjects planning holidays at popular destinations like Lake Balaton, hoping perhaps to locate a chink in the Iron Curtain and escape.

Occasionally East Germany's neo-Stalinists had opened their own tightly guarded border to let out dissenters, sometimes in chains, knowing that the West German state considered them "German citizens" and would issue passports. This self-ventilation caused the disappearance of vibrant oppositional milieus – for example, in Jena – but thanks to the Protestant churches, peace, civil rights, and environmental groups persisted, above all in East Berlin and Leipzig. Unlike opposition activists in Hungary and Poland, they and many GDR citizens were explicitly socialist. A poll from November 1989 showed that 67 percent of East Germans favored "socialism with a human face," while only 33 percent supported the West German economic and social model.[40] But the survey results reflected the horizon of expectations behind the Berlin Wall, a horizon that suddenly expanded beyond all imagination when the Wall fell. Perhaps alliance with the Soviet Union was not eternal as the propaganda had claimed; perhaps the West German social model was not so bad after all; perhaps Auschwitz had not forever settled the "German question."

East Germans had excellent reception of Western television reports of the rise to power of a Solidarity Prime Minister in neighboring Poland. That was August 24, 1989. Five days previously they had been riveted to TV sets as 500 fellow East Germans attended a "pan-European picnic" on the Hungarian-Austrian border, and after having their fill of goulash, picked up their bags, and leisurely walked across the border, with passports obtained at the German embassy in Budapest. The Hungarian organizers were celebrating their "return to free Central Europe," and now their guests from Saxony and Brandenburg, clutching bits of barbed wire as souvenirs, boarded buses taking them to new lives.[41] By early September the number of East Germans in Hungary exceeded 65,000, and the Hungarian government, ignoring appeals from Erich Honecker, permitted them to leave for Austria. Instead of contemplating reform, the SED sent hundreds of Stasi agents to Hungary to harass the refugees.[42]

Yet these were only the surface challenges of the new Hungarian border regime. East German communists justified their rule – and the fortified border to the west – through a grand narrative of constructing a social

---

[40] Lévesque, *The Enigma of 1989*, 154–55.

[41] The event was organized by Hungarian reform communists and Otto von Habsburg, see "'Rübergemacht' während des Paneuropa-Picknicks," Report of ARD News, Tagesschau (August 19, 1989), Online.

[42] Anonymous, "Und wenn sie die ganze Stasi schicken," *Der Spiegel* (August 21, 1989), 30–31.

system leading humanity forward not simply in Germany, but as part of a socialist world. How could two socialist neighbors suddenly evolve "backward," sacrificing the dictatorship of the proletariat? No one had an answer. The sense of crisis extended into the government's preparations to celebrate the fortieth anniversary of the founding of the GDR on October 7, 1989.

In late summer, challenges began to emerge from the increasingly desperate population within the GDR, above all from the southern city of Leipzig, where discontent swelled due to a regional environment devastated by chemical plants powered by pollutant soft coal and operating with minimal use of filters. On October 3 the government sealed the pressure cooker by closing the borders to Czechoslovakia. The point was to stem the tide of citizens southward to Hungary, but many feared their state would become a military dictatorship. A few dozen even tried to escape eastward – by swimming across the Oder into Poland![43]

But the steady growth of crowds also depended on something that was "contingent" and not "structural"; that is, the free decision of identifiable human beings. From the fall of 1982 Lutheran pastors Günter Johannsen and Christian Führer had been holding peace prayers on Mondays at St. Nicholas Church in central Leipzig, and the meetings continued even after the war panic of the early decade receded. In late summer of 1989, handfuls of demonstrators mixed in with the faithful and left the church proclaiming: "We want out!" They hoped to be arrested and "bought free" by the West German government. But many more streamed in to express hopes for change at home. From early September attendees began a march after the prayer around the circular road surrounding the old city center. They contended with police violence but their numbers grew.

Tens of thousands were expected for Monday, October 9, 1989, and television audiences across Europe wondered how the regime would respond. A few months earlier, Chinese leaders had crushed pro-democracy forces with no concern for casualties. Citizens of Leipzig knew that police had beaten demonstrators in East Berlin and Dresden two days earlier at the occasion of the country's fortieth anniversary. One thing the police could not stop was spontaneous chanting of "Gorbi, Gorbi" by the Free German Youth as they passed the reviewing stand of dignitaries in Berlin's Unter den Linden. At this the Polish guest Mieczysław Rakowski turned to Mikhail Gorbachev and said "they are

---

[43] Some 6,000 East German citizens had collected in Warsaw before they were permitted to travel to the FRG in early October, see Anke Hahn, "Die Botschaftsflüchtlinge von Warschau," Report of ARD News, Tagesschau (November 3, 2014), Online.

finished."[44] He meant the smiling Erich Honecker and his other comrades just a few feet away, unable to process what was happening.

The exception to violence on that October 7 was Plauen, a manufacturing town on the border to Bavaria, where some fifteen thousand demonstrated for reforms, and dispersed peacefully after the Protestant Superintendent Thomas Küttler secured promises that the local authorities would talk to them. Plauen was a place that was poorly provisioned, heavily polluted, and well aware of life in the West, but so were numerous other small towns in southern East Germany. That demonstration happened because one young man – the toolmaker Jörg Schneider – had distributed dozens of leaflets announcing that it would happen. But the curious onlookers who gathered in Plauen's center that rainy afternoon were transformed into a demonstration after police roughed up a man carrying a lonely banner reading: "we want reforms!" They were moved by anger, and without the superintendent's intervention might have stormed the city hall. That in turn would have produced fatalities and transformed the East German autumn.

The October 9 demonstration in Leipzig also ended peacefully, though thousands of well-armed militia stood by, and hospitals were given extra provisions of blood. Some 60,000 circled the city center protesting for free elections and free travel, chanting "We are the people!," a phrase more daring than it sounds. For decades the authorities claimed everything they did was for the "welfare of the people," yet here on the streets of Leipzig the people were speaking, and their words were not the regime's.

Without the example of a Soviet leader sanctioning change and surroundings that desperately needed it, the demonstrations of Plauen or Leipzig would not have happened. But they would also not have occurred without the courage of tens of thousands who knew that change would not come if they did not act. After this point the police and military seemed defanged, their ability to intimidate broken, and any claims that the demonstrators were "provoked" obviously false. Audiences around the world watched the footage captured by West Berlin journalist Roland Jahn: ordinary men, women, and children, hands raised in a sign of peace, could not be called traitors or agents. A little over a week later the leadership of eighty-year-olds resigned.

Now people throughout East Germany joined the Leipzigers in painting banners and demonstrating – usually on Saturdays – using eloquent German to tell of what they had come to detest in the state-socialist welfare state: it treated them like children; now they wanted to be "mündig," have a voice (literally mouth). One banner mocked Erich

---

[44] Wendy Tyndale, *Protestants in Communist East Germany* (New York, 2010), 2.

Honecker's successor, the youth functionary Egon Krenz, placing him in a crib above the inscription: "what big teeth you have, Grandma."

As in Hungary and Poland, organizations shot up, above all the New Forum, which was founded by Berlin-based dissidents, but then spread across the land. There were also the civic organizations "Democracy Now" or "Democratic Awakening," as well as a Social Democratic Party. The moribund parties that had cooperated with the Communists, like the Liberals and Christian Socials, also returned to life. Though led by the lackluster Egon Krenz, the Communists tried on the language of democracy and rights, and changed their name to the Party of Democratic Socialism. In late October East Germany's leaders learned that the country faced insolvency, and requested an emergency loan from the Federal Republic, thus heightening that country's leverage. One urgent demand was travel liberalization.[45]

On November 9, SED functionaries worked out new travel regulations permitting all citizens to leave the GDR, either permanently or with the intention of returning, but word leaked before they were to go into effect. During a free-wheeling press conference that evening, an Italian journalist asked government spokesman Günter Schabowski about plans for a law regulating travel. Having missed the Central Committee meeting where this was discussed, Schabowski mistakenly assumed the law had already been made public. Then he read the text he had been given on this matter by Egon Krenz just an hour earlier. East German citizens would be able to apply for private trips to foreign countries without conditions, and the police would approve these requests "promptly" (kurzfristig). A reporter for Bild-Zeitung then asked when the new rules governing travel would go into effect. The correct answer was the following morning at 10am, but Schabowksi said "immediately."[46]

At this news, crowds of East Berliners gathered at border crossing points. Just weeks earlier, the police would have nipped the problem in the bud by arresting the "ringleaders," but now officers stood by and watched as the numbers grew, growing concerned that some might be trampled. Attempts to get in touch with higher authorities produced no clear answers, and the ranking officer at the Bornholmer Strasse control point, Stasi lieutenant colonel Harold Jäger, ordered his men to let the noisiest through after putting a stamp on their ID pictures, with the understanding that they would not be let back in. Still the crowds grew, and so did the lines of cars. Western reporters were broadcasting the

---

[45] Lévesque, *The Enigma of 1989*, 158.
[46] M. E. Sarotte, *The Collapse: The Accidental Opening of the Berlin Wall* (New York, 2014), 116–18.

events as they happened, and by 11pm thousands were chanting "Open the gate," "We'll come back," and verbally confronting the uniformed guards who stood behind the barrier. Some who had been let through were trickling back and wanted to return home. One couple said they had left young children alone in their apartment.

By that late date in the annals of East German communism, both sides knew the "people" had lost fear and would not accept the explanation that travel was "verboten." They knew from Western television that the elite was permitting unregulated travel. Why wait any longer? Jäger collected his men and asked: "Should I shoot or let them go?" The answer was: "for heaven's sake." Moments later the gates at Bornholmer Strasse swung open wide; this border guard unit had nudged the Berlin Wall into history. Other checkpoints followed suit and soon travelers were moving freely in both directions for the first time in 28 years.[47]

Within a few weeks, the GDR was flooded with Western products like free newspapers as well as Western politicians anticipating the country's return to democratic political life. Many East Germans wanted the currency that would permit them to partake of West German prosperity, and in elections of March 1990 most voted for an alliance led by Helmut Kohl's Christian Democratic Union, which promised political and economic unification on the speediest timetable. The native New Forum faded into insignificance, and thereafter formed an electoral alliance with the Green Party. One dissident said a hippopotamus had come through from Bonn and crushed the tender seedling of East German democracy.[48]

The Soviet leadership did nothing to impede the process, but the outcome was not what it intended. To Gorbachev the SED had seemed the strongest East European communist party, with mid- and lower levels committed to socialism, presumably able to carry the country through "major domestic reforms," and move forward to new relations between the two German states.[49] And if rapid changes were possible in his country – an article of faith for Mikhail Gorbachev – why not in the smaller GDR?

End of Neo-Stalinism: Czechoslovakia, Romania, Bulgaria

With the Berlin Wall open, eyes turned to Czechoslovakia. Could it remain a neo-Stalinist island adjacent to the West? Like its East German

---

[47] M. E. Sarotte, *1989: The Struggle to Create Post-Cold War Europe* (Princeton, NJ, 2014), 42–43.
[48] This was Jens Reich, see Karsten Timmer, *Vom Aufbruch zum Umbruch: Die Bürgerbewegung in der DDR 1989* (Göttingen, 2000), 383.
[49] Lévesque, *The Enigma of 1989*, 156.

counterpart, the Czechoslovak government had been saying for years that Gorbachev's reforms were irrelevant, but now it was clear that the Soviet Union would not protect it from Czechoslovak society.

The reform movement of 1968 had been popular through all social strata and therefore Czech communists kept the lid on tight. If the Prague Spring was about decentralization and democracy then such words were "counterrevolutionary," and Alexander Dubček's successors extinguished any hopes for openness, criticism, or rational management, doing all they could to achieve the opposite: a "neo-Stalinist" command style, with orthodoxy dictated by a few men at the top. All those in power routinely examined their consciences to make sure nothing remained of desires for freedom of thought.

Take one glimpse of this mentality from December 1988, when a Czech delegation attended a meeting at the Diplomatic Academy of the Soviet Ministry of Foreign Affairs in Moscow. The Soviets admitted that the invasion two decades earlier had been a violation of international law, and encouraged the Czechs to speak freely about it. To their surprise, the guests rejected such "counterrevolutionary propaganda," and threatened to cancel their participation the following year.[50] Faced with this widespread mendacity syndrome Czech playwright Václav Havel produced a plea to fellow citizens to "live in truth."[51] Only from the standpoint of the Brezhnev-era gerontocracy could anyone call the Prague Spring a hostile counterrevolutionary act steered from Bonn and Washington.

Because of censorship few Czechs had read Havel's critique, but in 1989 they could not ignore thousands of East German refugees escaping through their country to Hungary, and when Hungary was placed off limits, the storming by thousands of East Germans of the West German embassy in Prague. On September 30, foreign minister Hans-Dietrich Genscher secured permission for them to travel to West Germany. From that day until October 4 the East Germans left by fourteen special trains from the Prague-Liben station, going northward to Dresden and the west via Plauen into Bavaria. (The GDR then closed its border to Czechoslovakia).[52]

In those autumn days, central Prague had resembled a camping zone for the East Germans, with their cars taking up virtually all the parking spaces on the city's left bank. Besides their tiny Trabants they left behind powerful images: of willingness to risk certainty and comfort for the sake of living freely. Take the recollection of Petr Pithart, historian, writer, and Charter 77 signatory, demoted with thousands of other Prague Spring

---

[50] Lévesque, *The Enigma of 1989*, 85.

[51] Václav Havel et al., *The Power of the Powerless*, ed. by John Keane (New York, 1985).

[52] The number in the embassy was estimated at 4,000, but many more waited outside, see Karel Vodicka, *Die Prager Botschaftsflüchtlinge 1989* (Göttingen, 2014).

supporters to manual labor in 1969: "the distance between freedom and unfreedom could be measured in the streets of Prague's left bank. I stood long night hours a few hundred yards from the West German embassy, packed tightly together with other Czechs, saying nothing but watching the spectacle: that's what you do if you want to take freedom for yourself."[53]

A tiny Czech opposition had managed to launch relatively small demonstrations in August and October 1988 and January 1989, all of which were suppressed, but gave a sense of unrest beneath the surface.[54] In light of evidence from Poland, Hungary, and the GDR that the USSR would not prop up Leninist regimes, only a spark was needed in the fall of 1989 to ignite a protest movement. As in East Germany, opposition forces could take advantage of a recurring event that brought people into the streets legally: in Prague it was the yearly commemoration of the November 17, 1939, Nazi arrests of over a thousand Czech students.[55] Ten to fifteen thousand young demonstrators took to the streets fifty years later and immediately went beyond the official script, singing patriotic songs and rattling keys at the police – a gesture meant to show the jailers that the inmates had the power to open their cells. They demonstrated peacefully, walking with open hands to show that they bore no arms. Still, the security forces moved to violently disperse the students, seriously injuring scores of them, and a rumor spread that one had been killed.

The spectacle of police beating and injuring defenseless students – who in the Czech national imagination played the role of a popular conscience – mobilized rage, driving tens and then hundreds of thousands of other Czechs onto the streets, shedding the fear that otherwise kept them indoors. Students as well as artists staged strikes and produced signs and posters, and within two days a new civil society group, "Civic Forum," inspired by the German New Forum, was formed at the Činoherní Klub Theater in Prague with dissidents from Charter 77 including Petr Pithart and Václav Havel.

On November 21 negotiations opened with the government at yet another "round table," though the premier had called Václav Havel

---

[53] Ct. in Jürgen Danyel, "Abschied von der DDR," in Martin Sabrow (ed.), *ZeitRäume: Potsdamer Almanach des Zentrums für Zeithistorische Forschung 2009* (Göttingen, 2010), 43–46.

[54] An estimated 10,000 demonstrated in Prague on August 21, 1988, and several thousands gathered on January 15, 1989 to commemorate the self-immolation of Jan Palach, see Milenko Petrovic, *The Democratic Transition of Post-Communist Europe* (New York, 2013), 106.

[55] Jan Gebhart and Jan Kuklik, *Dramatické i všední dny protektorátu* (Prague, 1996), 101.

a "zero" only weeks earlier.[56] Czechoslovak workers staged a two-hour general strike on November 27, and two days later the federal parliament did away with the leading role of the Communist Party in society. Ladislav Adamec's government resigned, and on December 10 a government with mostly non-communist ministers formed under the moderate Marian Čalfa. Non-communists were "coopted" into parliament, and on December 29 that body unanimously elected Václav Havel president.

By the end of January there were over 200 new political organizations legally recognized in Czechoslovakia, and Civic Forum (called VPN in Slovakia) received 46.6 percent of the vote in the June elections; the KSČ got 13.6 percent. Havel was confirmed as president, Čalfa as federal premier, Alexander Dubček as head of parliament, and Petr Pithart as prime minister of the Czech half of the country.[57]

Like its East German counterpart, the Czechoslovak regime discovered that it lacked the conviction to escalate beyond truncheon and tear gas to live ammunition. One more well-armed, hardline regime had gone to oblivion with little resistance. Save the beatings and arrests in the early East German demonstrations and the Prague "massacre" of November 17 in which no one died, the neo-Stalinist dictators departed the scene peacefully if not gracefully.

Yet if we look south to Romania we see massive violence verging on civil war. Tensions here were more severe because the previous decade had been a time of extreme hardship imposed by the megalomaniacal clique of Nicolae Ceaușescu, a national-Leninist who came to power in the 1960s with much popularity, but then became attracted to the discipline of North Korea, and decided to reduce his country's reliance on foreign imports. Money and goods needed for basic consumption were sent to the West to repay loans, and the population's living standards dropped, so that by the early 1980s basic foodstuffs were on ration cards and use of electricity and gas limited to a few hours a day.

At the same time Ceaușescu sought no understanding with diverse groups within the party, let alone beyond the party, and, in contrast to the countries further north, virtually no interest articulation developed in civil society. Ceaușescu regularly "cleared the terrain of contenders" and destroyed all loci of opposition, producing a "remarkable atomization of Romanian society, in which fear and distrust became the currency of human relations."[58]

[56] JiříVykoukal, Bohuslav Litera, and Miroslav Tejchman, *Východ: Vznik, vývoj a rozpad sovětského bloku 1944–1989* (Prague, 2000), 722.

[57] Vykoukal, Litera, and Tejchman, *Východ*, 726.

[58] Katherine Verdery and Gail Kligman, "Romania after Ceausescu: Post-communist Communism?," in Banac (ed.), *Eastern Europe in Revolution*, 117–48, 118.

Nevertheless periodic explosions of discontent occurred in working-class areas, the most notable in Brasov in November of 1987 involving some 40,000 workers from tractor and truck-making plants. Much like the protests that shook Plzeň in 1953, Poznań in 1956, or the Baltic coast in 1970, economic grievances had led to political demands, and even the singing of anthems from 1848.[59] In 1989 the turning point toward collapse was reached when revolts in Transylvanian Timişoara were sparked by the threatened arrest of the popular Hungarian Calvinist pastor László Tőkés. When authorities moved to seize him, thousands of supporters blocked them with a human chain, and by December 16 the city was virtually in the hands of protesters. The region's many Hungarian-speakers had access to informative media broadcasts from Hungary and Yugoslavia, and when railway workers carried word of the demonstrations eastward to international media, authorities rotated troops out of the city.[60]

On December 18 Ceauşescu left Romania to visit his last supporters, the theocratic rulers of Iran. Witnessing the growing turmoil on his country's western border, Soviet foreign minister Shevardnadze said he would welcome Ceauşescu's fall. Upon returning on December 20, Ceauşescu declared a state of emergency in Timişoara, branding the demonstrators terrorists, and organized demonstrations in his own favor in Bucharest the following day.[61] The masses turned against him, however, with calls emerging for his resignation. Security forces injured hundreds when trying to disperse the demonstrators. The next day the army went over to the people and Ceauşescu and his wife Elena fled the capital by helicopter, touching down in the countryside. They were apprehended, placed before a military tribunal, and executed before running television cameras on Christmas Eve.

One explanation for the haste in doing away with the rulers was concern that they might lead a counterrevolution against the "Front of National Salvation" that suddenly announced its existence over the airwaves on December 22, just as crowds were seizing the Communist Central Committee building and television station in Bucharest. The Front consisted not of dissident leaders – none existed – but of former high placed Communists, some of whom Ceauşescu had disgraced. Prominent was Ion Iliescu, a once-top apparatchik who had influential supporters in the police and the army. In his first speech Iliescu called Ceauşescu a "man without a heart or soul or common sense, a feudal

---

[59] Denis Deletant, *Romania under Communist Rule* (Portland, OR, 1999), 135.
[60] Verdery and Kligman, "Romania after Ceausescu," 120.
[61] Vykoukal, Litera, and Tejchman, *Východ*, 733.

fanatic, who destroyed the country" and "perpetrated the worst crimes upon the people."[62]

Bulgaria was the final country to depart the neo-Stalinist camp. Its leadership under Todor Zhivkov had a line of succession dating back to the 1950s, broken by no period of reform. Like Ceauşescu, Zhivkov promoted family members to top positions in the party and state hierarchy; for example, his daughter Lyudmila became Minister of Culture before dying under mysterious circumstances in 1981.

Reminiscent of the Romanian regime of the 1980s, Zhivkov's rule was characterized by an ethnic chauvinism that aroused protest even from East Bloc neighbors. From 1984 the leadership attempted to forcibly assimilate members of the Turkish minority living to the south and northeast. The first measures involved making their names sound Slavic, but opposition necessitated calling in tanks in the largest military operation in Bulgaria since the Second World War.[63] As in Romania, the leadership turned to nationalism as a way of inflating popular support in a time of economic trouble.

Yet unlike Romania the dictators in Sofia had no history of defying Moscow. Quite the opposite: the imitation of Soviet ways was so slavish that Soviets called Bulgaria a "sixteenth republic." That made the advent of Gorbachev particularly embarrassing. After initially claiming that Bulgaria had reformed its economy and did not need perestroika or glasnost, Bulgaria's ruler paid lip service, but in fact, as Gorbachev later recalled, "as for real democratization and glasnost, there was not a whiff of that."[64] To the end, Bulgaria's leaders maintained camps for political prisoners, and a huge police apparatus.

Yet they were not as repressive as their Romanian counterparts, and in early 1989 small opposition groups sprouted up, some seeking to cover themselves with overtly pro-Soviet platforms, like the Discussion Club for the Support of Perestroika and Glasnost or Ecoglasnost, but there was also an Independent Association for Human Rights, an independent trade union, and a Committee for the Defense of Religious Rights. The fate of the oppressed Turks had given the Bulgarian intelligentsia something to rally around, and in early November opposition leaders met in Sofia, supporting a program of human rights.[65]

Mass demonstrations had broken out in Turkish areas in the spring; the regime's response was brutal repression, but also an offer to ethnic Turks to leave. Contrary to what Zhivkov expected, some 344,000 took up his

---

[62] Ibid., 732 and 734.
[63] R. J. Crampton, *A Concise History of Bulgaria* (Cambridge, 1997), 209.
[64] Gorbachev, *Memoirs*, 485.   [65] Crampton, *A Concise History of Bulgaria*, 214.

offer, so many that Turkey had to close its borders (August 22). The fiasco reached the foreign press, costing Zhivkov any lingering support in Moscow. On November 10, his rivals in the party leadership ousted Zhivkov after first clearing the move with Mikhail Gorbachev.

Now Bulgaria'a streets filled with demonstrators: as early as November 18, 50,000 protested in the capital, demanding democracy and free elections. What followed – again reminiscent of Romania – was a transformation largely under the control of the old apparatus, now speaking of the virtues of democracy. A Union of Oppositional Forces was founded on December 7, almost a month after Zhivkov's fall – in contrast to the situation in Poland, Hungary, Czechoslovakia, the GDR, and even Romania, where political opposition formed while the dictator still ruled.[66] This was a harbinger of later difficulties of transition to democracy.

The Communists' successor organization, the Bulgarian Socialist Party, won the elections in June 1990, beating their main rival, the Union of Democratic Forces, with 211 seats to 144 in parliament (of a total of 400).[67] They prospered thanks to leftist and pro-Russian traditions extending into the countryside, but also the cohesion of new leadership around former Foreign Minister Petar Mladenov. They did not seem a foreign force, and the opposition was divided, failing to produce a strong leader. Because the elections were fair, this was a definitive end to communist Bulgaria.[68]

Concluding Thoughts

The transition to something new was just beginning, and this was true of the region as a whole. We started by noting that in 1989 revolution was incomplete in some places and hardly evident in others, but the process of transformation extended before that year and went far beyond it, into our present moment. The earliest revolutionary event occurred in August 1980 when Poles launched a ten-million-strong protest movement that authorities outlawed but never crushed. When strikes broke out late in the decade, reform communists called upon Solidarity's leaders to negotiate the "solution" of partly free elections. The event's resonance went beyond Poland, however, because the trade union's continued strength showed people

---

[66] György Dalos, *Der Vorhang geht auf: das Ende der Diktaturen in Osteuropa* (Munich, 2009), 169.

[67] Crampton, *A Concise History of Bulgaria*, 219; and Vykoukal, Litera, and Tejchman, *Východ*, 731.

[68] Vykoukal, Litera, and Tejchman, *Východ*, 730–32.

across the Bloc that state socialism was irreparably dysfunctional and needed reforms that went beyond and indeed contradicted Leninism.

Important in Poland and Hungary were even older histories of pressure from below, often suppressed but never extinguished, given expression through opposition groups, party reforms aiming at appeasement of mass desires, but also the rise of civil society, especially in Poland. Poland stands out as the place where society had self-organized in complex and substantial ways by 1989, meaning that groups existed that could involve themselves in political contests from the start. A ubiquitous grey and black market also played a role; meaning that formerly illicit trade and production could come above ground and contribute to rapid economic growth after an early bout of hyperinflation. Though the opposition was much smaller in East Germany and Czechoslovakia it also quickly self-organized in 1989, and elections of representatives of new groups were held within months of the rupture in power. By contrast, the emergence of independent spheres was much slower in Bulgaria and Romania, where the opposition movements were small. Though initially this south-eastern tier lagged in democratization, by 2007 the entire former Soviet Bloc had entered both NATO and the European Union.

That is one level of the story: how some East Europeans showed others the character of their common predicament and how to escape. Another level was change in the communist parties themselves, when liberals, most importantly Mikhail Gorbachev, but also Hungarian and Polish comrades, discussed and prepared for change; for example, through legal reforms. Without Gorbachev the communist system could have continued, and perhaps transformed into something different – market-oriented but less democratic. Polish and Soviet communists attempted to learn from János Kádár's decades-long economic reforms; but the important slogan transmitted by the Soviet leader was of a common European home. In the spring of 1989 Hungarians concluded that the rooms could not be separated by barbed wire, and their mostly symbolic effort to erase "Cold War"-style fortifications to the west had the starkly real effect of causing the GDR to implode in the summer and fall.

Symptomatically reformers were absent in the GDR, Czechoslovakia, Bulgaria, and Romania, and that is why the events of 1989 appeared more explosive (and revolutionary) than in Hungary and Poland; of course once the GDR had disappeared hardliners in all three countries had to count their days as numbered, and they adjusted more (Bulgaria) and less (Romania) successfully. The Bloc had come into existence as a unit, and it entered oblivion as a unit.

But there is a third level to the transnational agitation and ferment: the role of the West in the East, beginning with the work of consular officials promoting dissenters as well as reform communists in the 1980s, but continuing in the careful monitoring of political change in the 1990s. Was there a chain-reaction of self-liberation among the societies of Eastern Europe? We can take for granted that people in various places knew well what was happening elsewhere, but the exact impact is difficult to gauge. The suppression of Solidarity in Poland in 1981 convinced many East Germans and Czechs that resistance was pointless; yet we know that East Germans inspired many Czechs on the virtues of mass action eight years later. The failure of Poland ever to be properly reintegrated in the Bloc during the 1980s hinted at profound deficiencies of economic and political structure; but that country's deepening recession was only the most extreme case of a debt crisis that touched Hungary, the GDR, and even the Soviet Union.

What the leaders and societies learned from each other – with the exception of Nicolae Ceaușescu – was that reform (the intention of the former) and revolution (implicitly the goal of the latter) required compromise. If one focuses on the negotiations of 1989 one notices that the revolutionary process had a self-limiting aspect that made the changes possible, and perhaps enduring. Had each side in roundtable talks not stepped back from extremes and met in the middle, change may have stalled or stopped. Here seemingly non-revolutionary practice could itself, on a broader background, be seen as revolutionary.

Ideas were undoubtedly flowing across borders, but to say that the flow of ideas prompted or generated action would be incorrect. By the fall of 1989, the flow was a torrent, a gushing stream with much noise and power whose work evades careful analysis. But the idea carried was one: it was democracy. Everything else had been tried, and democracy seemed not only a natural step, it was the only step. The year was called "miraculous," but the path forward seemed straight and predestined, carried by the hope and idealism that we can read in slogans transmitted in dozens of permutations, captured perhaps best by an unknown Prague shopkeeper who put the following in her window in December 1989: "The heart of Europe cries for freedom."[69]

---

[69] Timothy Garton Ash, "The Revolution of the Magic Lantern," *New York Review of Books* (January 18, 1990).

10 The Arab Uprisings

James L. Gelvin

On December 17, 2010, a Tunisian street vendor, Muhammad Bouazizi, set himself on fire in front of the local government building in Sidi Bouzid, a small town in central Tunisia.[1] Earlier in the day, a policewoman had confiscated his wares and publicly humiliated him. He tried to complain at the local municipality, but to no avail. It was then that he went to the local market and bought the flammable liquid with which he doused himself.

Bouazizi's act struck a chord among Tunisians, and protests quickly spread from Sidi Bouzid across the country. Tunisian protesters brought a number of issues to the table: unemployment, food inflation, corruption, poor living conditions, lack of freedoms, and lack of government responsiveness. The Tunisian General Labor Union (UGTT), the sometime lapdog of the regime, saw which way the wind was blowing and threw its support behind the protests. The UGTT had more than six hundred thousand members. At first, Tunisian president Zine al-Abidine Bin 'Ali, who had ruled for a quarter century, tried to pacify the protesters. In a pattern that would be repeated time after time in the Arab world, he promised three hundred thousand new jobs, new parliamentary elections, and a "national dialogue." This did little to mollify them. By January 14, 2011 – less than a month after Bouazizi's self-immolation – military and political leaders decided to take matters into their own hands. With the army surrounding the presidential palace, Bin 'Ali resigned and appointed his prime minister to head a caretaker government. Continued protests forced the appointment of a different prime minister, not as closely identified with the old regime,

---

[1] Parts of this article are drawn from previously published or forthcoming works, including my "Conclusion: The Arab World at the Intersection of the National and Transnational," in Mark L. Haas and David W. Lesch (eds.), *The Arab Spring: The Hope and Reality of the Uprisings*, (Boulder, CO, 2017), 288–305, which was first published in 2016; *The Arab Uprisings: What Everyone Needs to Know* (New York, 2015), which was first published in 2012; *The New Middle East: What Everyone Needs to Know* (New York, 2017); "Reassessing the Recent History of Political Islam in Light of the Arab Uprisings," in Fahed Al-Sumait, Nele Lenze, and Michael C. Hudson (eds.), *The Arab Uprisings: Catalysts, Dynamics, and Trajectories* (Lanham, MD, 2014), 115–34.

shortly thereafter. The uprising in Tunisia was the first ever in the modern Arab world to bring down an autocrat.[2]

About a week and a half after Bin 'Ali resigned, protesters, many of whom belonged to the "April 6 Youth Movement," began their occupation of Tahrir Square in Cairo.[3] (While Tahrir Square was but one site of many in Egypt where protests were held that day, it emerged as the symbolic center of the Egyptian uprising.) The April 6 Youth Movement got its name from a date in 2008 when young people, using Facebook, called for a general strike to support striking workers at a state-run textile factory. The general strike failed, giving lie to the miraculous powers frequently ascribed to Facebook and other social media by breathless Western commentators.

That was 2008. This time around protesters were more successful. The security forces and goons-for-hire failed to dislodge them from the square. Then the army announced it would not fire on them. Strikes and anti-government protests spread throughout Egypt. On February 11, 2011, the army took matters into its own hands. It deposed President Hosni Mubarak and established a new government under the Supreme Council of the Armed Forces. This phase of the Egyptian uprising – what might be called the first street phase of the Egyptian uprising – was over in a mere eighteen days.

Soon after the Tunisian and Egyptian uprisings seemingly demon-strated what could be done, populations elsewhere in the Arab world began to smell blood in the water and followed suit. In spite of the obvious influence the first two uprisings had on those that followed, however, it would be wrong to view them through the lens of the first two. For example, after the outbreak of the Egyptian uprising, a similar-style protest movement emerged in Yemen. Nevertheless, it had very un-Tunisian, un-Egyptian results. As supporters of the regime squared off against social networking youths and labor, along with military officers, disgruntled tribesmen, and opposition members of parliament whom the regime had neglected to buy off, Yemen descended into chaos and violence. Ever since, Yemen has suffered through extended periods of bloodshed intermittently interrupted by outside attempts to broker national reconciliation.

---

[2] Perhaps the best account of the Tunisian uprising – one which puts it in its historical and geographic contexts – is Julia Clancy Smith, "Lessons from a Small Place: The Dignity Revolutions in Tunisia, North Africa, and the Globe," in Haas and Lesch (eds.), *The Arab Spring*, 10–39.

[3] Although Western media referred to the protesters as "youths," a term they borrowed from the name "April 6 Youth Movement" – 59 percent of those who occupied Tahrir Square were between the ages of 25 and 44, see James L. Gelvin, "Everything You Think You Know about the Egyptian Revolution is Wrong," *History News Network* (February 11, 2014), Online.

Uprisings in both Libya and Syria also turned into long, violent affairs. In Libya, dissidents called for a "Day of Rage" after the arrest of a prominent human rights lawyer. He represented families of the twelve hundred "disappeared" political prisoners who had been murdered in cold blood in one single incident in 1996. A six month civil war followed, which only ended after a fierce NATO air campaign targeted the regime. And after months of predictions that "it couldn't happen in Syria," it did.[4] As in Libya, a spontaneous uprising in a town far from the capital sparked a bloody anti-government insurrection. However the Syrian uprising ends, it is unlikely the Syrian people nor the villages and cities in which they live will ever return to their pre-uprising condition.

Protesters challenged monarchies as well. After protests modeled on those of Egypt broke out in Bahrain, the government struck back violently. Using the excuse that Iranian subversion was behind the protests, it invited in troops and police from neighboring Saudi Arabia and the United Arab Emirates to help "restore order." A period of fierce counter-revolutionary repression followed. As in Libya, outside intervention determined the course of an uprising. In Saudi Arabia and Morocco, kings who had presented themselves as "reformers" faced protesters who demanded expanded representation, an end to corruption, and constitutional checks on monarchic power. Significantly, protesters did not demand the replacement of the regime, as protesters elsewhere had done. Both governments sought to calm the waters by offering their citizens inducements. The Saudi government promised a $130 billion benefits package for its citizens. The Moroccan government agreed to some reforms.

These were the main sites of contention from December 2010 through March 2011 – the period commonly associated with the so-called "Arab Spring." There were other sites as well. There were also sites where populations took to the streets after the initial wave had crested. All told, since Bouazizi's suicide, protests or uprisings have broken out in at least eighteen of the twenty-two states which consider themselves part of the Arab world. This chapter explores those uprisings, first looking at their connections, then at their differences.

A Revolutionary Wave

What took place in the Arab world was a revolutionary wave, both in temporal and spatial terms. Temporally, the protests and uprisings that

---

[4] Anonymous, "Interview with Syrian President Bashar al-Assad," *Wall Street Journal* (January 31, 2011), Online.

took place during those four months in 2010–2011 were, in fact, the culmination of thirty years of struggle in the Arab world for human and democratic rights, on the one hand, and social and economic justice, on the other. The demand for human rights lay at the heart of the "Berber Spring" of 1980, the fight by Algeria's largest ethnic minority for their rights. Eight years later, the Algerian "Black October" riots led to the first democratic elections in the Arab world (unfortunately, the government overturned their results). The Bahraini *intifada* of 1994–1999 began with a petition signed by one-tenth of Bahrain's inhabitants demanding an end to emergency rule, the restoration of rights revoked by that rule, release of political prisoners, pardons for political exiles, and the expansion of the franchise to women (the word *intifada* is Arabic for shaking off, and is now commonly used to mean rebellion). Petitioners also demanded a restoration of the 1973 constitution, which provided for a parliament in which two-thirds of the members were elected.

The death of Syrian dictator Hafez al-Assad in 2000 spawned the rise of political salons throughout Syria. Participants in those salons expanded their movement through the circulation of the "Statement of the Ninety-Nine," then the "Statement of a Thousand," which made many of the same demands made during the Bahraini *intifada*, along with multi-party elections and freedom of speech, assembly, and expression. Even after the "Damascus Spring" turned into the "Damascus Winter," aftershocks of the mobilization continued. Among those aftershocks was the Damascus Declaration Movement of 2005, which (initially) united the secular and religious opposition in a common demand for democratic rights.

These movements were only the tip of the iceberg. Following the spread of the pro-democracy *diwaniyya* (civic council) movement in the wake of the expulsion of Iraqi troops in 1991, Kuwait experienced two "color revolutions." The first – the "Blue Revolution" – lasted from 2002 to 2005. It won for Kuwaiti women the right to vote. A year later, Kuwaitis organized the "Orange Revolution" to promote electoral reform. In 2004, secular and Islamist Egyptians banded together to form a group called "Kifaya" ("Enough"), which called on Mubarak to resign. In Morocco, popular agitation led to the establishment of the Equity and Reconciliation Commission in 2004 to investigate human rights abuses that had occurred during the previous thirty years – the so-called "Years of Lead." Lebanese took to the streets in 2005 in the so-called "Cedar Revolution," demanding the withdrawal of Syrian forces from that unfortunate country and parliamentary elections free from Syrian interference. In 2004, 2008, and 2010 Kurdish citizens protested for minority rights in Syria. And the list goes on.

Alongside protests and uprisings for human rights and democratic governance were protests and uprisings for social and economic justice. These began in the 1970s with a series of "IMF riots" in the region – the sometimes regime-threatening protests against the "economic reforms" demanded by the International Monetary Fund in exchange for bailing out cash-strapped states. The IMF demanded, among other things, that states cut expenditures, balance their budgets, remove price controls, deregulate business, privatize public enterprises by selling them off to the highest bidder, and end across-the-board subsidies on consumer goods – unpopular measures, to say the least. IMF riots spread from Egypt (1977) to Morocco (1983), Tunisia (1984), Lebanon (1987), Algeria (1988), and finally Jordan (1989, 1996).

But IMF riots were not the only way populations expressed outrage over economic and social issues. There was an upsurge in labor activism as well. In 2008, for example, unemployed phosphate miners in the Gafsa region of Tunisia sparked a general strike that lasted six months. Using a variety of tactics – including demonstrations, sit-ins, the blockage of railroad tracks, and attacks on police – tens of thousands of protesters shut down the region until the army reimposed government control. Then there was the surge in Egyptian labor activism. From 2004–2010, two million Egyptian workers and their families participated in more than three thousand strikes, sit-ins, and walkouts. Sometimes protesters framed their demands in class terms; at other times, they framed them in human rights terms, as in the 2008 and 2011 Tunisian slogan, "A job is a right."[5]

The protests and uprisings of 2010–2011 amplified these earlier protests and uprisings in two ways. First, by combining demands for human and democratic rights with demands for social and economic justice, they involved broader segments of the population wherever they broke out. Second, they were more widespread. During the wave of 2010–2011, protests and uprisings unfolded in near simultaneity across national boundaries until they engulfed almost the entirety of the region.

This brings us to the spatial aspect of the Arab uprisings of 2010–2011. That uprisings should spread from Arab state to Arab state so rapidly is not difficult to explain: Over the course of the last half century, all Arab states came to share similar characteristics, and over the course of the last two decades all Arab states have faced similar conditions and shocks that made them vulnerable to popular anger.

---

[5] Joel Beinin, *Workers and Thieves: Labor Movements and Popular Uprisings in Tunisia and Egypt* (Stanford, CA, 2015), 2, 87, 101, and 136.

Overall, there are five factors that made all states in the Arab world vulnerable to popular anger. First, beginning in the late 1970s, and accelerating over the course of the last decade and a half, the United States and international banking institutions persuaded or coerced regimes throughout the region to adopt social and economic policies associated with neoliberalism. These policies shredded the post–Second World War ruling bargain that had connected Arab governments with their populations.

Before the 1980s, states throughout the Arab world had played an uncontested role in their national economies in an effort to force-march economic development. They also provided a wide array of social benefits for their populations, including employment guarantees, health care, and education. In addition, consumer goods such as food and petroleum products were subsidized by the state. In some states – Nasser's Egypt, post-independence Algeria, Qadhdhafi's Libya, post-1958 Iraq, Syria at various times, and others – regimes justified their policies using a populist discourse that extolled anticolonialism and the virtues of the revolutionary masses. In others – in the monarchies of Jordan and Saudi Arabia, for example – rulers appealed to tradition or efficiency. Whether "revolutionary" or "reactionary," however, governments came to the same destination, although via different routes. In return for their generosity, Arab states expected obedience. Overall, then, the ruling bargain connecting states with their populations might be summed up in three words: benefits for compliance.[6]

During the last quarter of the twentieth century, as development stalled and economies stagnated, neoliberalism came to replace *dirigisme* as the dominant economic paradigm globally. Neoliberalism got its tentative start in the Arab world in December 1976, when Egypt negotiated a $450 million credit line with the International Monetary Fund. In return, the Egyptian government pledged to cut commodity supports and direct subsidies. Over the course of the next three decades, the IMF negotiated ever-more-expansive agreements with cash-strapped governments in the region. These agreements were fairly consistent across the board: Governments agreed to cut and target subsidies, remove price controls, privatize government-owned assets, balance their budgets, liberalize trade, deregulate business, and the like. Neoliberalism thus violated the norms of the ruling bargain.

[6] James L. Gelvin, "American Global Economic Policy and the Civic Order in the Middle East," in Michael Bonine, Abbas Amanat, and Michael Gasper (eds.), *Is There a Middle East?: The Evolution of a Geopolitical Concept* (Palo Alto, CA, 2011), 191–206; and Steven Heydemann, "Social Pacts and the Persistence of Authoritarianism in the Middle East," in Oliver Schlumberger (ed.), *Debating Arab Authoritarianism: Dynamics and Durability in Nondemocratic Regimes* (Palo Alto, CA, 2008), 21–38.

As previously noted, populations throughout the Arab world confronted the new dispensation by engaging in acts of resistance. Those populations found two aspects of neoliberalism particularly repellent. The first is the fraying of the social safety net and threats to middle-class welfare, particularly threats to across-the-board subsidies for food and fuel. At the recommendation of the IMF, those subsidies were replaced by subsidies targeted to those who live in "absolute poverty." The second aspect of neoliberalism populations found repellent was the sell-off of publicly owned enterprises. For many, privatization threatened state employment guarantees. Furthermore, privatization did not lead, as promised, to free-market capitalism, but rather to crony capitalism, as regime loyalists took advantage of their access to the corridors of power. The worst of the crony capitalists – Ahmad Ezz in Egypt, Rami Makhlouf in Syria, anyone named Trabelsi in Tunisia – thus came to symbolize systemic corruption in the buildup to the uprisings.

Accompanying the neoliberal revolution was the so-called "Human Rights Revolution" which began in the mid-1970s – the second factor that made states in the region vulnerable to uprisings. Between 1948, when the UN General Assembly adopted the Universal Declaration of Human Rights, and the late 1970s, "human rights" referred to a bundle of rights, including collective rights (such as the right of national self-determination), economic rights, and individual rights. In the wake of the Human Rights Revolution, whenever the subject of human rights was broached in international conferences and legal proceedings, the point of reference was inevitably individual political, civil, and personal rights.

As I have argued elsewhere, neoliberalism and this restrictive definition of human rights were cut from the same cloth.[7] Both counterposed a system which gave autonomous, decision-making, rights-bearing citizens pride of place against one in which autonomy, decision-making, and rights-bearing were attributes of the state. Both pit the individualism of the West against the collectivism of the Soviet and the increasingly assertive Third World blocs. Indeed, both were used by the United States to undercut the foundations and very raison d'être of states within the two blocs. This was particularly important in the mid- to late 1970s, when Third World states threatened the global economic order by asserting such collective rights as the right to economic development, the right to compensation for colonialism's legacy, and the right to own and set the price for the raw materials they exported themselves.

---

[7] James L. Gelvin, *The Modern Middle East: A History* (New York, 2020), 267–68, which was originally published in 2005.

The Arab world was not impervious to the new dispensation. A wide variety of individuals, from leftists and liberals to members of the loyal opposition and even Islamists, found human rights to be an effective tool in the struggle against their autocratic governments. Hence, the proliferation of NGOs tasked to monitor their government's compliance with the new norm. And hence, the protests and uprisings for human and democratic rights and against autocratic regimes alluded to earlier. It was no accident, then, that the uprisings of 2010–11 initially spoke in the language of human and democratic rights, no matter how they evolved over time.[8]

The third structural factor that made regimes vulnerable was their brittleness. The years between the onset of the economic crisis of 2008 and the first uprising were not good ones for governments throughout the world. Governments found themselves caught between bankers and economists recommending austerity, on the one hand, and populations fearing the end of the welfare state they had come to know, on the other. While uprisings were spreading in the Arab world, governments fell in the United Kingdom, Greece, Ireland, Portugal, Spain, Iceland, Italy, and elsewhere, and were challenged in France and the United States. Throughout it all, not one government was overthrown, nor were political institutions uprooted. Blame fell on politicians and parties and the policies they pushed.

In the Arab world, popular representatives could not be turned out of office because there were no popular representatives. This is why populations throughout the region took to the streets as their first option. This also explains why the most common slogan during this period was "Down with the *nizam* [regime]," not "Down with the government [*hukuma*]."

In addition to these three deep-seated structural factors, there were two contingent ones that made regimes in the Arab world vulnerable. The first of these was demography. In 2011, approximately 60 percent of the population of the Arab world was under the age of thirty. Even more telling is the percentage of youth between the ages of fifteen and twenty-nine, the period during which most enter the job market and compete on the marriage market. In 2010, youths between the ages of fifteen and twenty-nine made up 29 percent of the population of Tunisia, 30 percent of the population of Egypt, and 34 percent of the population of Libya. They also made up the bulk of the unemployed (for example, in Egypt they made up 90 percent of the unemployed).[9]

---

[8] Gelvin, "Reassessing the Recent History of Political Islam."

[9] Farzaneh Roudi, *Youth Population and Employment in the Middle East and North Africa: Opportunity or Challenge* (New York, 2011), Online; and *Egypt Human Development Report 2010: Youth in Egypt: Building Our Future* (Cairo, 2010).

Demography is not, of course, destiny, and frustrations about job or life prospects do not necessarily translate into rebellion. And youth was hardly the only segment of the Arab population that mobilized during the uprisings: In Tunisia and Egypt, labor played a major role; in Libya and Syria, parents protesting the way the state had dealt with their children sparked them. Nevertheless, by 2010 there was a cohort of youths throughout the Arab world with a significant set of grievances. Under the proper circumstances, this cohort was available to be mobilized for oppositional politics.

The final factor that made regimes in the Arab world vulnerable was a global rise in food prices. Between mid-2010 and January 2011, the world price of wheat more than doubled. Economists attribute this price rise to a number of factors, from speculation to drought to more acreage in the United States and Europe devoted to growing corn for biofuel.[10]

The Arab Middle East is more dependent on aggregate food imports than any other region in the world. At the time of its uprising, Egypt was the world's largest wheat importer. In addition to its dependence on food imports, however, there are two other reasons that skyrocketing food prices were a particular burden in the Arab world. First, the portion of household spending that went to pay for food in the Arab world ranged as high as 63 percent in Morocco. Compare that to the average percentage of household spending that goes to pay for food in the United States: 7 percent – a figure that includes eating as entertainment (that is, dining outside the home).[11] The second reason the damage caused by skyrocketing food prices in the Arab world was particularly punishing is neoliberalism: Pressure from the United States and the IMF has constrained governments from intervening into markets to fix prices and has forced governments to abandon across-the-board subsidies on food.

These five factors, then, made all regimes throughout the Arab world vulnerable to popular anger. They did not, of course, cause the uprisings. To attribute causation to these or any other factors overlooks a key variable – the human element – that determines whether an uprising will or will not occur. Furthermore, the fact that these factors were at play in all Arab states does not explain why the protests and uprisings followed different trajectories and resulted in different outcomes, at least in the short term. Whatever the region-wide elements that went into the

---

[10] Elena Ianchovichina, Josef Loening, and Christina Wood, *How Vulnerable Are Arab Countries to Global Food Price Shocks?* (Washington, DC, 2012), Online.

[11] "Eight Reasons Food Prices Are Rising Globally," *Rediff Business* (October 17, 2011), Online; and Gregory White, "The Twenty-Five Countries That Will Be Screwed by a World Food Crisis," *Business Insider* (September 17, 2010), Online.

making of the protests and uprisings of 2010–2011, local factors – variations in local history, state structure, and state capability – shaped them. Those variations made it impossible for Libyans, Yemenis, or Syrians, for example, to replicate the relative peacefulness and quick resolution that marked the initial phases of the Tunisian and Egyptian uprisings. And there was an additional factor that played a significant role in determining the course of an uprising, as shown in the previous chapters of the volume: foreign intervention (or lack thereof). States both outside and within the region had an interest in the outcomes of the various uprisings and acted accordingly. Indeed, in Libya, Yemen, Bahrain, Syria, and even Egypt, foreign assistance proved decisive for successes enjoyed by insurgents (Libya), counterinsurgents (Yemen, Bahrain, Egypt), or both (Syria).

The Anatomy of the Uprisings: Comparisons

Once uprisings began to break out in the region, they took a number of forms. In the main, the uprisings that have broken out thus far might be placed into five clusters. The first cluster consists of Tunisia and Egypt, where militaries stepped in to depose long-ruling autocrats who faced widespread disaffection. The militaries thus cut the revolutionary process short. This prevented a thorough housecleaning in both states.

Tunisia and Egypt are unique in the Arab world: Beginning in the nineteenth century, both experienced two centuries of continuous state-building. As a result, in both there were long-lived, functioning institutions autonomous from the executive branch of the government. The military is one of those institutions, but there are others as well, including the judiciary and security services. Together, these institutions make up what political scientists call the "deep state."[12] When faced with an unprecedented crisis, the institutions of the deep state closed ranks to protect the old order.

The struggle between the deep state and the forces promoting change in both places defined the course of the two uprisings. When moderate Islamist organizations – Ennahda in Tunisia, the Muslim Brotherhood in Egypt – won popular mandates to form governments, the deep state joined forces with remnants of the old regime and more secular-oriented groups within the population in defiance. In Egypt, the Brotherhood believed itself locked in a battle to the death with its adversaries, who believed likewise. It therefore refused to share power with them, and even pushed through a constitution it drafted when it appeared

---

[12] For a nuanced exploration of the deep state phenomenon in Egypt, see Nathan J. Brown, "Egypt's Wide State Reassembles Itself," *Foreign Policy* (July 17, 2013), Online.

that the judiciary was about to dissolve the constitutional assembly on procedural grounds. As the crisis escalated – and as the Egyptian economy went into a free fall – hundreds of thousands of Egyptians took to the streets. Once again, the military stepped in, dissolved the Brotherhood, had a constitution drafted that enhanced the power of the deep state, and established a regime far more repressive than Mubarak's: According to the Egyptian Centre for Economic and Social Rights, between July 2013, when the military retook power, and November and December 2013 the military killed 2,665 of their fellow citizens, wounded 16,000, and arrested 13,145.[13]

Things in Tunisia did not end up as badly. Unlike the Egyptian Muslim Brotherhood, Ennahda did not overplay its hand. As a matter of fact, from the beginning Ennahda reached out to opposition parties and brought them into the government. And when faced with the same crises and oppositional forces faced by the Egyptian Muslim Brotherhood, Ennahda, as well as its opponents, stepped away from the precipice. Ennahda not only dissolved the government it dominated and called for new elections, it signed on to the most liberal constitution in the Arab world.

The second cluster of states undergoing uprisings consists of Yemen and Libya, where regimes fragmented, pitting the officers and soldiers, cabinet ministers, politicians, and diplomats who stood with the regime against those who joined the opposition.

The fragmentation of regimes in the two states is not surprising: In contrast to Tunisia and Egypt, both Yemen and Libya are poster children for what political scientists call "weak states."[14] In weak states, governments and the bureaucracies upon which they depend are unable to assert their authority over the entirety of the territory they rule. Nor are they able to extend their reach beneath the surface of society. It is partly for this reason that populations in weak states lack strong national identities and allegiances. Such is the situation in both Yemen and Libya.

To a certain extent, the weakness of the Yemeni and Libyan states came about as a result of geography. Neither country has terrain which makes it easy to govern – Yemen because of the roughness of its terrain, Libya because of its expansiveness. To a certain extent, the weakness of the Yemeni and Libyan states is a result of their history (or lack thereof). Both states are relatively recent creations, artificially constructed from disparate elements. Yemen had been divided between North Yemen and South

---

[13] Anonymous, "Statistics Reveal Casualties since Military Coup in Egypt," *Middle East Monitor* (February 5, 2014), Online.
[14] Arjun Chowdhory, *The Myth of International Order: Why Weak States Persist and Alternatives to the State Fade Away* (Oxford, 2018), 1–4.

Yemen until 1990. Contrasting social structures found in each Yemen reflect the legacies of formal imperialism (until 1967) in the south and the absence of formal imperialism in the north. The United Nations created an independent federated Libya in 1952 from the remnants of three former Italian colonies that had been kept separate until 1934. Even then, regional differences remained. Finally, the weakness of the Yemeni and Libyan states was a product of the ruling styles of their leaders: Both President 'Ali 'Abd Allah Salah ('Ali Abdullah Saleh) of Yemen and Mu'ammar Qadhdhafi of Libya purposely avoided establishing strong institutions in favor of a personalistic style of rule which gave them more leeway in playing off tribes and other internal groupings against each other.

Because regimes in both states fragmented, there was no unified military to step in to end the uprisings, as had happened in Tunisia and Egypt. As a result, uprisings in both states were both violent and invited foreign meddling. In the case of Yemen, the Gulf Cooperation Council, the United States, and the United Nations intervened to foster a "national dialogue" which, since the outside world was more interested in stability than democratic transition, mainly included the pre-uprising political elites interested only in claiming their share of the pie. In the end, foreign powers got neither democratic transition nor stability. Not only did a Southern secessionist movement reassert itself, the northern Houthi movement, which represents Yemen's Zaidi religious minority, joined forces with 'Ali Abdullah Saleh to take control of the capital and depose the government that the Gulf Cooperation Council, the United States, and the United Nations had installed (Zaidis – the followers of a sect of Islam that is a branch of Shi'ia Islam – make up an estimated 35–45 percent of the Yemeni population). Once again, a counterrevolutionary international coalition led by Saudi Arabia intervened to restore the pre-uprising system – only this time it was with a Libya-style air campaign. Four years after the initial uprising, Yemen became a humanitarian nightmare facing continued civil war and dysfunction, if not breakup.

As for Libya, locally based militias – some Islamist, some not – vied for control over resources, territory, and political power in the immediate aftermath of the uprising. Over time, Islamist militias, on the one hand, and non-Islamist militias and regime holdovers, on the other, coalesced into two opposing camps represented by two different governments. And, over time, the battlefield became even more complex, as forces under the command of a UN-brokered Government of National Accord and the "Islamic State" movement (ISIS) joined the fray.

As in Tunisia and Egypt, then, the main fault line in Libyan politics in the aftermath of the February 2011 uprising became one separating

Islamists from their anti-Islamist opponents. Unlike the case of Tunisia, however, outside powers have fueled the Libyan flames. First, there was NATO. Then Qatar supplied Islamists with weaponry while Egypt and the UAE spearheaded military intervention on behalf of anti-Islamist opponents. Finally, as ISIS consolidated its position there, Libya became another front in the American-led war on terrorism in general and the war on ISIS in particular.

A third cluster of states includes Syria and Bahrain, where regimes maintained their cohesion against the uprisings. One might even say that in Syria and Bahrain regimes had no choice but to maintain their cohesion against uprisings. Thus, once uprisings broke out in these states, there was little likelihood that one part of the ruling institution would turn on another, as happened in Tunisia or Egypt, or that the ruling institution would splinter, as happened in Libya and Yemen.

In Syria and Bahrain rulers effectively "coup-proofed" their regimes by, among other things, exploiting ties of sect and kinship to build a close-knit, interdependent ruling group.[15] In Syria this group consisted of Bashar al-Assad, his extended family, and members of the minority Alawite community (Alawites make up approximately 12 percent of the Syrian population; about 75 percent is Sunni Muslim). Thus, at the time of the outbreak of the uprising President Bashar al-Assad's cousin was the head of the presidential guard, his brother was commander of the Republican Guard and Fourth Armored Division, and his now-deceased brother-in-law was deputy chief of staff. None of them could have turned on the regime; if the regime went, they would go too. As a matter of fact, few persons of note have defected from the regime and, of those who have – one brigadier general, a prime minister (which in Syria is a post of little importance), and an ambassador to Iraq – not one was Alawite.

The core of the regime in Bahrain consists of members of the ruling Khalifa family who hold critical cabinet portfolios, from the office of prime minister and deputy prime minister to ministers of defense, foreign affairs, finance, and national security. The commander of the army and commander of the royal guard are also family. As in Syria, members of a minority community – Sunni Muslims, who make up an estimated 30–40 percent of the population – form the main pillar and primary constituency of the regime. The regime has counted on the Sunni community to circle its wagons in the regime's defense, although the uprising started out as non-sectarian in nature, as had Syria's. But as happened in Syria, repression by a regime identified with a minority community, along

---

[15] James T. Quinlivan, "Coup-Proofing: Its Practice and Consequences in the Middle East," *International Security* 24, 2 (1999), 131–65.

with the regime's deliberate provocation of intersectarian violence to ensure their communities would stick with the regime until the bitter end, sectarianized the uprisings and intensified the level of violence.

Foreign intervention has played a critical role in determining the course of the uprisings in both Bahrain and Syria. The one thousand Saudi and Emirati soldiers and policemen who crossed the causeway connecting the island nation with the mainland took up positions throughout the capital, Manama. This freed up the Bahraini military and security services (led by members of the ruling family and made up of Sunnis from Pakistan, Jordan, and elsewhere) to crush the opposition. The regime then embarked on a campaign of repression that was harsh by even Gulf standards. Regime opponents have faced mass arrests and torture in prison, all demonstrations have been banned, insulting the king can result in a prison sentence of up to seven years, and security forces armed with riot gear have cordoned off rebellious Shi'i villages, terrorizing residents with nighttime raids. It is also illegal to possess a Guy Fawkes mask, the accessory of choice of anarchists and members of Occupy movements the world over.[16] All the while, the regime has hidden behind the façade of a series of national dialogues whose outcomes the regime fixed.

While foreign intervention helped curtail the Bahraini uprising, it had the opposite effect in Syria. Both supporters of the regime – Iran, Russia, and Hizb Allah (Hezbollah) – and supporters of the opposition – the West, Saudi Arabia, Qatar, Turkey, and others – have funneled arms and money to their proxies, while Hizb Allah fighters and Iranian soldiers joined the fray. This has not only served to escalate the violence; it created the environment in which ISIS might incubate before it set out to create its caliphate from portions of Iraq and Syria. The foreign backers of the government have been more effective in their efforts than the foreign backers of the opposition for two reasons. First, the latter group supports a number of groups acting at cross-purposes – ranging from the inept "moderate" forces supported by the West to hard-line Islamists supported by the Qataris and Saudis. Second, they themselves act at cross-purposes: The West, fearing a sectarian bloodbath and the strength of Islamist groups within the opposition, has been ambivalent, at best, about facilitating a clear-cut opposition victory. On the other hand, the Saudis and Qataris have supported groups that seek to rule post-uprising Syria according to a strict interpretation of Islamic law.

All told, within three years Syria hosted 100,000–120,000 opposition fighters who joined upwards of one thousand opposition groups, many of

---

[16] Samuel Muston, "Anti-protest: Bahrain Bans Import of Plastic Guy Fawkes Masks," *The Independent* (February 25, 2015), Online.

which have taken control over villages and towns and the surrounding countryside.[17] The fact that the Syrian uprising turned into a proxy war which outside powers on both sides were willing to escalate when the need arose means that a negotiated settlement is unlikely. As the United Nations and Arab League special envoy to Syria, Lakhdar Brahimi, put it, in the end the uprising will quite possibly lead to the "Somalization" of Syria.[18] That is, like Somalia, Syria will remain a state on paper only, while real power will be divided among the government and rival gangs which control their own fiefdoms.

The fourth cluster of states consists of four of the seven remaining monarchies – Morocco, Saudi Arabia, Kuwait, Oman – in which uprisings occurred. Here the word uprising is a misnomer: With the exception of the uprising in Bahrain and, arguably, Jordan, *protests* in the Arab monarchies share two important characteristics that set them apart from *uprisings* in the Arab republics: They have, for the most part, been more limited in scope, and they have demanded reform of the *nizam*, not its overthrow.

It is not altogether clear why this discrepancy has been the case. Some political scientists have maintained that the reason why the demand in monarchies has been for reform and not revolution is that monarchs have an ability presidents – even presidents for life – do not have: They can retain executive power while ceding legislative power to an elected assembly and prime minister. As a result, the assembly and prime minister, not the monarch, become the focal point of popular anger when things go wrong.[19] Unfortunately, this explanation rings hollow. While it might hold true for Kuwait, which has a parliament that can be, at times, quite raucous, Saudi Arabia does not even have a parliament and the king *is* the prime minister. Others argue that oil wealth enables monarchs to buy off their opposition or prevent an opposition from arising in the first place. This might explain the Gulf monarchies, but Morocco (which had an uprising that the king enfeebled with a few cosmetic reforms) does not have oil, while Bahrain – which has had a long history of rebellion and had a full-fledged uprising in 2011 – has been hydrocarbon rich.

It is entirely possible that in the future it might be necessary to reassess whether a monarchic category even exists. Bahrain was not the only

---

[17] UK Home Office, "Country Information and Guidance, Syria: The Syrian Civil War" (August 2016), Online.

[18] UN News Centre, "Transcript of press conference by Joint Special Representative for Syria, Lakhdar Brahimi, with Secretary-General of the League of Arab States Dr. Nabil Al Arabi-Cairo" (December 30, 2012), Online.

[19] See, *inter alia*, Jack A. Goldstone, "Understanding the Revolutions of 2011: Weakness and Resilience in Middle Eastern Autocracies," *Foreign Affairs* (May-June 2011), Online.

monarchy in which opposition leaders called for the removal of the king. The same occurred in Jordan during demonstrations in November 2012, and although those demonstrations soon ran out of steam there is no way to determine how deep the sentiment runs or whether it might reemerge in the future. And while the world was focused on the anemic demonstrations of social-networking youths in Saudi Arabia's capital, violent protests, which met with violent suppression, broke out in the predominantly Shiʿi Eastern Province of the country. Taking these latter protests into account challenges the notion that protests in the monarchies were limited in scope. Ultimately, the small number of monarchies included in this category (four out of eight in the region) makes any conclusions about a monarchic exception problematic.

The fifth and final cluster includes the only three states in the Arab world which, at the end of 2010, *The Economist* Intelligence Unit listed as governed by "hybrid regimes": Iraq, Lebanon, and Palestine. According to *The Economist*, hybrid regimes maintain a democratic façade: There are, for example, elections, but those elections have substantial irregularities and are hardly free and fair. Rampant corruption and clientelism further erode the rule of law and frustrate the popular will.[20]

The uprisings in the three states share characteristics that reflect regime structure: Populations had relative freedom to mass on the streets (often alongside disgruntled members of the ruling elite) demanding accountability from dysfunctional elected governments. Protests unfolded over time, and as governments proved unable or unwilling to break the political gridlock and answer even the most rudimentary needs of their populations, those populations expanded their demands to include an overhaul of the entire political system. Hence, demonstrations that began throughout Iraq on February 25, 2011 protesting the lack of potable water, electrical shortages, and high unemployment, along with those that began in Beirut in August 2015 protesting the government's inability to secure the removal of garbage (hence the campaign's evocative name, "You Stink") and other services, morphed into demonstrations demanding the removal of oligarchs and an end to the sectarian systems in which they bred.[21] Because ruling elites in Iraq or Lebanon would hardly consent to changes that would result in their disempowerment, their options were to stall until protests ran out of steam, crush the protest

---

[20] Economist Intelligence Unit, "Democracy Index 2010: Democracy in Retreat," Online.

[21] Anne Barnard, "Lebanese Protesters Aim for Rare Unity Against Gridlocked Government," *New York Times* (August 29, 2015), Online; and Tim Arango, "Protests in Iraq Bring Fast Promises, but Slower Changes," *New York Times* (August 31, 2015), Online.

movement, or attempt to co-opt it. Lebanon went the first route; Iraq, the second and third.

It should also be mentioned that in Iraq a separate protest movement began in the winter of 2014 in the Sunni areas of the country. Protesters demanded the end of discriminatory policies against their community perpetrated by the Shi'i government of Prime Minister Nuri al-Maliki. The government met those protests with extreme violence (as it did the initial protests), encouraging many Sunnis to sit on their hands or openly support the Islamic State when it began its conquests.[22]

Since Palestinians live under exceptional conditions, the uprising in Palestine naturally followed a different path. In January 2011, a group calling itself "Gaza Youth Breaks Out" issued its first manifesto, which stated, "There is a revolution growing inside of us, an immense dissatisfaction and frustration that will destroy us unless we find a way of canalizing this energy into something that can challenge the status quo and give us some kind of hope."[23] That energy was "canalized" through the March 15 Youth Movement, a loose association of social media–savvy young people similar to Egypt's April 6 Youth Movement that had sparked the uprising there. Like the April 6 Youth Movement, the March 15 Youth Movement began its protests with a "Day of Rage" in which tens of thousands of Palestinians took part. Rather than demanding the ouster of the regime as their Egyptian neighbors had done, however, movement leaders demanded reconciliation between Fatah and Hamas – two branches of the Palestinian national movement, which had gone their separate ways in 2007.

A second stage in the Palestinian uprising took place in the West Bank in September 2012 after the government raised prices on food and fuel. Spurred on by the same sort of labor activism that had proved decisive in the Egyptian uprising, protesters soon escalated their demands from the economic to the political: They called for the dismissal of the prime minister of the Palestinian Authority (and, in some cases, the resignation of its president, Mahmoud Abbas); the dismantling of the Authority; the renunciation of the Oslo Accord (which had empowered the Authority) along with its associated economic protocols; and the establishment of a Palestinian state within the 1967 borders with East Jerusalem as its capital.[24] The protest deeply shook the Palestinian leadership. It not only led to the firing of the Palestinian Authority prime minister, it encouraged President Mahmoud Abbas to seize the initiative by bypassing direct

---

[22] Dexter Filkens, "What We Left Behind," *New Yorker* (April 28, 2014), Online.

[23] Gaza Youth Breaks Out, "GYBO Manifesto 2.0," n.d., Online.

[24] Arab Centre for Research and Policy Studies, "The Palestinian Protests of September 2012: The Birth of a Social Movement" (Doha, 2012), Online.

negotiations with the Israeli government and taking the case for Palestinian statehood to the General Assembly of the United Nations.

The Uprisings as History

Overall, the scorecard for the uprisings that began in 2010–2011 is disheartening. In Egypt and all the monarchies the forces of reaction snuffed out the demands for change. Although the state system as a whole is not threatened – thanks in large measure to the support of both great and regional powers for the status quo – the inhabitants of Libya, Yemen, and Syria did not get functioning governments that rule over the entirety of their territories.

Across the region, there has been a rise in sectarianism, fueled by a combination of the Syrian civil war, the Iranian-Saudi rivalry over which regional power would determine the fate of embattled regimes and the regional order, and the Islamic State's war on everyone who does not follow the group's rigid interpretation of Islam or bow to its will. And however much protesters in Lebanon and Iraq might aspire to end sectarianism, once people segregate themselves among "their own kind," or representation or employment opportunities are allocated according to religious affiliation, sectarianism is unlikely to disappear.

In some states – Egypt, Bahrain, much of the Arabian peninsula – populations face the heavier hand of regimes that, for a brief moment, had caught a glimpse of their own vulnerability. Elsewhere – Syria, Libya, Yemen, Iraq, even Tunisia and the Sinai – the weakening of regimes or the diversion of their attention elsewhere created an environment in which violent Islamist groups, from ISIS and al-Qa'ida to Syria's Ahrar al-Sham and the former al-Qa'ida affiliate Jabhat al-Nusra, might breed. Again, the Saudi-Iranian competition has made matters worse. In their efforts to combat the expansion of Iranian influence in the region and uphold Sunni dominance in the Arab world, Saudi Arabia and its Gulf allies have supported a number of violent Islamist groups on the battle-fields of Syria and elsewhere. They have also financed mosques and schools that spread doctrines similar to those espoused by violent Islamists, thus normalizing those doctrines.

In the aftermath of the uprisings the region has experienced one humanitarian crisis after another. In the most brutal war zones – Syria, Libya, Yemen, Iraq – entire towns and cities have been laid waste, their populations scattered. War and civil disorder have not only taken their toll in terms of civilian casualties, but have destroyed billions of dollars of infrastructure in the region and created a public health nightmare. And particularly in Syria and Yemen, mass starvation – both an accident and tool of war – is an ongoing threat, endangering hundreds of thousands.

Tunisia was the one possible success story of the 2010–11 uprisings. Although the challenges it faces are daunting, it has bucked the counter-revolution, repression, and violence experienced by many of its neighbors.

The fact that so much of the region has experienced state breakdown, expanded repression, unprecedented levels of bloodshed, and sectarianization and intersectarian violence begs an obvious question: Were the Arab uprisings doomed to fail? For anyone watching the Egyptian uprising, it was difficult not to get caught up in the moment. Nevertheless, it is not unreasonable to ask how anyone could have thought that a regime as strong as the Egyptian – with its entrenched institutions and power-brokers, its far-ranging patronage networks, its anti-democratic but oil-rich allies, its one-million-man army (including reserves) and two-million-man security apparatus – would throw in the towel after eighteen days without putting up more of a fight.

From the beginning, protesters and rebels throughout the Arab world faced overwhelming odds, foreign intervention, and extremist groups out for their own ends. Since participants in the uprisings were, more often than not, united by what they were against – the regime – than what they were for, they also disagreed among themselves about goals. In all cases but that of Libya (and, to a far lesser extent, Syria), they faced the indifference or hostility of the United States. Finally, the very spontaneity, leaderlessness, diversity, and loose organization on which the uprisings thrived proved to be their Achilles heel as well. True, these attributes kept regimes off guard and impeded them from reining in rebellious activity. But they also prevented protesters and rebels from agreeing on and implementing coordinated policies with regard to tactics, strategy, and program.

There is one further factor that might have doomed the protests and uprisings to failure even had they been able to upturn or overthrow the old order: the wretched state of the economies of the non-oil-producing states and the absence of a blueprint other than the widely loathed neoliberalism to fix them. Throughout the region, economies went from bad to worse after uprisings broke out. This was the result of interrupted production, strikes, a lack of security that discouraged commerce and tourism, damage to infrastructure and sites of production, and displacement and migration.

In 2013, hundreds of thousands of Egyptians, angered by fuel shortages, electricity blackouts, and higher food prices, went out on the streets to demand the incompetent, but democratically elected president, leave office. Most cheered on as the army first gave him an ultimatum, then arrested him and assumed power.

Yet there is another way to look at the "Arab Spring" protests and uprisings of 2010–2011 and, indeed, the spate of protests and uprisings that have erupted throughout the Arab world since 1980. The first time the "Spring" metaphor was used to describe a political upheaval was in reference to the revolutions of 1848. Just as no revolution during that "Springtime of Nations" ousted any autocrat, with the exception of Louis Philippe, its outbreak signaled in retrospect that the field of political contestation in Europe had opened up to include liberal and nationalist alternatives to the old order. While historical analogies are inevitably deficient, a corresponding lesson might be drawn from the more recent wave of uprisings, only this time uprisings have signaled that global norms of human and democratic rights remain on the table in the Arab world. This cannot but disturb the sleep of kings and dictators there and beyond.

Islands of Global Revolution

Anne Eller

As Odd Arne Westad observes in this volume, we live in a present profoundly shaped by anticolonial struggle. Western colonialism has
wreaked such a profound impact on global history and the present that
the study of revolutions outside of the North Atlantic is frequently
enveloped within models seeking influence and diffusion from power
centers to putative peripheries. As scholars, politicians, and others have
long observed, however, colonized sites were not peripheral to the modern world but rather constitutive of its very foundation, in moments of
peace and war, profit and downturn, and especially in fomenting the
greater preconditions that sparked apparently metropolitan revolutions.
That these deep colonial connections might have been obfuscated in
Europe, even at moments of revolutionary rupture, only highlights the
distortions of national political discourses, the hermetic fiction of the
national frame, and the success of colonial power in disguising itself.
Historically, scholars' "methodological nationalism" amplified this silen-
cing, as did neat linear telos of expectations that long understood industrialized, powerful nation-states as the ascendant, and triumphant,
political form.[1] Analyzing the thick connections between revolutions
across oceans and hemispheres, then, promises to connect the material
to the political, to betray long-held geographic fictions, and reassess the
distribution of rights contested in these movements.

Heeding David Motadel's call to analyze the value of a territorialized
lens in the opening pages of this volume, the Caribbean once again
emerges as one of the clearest and longest-enduring examples of the
foundational, inextricable, and fraught interrelation of different revolutionary sites and the modern order.[2] Stated clearly, understanding
Caribbean centrality to a number of modern global revolutions promises
to reorder and deepen analyses of political contests of the past 400 years.

---

[1] Andrew Zimmerman, "Conclusion: Global Historical Sociology and Transnational
History – History and Theory against Eurocentrism," in Julian Go and George Lawson
(eds.), *Global Historical Sociology* (Cambridge, 2017), 221–40.

[2] Eric Williams, *Capitalism and Slavery* (London, 1944).

The Caribbean represents a site where fundamental social and political questions met repeated and profound contestation, where the preconditions against revolutionary success were sometimes the most extreme, and where stale analytical frameworks of supposed diffusion or mimesis of revolutionary thought dissolve into new perspectives entirely. Such an analysis centers an analytic of racist thought at the heart of a number of liberation contests, highlights the unevenness of freedom and economic expansion inherent in trans-oceanic colonial projects, and restores a historicity to Western revolutionary struggles that is impossible without analyses beyond their borders.

Despite a rich revolutionary literature, the study of the eighteenth- and nineteenth-century Caribbean challenges the limitations of an Atlantic "Age of Revolutions" itself, as revolutionary activity in the region exceeded what the paradigm has come to contain. Of course, the tremendous value and gains of the Atlantic frame are clear: intercolonial studies of the past twenty years have benefitted greatly from analyses of some struggles as unfolding within an "integrated space of debate," in which the vision and actions of subaltern actors, particularly the enslaved in the Caribbean, are shown to have shaped metropolitan European politics that were previously analyzed in isolation.[3] As David A. Bell observes in this volume, analyses of the toppled monarchies and swift revolutionary change has become truly transimperial and even global.

What analyses of an Atlantic "Age of Revolutions" achieve best – that is, highlighting the severing of certain colonial ties and the formation of new nation-states within rights-based discourses – does not begin to account for the upheaval or the intellectual ferment of the age within the Caribbean itself. As others observe, the first limitation of "Atlantic Revolutions" within global analyses is geographic fallacy of the name, as studies usually fail to include the enormous political transformations in West and Central Africa in the very frame bound by crises provoked by Europeans on African soil, or they tend to elide deep, local political logics beyond the reach of any boat.[4] What's more, a state-centric revolutionary lens often disappoints. Even the

---

[3] Laurent Dubois, "An Enslaved Enlightenment: Rethinking the Intellectual History of the French Atlantic," *Social History* 31, 1 (2006), 1–14.

[4] Boubacar Barry, *La Sénégambie du xve au xixe siècle: traite negrière, Islam, et Conquête coloniale* (Paris, 1988); Joseph Inikori and Stanley L. Engerman (eds.), *The Atlantic Slave Trade: Effects on Economies, Societies and Peoples in Africa, the Americas, and Europe* (Durham, NC, 1992); Joseph C. Miller, "The Dynamics of History in Africa and the Atlantic 'Age of Revolutions'," in Sanjay Subrahmanyam and David Armitage (eds.), *The Age of Revolutions in Global Context, c. 1760–1840* (New York, 2010), 101–24; Paul Lovejoy, *Jihād in West Africa during the Age of Revolutions* (Athens, OH, 2016); Bronwen Everill, "Demarginalizing West Africa in the Age of Revolutions," March 19, 2018, "Age of Revolutions" Website (Online).

very best of work that follows political transformations from Africa into the Americas remains outside regular conceptions of an Age of Revolutions, for example. Anti-slavery liberation struggles, one of the most foundational and enduring political contests of the plantation Americas, proliferated outside of a statist framework. Political analyses of some struggles against slavery, like Tacky's War in Jamaica, are gaining centrality alongside study of the Haitian Revolution, but much non-state resistance in Caribbean colonies remains deleteriously out of the Atlantic revolutionary frame.[5] A metric of "success" or "failure" – occasionally applied to the Haitian Revolution as "the only successful revolution of the enslaved in Atlantic history" – contributes to obscuring more complicated and profound analyses of daily life and ferment, as well as the impact on metropolitan societies.

Wholly different epistemologies of freedom also demand attention. Placing too much focus on European revolutions or archives, for example, and one distorts the Haitian Revolution beyond recognition. Revolution against slavery and for self-rule in a vicious plantation society did not necessarily follow a path of diffusion or "radicalization" from other revolutions. Debates of the Colonial Committee were important, and related contests had precipitated visible, exploitable fissures in Saint-Domingue for several decades, but foregrounding these obscures decades of resistance in the colony itself, as well as the intellectual vision of the overwhelming majority of those fighting, which sprang from elsewhere altogether. First, rebels called heavily on contemporary epistemologies of retribution and justice forged in the crisis of the trans-Atlantic human trade but also with much deeper roots. Furthermore, on Saint-Domingue plantations, once begun, revolution was entire and immediate. The storied Bwa Kayiman ceremony offers one entry into the epistemology and praxis of total revolution in Saint-Domingue that bypasses France entirely.[6] Critically expanding on the massive importance of this fighting – and, next, the specific challenge of Black humanity and freedom embodied in the birth of Haiti to other revolutionary projects in the hemisphere and Europe – better highlights the anti-blackness that remained at the heart of other burgeoning Atlantic sovereignties. Scholars must also engage with the rich literature on African diasporic geopolitical visions that insisted that new nations live up to tepid and contradictory promises of liberty or imagined different salvation entirely.[7]

---

[5] Vincent Brown, *Tacky's Revolt: The Story of an Atlantic Slave War* (Cambridge, MA, 2020); See also João José Reis, *Slave Rebellion in Brazil: The Muslim Uprising of 1835 in Bahia* (Baltimore, 1993).

[6] One recent analysis: Robbie Shilliam, "Race and Revolution in Bwa Kayiman," *Millennium: Journal of International Studies* 45, 3 (2017), 269–92.

[7] Once again, the literature is far too extensive to encapsulate here. Signal texts might include, for example, Tiffany Patterson and Robin D.G. Kelley, "Unfinished Migrations: Reflections on the African Diaspora and the Making of the Modern

Clearly, analyses of global revolutions through a Caribbean lens demands that racism features more prominently in analyses of revolutionary freedoms. Slavery did not merely "survive" the late-eighteenth-century revolutions, as some triumphalist narratives of those processes occasionally contend; rather, it continued to metastasize at the foundation of Atlantic societies and beyond. Like settler violence, this insurgent racism centrally facilitated subsequent colonial expansion. In the middle decades of the nineteenth century, Caribbean societies plunged into dynamic contests that highlight how freedom and unfreedom remained very much mutually constitutive. As residents of different islands won emancipation, the response of planters was swift and forward-looking: they sought to limit the political and socioeconomic rights of the newly free, to repress small farming, and, in many places, to bring in indentured men and women from China and India to drive plantation wages lower.[8] No elite intended for Caribbean civil society, or political independence, to flourish.

As the only independent Caribbean state, Haiti bore the enormous symbolic – and financial – weight of Black sovereignty in the hemisphere, its president signing an inimical "indemnity" to France in exchange for recognition in 1825. First joined with Haiti for twenty-two years, then a separate nation from 1844, leaders in the Dominican Republic excoriated Haiti as they angled for favor, keenly discerning the pressures against Black nationhood. When one Dominican president offered the Dominican nation back to Spain, however, the people rose up, massively and fast. The Dominican War of Restoration of 1863–1865 represented not only an affirmation of nationhood but also a revolution against the potential reimposition of slavery. These and other Caribbean emancipation contests – in other islands, where planters and allies purposefully preferred to maintain imperial ties rather than seek national independence – demonstrate the local elite and global opposition to Caribbean self-rule, relative to other new republics. These struggles also highlight an ongoing commitment to plantation export – and racist hierarchy – that prefigured European expansion in Africa in these same decades.[9]

World," *African Studies Review* 43, 1 (2000), 11–45; Ada Ferrer, *Freedom's Mirror: Cuba and Haiti in the Age of Revolution* (New York, 2014); and Kendra Field, *Growing Up with the Country: Family, Race, and Nation after the Civil War* (New Haven, CT, 2018).

[8] Clarion texts include Michel-Rolph Trouillot, *Peasants and Capital: Dominica in the World Economy* (Baltimore, 1988); and Natasha Lightfoot, *Troubling Freedom: Antigua and the Aftermath of British Emancipation.* (Durham, NC, 2015).

[9] Jeremy Adelman, *Sovereignty and Revolution in the Iberian Atlantic* (Princeton, NJ, 2006); and Anne Eller, "Rumors of Slavery: Defending Emancipation in a Hostile Caribbean," *American Historical Review*, 122, 3 (2017), 653–79.

External factors severely vexed struggles for nationhood in the Caribbean in future decades, too: namely, the outsized weight of foreign capital and the direct interference of the United States and other imperial powers. Just before the turn of the twentieth century, Cuban and Puerto Rican movements were overcome by this northern neighbor, whose influence had grown steadily for decades. As the Great War began in Europe, US forces tested aerial bombardment for the first time – in Haiti, which they occupied (alongside Nicaragua, the Dominican Republic soon to follow).[10] Tens of thousands of Caribbean men and women collaborated in the European war effort, making new claims on empire and contributing to steadily growing nationalist movements. Massive labor movements rocked the British Caribbean in the 1930s; recent scholarship underscores how original and total these efforts were in small islands like St. Kitts.[11] In the Caribbean, anticolonialism had long found vocabulary in anti-capitalism. In the wake of the Second World War, few writers offered more roundly critical or more lucid critiques than writers like Aimé Césaire; he critiqued the real fruit of several hundred years of European colonialism in the Caribbean and elsewhere as rotten, racist, and criminal.[12]

Revolutionary experiments and independence movements in the mid-twentieth-century Caribbean typified the growing global debates over whether or not national units were the redemptive vehicles they once seemed. Despite controversy, Césaire and his political contemporaries in Martinique and Guadeloupe leaned toward ongoing association with France as overseas departments. Meanwhile, Cuban revolutionaries argued that the triumph of the M-26 movement in 1959 represented true independence at long last – the vindication of the nation from US dominance – even as it plunged the island immediately into gale-force Cold War hostilities. A mid-century West Indies Federation dissolved after only a few years. Some revolutions, like Grenada's, succumbed to direct US hostility. Others fractured. Neoliberal economic treaties proliferated by the late 1970s and early 1980s, meanwhile, even as new nations were still being born.

Studying Caribbean political philosophies across time highlights how analytical models of revolutionary diffusion represent barely half of any global story. First, these models often dwell on ideas where they might more fruitfully analyze interference: that is, they might more appropriately focus on guns, threats, and extraction,

[10] Laurent Dubois, *Haiti: The Aftershocks of History* (New York, 2012), 258.
[11] Hermia Eddris Morton Anthony, *Decolonizing Narratives: Kittitian Women, Knowledge Production, and Protest* (Ph.D. University of Toronto, 2018).
[12] Aimé Césaire, *Discourse on Colonialism* (New York, 2000).

rather than pamphlets, markets, or exchange. As Christopher Clark writes in his chapter about nineteenth-century Martinique, Caribbean actors weighed constrained choices carefully and made opportunities where there were none. Far from a diffuse or diluted revolutionary model, these heterogenous strategies challenged the fictions of racelessness and betrayed the paternalism of global revolutions more fully than actors in European sites. Jamaican migrants of the mid-century migration to Great Britain known as the Windrush Generation called on the metropole to live up to its antiracist mythology, for example, invoking and confronting narratives about imperial abolition and benevolence that were by then many generations old. Such movements, organized and unrelenting, call on metropolitan societies to make their egalitarian language more real and to reconcile incomplete revolutions for freedom with the global history of European colonialism at long last.[13]

Revolutionaries in the Caribbean, a region colonized longer than almost any other, also articulate a vocabulary for revolutions that are yet to come. Some argue that the predicaments emerging from Cuba's Special Period, the diffusely demarcated period of crisis in Cuba that followed the collapse of the Soviet Union, represent the world's future, not socialism's past: confronting survival after oil, after the possibility of large-scale food imports, and social stability, even survival, in the face of extraordinarily trying circumstances.[14] From Guadeloupe to Puerto Rico to the Netherlands Antilles, communities debate the true meaning of sovereignty, drawing old forms of nationhood – and our relationship to the environment, to food production, to meaningful autonomy – into question.[15] They do so under the trying conditions and manmade precarity of neoliberalism. The vexed solidarity– but shared experiences – that are emblematic of Caribbean political movements encourage scholars to multiply and pluralize local analyses of their own. These will reveal deeper and more original local histories of revolutions unrealized or simply unwritten. They will also encapsulate contradictory experience of revolutions themselves, of the pain and possibility of "splintered national conscience" alongside the "expectation of flight."[16]

[13] Kennetta Hammond Perry, *London Is the Place for Me: Black Britons, Citizenship, and the Politics of Race* (Oxford, 2015).

[14] Reinaldo Funes, Roundtable, "The Cuban Revolution at 60: New Directions in History and Historiography," New York University, March 8, 2019; and Julia E. Wright, *Sustainable Agriculture and Food Security in an Era of Oil Scarcity: Lessons from Cuba* (London, 2012).

[15] Yarimar Bonilla, *Non-Sovereign Futures: French Caribbean Politics in the Wake of Disenchantment* (Chicago, 2015).

[16] Rosario Ferré, *Sweet Diamond Dust and Other Stories* (London, 1988), ix.

Just as hierarchies of incorporation into a nation-state are most visible in national borderlands, so do non-industrial territories and nations clearly lay bare all of the limits of national revolutionary promises past.[17] Processes of domination, and liberation, are interconnected here. In analyzing these interconnections fully, we are attentive to dialectics, ideas, processes, and hopes that might otherwise be effaced.

[17] Nicole M. Guidotti-Hernández, "Borderlands Scholarship for the Twenty-First Century," *American Quarterly* 68, 2(June 2016), 487–98.

Index

Lightning Source UK Ltd.
Milton Keynes UK
UKHW022354180321
380617UK00009B/89